GAME FISHING *in* SCOTLAND

GAME FISHING
in
SCOTLAND

BRUCE SANDISON

MAINSTREAM
PUBLISHING

First published in Great Britain in 1988 by
MAINSTREAM PUBLISHING COMPANY (EDINBURGH) LTD,
7 Albany Street,
Edinburgh EH1 3UG.

ISBN 1 85158 152 9 (cloth)

British Library Cataloguing in Publication Data
Sandison, Bruce
    Game fishing in Scotland.
    1. Scotland. Game fish. Angling
    I. Title
    799.1′2
    ISBN 1-85158-152-9

Back cover photograph courtesy of Ann Sandison.
Typeset in 11 on 12 Imprint by C. R. Barber & Partners, Fort William.
Printed and bound in Great Britain by Richard Clay Ltd, Bungay, Suffolk.

For Ann

'Where white flows the river and bright blows the broom'

CONTENTS

INTRODUCTION

I am often asked which is my favourite loch or river, where do I most enjoy fishing, and I find it difficult to respond with conviction. There is so much wonderful fishing in Scotland that I find it impossible to prefer one place to another. Which of my children should I love most? Do I prefer Mozart to Beethoven? Tweed or Tay? North Uist or Caithness? They are all dear to me, equally precious.

If therefore, I have not given due credit to some of your favourite fishing locations, or if my opinions vary from yours, then I apologise sincerely. Fishing is and always will be a personal, almost private matter. At least it is for me; and this book is very much a personal account of the places I have enjoyed fishing over the past 40 years.

I have also prepared location maps and a fishing directory for the areas described and, together with the text, this should help you find the fishing that suits you best. Most of the local tourist organisations will also be able to offer help and guidance; some more than others, particularly Perthshire, the Borders, Sutherland and Orkney.

Fishing tackle shops are an excellent source of information and institutions such as John Dickson's in Edinburgh and Glasgow, Grant Mortimer's in Grantown-on-Spey, the Rod and Gun Shop, Fort William, Pattie's in Dumfries, Sandy Harper in Thurso, Angler's Choice in Melrose and Sommer's in Aberdeen are a Mecca for anglers visiting these areas. My own organisation, Scottish Sporting Services, offers a full-scale fishing holiday planning service, so there is plenty of advice available; all geared to making sure that a fishing trip in Scotland is everything you desire.

Scotland is a very special place and it offers perhaps the greatest variety of game fishing in the world. Most is easily accessible to visiting anglers, reasonably priced and of high quality; a magnificent asset, to be valued,

9

protected and treasured for the pleasure and enjoyment of future generations. Anything that damages that asset, damages us all; and everyone who values the quality of Scottish game fishing is responsible for its protection.

If I appear unreasonably concerned about the activities of the Forestry Commission and private tree-farmers, then it is because I am convinced that mass-afforestation is seriously damaging Scotland's game fishing. From the Flow Country of Caithness and Sutherland to the Border lands, rivers, streams and lochs are becoming increasingly subjected to higher levels of acidity, flash flooding and diminishing stocks of fish. Our hills, mountains and moorlands are fast disappearing under a blanket of monotonous conifers in the name of spurious progress. Whereas Upland England, the Yorkshire Dales, Lake District and Cotswolds are jealously protected from the ungentle administrations of the tree-farmers, it appears that, as far as Scotland is concerned, anything goes.

If you agree with me, do something about it. Write to the Scottish Secretary, demanding that all planting in the vicinity of headwaters and catchment areas of rivers and lochs is stopped. Support the work of the Royal Society for the Protection of Birds and other conservation bodies who are at present fighting a losing battle against faceless accountants and private commercial interests.

On the credit side, the work of the Atlantic Salmon Conservation Trust has had a dramatic impact on the survival prospects of our mighty friend, Salar the leaper. Far more so than the feeble, half-hearted attempts of successive governments; and every angler in the land owes a debt of gratitude to the Trust for their success in buying out netting interests round Scotland's estuaries and rivers.

There is no public right of fishing in freshwater for brown trout or other species in Scottish rivers, streams, burns or lochs. The right to fish belongs to the owner of the land bordering the water. In tidal water, there is a public right to fish for white fish and brown trout but this right does not apply to salmon and sea-trout.

Therefore, before fishing, you must have written permission from the owner of the water concerned. To fish for brown trout without such permission is a civil offence; to fish for salmon or sea-trout without permission is a criminal offence, as it is to fish for any species without proper permission in an area covered by a Protection Order, granted under the provision of The Freshwater and Salmon Fisheries (Scotland) Act (1976).

Describing where to catch salmon, sea-trout and brown trout is one thing; how to catch them is quite another matter. There are countless learned tomes which will give you a clue: techniques, tackle, methods, all you need to know. However, the most certain fact is that nothing is as uncertain as fishing and you will have to make your own decision concerning which of the hundreds of patterns of flies and lures you offer the brutes.

I believe that a small number of standard patterns cover most eventualities 'frae Berwick to the Clint's o' Dee' and, for what they are worth, I offer them to you. Salmon: Jock Scott, Stoat's Tail, Munro Killer, Blue Charm, Shrimp Fly, Garry Dog, Red and Orange Waddingtons, Black Doctor, Thunder and Lightning, Hairy Mary and General Practitioner. Vary the size according to water levels.

Baits which work well throughout Scotland include: Rappalla, Kynoch Killer, Devons in brown, gold, blue and yellow, Toby, Mepps and spoons. Offer sea-trout: Black Pennel, Ke-He, Loch Ordie, Teal & Green, Teal Blue & Silver, Grouse & Green, Grouse & Claret, Dunkeld, Peter Ross and Butchers. For brown trout: Soldier Palmer, Invicta, Black Pennel, Ke-He, Loch Ordie, Black Zulu, Blue Zulu, March Brown, Greenwell's Glory, Grouse & Claret, Woodcock & Hare-lug, Dunkeld, Alexandria, Peter Ross, Silver Butcher and Silver Invicta.

Crossing the fingers, legs, arms and anything else available can also sometimes help. As can cursing, looking the other way, singing and a general lack of attention. Of course, luck is probably responsible for 95 per cent of all fish landed.

Game fishing in Scotland need not be expensive, although the best salmon fishing always is; but that is a relative statement because frequently, less well-known rivers and streams often produce just as good sport as their more famous brethren. Expect to pay up to £15,000 for five rods for a week on top beats of Tweed or Tay; but even then, they are rarely available.

Recognised salmon rivers will cost between £100 and £300 per rod per week; lesser rivers and streams, about £10 to £25 per rod per day. Sea-trout fishing is available at reasonable cost throughout Scotland and varies from £5 to £10 per rod per day up to £250 per rod for a week on one of the classic waters such as Eachaig or Eilt. Brown trout fishing probably represents the best value-for-money sport and costs from as little as £5 for a boat and two rods on a hill loch to £25 per day for a boat and two rods on a managed fishery.

In preparing the text of this book I have been greatly helped by a number of people throughout Scotland who have given freely of their advice and time. Much of the material in the book has appeared in my *Scotsman* fishing column, written over the past seven years, and I have tried, with the best will in the world, to be as accurate as possible. Please don't be furious if there are mistakes. I'm only human, in spite of what so-called friends and members of my family claim.

Certainly, without their help, I could never have finished this guide and I would like to thank them, from the bottom of my waders. Daughter Lewis-Ann who came north for a few days to visit her mother and found herself immediately chained to a desk and relegated to detail more than 2,000 lochs in the Outer Hebrides. Her long-suffering husband, Mike, condemned to solitude and self-cooking for nearly two weeks.

My own mother, who thought that she had been invited for rest and relaxation but spent her time copy-editing the script and numbering pages far into the night; and of course my wife Ann, whose constant support and encouragement over the years has made all my work possible. To them, and all the anglers and friends who helped, my thanks; I am forever in your debt.

Bruce Sandison,
Ruther House,
Watten,
Caithness.

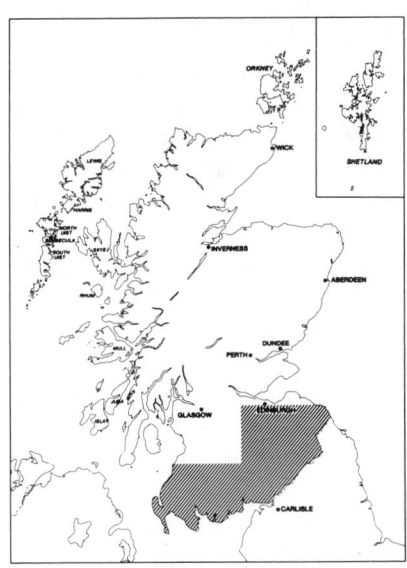

THE BORDER LINE

From Tweed to Solway

Tweed is part of me. Wrapped close about my soul; and I wear the smell of Tweed like a treasured garment no matter where I roam. By Arabian streams, grown proud with mountain rain; African rivers, flowing softly into antelope-sipping pools; pine-canopied Finnish torrents or sweet English chalk-streams; all shimmer and change before my gaze, reminding me of glorious Lady Tweed, Queen of Scottish rivers.

My fishing memories were born on the Tweed in the cool, clear streams of its little tributary, Lyne Water, where I first committed the sin of angling nearly 40 years ago. Bus from St Andrews Square, Edinburgh, bristling with rod, landing net, picnic and waders. That wonderful sense of anticipation, walking to the river by Romanno Bridge. Catching my first trout. It flew past my ear on a particularly violent back-cast and I spent frantic seconds on hands and knees, searching for it in long grass. The fish was about four inches long, sparkling silver, red-spotted and gasping; and I felt that I had never seen anything quite so beautiful nor felt such extreme excitement. With reverent care I removed the fly and returned the trout to the water, watching breathlessly as it darted off into the depths.

Unbeknown to me, that same warm, endless summer, two miles upstream, my future wife was busy catching her first fish. It was to be another seven years before we met but, when we did, Tweed, Lyne and fishing formed an instant bond between us. Now, many years and four children later, we still share the same affection for the Tweed and our offspring were introduced to fly fishing almost as soon as they could walk. Far better than putting money in the bank for children. Money comes and goes, but a love of fishing gives a lifetime's joy and pleasure.

I introduced my father to fishing on Lyne Water. One evening, after his

13

golf match had been cancelled, he decided to drive down and collect me. I was fishing a wide pool near Flemington and saw Father park the car by the side of the road. He waved and walked down to where I was busy casting. 'Here son, give me a shot at that.' Not long afterwards he sold his golf clubs and for the rest of his life dreamt of little else than fishing.

Once I had mastered basic fishing techniques, such as filling wellington boots with water, falling in, retrieving flies from underwater obstructions, the back of my neck and passing cattle, I moved downstream to Lyne Station, where the Lyne mingles with Tweed. Dr Beeching took his axe to the railway many years ago, but there is still a Victoria Regina letter-box set into the wall of the roadside cottage where we parked.

One evening, full of the scent of meadow-sweet and honeysuckle, I was fishing upstream from the railway bridge, the light fading. First dusk bats flicked by and I was engrossed in trying to remove a Grouse and Claret from the back of my jacket. The river had that heady, lingering, evening smell; water bubbling by, caressing moss-capped stones, urgent for the sea. As I twisted and turned, cursing the loss of a few more moments' fishing, the water by my feet exploded in a shower of crystal droplets. A huge, silver and golden shape rose majestically from the river and arched back into the water, almost in slow motion, the broad tail, sail-like, powering the salmon, on upstream. The noise of its landing echoed through the night, sending moorhens clucking angrily amongst reeds, cross at being disturbed.

I slumped to the ground, following the salmon's arrow-wake into the distance until it faded from view and silence settled once more over the river. In that moment, I was confirmed into the angling fraternity and have remained so ever since. Everything I had ever wanted lay around me and I knew that no matter what outrageous slings and arrows fortune flung, I could always escape to the river.

The Tweed rises deep in the Lowther Hills, north of the Devil's Beef Tub, close to the source of that other great Scottish river, the Clyde and almost within view of the birthplace of Annan, Nith and Esk. Tweed's headwaters have been trapped by flooding the valleys of Fruid and Talla and both these reservoirs provide brown trout fishing in wonderful surroundings, edged by steep, green hills.

Broad Law (840m), second only to Merrick in Lowland height, crowds the east shoreline of Talla and it is possible to walk above 2,000 feet for miles on these gentle slopes. It is sheep-farming country, and the home of curlew, lapwing and meadow pipit. This is also John Buchan country. Buchan is perhaps most remembered for his stirring novel *The Thirty-nine Steps*; we anglers love him best for *John McNab* and the poem *Fisher Jamie*: 'He lo'ed nae music, kenned nae tunes, Except the sang o' Tweed in spate, or Talla loupin' ower its linns.'

Tweed flows for a distance of 100 miles through the Scottish Borders, by salmon beats whose names are synonymous with the finest sport: Bemersyde, Mertoun, Makerstoun, Upper and Lower Floors, Junction Pool, Hendersyde, Birgham past the grandeur of Sir Walter Scott's home at Abbotsford and through the deep pool near Ladykirk, where James IV nearly drowned in 1500 AD.

Gathering in waters from almost 2,000 square miles, it hurries past Fruid, Talla, Lyne, Eddlestone, Ettrick, Yarrow, Gala, Leader, Teviot, Eden, Whiteadder, and Till to the sea past Berwick and Tweedmouth. The Tweed and its tributaries offer more than 300 miles of salmon, sea-trout and brown trout fishing to visiting anglers and to know Tweed is to know the best of Scotland's river fishing.

Salmon and sea-trout fishing is administered by the River Tweed Commissioners and they represent 128 owners who have 204 fishings. The season opens on 1 February and lasts until 30 November with trout fishing from 15 March until 30 September. Salmon and sea-trout run the river throughout the year and in days past the Tweed was noted for the quality of its spring fishing. These days vanished during the 1960s, '70s and early '80s but there are now signs that spring runs are improving once more.

In spring 1988 Mrs Watson from London landed a fine 18-lb salmon from Sprouston and the week ending 20 February produced 70 fish for Ednam House Hotel guests; and Mr David Brimms from Heddon-on-the-Wall took a wonderful fish of 21 lb from Pavillion near Ettrickmouth.

Tweed trout-fishing is at its finest in May and June when Canon Greenwell's fly is busy amongst large, hungry brown trout. When I used to stumble about the Tweed as a boy, the river was very quiet and seeing other anglers was the exception, rather than the rule. I experimented with horse-hair casts and tiny dry flies, often producing good baskets of trout, even in high-water conditions. Now, Tweed trout-fishing is a busy affair and, as in other areas of Scotland, a Protection Order has had to be obtained to protect the quality of stocks and control the hundreds of anglers who fish the river and its tributaries. However, I have always found that if you are prepared to walk away from the main centres, you may still find peace and quiet, corners far from the crowds where you, nature and trout can commune.

Tales and stories of the Tweed's mighty fish are legendary and the heaviest spring fish landed was caught on 23 April 1920 and weighed 43 lb. Today, early fish are generally smaller and average 8 lb in weight with most of the spring runs swept up by estuary and river netting stations. Recently, the nets have been bought out and all returning fish have freedom of access to their spawning grounds. Apart, that is, from the 50,000 to 80,000 salmon and unspecified numbers of sea-trout taken by the Northumberland coastal drift-net fishery, surely one of the most misguided, malevolent blights on Scottish east coast salmon fishing. The majority of fish taken are heading for the Tweed, Tay, Esks, Dee and Don and that such massive depredations should be allowed to continue is unbelievable, given the

15

damage they cause to Scottish salmon stocks.

After a summer run of grilse, huge autumn salmon run the Tweed and these fish used to be of enormous proportions. In 1743 Lord Home was reported to have landed a salmon which weighed 69 lb 12 oz and William, Earl of Home, had a fish of 61 lb. Because of uncertainty about matters avoirdupois, the authenticity of these weights cannot be confirmed. However, there is no doubt about the heaviest salmon taken in modern times—a fish of 57 lb 8 oz, caught by Mr Pryor on 27 October 1886 in Upper Floors on a Silver Wilkinson. Seven other fish weighing over 50 lb were taken up until 1925 and the heaviest salmon of recent times was a fish of 43 lb, caught by Lady Burnett in the Pot Pool at Tillmouth in 1977.

The Tweed is also famous for the numbers of rod-and-line-caught fish taken during the course of a single day. G. McCulloch took nineteen salmon on 20 November 1903 weighing a total of 389 lb 8 oz with the heaviest being 39 lb. 'Hey, mon, sic a fish!' In more recent times, Mr Dixon, fishing with the Michael Chapman, caught six fish in a morning on Beat 6 of the Tillmouth Park Water. Their total weight was 121 lb and the heaviest weighed 24 lb 8 oz.

Sea-trout of great size are also taken on the Tweed most seasons, and in 1985 fish of 18 lb and 17 lb were caught. A sea-trout of more modest size was landed in 1957, below the bridge of Innerleithen. My father had his first encounter with sea-trout there and caught a fine specimen weighing 4 lb. He was so excited by his success that he telephoned to tell me the news. At that time I was in the army, stationed overseas on the Isle of Wight, and my heart ached for the feel of a fishing rod in my hand, bent double in action on the Tweed.

Splendid sea-trout are taken on the Tweed, almost from the beginning of the season, and in 1988 Mr K. Smalley had a fish of 6 lb from The Little Stream and fish of 5 lb were taken from Otter Rock on the same beat. The best spring sea-trout in 1988 was caught by Dr C. T. L. Peach from London, and weighed 8 lb.

The definitive description of salmon fishing pools on the Tweed is contained in an old book, published in 1860 by John Younger, listing 347 pools from Manor Water down to the estuary; the most famous of these pools are in the vicinity of Kelso, including: Birgham Dub, Sprouston, Reddenhaugh, Maxwheel, Junction, The Shot, The Goat Mouth, The Red Stane, North and South Clippers, Lover's Leap and Mill Stream. All the money in the world cannot buy you fishing here and for most anglers, casting over these magnificent streams will probably remain an unattainable dream. The fishings are let to the same tenants, year after year, and little short of murder, or incredibly good luck, will provide an opportunity of obtaining a rod.

Even if you are fortunate enough to be offered a week, then be prepared to pay upwards of £12,000 for four to five rods for peak autumn fishing.

Nor, these days, is there any guarantee of catching fish. Recent years have seen a severe drop in catches on the Tweed, most markedly in the spring but also now in September, October and November. Everyone hopes that matters will improve, post-netting. Particularly those who fish these most expensive waters. These twin evils, drought and spate, might also play havoc with your sport and success is very much a matter of chance. Nevertheless, there is an ever-increasing queue of hopeful anglers, all waiting, cheque-books poised, to grab the first opportunity of fishing these famous beats.

But good Tweed salmon fishing need not cost an arm and a leg and there are times and places where visiting anglers will find excellent fishing with a good opportunity of catching fish. In summer months, the owners of even the best beats let them on a day or weekly basis to visitors. The charges range from £10 per rod per day up to £30 and, for the Tweed, this represents value for money. Even more so now that all river and

The Border Esk at Canonbie

estuary netting has ended. Granted, the water levels must be reasonable but it is worth taking the chance and when conditions are right, you may catch as many fish as the more affluent autumn anglers.

In July 1988, when the Game Fair visited Floors Castle at Kelso, home of the Duke of Roxburghe, conditions were most definitely unfavourable. The rain poured down and 'made the ground quite muddy'—in fact about a foot deep. The Tweed threatened to retaliate against the intrusion of 90,000 visitors to its banks by flooding the show ground and for three days people plodged around dragging miserable dogs and children through a sea of mud. The river hurtled angrily by, red and brown with rage, absolutely unfishable.

Several local angling clubs offer fishing permits on the Tweed for salmon, brown trout and sea-trout: Norham Angling Club; Coldstream and District Angling Club; Kelso Angling Club; Newton St Boswell's and District Angling Club; Melrose and District Angling Club; Galashiels Angling Club; Peebles Trout Fishing Association and Peebles Salmon Fishing Association. A number of local hotels also offer their guests Tweed fishing, including Tillmouth Park Hotel, Tweed Valley Hotel, Tontine Hotel and the Crook Inn, by the side of the A701 Moffat/Broughton road, which has seven miles of salmon, sea-trout, and brown trout fishing on the Upper Tweed.

Most of my early days of salmon fishing were spent on the stretch between Walkerburn Cauld and Manor Bridge, some twelve miles of super fishing. Salmon rarely reached that far upstream before June, but from then on there was always the chance of a fish and over the years I had some amazing tussles with salmon, often on trout tackle. My first encounter came in Long Pool, above Innerleithen, one warm June morning when I had been trying to tempt trout from the other side of the rushing stream that feeds the pool from New Water. The fish took gently and it was a moment or two before I realised what I had hooked. I was fishing with 2 lb breaking-strain nylon and the nearest I came to the fish, which in my young opinion, estimated to have weighed at least 64 lb, was when he casually swam almost within touching distance and sulked by my feet. The moment I tried to put pressure on, he ran upstream, breaking my cast, and disappeared, heedless of all my despairing cries.

If you are a sea-trout running the Tweed, you will know that first left after Berwick brings you into the River Till. This river rises in Northumberland, flowing past the market town of Wooler and Flodden Field, joining the Tweed near Twizle Bridge and the Tillmouth Park Hotel. In recent years, catches of salmon have declined but the Till is still popular with sea-trout and good numbers are taken most seasons. Sea-trout are caught throughout the system and even as far upstream as south of Wooler. Bowmont Water is the most important tributary of the Till and this stream is a noted grayling fishery. We once saw in the New

Year at Town Yetholm and had a few casts for Bowmont grayling. Either the weather was too bitter or the prospect of good cheer in Yetholm too tempting, but we lasted barely an hour before snow drove us home.

Some years ago, whilst researching my book *The Sporting Gentleman's Gentleman,* I had the great privilege of meeting Jimmy Wallace, one of the best known and respected Tillmouth gillies; it was with pleasure that I heard him tell me he caught his first salmon not on the Till but on the Whiteadder. This lovely little river is best known as a trout stream and when I finally got hitched to my angling friend, we spent the first week of our married life in a cottage at Abbey St Bathans. It was spring, river banks nodding with daffodils, shy primrose blinking in April sunlight. The river flowed sweetly by Mrs Gillan's cottage and all was right with the world. We had long days by the waterside, clear pools dimpled with rising fish. Trout for breakfast, trout for dinner, trout for tea. Happy days.

'March, march, Ettrick and Teviotdale!' go the stirring words of the old Scots song, *The Blue Bonnets.* The bonnets were being encouraged over the border, for yet another attack on their English neighbours, for the history of the borders is one of continual feuding between rival families: Armstrong, Beattie, Bell, Collingwood, Elliot, Forster, Irvine, Kerr, Lowther, Ridley Scott, Storey, Trotter and Turnbull. The Teviot, longest of the Tweed's tributaries, flows serenely through the mists of bloody border history; rising to the south of Hawick deep in the Cheviot Hills by Black Burn Head and Haggis Side, it flows through an area now covered by the forests of Eskdalemuir.

My wife Ann spent her childhood in these hills, eastwards at Riccarton Junction on the Waverley Line. Riccarton was an exchange platform, serving the line southwards to Carlisle and eastwards over the moors to Hexham. The only way either in or out of Riccarton was by train or on foot. Returning now and seeing those once open moorlands obliterated by endless rows of conifers is a nightmare, a physical, sickening shock; in my opinion, an act of mindless, wanton, environmental vandalism.

The Teviot collects in the waters of Allan, Borthwick and Slitrig which run north by the old railway line, Trow, Dean, Rule and Ale. I used to stop by the old bridge over the river near Ancrum and 'dreep' down to see what I could see. For several seasons, a large trout of about 2 lb in weight used to live by one of the pillars. I never managed to have a cast at him and in time realised I would never do so. How could I hurt such a good friend?

The slow-moving Jed Water joins the Teviot near Jedburgh, wandering in by red-scarred cliffs, past the Capon Tree, where tenants used to pay rent in kind and where the river often floods the fields surrounding the graceful Abbey town. Oxnam and Kale add their worth next and the Teviot eventually makes its grand entrance to the Tweed in the famous Junction Pool.

Salmon and sea-trout fishing on the Teviot is readily available to visitors, as is brown trout fishing and, given the right water levels, sport can be very good indeed. Upper Teviotdale Fisheries Association, Hawick Angling Club and Lothian Estates all offer permits as do a number of hotels along the way. Spring fish enter the system early in the season but the best sport is with summer sea-trout and autumn salmon.

The Ettrick and Yarrow are two of Tweed's principal hand-maidens, flowing northwards to join at the Cauld, near Philiphaugh where the great Montrose was savagely defeated by Commonwealth forces commanded by General Leslie in 1645. Upstream from Philiphaugh, across from the ruins of Newark Castle is the birth place of Scottish explorer and doctor, Mungo Park who wrote *Travels in the Interior of Africa* and was drowned when attacked by natives on the Upper Niger River. The Ettrick offers the best fishing, particularly with sea-trout whilst Yarrow is reported to be improving. Without the nets at the mouth of Tweed, these delightful streams may once more recover their former stature as exciting and rewarding fisheries.

Trout lochs are few and far between in the borders. The Tweed Valley Hotel has fishing on Stantling Craig Reservoir and the Hawick and District Angling Club has fishing available on a number of waters including Acremoor, Hellmoor, Williestruther, Alemoor and Ackerknowe Reservoir.

The most remote of the border lochs is Skeen, lying in the folds of the hills above the Grey Mare's Tail waterfall, six miles north of Moffat. Catch your breath on the way up and look out for action with lots of small, hard-fighting trout. For sterner stuff, travel eastwards towards the dramatic cliffs near St Abbs. One of Scotland's oldest and best-managed fisheries, Coldingham Loch, lies on the heights—22 acres in extent with fine brown and rainbow trout which average 1 lb 8 oz.

The heaviest fish taken in recent years weighed over 7 lb and Coldingham is a great place for a family holiday. There are a number of well-furnished cottages and, nearby, lovely beaches and places of interest for the tribe to visit whilst you fish. My favourite property is the Boat House, on the far side of the loch. Peaceful and private with first-class fishing, from the lounge window.

The most romantic and best loved of the border lochs is however St Mary's, lying to the south of Innerleithen, famous for both angling and literary association, centred upon Tibbie Shiels Inn. Robert Burns, who knew a thing or six about human nature, once remarked,

A chiel that's aye sober is damned ill tae ken,

Keep him wat wi good drink and you'll find him out then.

Tibbie Shiels Inn on the banks of St Mary's Loch has been finding out 'chiels' for more than 200 years and is one of the oldest hostelries in the Scottish Borders. James Hogg, the Ettrick Shepherd, author of *Private Confessions of a Justified Sinner*, was a regular visitor, as was Sir Walter

Scott, the 'Wizard of the North', whom Hogg described as 'the best and most steady friend that I ever had to depend on'.

Another of Hogg's steady friends was Thomas Tod Stoddart, Scottish fisherman and angling author. Tom was once stopped on the road by the local magistrate who asked him what he was doing with himself these days. Outraged, Stoddart roared, 'Doing, man? Doing? I'm an angler!' Stoddart and James Hogg shared a boat on St Mary's on 4 May 1833 and reported catching 79 trout weighing 36 lb and no doubt they celebrated their victory with their friends and Tibbie over a dram or two or three.

Tibbie Shiels was the nickname given to Isabella Richardson, widow owner of the inn; the redoubtable lady saw most of her more famous customers off into that 'great trout loch in the sky' before departing hither herself in 1878 in her 96th year. She is buried in Ettrick churchyard but her memory lives on in the name of the inn by the shores of the gentle loch.

West of Tibbie Shiels is a statue of James Hogg holding his shepherd's crook, stone-deep in infinite thought, watching rising trout he may no longer catch; opening of doors that he may no longer enter; hearing new voices telling old stories of ones that got away. In his hand is a scroll inscribed with words from his poem *The Queen's Wake*: 'He taught the wandering winds to sing.'

The Tweed valley holds many dear memories for me; of battles fought and lost with salmon and trout; long walks by red-decked rowans, heavy with berries; the wonderful glory of autumn trees, beech, oak and sycamore ablaze with colour; brown and gold fragments, nodding in gentle breezes; days lazy and drowsy, lulled to sleep by the sound of larks, and the ever-murmuring stream.

When Scots tired of fighting amongst themselves they could always rely on their southern neighbours to provide good sport. Most of the action took place along the border between England and Scotland and for centuries the actual border line was a matter of hot, often bloody, dispute between the two nations. The steel bonnets of the border reivers were a common, unwelcome sight to the people of the Marches, and towns and villages were frequently subjected to wholesale slaughter, burning, murder and rape. Living was not easy. Families went to bed at night never certain if they would awake the following morning in their own beds or trying to explain to St Peter the reason for their sudden appearance at the Pearly Gates.

The Wardens of the Marches met to try and settle arguments and one of their meeting places was at Lochmabon Stone, west of anvil-married Gretna Green. A single stone marks the site today. There used to be others, but an enterprising local farmer arranged that most of the other great obelisks went under ground because they interfered with his ploughing. Fortunately, the local laird appeared on the scene in time to save the last stone. The boundary between England and Scotland follows the line of the Border Esk, a prolific salmon and sea-trout river which enters the Solway Firth at Sarkfoot Point, six miles north-west of Carlisle. The Esk is formed by two main tributaries, the Black and White Esks. The White Esk rises amongst the forests and hills of Carrick and Eskdalemuir, beginning life as the Tomleuch Burn and flowing southwards to a meeting with its dark partner at the Deil's Jingle, by the disused railway.

The Black Esk headwaters are completely afforested and flow from the impounded waters of Black Esk Reservoir, now a useful brown trout fishery, through Castle O'er Forest. At Langholm, on the A7 Carlisle/Hawick road, the Esk collects in Wauchope and Ewes Waters; downstream at Irvine House, Tarras Water tumbles in from Arkleton Hill (521 m) and Watch Hill (500 m). South from Canonbie, above Scotsdike, the Esk's principal stream, Liddel Water, flows in forming the best pool of the Esk, Willow Pool; and this junction of the waters is at the centre of the area known as the Debatable Land.

These lands were the cause of most of the trouble between Scotland and England because neither side could agree which country owned them. Consequently, in order to avoid anyone settling there permanently, the Debatable Land was declared 'open country' for acts of violence. The law did not apply and if people were foolish enough to live there then they had only themselves to blame if they were murdered, robbed or beaten. Which they often were.

Old habits die hard and even today, poaching and illegal fishing is an ever-present hazard to Esk salmon and sea-trout; but as long ago as 1278 AD, concern was being expressed about over-netting of salmon. At the Carlisle Assizes in that year it was agreed that due to 'great destruction in the water of Esk of salmon coming up to spawn it was unanimously determined that from Michaelmas to St Andrew's day, no net shall be drawn or placed at weirs, pools or mills'.

Another strange tale shows just how important Esk salmon fishings were in days past. A fish garth, salmon trap, was erected by the English on their side of the river in about 1470. From then until 1543 it was a source of constant and bitter dispute. As soon as the Scots raided and pulled it down, the English rebuilt it. Such was the anger aroused by the garth, that before the Battle of Flodden in 1513, King James IV of Scotland challenged the Earl of Surrey to single combat, to resolve their dispute. Although the fight did not take place, Surrey saying that he was too humble to fight with a king, one of the rewards that James sought, should he have won, was the removal for all time of the Esk fish garth.

Battles still rage along the banks of the Esk and Liddel today but these are between man and fish, rather than Scots and English and the Esk is renowned for the quality of its fishing, particularly, sea-trout with as many as 4,000 fish taken each season. Spring salmon runs have virtually disappeared but in the autumn months, grey-backs, the huge salmon for which Solway rivers are famous, still run the river.

Much of the Esk fishing is controlled by the Esk and Liddel Fishery Association and angling returns for 1987 were based upon the 25 per cent of anglers who completed the required details after fishing. Even then the figures are outstanding. Of the 4,228 sea-trout taken by members, 2,045 were from 'all waters permits'. Canonbie produced 830 fish, Langholm 448, and Lower Liddel 870. Even as far upstream as Newcastleton 35 sea-trout were caught.

The heaviest sea-trout caught that year weighed 12 lb and another good fish weighing 10 lb 8 oz was landed by Mr W. Tweedle at Langholm. Salmon returns were 272, compared with 477 in 1986 and 25 were caught on fly, 162 by spinning and the remaining 85 succumbed to 'the garden fly' worm. Spring fish averaged 13 lb in weight, summer salmon 7 lb. September and October were the peak months, producing a total of 223

River Nith at Auldgirth

salmon. The heaviest salmon caught during 1988 weighed 24 lb and was landed by Mr T. Wightman, from Canonbie.

Canonbie and Langholm, birthplace of Thomas Telford, the famous road and bridge builder, are the principal centres for visiting anglers and there is good accommodation available locally. It is best to book in advance because, as you can imagine, Esk fishing, particularly for summer sea-trout is always in demand. Avoid debate and dispute, other than with fish. There are long memories in the dales and hills of border lands. Or take along a steel bonnet. Don't say you haven't been warned.

The River Annan rises close to the source of the Tweed, near the Devil's Beef Tub and flows through border lands for a distance of 35 miles before reaching the sea, south of the town of Annan. Thomas Carlyle, Scottish writer and historian was born at the little village of Ecclefechan nearby, and in 1814 was appointed Rector of Annan Academy. Another, earlier, wanderer through these lovely south-west lands was Robert the Bruce, eventually King of Scotland. It was in the south-west that Bruce regrouped and consolidated his forces, drawing on the inner strength that eventually led him to victory at Bannockburn in 1314, much helped by sitting in a damp cave near Ecclefechan, watching a spider trying to spin a web.

As on the Esk, spring runs of Annan salmon are minimal but autumn runs often produce good catches, with October and November providing great sport with the large salmon for which the Annan is noted. The average weight of autumn salmon is in the order of 13 lb but each season fish of 20 lb and heavier are taken. In 1979 a fish of 38 lb was caught during November and on the last day of the season in 1984 a salmon of 34 lb 8 oz was landed from Cauld Pool.

The Annan is famous as a sea-trout river and on Newbie Beat in 1984 1,114 sea-trout were caught with many of these fish being 3 lb and more in weight. Night fishing for sea-trout is one of Annan's principal delights, provided that you are well organised and know the river. Otherwise, you may get a closer look at the pools than you had anticipated.

Castle Milk Water starts six miles south of Lockerbie and offers two and a half miles of good fishing, including some excellent pools such as Manse Pool and Jimmie's Stream. The Royal Four Town's Water has some of the best and most readily available fishing on the Annan and fishing is also open to members of the public on the Upper River where the Upper Annandale Angling Association controls two stretches of the river.

Fishing closes on the Annan on 15 November and very often the first two weeks of November, given decent water levels, can produce fine sport. In 1987, Edinburgh angler Mike Shepley landed a 20 lb fish, Mr Chisholm one of 19 lb and Mr J. Black a salmon of 18 lb 8 oz.

The best news from Annan is that negotiations have begun to try and buy out netting rights in the estuary and this should help to improve salmon runs which have seriously declined during recent years. In the meantime, the close time for nets at weekends has been increased to eighteen hours and this means that there will be only 40 hours of netting, rather than the previous 60. As far as I am concerned, one hour's netting is still one hour too many.

The River Nith is the longest and most productive of the south-west salmon and sea-trout systems, draining an area of 435 square miles. The Nith rises to the east of the old mining town of Dalmellington. I remember visiting one of the two pubs in Dalmellington. The roof was so low that I had to sit down before I could raise the pint glass to my thirsty lips. Short of stature, Dalmellington men.

The headwaters of the Nith, like so many of the streams and lochs of the south-west, are afforested, and Nith begins its long journey to Solway in the Kyle Forest by Nith Lodge. The principal tributary is Cairn Water, a useful salmon and sea-trout fishery in its own right, which joins the Nith just north of Dumfries, and the only other significant feeder stream is Scaur Water, offering principally sea-trout fishing, which meets the Nith at Whitegate, south from Thornhill.

The Nith Fishings Improvement Association has been responsible for bringing the river back from the brink of being a 'well remembered, fine fishery' to its present state of excellence; and sport seems to be improving all the time. Even spring runs appear to be returning and in spite of a savage attack of UDN (Ulcerative Dermal Necrosis) in the mid-1960s, in 1983 the Nith System recorded a total catch of 1,238 salmon and 4,612 sea-trout. The best year for the Nith was 1966, prior to UDN, when the system produced 2,251 salmon, 559 grilse and an astonishing 9,502 sea-trout.

Sadly, the Nith is much beset by poachers and association bailiffs fight a constant battle to protect their fishery. Bailiffs are assaulted, not only by the river, but also in the court at Dumfries after being convicted. In July 1988 the police had to intervene with handcuffs to restrain the disgruntled poachers' friends.

The Nith flows through Dumfries and the Royal Town is forever linked with the name of Scotland's greatest poet, Robert Burns, who lived there after becoming an excise man, when his various agricultural enterprises failed. There is a Burns Heritage Trail and Scotland's Bard lies buried at Dumfries: 'Lord grant that I should lead a good life, for a good life makes for a good end.'

Another famous figure, born near Dumfries at Arbigland, was John Paul Jones, credited with founding the American Navy and encouraging thousands of people all over the world to dance round in circles, changing partners as often as possible. Dancing round the banks of the Nith is a more rewarding pastime for anglers and much of the salmon and sea-trout fishing is available to visiting anglers.

Nithsdale District Council, Dumfries and Galloway Angling Association, Mid-Nithsdale Angling Association and Upper Nithsdale

Angling Association all offer day and weekly permits to visitors. Some of the best Nith fishing is controlled by Buccleuch Estates and beats on their water are sometimes available. Buccleuch Estate fishing is divided into three beats, Upper, Middle and Lower and there is also fishing on Nith Linns. There are a number of good pools: Ivy Lee, Mermaid's Shoe, Drumlanrig Brig, Priests Pool, Buchts, Dovecote Knowe, Isla Holm Stream, Crowbank, Lower Crowbank, Willowholm, Carronfoot, Quarry Pool, Whitehill, Bullackholm, Doctors and Nith Bridge.

On Nith Linns the pools are: Hell's Cauldron, Long Straight Pool, Milestone, Auchensell, Palmtree, Cow and Otter Pool. Some of these beats are fairly inaccessible and involve some mountaineering but, when conditions are right and fish running, who minds a bit of a scramble to get to the river? Plan your scramble for sea-trout during June, July and August; wait until September and October to attack Nith salmon.

To the west of Dumfries lies the little River Urr, unattractive to sea-trout but with runs of salmon and some large Solway grey-backs in the autumn months. The river rises north of the village of Corsock and much of the headwaters have suffered from the effects of afforestation. Because of this, the river is subjected to flash-flooding and this makes angling difficult. Once again, being in the right place at the right time is all-important. Getting it all together can be worth while for fish of up to 30 lb have been taken from the Urr. The two angling associations which control much of the river issue day and weekly permits to visitors and they regularly stock their waters.

The story of the River Ken, Urr's neighbour which runs into the sea by Kirkcudbright, is a sad tale of afforestation, hydro electric schemes, reservoirs and water impoundment. What is left of salmon fishing on the Dee is of little quality although some fish are taken each season. The main source of the Dee is from Loch Ken and in recent years this has become almost fishless. Now, the interested parties are attempting to establish exactly why this has happened and the Forestry Commission is studying various schemes in an attempt to put matters right. Needless to say, the long-suffering tax-payer will be picking up the 'tab' and one can only despair that proper consideration was not given to the effects of their works before they started planting.

Sandy, shallow Fleet Bay, west from Kircudbright, receives the waters of the River Fleet, spreading them out amidst the small islands and rocky outcrops that scatter the bay. The river is composed of two streams, Big and Wee (small) Fleet and both rise in the once lovely Galloway Hills. Once lovely, because they are now virtually all afforested and consequently the Fleet is much affected by flash-flooding. Worse, the lochs at the headwaters of both streams have become increasingly acid over the years since afforestation took place and as a result Lochs Grannoch and Fleet are to all intents and purposes now fishless.

26

Salmon run the Fleet and fishing throughout the whole system is available to visiting anglers from the owners who offer day and weekly tickets. The river is noted more for the quality of its sea-trout fishing than salmon, although Fleet occasionally produces surprises with salmon of up to 20 lb. Autumn fishing is most productive and most seasons about 20 salmon and 60 sea-trout are caught.

Newton Stewart in Galloway is the angling centre for the far south-west of Scotland and offers visiting anglers a wide variety of sport with good river fishing for salmon and sea-trout and some fine trout fishing in a number of easily accessible lochs. To the south of Newton Stewart, on Burrow Head, is the quaintly named Isle of Whithorn, really a peninsula rather than a proper island; but it is considered to be a 'cradle of Christianity'. The parish church stands on the site of a priory founded by St Ninian in 397 AD and the small town was the seat of the Bishops of Galloway until the Reformation. The process of 'Reformation' in Scotland was much harsher than the gentle word implies. Two women, aged 18 and 65, were tied to stakes in Wigtown Bay and left to drown in the incoming tide. They refused to betray their religious beliefs and were thus 'reformed'.

However, for me, the greatest tragedy of modern times is the extensive afforestation that has taken place and now covers more than 50 per cent of Galloway. I recently climbed Merrick (2,764 ft), lowland Scotland's highest peak and, for as far as the eye could see the dark green of conifers sprawled across the horizon, except to the west, where the sea stops them.

The principal river is the Cree, 18 miles long, rising, draining Minnoch, Trool, Penkiln and Palnure, all afforested. Apart from in its headwaters, above the falls at Bargrennan, the Cree offers good fishing with some delightful pools where fly fishing is the best method of hooking salmon.

The Newton Stewart Angling Association and Galloway Estates make fishing available to the public, including fishing on the tributaries, good little salmon and sea-trout streams which fish well in decent water levels. Opening day on 1 March can often produce fish, as it did for John Lyons in 1988. He landed a beautiful, sea-liced 9-lb fish in the association's tidal waters. The most famous pool on the river is High Leaire, a first-class holding pool and others of note are Linlaskin, Ghyll Pool, Steeps, Cunningham's Ford and Cardorchan.

The best of the Cree fishings is in the hands of the Galloway Estate which regularly stocks its waters which is of benefit to the whole system. In 1988 they introduced 20,000 one-inch-long stock fish, purchased from the Girvan hatchery. Galloway Estate Waters produce about 150 salmon each season with autumn months giving most: October, 37; September, 28; July, 34 and April and May, 15. These waters are always in demand but some weekly lets are available. However, don't despair, for the Angling Association will introduce you to this very lovely river for a modest charge. As on most of the Solway rivers, sea-trout fishing on Cree is excellent and for an all-round summer family holiday Newton Stewart is an ideal centre.

The River Bladnoch is Cree's neighbour and joins Wigtown bay south of the country town of Wigtown. This is a modest stream, also affected by forestry operations but it can fish well, particularly during autumn months. There is also a small run of summer grilse but, for some reason best known to themselves, sea-trout tend to give Bladnoch a miss. The most productive of the Bladnoch fishings is at Mochrum Park and there is an added attraction here in that the owners also offer self-catering accommodation of the highest standard, close to the river. Charges are modest and the river is carefully managed and also stocked with brown trout. Given the chance of salmon and with alternative trout fishing in river and lochs nearby, the Bladnoch would be high on my list of venues for a relaxing holiday.

Bladnoch salmon are not large, but playing a fresh run fish in the narrow confines of the stream is an exciting prospect. In June 1988 Mr R. Luckin was lucky and took three fish, two from Tinto's Pool and one from Nit Bank: total weight 27 lb. June also produced a number of other salmon in the order of 9–10 lb and results seem to indicate that the summer run of salmon and grilse of this delightful river is improving.

The most westerly of the principal south-west salmon and sea-trout streams is the Water of Luce which rises in Ayrshire in yet another southern forest, Arecleoch, to the east of Ballantrae. There are two feeder streams: Main Water of Luce, rising to the east of Arecleoch Forest and Cross Water of Luce which begins life near the Martyr's Tomb at Barhill and almost joins Duisk River and Girvan. Main Water of Luce draws strength from Penwhirn Reservoir and meets Cross Water at the village of New Luce.

Salmon fishing is best from New Luce down to Glenluce where the river enters the Solway by St Helena Island and the golf links; but most of this fishing is reserved for the owners, Stair Estates. The Stranraer & District Angling Association have good fishing starting from about four miles upstream of New Luce and extending for a distance of eight miles of Cross Water of Luce.

The Luce is very much a spate river and it is often September before salmon arrive on the association waters in any numbers. Sea-trout also run the Luce, from July onwards, when evening and night-time fishing can be excellent and sea-trout seem to prefer Main Water. In spite of a general lack of good holding pools, the Luce seems to be an improving salmon fishery. With netting coming to an end on much of the Solway, this little river should benefit even further.

And description of trout fishing in south-west Scotland must be prefaced by a warning that mass-afforestation has, in my opinion, severely damaged the quality of sport. Several once prolific waters are now virtually fishless and concern is being expressed about the future of many more.

The high lochs of Merrick were never noted as being prolific trout fisheries; but they always contained fish. Now, waters such as Enoch, Neldricken, Valley, Glenhead and Dungeon are hardly worth a cast increasingly in recent years. Where once trout bred naturally, sport in the south-west depends upon artificial restocking.

Sproustow Dub, River Tweed

There are now almost no natural fisheries and the trout angler must be prepared to accept largely put-and-take fishing to find reasonable sport. Nevertheless, local angling clubs and associations work hard to maintain as high a level of fishing as possible and providing you don't mind much of your angling surrounded by vast conifer plantations, there is still splendid sport to be found.

Perhaps my favourite waters are the Drumlanford lochs, Morton Castle, Starburn, Kettleton and Ettrick. They are in a more natural setting, small, intimate and offering a considerable degree of privacy. Afton Reservoir to the north is also worth a visit and this water contains both brown trout and brook trout. Afton is regularly stocked and every two years upwards of 1,000 fish are released.

The Forestry Commission owns most of the forest waters, including Bradan, Skelloch, Dee, Dhu, Breckbowie, Lillie's, Loch of the Lowes, Black Loch, Barnbaroch and Clatteringshaws, situated in the vicinity of Newton Stewart. The Newton Stewart Angling Association will direct you to most of these waters and Pattie's, the excellent tackle shop in Dumfries, will keep visiting anglers right.

Hotels in the area also offer trout fishing and I can heartily recommend Barscobe Loch as one of the most productive and beautiful waters in the area, stocked with brown, rainbow and American brook trout. The New Galloway Angling Association has the fishing on Loch Lochinvar and this is also stocked with both brown and rainbow trout.

G. M. Thomson in Castle Douglas offer visitors fishing and accommodation on Loch Mannoch, 72 acres in extent and full of hard-fighting 8-oz trout. Thomson's also have a good little water north of Castle Douglas, Loch Ervie, which is stocked with larger trout but they are much more difficult to catch.

Trout fishing is available to visitors on Dalbeattie Reservoir, two miles west of the town and Loch Roan, north of Castle Douglas has produced fish of over 4 lb in recent years. Loch Whinyeon at Gatehouse of Fleet has four boats available and bank fishing for visitors; but if you are looking for specimen fish, then Jericho Loch is the best place to cast your fly. This is a first-class put-and-take fishery, north of Dumfries, and trout average just under 2 lb in weight with fish of over 5 lb not uncommon.

In the Stranraer area, the local angling club have trout fishing on a number of reservoirs including Soulseat which can produce trout of up to 5 lb; Penwhirn and Loch Ree are full of small native brown trout; and out towards Port Patrick visitors may find good sport on several delightful, remote waters, such as Knockquhassen and Dindinnie Reservoirs and Lochnaw Castle Loch and Dunskey Loch.

South-west Scotland has fine game fishing, set amidst attractive scenery, particularly along the Solway coast. Whilst trout anglers and salmon anglers may struggle at times for sport, there are few areas in Scotland to match the high quality of its sea-trout fishing. If I were asked to name that place where you are most likely to have success with sea-trout, then Solway rivers would be top of my list.

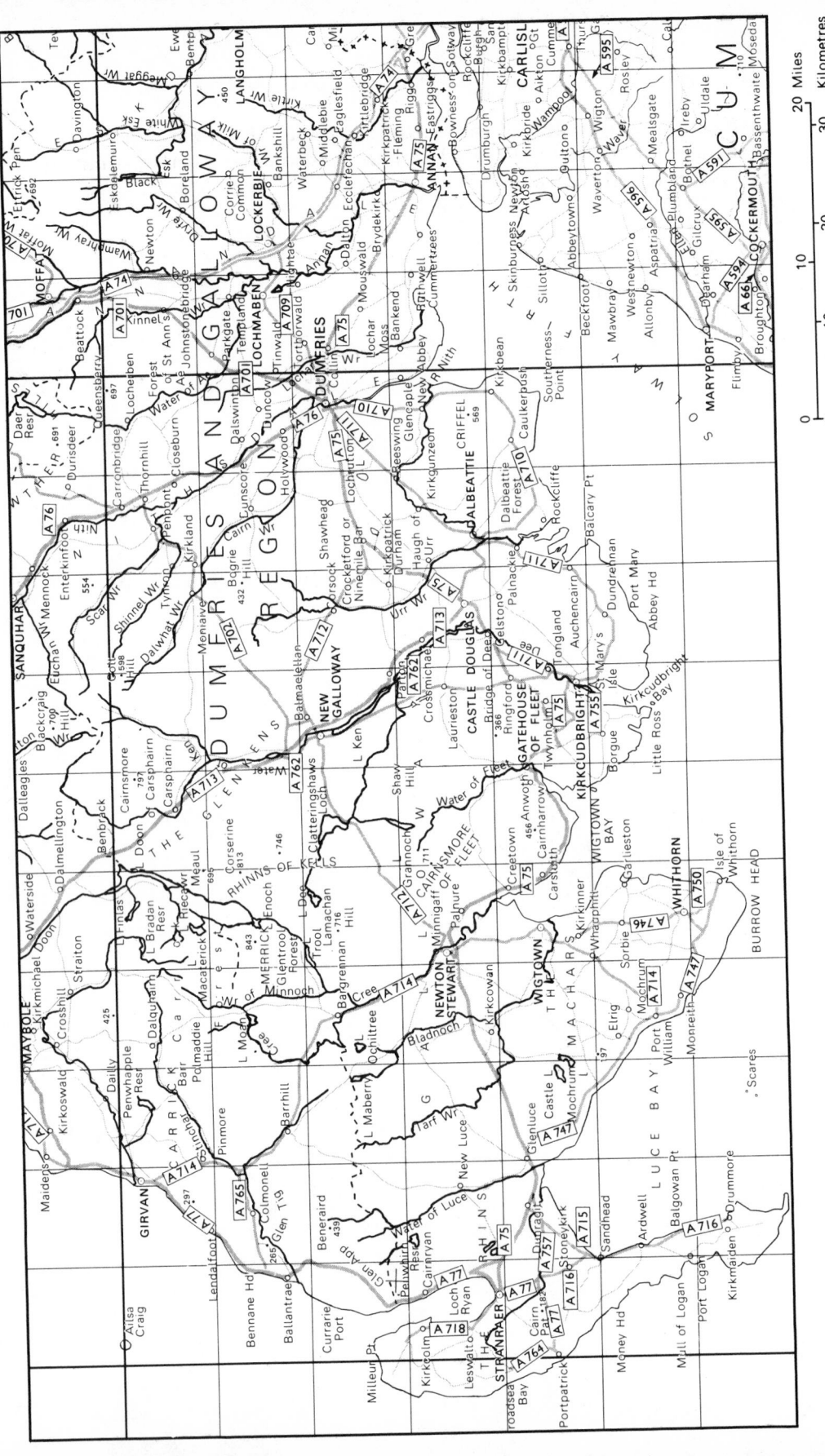

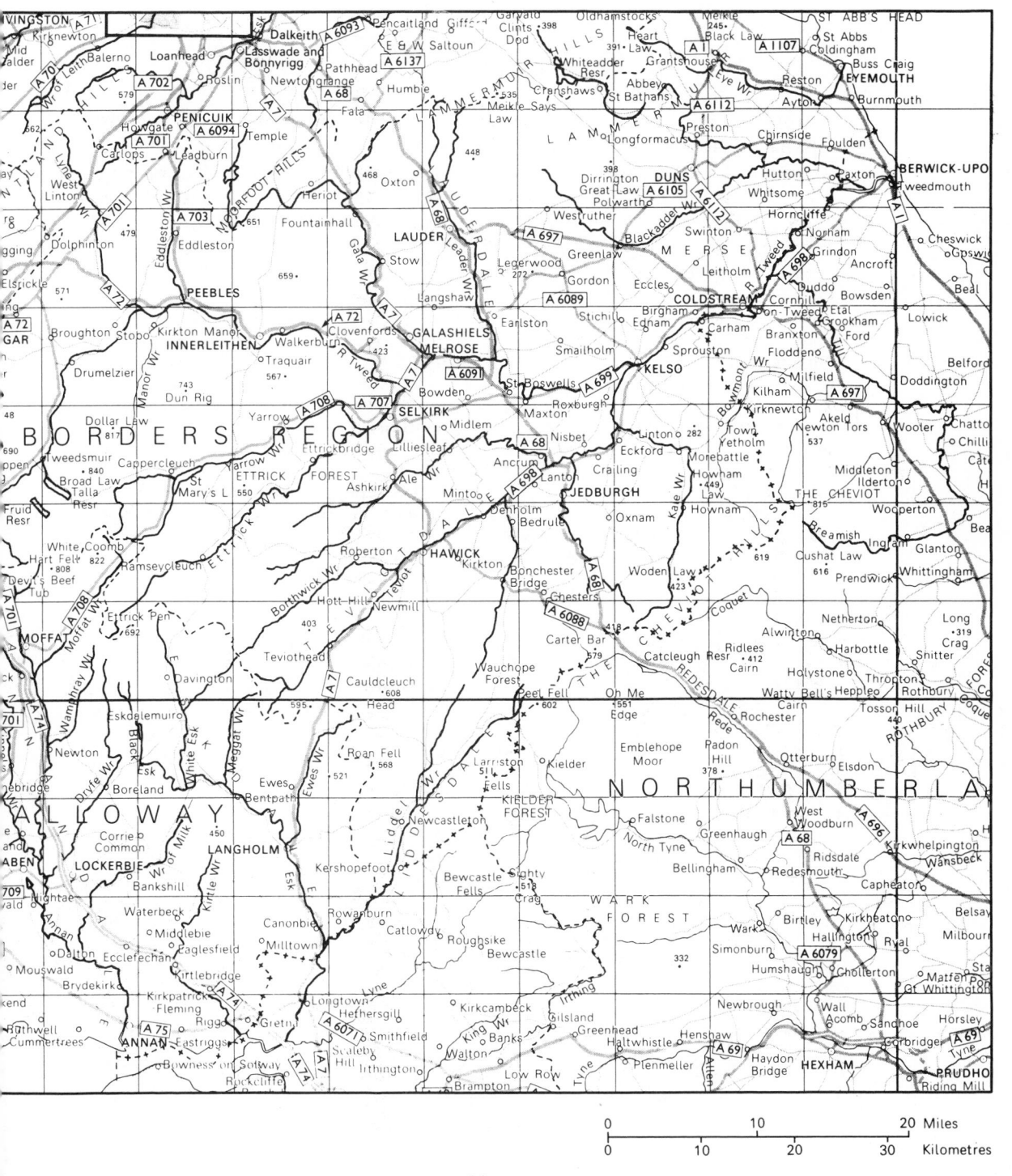

THE BORDERLINE

FISHING DIRECTORY

Fishing on Tweed and her tributaries is controlled by estates, local angling clubs, associations and hotels. Tackle shops issue permits for all the club waters and these are listed below; as are hotels which arrange fishing and also a number of locations which offer self-catering accommodation with fishing. Decide which part of Tweed you wish to visit and contact the appropriate person for details.

Anglers Choice,
High Street, Melrose
(089682) 3070
John Dickson & Son,
35 The Square, Kelso
(05732) 24687
Ian Fraser Sports,
Northgate, Peebles
(0721) 20979
Game Fair,
12 Marygate, Berwick-upon-Tweed
(0289) 5119
R Greive & Son,
High Street, Eyemouth
(0390) 50270
Gun & Sports Shop,
Kenmore Toll, Jedburgh
(08356) 2377
D & H McDonald,
9-11 High Street, Selkirk
(0750) 21398
Sports Shop,
29 High Street, Innerleithen
(0896) 830806
A Murray, Pet Shop,
Union Street, Hawick
(0450) 3543
Messrs J Stothart,
6 High Street, Hawick
(0450) 2231
J & A Turnbull,
30 Bank Street, Galashiels
(0896) 3191
Redpath & Co,
55/57 Horsemarket, Kelso
(089682) 24578
The Factor,
Lothian Estates Office, Jedburgh
(08356) 2201

J P Campbell,
Glenrath Farm, Kirkton Manor
(07214) 221
Mrs Richard,
The Garden House, Kailzie, Peebles
(0721) 20007
The Manager,
Milne Garden, Coldstream
(0289) 82245
Mrs H Dunlop,
Whitmuir, Selkirk
(0750) 21728
Dr E J Wise,
West Loch House, Coldingham
(03903) 270
Douglas Hotel,
Channel Street, Galashiels
(0896) 2189
Abbotsford Arms Hotel,
63 Stirling Street, Galashiels
(0896) 2517
Kingsknowes Hotel,
Galashiels
(0896) 3478
R Smyly,
Sunderland Hall, Galashiels
(0350) 21298
L Bald,
Fisherman's Cottage, Boleside
(0896) 2792
L B Smith,
Darnlee, Darnick, Melrose
(089682) 2261
J Broomfield,
Ravensbourne, Douglas Road, Melrose
(089682) 2308
George & Abbotsford Hotel,
Melrose
(089862) 2038

Bel Ingram Limited,
7 Walker Street, Edinburgh
031 225 3271
(Mertoun & Makerstoun Beats)
The Hon Caroline Douglas-Home,
Douglas & Angus Estates, The Hirsel,
Coldstream
(Birgham/Lower Birgham Beats)
Tillmouth Park Hotel,
Tillmouth, Cornhill, Northumberland
(0890) 2255
Ednam House Hotel,
Kelso
(089682) 24168
The Crook Inn,
Tweedsmuir
(08997) 272
Ettrickshaws Country House Hotel,
Ettrick Bridge, Nr Selkirk
(07505) 229
Tweed Valley Hotel,
Walkerburn, Peeblesshire
(089687) 220
Elm House Hotel,
17 Bridge Street, Hawick
(0450) 2866/4175
Dryburgh Abbey Hotel,
St Boswells, Roxburghshire
(0835) 22261
Phililburn House Hotel,
Selkirk
(0750) 20747/21690
Blackwood & Smith, WS
39 High Street, Peebles
(0721) 20131
J H Leeming, ARICS
Stichill House, Kelso
(05737) 280
Various Beats on Lower, Middle and Upper
Tweed.

Fishing in south-west Scotland is widely
available through estates, local angling clubs
and hotels; the Forestry Commission owns
a large number of trout lochs.

RIVER NITH & CAIRN
Director of Finance,
Municipal Chambers,
Dumfries
(0387) 53166

**Dumfries & Galloway Angling
Association,**
W McMillan, 6 Friar's Vennel,
Dumfries
(0387) 52075
Mid Nithsdale Angling Association,
R W Coltart, Shoe Shop, Thornhill
(0848) 30464
Buccleuch Estates Ltd,
Drumlanrig Mains, Thornhill
(08486) 283
Upper Nithsdale Angling Association,
W Forsyth, 100 High Street, Sanquhar
(06592) 241

RIVER ANNAN
Mr A Bailey,
Newbie Mill, Annan
(04612) 2608
Ecclefechan Hotel,
Ecclefechan
(05763) 213
(Hoddom Water)
McJerrow & Stevenson,
Lockerbie, Dumfriesshire
(05762) 2123
(Hallheaths Water)
K Ratcliffe,
Jay-Ar, Preston House Road, Hightae,
Lockerbie
(038781) 220
Castle Milk Estate Office,
Norwood, Lockerbie
(05765) 293
Hoddom & Hoddom,
Water Bailiff, Bridge Cottage, Hoddom
(05763) 488
(Kinmount Beat)
Upper Annandale Angling Association,
J Black, 1 Rosehill, Grange Road, Moffat
(0683) 20104

RIVER ESK
Esk & Liddle Fisheries,
J I Wylie, Byreburnfoot, Canonbie
(05415) 279
(enclose a large, sae)

RIVER WHITE ESK
Hart Manor Hotel,
Eskdalemuir, by Langholm
(05416) 217

RIVER URR
Tommy's Sports Shop,
King Street, Castle Douglas
(0556) 2861
Dalbeattie Angling Association,
N Parker, Dalbeattie
(0556) 610448

RIVER BLADNOCH
J Haley,
Riverview Cottage, Spittal Bridge, Nr
Kirkcowan, Wigtownshire
(067183) 471

RIVER CAIRN
**Dumfries & Galloway Angling
Association,**
D G Conchie, 46 Barrie Avenue, Dumfries
(0387) 55233
D McMillan,
6 Friar's Vennel, Dumfries
(0387) 52075

RIVER CREE
Newton Stewart Angling Association,
Galloway Guns & Tackle, Albert Street,
Newton Stewart
(0671) 3404

CROSS WATER OF LUCE
McDiarmid Sports Shop,
90 George Street, Stranraer
(0776) 2705

RIVER FLEET
Murray Arms Hotel,
Gatehouse of Fleet
(05574) 207

BARBARROCH LOCH
Forestry Commission,
Hazelbank, Kilstruie, Sorbie, Newton
Stewart
(09885) 238

BARSCOBE LOCH
BRACK LOCH
MOSSRODDOCK LOCH
Mrs Kirk,
Barscobe Cottage, New Galloway, Castle
Douglas, Kirkcudbrightshire
(06442) 245

Milton Park Hotel,
Dalry, Castle Douglas, Kirkcudbrightshire
(06443) 286

BLACK ESK RESERVOIR
Hart Manor Hotel,
Eskdalemuir
(05416) 217

THE BLACK LOCH
CLATERINGSHAW LOCH
LOCH DEE
LOCH OF THE LOWES
LILIE'S LOCH
Forestry Commission,
Galloway Deer Museum, New Galloway,
Castle Douglas, Kirkcudbrightshire
(06442) 285

BRUNTIS LOCH
Gun & Tackle Shop,
40 Queen Street, Newton Stewart,
Wigtownshire
(0671) 2570

DALBEATIE RESERVOIR
N Parker,
30 High Street, Dalbeattie,
Kirkcudbrightshire
(0556) 610448

DINDINNIE RESERVOIR
KNOCKQUHASSEN RESERVOIR
LOCH REE
PERWHIRN RESERVOIR
SOULSEAT LOCH
J L Johnstone,
13 Dalrymple Court, Stranraer,
Wigtownshire
(0776) 4554
McDiarmid's Sports Shop,
90 George Street, Stranraer, Wigtownshire
(0776) 4554

LOCHNAW CASTLE
Lochnaw Castle Hotel,
Leswalt, by Stranraer, Wigtownshire
(077687) 277

DUNSKEY LOCH
The Keeper,
Dunskey Kennels, Portpatrick,
 Wigtownshire
(077681) 486

BAREND LOCH
Barend Properties,
Sandyhills, Dalbeattie, Kirkcudbrightshire
(038778) 663

LOCHENBRECK LOCH
D Twiname,
52 High Street, Gatehouse of Fleet
(05574) 222

LOCH WHINYEON
Murray Arms Hotel,
Gatehouse of Fleet, Castle Douglas,
 Kirkcudbrightshire
(05574) 207

LOCH MANNOCH
LOCH ERVIE
G M Thomson & Co,
27 King Street, Castle Douglas,
 Kirkcudbrightshire
(0556) 2701/2973

GLENKILN RESERVOIR
The Water Engineer,
South-West Scotland Water Board,
70 Treeglas Street, Dumfries
(0387) 63011
Galloway Arms Hotel,
Crocketford, Dumfries
(055669) 240

LOCH ROAN
Tommy's Sports Shop,
178 King Street, Castle Douglas,
 Kirkcudbrightshire
(0556) 2851

MOSSDALE LOCH, LOCH KEN
Cross Keys Hotel,
New Galloway, Kirkcudbrightshire
(06442) 494

JERICHO LOCH
Baird & Stevenson,
Lochanbriggs, Dumfries
(0387) 710237

CARSFAD RESERVOIR
EARLSTOUN LOCH
Glenkens Cafe,
14 Main Street, Dalry, Castle Douglas
(06443) 427

LOCHINVAR LOCH
Lochinvar Hotel,
Dalry, Castle Douglas
(06443) 210
Mr Armour,
Lochinvar Lodge, Castle Douglas, Dalry
(06443) 427

LOCH OCHILTREE
KIRRIEREUCHLOCH
R W McDowall,
9 Victoria Street, Newton Stewart,
 Wigtownshire
(0671) 2163

DRUMLAMFORD LOCH
A McKeand,
Head Keeper, the Kennels, Barrhill,
 Ayrshire
(046582) 256

LOCH BRADAN, LOCH SKELLOCH
Forestry Commission,
Ayrshire District Forest, Forest Office,
 Dalmellington Road, Straiton, Ayrshire
(06557) 637

KETTLETON RESERVOIR
Messrs Pollock & Oag,
1 West Morton Street, Thornhill,
 Dumfriesshire
(0848) 30207

LOCH ETTRICK
The Keeper,
Blawbrae Cottage, Thornhill,
 Dumfriesshire
(0848) 31304

AFTON RESERVOIR
Stanley Stores,
Unit 9, Glaisnock Shopping Centre,
Cummnock, Ayrshire
(0290) 22467

STARBURN LOCH
MORTON CASTLE LOCH
Buccleuch Estates,
Estate Office, Drumlanrig Mains,
Thornhill
(08486) 283/284

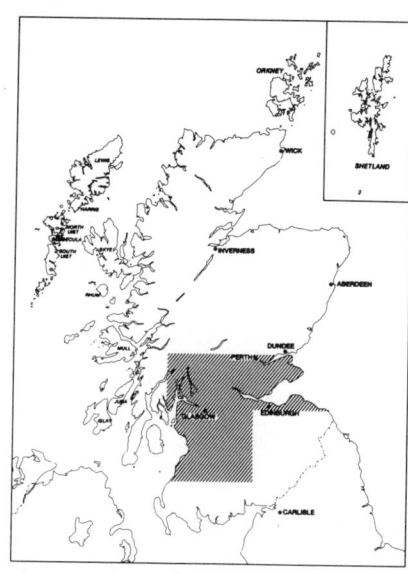

THE HEART
OF SCOTLAND

*Fife, Lothian, Clyde
and Carrick*

King James V of Scotland did not get on very well with his English
counterpart, Henry VIII. In fact, poor James didn't get on well with his
own knights and nobles either, let alone overbearing neighbours. Matters
came to a head in 1542 when Henry VIII invaded Scotland and defeated
James's hastily gathered forces at the rout of Solway Moss. James retired
hurt to his favourite home, Falkland Palace in Fife and took to his bed. As
he lay dying, news was brought to him of the birth of a daughter, Mary,
born at Falkland Palace. On receiving the news, James is reputed to have
muttered the prophetic statement 'God's will be done. It cam wi' a lass and
it'll gang wi' a lass.'

The House of Stuart ruled Scotland through Walter Stuart, who
married Margaret, daughter of the architect of Scottish independence,
King Robert the Bruce. The family had been Stewards of Scotland since
the time of King David I. Walter's son, Robert, became king of Scotland
in 1371 and from him the royal line descended in male succession until
James V. The luckless lass who ushered in the fall of the House of Stuart,
was Mary, Queen of Scots, born five days before her father's death and
shipped to France in 1547 to escape infant marriage to English Edward VI.
Her mother, Mary of Lorraine, stayed in Scotland and ruled on her
daughter's behalf. Mary returned to Scotland in 1561 to be confronted
with a host of political and religious problems, much fuelled by her
bickering, ambitious nobles and the preaching of John Knox.

After defeat at the Battle of Carberry Hill in 1567, Mary was imprisoned
in Loch Leven Castle and forced to abdicate in favour of her son, James
VI. Mary spent the rest of her mortal existence incarcerated in various
castles and finally ended her unhappy life on the headsman's block at
Fotheringhay on 8 February 1587, executed on a warrant signed by her

cousin, Queen Elizabeth of England.

I never fish Loch Leven without thinking of Mary. In retrospect, I suppose she never really stood a chance. Tall, regal, opinionated, she must have been anathema to her chauvinistic Scottish barons. That she lasted so long is remarkable in itself; but I believe her fate was almost a foregone conclusion.

Castle Island on Loch Leven was a secret, silent place. As a boy, I used to wander among the grey ruins, through the tangled undergrowth, rehearsing the sad facts of Mary's life. How she escaped from the castle, helped by one of the servants, rowed across the loch and cantered off smiling, to meet her grim fate so many harsh, friendless years later. I like to think that she found some pleasure amidst the beauty of Loch Leven and even imagine her dining off the magnificent trout for which this most special of all Scottish lochs is justly famous. Scotland, without Loch Leven, would not be Scotland and for decades anglers from all over the world have made their pilgrimage to this centre of all things excellent in angling.

Loch Leven has always offered anglers top-quality sport. When I fished it regularly during the late 1950s and early 1960s upwards of 50,000 trout were taken each season. The best recorded catch came in 1960 when 80,000 fish were caught and the most remarkable fact about these figures is that the loch was rarely stocked; because of the superlative quality of both water and insect life, trout maintained their numbers naturally.

In the 1930s fishing was leased for a time to the Perth angling family of Malloch and for several years they stocked the loch with fish reared in the old ponds on the north shore. However, when it became clear that their efforts were having little effect on numbers of fish taken, this practice was discontinued.

Biologists estimate that Loch Leven supports a population of about 120,000 fish and in the old days these lovely creatures, trout, not biologists, used to rise readily to surface flies and give great sport. Fishing was from long, heavy boats, propelled by two gillies, each wielding an oar and blank days on Loch Leven were virtually unknown. Sadly, things are very different now and to see fish rising is the exception rather than the rule. In times past, a June rise on Loch Leven was a miracle of nature, with the whole surface covered by hungrily feeding fish, and eagerly casting anglers. Today, fish tend to feed on the bottom and fishermen now have to resort increasingly to raking the depths with reservoir-type lures in order to catch them.

Even these methods are often fruitless. The Central Scotland Angling Championship in 1988 was fished by 126 competitors who managed to land only five trout between them during the course of a whole day's fishing. Frequently, more than 20 boats will return to the pier with but a single fish. The average annual catch in the early 1980s has dropped to below 10,000 trout and fishing is now very much dependent upon good weather conditions for best sport. This alteration to bottom feeding has been caused by intensive agricultural methods round the shores of the loch. Sewage, industrial waste, insecticides and fertilisers are washed into the water causing an alarming degree of 'eutrophication'. In the late 1960s, the water was heavily clouded with algal growth and this situation has often been repeated in recent years causing alarm to anglers.

In 1988 the Kinross firm of Todd & Duncan were fined £1,000 at Perth Sheriff Court after admitting that they had allowed chemicals to be discharged into the loch via the South Queich. More than three times the permitted level of ammoniacal nitrogen and twice the level of phosphorous; certain to increase algal growth.

Sir David Montgomery, whose family has owned the fishing rights on Loch Leven since the days of James IV, instigated a major restocking programme and this seems to be producing results with improved numbers of fish being caught. In 1988, 150,000 trout were released into the loch and the hatchery had some 350,000 eggs, collected during the autumn for rearing. Given this level of commitment, there is every chance that Loch Leven might, some day, return to its former glory; 1985 saw 23,000 trout caught. But the root-cause of the decline, intensive agriculture and effluent discharge, remains and until this problem is properly addressed, it is doubtful if the restocking programme will be successful and perhaps Loch Leven in the future will always have to rely upon artificial stocking methods.

In the meantime, do your best. Good baskets are taken. The St Serf's Ladies Angling Club, a three-strong team of experienced lady anglers, fishing in a 1988 Inter-club Competition, had eight fish weighing 9 lb 8 oz and the ten boats taking part had a total catch of 50 trout weighing 45 lb 14 oz. The best fish caught during 1988 weighed 4 lb, taken by David Hunter of the Howff Angling Club and Loch Leven is a popular venue for competitive events.

Loch Leven covers an area of 4,300 acres and is generally a shallow loch, the deepest part being to the west of St Serf's Island where the water drops to a depth of 80 ft. Over the years a number of classic drifts have been established, related to wind direction, and the most productive of these are well noted.

In a west wind fish Thrapple Hole; from the Beech Hedge to the Start; Hole o' the Inch; Duncan's Corner; East Point; Castle Island to Sunken Rock; Paddies Point to Garden Point.

In a north-west wind fish The Shallows and in a north wind, concentrate from the Old Manse to the Elbow. In a north-east wind, fish Rough Hole over the face of the bank; Portmoak Point to the Hole of the Inch; Back o' the Yairds; Green Myres to the Elbow. When an east wind blows, try Horse Shoe to Castle Island; and the Shallows, which can also be fished with a steady breeze from any direction; anglers are advised to fish the South Shore, particularly in the afternoon.

In a south-east wind, fish The Narrow Neck; Horse Shoe to the Elbow;

Leven Mouth to St Serf's and the Brox Hole by the sluices. South wind, fish South Shore; Vain Dyke; Garden Point and Alice's Bower to Green Isle. Finally, in a south-west wind, fish South Shore to Reed Bower and Castle Island; Clay Hills to the Mary Knowe; Mary Knowe to Green Isle past the Queich Mouth.

The River Leven drains the loch eastwards, flowing through industrial Fife, past Leslie, Glenrothes and Markinch to reach the Firth of Forth at Leven in Largo Bay. The river has excellent brown trout fishing and in the first few miles there can be decent sport with sea-trout. The River Leven Trust and the Methilhaven and District Angling Club manage the fishing and issue day tickets to visiting anglers. They fight a constant battle against pollution and have carried out much improvement works to the lower river.

The area to the north of Leven is a good base for anglers who have non-fishing family members to keep happy. The wide, golden sweep of Largo Bay offers splendid bathing and sand-castle building opportunities and there is a large, well-laid-out caravan site near Shell Bay which is ideal for little ones. The area also has several golf courses and places of interest to visit, including the birth place of Andrew Selkirk, Daniel Defoe's model for Robinson Crusoe, at Lower Largo.

Fife offers visiting anglers a number of good brown trout waters, well stocked and with permits readily available. The majority of these waters are owned by Fife Regional Council and are leased to local angling clubs and associations. In the Lomond Hills, east of Loch Leven, there are a number of reservoirs, including Harperleas, Ballo, Holl and Arnot. The best of these is the smallest, Arnot Reservoir, privately owned and extending to an area of forty acres. The fishing is managed by two angling clubs and the quality of sport is very high. Permission to fish is sometimes available and you might well be rewarded with trout of over 3 lb for your trouble.

South of Loch Leven is Loch Ore, the site of an opencast coal-mining operation in days gone by and now redressed as a country park and the largest freshwater loch in Fife. Facilities are provided for a number of activities: cafeteria, display area, slide shows and talks, guided walks, fishing, bird-watching and an area of the loch has been reserved for instruction in dinghy and canoe sailing. A ranger is on hand to assist visitors and make them welcome.

Loch Ore is stocked with brown and rainbow trout and their average weight is 12 oz. The Regional Council have also provided facilities for disabled anglers and the heaviest fish taken recently was a trout of 5 lb 12 oz, caught by Mr Andrew Herd in June 1988.

Lochmill Reservoir, south of Newburgh on the Firth of Tay, offers both boat and bank fishing to visitors. Nearby Lindores Loch has the reputation of containing some very large pike; and excellent brown trout with fish of 5 lb sometimes caught.

Cameron Reservoir, south of St Andrews has brown trout and a few rainbow trout and is managed by the St Andrews Angling Club. There is a bag limit of nine fish and this is frequently achieved. Trout fishing is also available at Upper Carriston, near Methilhill.

Little Clatto Reservoir, between Kennoway and Cupar is leased to Crawford Priory Estates and offers the chance of sport and in the vicinity of Burntisland is Stenhouse Reservoir, leased to the Burntisland Angling Club, perhaps the best of the Fife trout waters, with fish of over 5 lb sometimes caught and an average weight of 1 lb 8 oz.

In the Dunfermline area the council lease Cullaloe to the Civil Service Sports Association and this water has fish which average 12 oz; the association also lease Loch Glow, to the west of Kelty and both these waters can provide good sport. The Black Loch adjoins Loch Glow and regularly produces trout of over 3 lb and in 1983 a magnificent fish of 7 lb 2 oz.

Fishing is also available on a number of other council reservoirs, including Castlehill, Upper and Lower Glendevon, Glenfarg, Glenquey and Craigluscar. Craigluscar is the most productive of these and offers a real challenge to anglers. The water is stocked with brown and rainbow trout and fish of up to 7 lb have been caught in recent years. But I suppose my favourite is Lower Glendevon which has all the characteristics of a Highland loch and none of the gloom usually associated with reservoir fishing. There are interesting weed beds and fishing corners and in autumn months this is a very lovely place to spend a day. Trout are not large but fight well. Neighbouring Upper Glendevon suffers much in appearance when water levels are low and intending visitors should check this point before booking.

The most notable put-and-take fishing in Fife is to be found at Loch Fitty, close to Dunfermline, Scotland's old capital city and the last resting place of King Robert the Bruce. Well, that's not strictly true because only his body lies there. His heart was removed and carried in a silver casket on crusade to the Holy Land by his life-long friend and supporter, the Black Douglas. Unable to resist the temptation of a good brawl, Douglas stopped off along the way to give the Spaniards a bit hand in a fight with the Moors. Rising in his stirrups, Douglas flung the casket ahead of him, into the thickest of the fray and galloped after it in hot pursuit. He was killed in the battle and his corpse was found, lying over the heart of his dead king. The casket was taken back to Scotland and buried somewhere in the grounds of Melrose Abbey in the Borders where it remains, undiscovered to this day.

This is less than can be said for the brown trout and rainbow trout in Loch Fitty which are found all the time, much to the delight of the many anglers who patronise its 160 acres. Fitty is a shallow water with excellent natural feeding which produces high-quality, pink-fleshed fish.

The loch is under the day-to-day management of a fishery manager who is always in attendance ready to give the best possible advice on flies and fishing areas. There is also a fully stocked tackle shop where anglers can try out their intended purchases, before walloping their wallets.

More than 20,000 trout are introduced each season and opening day, 27 February, generally produces good sport. In 1988 the first fish of the season was netted within ten minutes of the boats setting out and the best catch of the day fell to Edinburgh angler Kevin Burns and his two sons who took 15 fish weighing 20 lb. A total of 138 trout weighing 155 lb 8 oz were landed, including fish of 5 lb 2 oz, 4 lb 8 oz and 3 lb 2 oz.

Although Kinross and the Wee Kingdom of Fife may not be able to boast of outstanding salmon and sea-trout fishing, it does offer good sport with brown trout; above all, on that majestic, inner sanctum of Scottish trout fishing, Loch Leven. Furthermore, ease of access and variety of waters make the lands north of the Firth of Forth well worth while visiting.

As a centre for a combined fishing/family holiday, the area has few rivals. The coastal towns and villages are of great beauty; charming, charismatic, picturesque and unspoiled. Anstruther is the home of the unique Scottish Fisheries Museum, and start-point for visiting the RSPB bird sanctuary on May Island in the Firth of Forth. Crail, with its beautiful little harbour, and well-preserved buildings is also worth a visit. Then there are Elie and Lundin Links with their famous golf links, and that most famous of all the world's golf courses, the Old Course at St Andrews, with its 12th-century cathedral and university, the oldest in Scotland, founded in 1411. Fife has many dear memories for me. As children, we were taken, steam-trained from Waverley for summer holidays on the north shore of the Forth. Later, I travelled brighter-eyed, full of hope, hurrying to every trout fisherman's destiny; a date with the wonderful fish of Loch Leven.

Throughout the centuries, the Firth of Forth has been the principal sea gateway to Scotland; 50 miles long by up to 17 miles wide, scattered with the islands of Cramond, Inchcolm, Inchmickery, Inchkeith, May and gaunt, basalt-core Bass Rock.

Inchcolm, 'the island of St Columba', is the holy island of the firth, where King Alexander I established a monastery in 1123 AD. Alexander had been caught in a storm and shipwrecked on Inchcolm, then known as Emonia, and he built the Abbey as a 'thank you' for his deliverance. The ruins of the Abbey still grace the little isle today and visitors sail from Aberdour to spend a few hours wandering amidst old ruins and more modern gun emplacements left over from fortifications built during two world wars. On the way over to the island, the boat crosses Mortimer's Deep, named after Alan de Mortimer who gifted much of his lands to the Abbey, on condition that upon his death, he might be buried there. In due course the monks collected his coffin and rowed towards Inchcolm;

but a wind got up and in their struggle the monks lost the coffin overboard—hence, Mortimer's Deep.

At the southern entrance to the Firth, Bass Rock had a less peaceful purpose and was the watch-dog of the Forth, the lookout for incursions by ships of the old enemy, England; the assembly point for the Scottish fleet. The rocky promontory thrusts aggressively, 350 ft above sea-level and is only seven acres in extent. Solan geese and myriad sea-birds crowd sheer crags. It was said that James IV had two new-born children incarcerated on the rock, tended by a deaf and dumb nurse, in order to see what language the children would naturally speak; and the story is that the infants began to speak Hebrew. In 1671 Bass Rock was converted into a prison for Covenanters and in later years rebellious Jacobites cooled their heels on Scotland's 'Devil's Island'.

Fishing was and is a major source of employment in the Firth and the small harbours on either shores of the estuary still boast sizeable fleets, although the grand days of the herring fishings are long gone and even inshore boats have a difficult time making a living. Crab and lobster have virtually disappeared and for the past two hundred years pollution in the firth has played havoc with fish stocks.

The Industrial Revolution brought increased prosperity to the Forth and Clyde Vallies but in its wake the rivers and streams that fed the firth were choked with effluent and in many places the river and estuary were little better than an open sewer. Runs of salmon and sea-trout declined and a once superlative fishery slipped towards disaster. A few migratory fish still managed to reach upstream spawning grounds, swimming swiftly through the filth on the clean top-waters of spates, but the days when the Forth System ranked as a major salmon river, on a par with Tay and Tweed, vanished.

Much-needed improvement has been brought about in recent years; by stricter control of the disposal of sewage and industrial waste and salmon and sea-trout are returning to the river in ever-increasing numbers. However, a new problem confronted returning fish: illegal drift-netting in the estuary and it has been estimated that these nets have accounted for as many as 20,000 fish each season.

Perhaps because of its reputation as being heavily polluted, and consequently of limited value as a fishery, it has taken a long time for the Forth District Salmon Fisheries Board to waken up to the fact of illegal drift-netting, and act to protect stocks of fish. Previously, the river was patrolled by Maj Clifford Fordyce-Burke, who retired in 1988 at the age of 75. The Major had been expected to carry out his duties—by car—from Torness to Balquhidder and never stood a chance of making any real impact on the poachers. Now, two fast launches operated by a number of honorary bailiffs have imposed their will on the netsmen and in 1988, 33 nets, six boats and three rods were confiscated.

Talla Reservoir, Tweedsmuir

All this is good news for rod and line anglers, who have been experiencing the best sport for years on the Forth and Teith and provided that this surveillance is continued, there is no reason why, given time and care, the system should not once again become a major salmon fishery, offering pleasure and profit to hundreds of anglers and hotels and guest houses in central Scotland.

The River Forth begins life in Loch Chon and Loch Ard, deep in the Queen Elizabeth Forest. Both these lochs were once excellent trout waters but, sadly, in recent years, the effects of afforestation have seriously diminished the quality of fishing. The Forestry Commission have now instituted a restocking programme on Loch Ard and I believe that they suspect that the damage was caused by planting their trees too close to the margins of the loch.

Some salmon manage to reach Loch Ard but there is concern over the fate of their progeny. Low pH water, caused by a combination of afforestation and acid rain, damage insect life in the spawning streams and the survival rate of parr and smolts must be greatly reduced in consequence. Best sport on the Forth comes in the autumn with good runs of fish entering the river from August onwards and fishing is available to visitors near Gartmore and at Stirling.

The headwaters of the Forth/Teith system have been much affected by water-impounding schemes to meet the demand from Central Scotland and this obviously means that fishing on the rivers, other than in times of spate, is dependent upon compensation flows. The Teith had its beginnings in one such water, lovely Loch Katrine in the Trossachs.

Loch Katrine used to flow eastwards to the River Forth until it was diverted to help supply Glasgow with water. Queen Victoria opened the new system in 1859 when Royal Cottage near Stronachlachar was built for her 'amusement'. This striking building, more lodge than cottage, is surrounded by fine woodlands, skirted by neat, well-trimmed lawns and enclosed by angular, clipped hedges with magnificent views over Katrine towards Stob Ardrain and Beinn Tulaichean.

Fishing on Loch Katrine is managed by Strathclyde Regional Water Department who stock the loch with brown trout from their hatchery on nearby Loch Arklet. Trout average 12 oz in weight and fishing is by fly only, from boats. Heavier fish are taken most seasons and trout of over 6 lb have been caught. The best sport is found at the west end of the loch, in the last, narrowing two miles, from Stronachlachar past Black Island and up to where Glengyle Water tumbles down from Parlan Hill. The south end is particularly attractive to fish, being edged with numerous headlands and bays where fish lie in shallow waters. Arrange your drift accordingly, close to the shore, fingers crossed.

My ancestors fished Loch Katrine more than 300 years ago but I doubt if they asked permission first. Clan Gregor were not much given to asking. The 'Children of the Mist' considered anything not actually nailed down to be fair game, including salmon and trout. Also cattle, sheep, horses, the Laird's factor, odd wealthy females and, of course, that most portable of all property, hard cash. The most famous of their kilted race was Rob Roy Macgregor, born at Glengyle at the west end of the loch in a house below the black crags of Meall Mor and Stob an Duibhe. A tiny graveyard still marks the final resting place of many of the clan although Rob himself lies asleep further north, on the cold Braes of Balquhidder overlooking Loch Voil.

The lands of Rob Roy are guarded by Loch Lomond in the west and Loch Katrine in the east; a magnificent wilderness of sudden peaks and secret corries, surrounded by mighty Ben Lomond, Ben Venue and Ben Ledi. My grandmother was a MacGregor from Callander and I feel a special kinship with the men who ruled these rugged lands of the 'bristling country', the Trossachs.

The River Teith now depends upon the waters of Lochs Venachar, Voil and Lubnaig and since the last two of these waters remain unaffected by dams, salmon fishing in the Teith is much better than the Forth. The Teith rises from remote, trackless wastes, west of Inverlochliarg, near the home of Rob Roy. Munros, mountains over 3,000 ft, crowd round: Beinn Tulaichean (945 m), Cruach Ardrain (1045 m), Beinn a'Chroin (946 m), An Caisteal (995 m) and Beinn Chabhair (931 m).

The infant river slips through ancient spawning redds into Lochs Doine and Voil, both good brown trout fisheries, hurrying by Balquhidder and the Balvag River, past Bonnie Strathyre to long Loch Lubnaig. Ben Ledi (879 m) and Ben Vorlich (983 m) enclose the leaden waters of the loch and much of the lower slopes of these two majestic peaks have been afforested. The dozens of mountain streams that feed through the forest into Lubnaig now probably carry unwelcome silt and sediment, scoured out of the hillsides during heavy floods. Lubnaig can produce good trolling for salmon and the most productive area is at the north-east end. The loch also holds good stocks of brown trout and some very large specimens have been taken over the years, mostly by anglers trolling for salmon.

Ann and I have never had much success on Lubnaig and our most famous catch was a large honey bee, found afloat in the middle of the loch on a leaf-raft. But don't let that deter you. Lubnaig is still very beautiful, in spite of the encroachments of the tree-planters and somewhat dour character of the fish.

Lubnaig charges south-east past St Brides Chapel, over the Falls of Leny, urgent to gather in the slow-flowing waters of Eas Gobhain from Venachar to burst into the Teith at Callander. The best of Teith salmon fishing is from here downstream to where the Forth and Teith join hands west of Stirling at Drip, before meandering through the sluggish loops south of Cambuskenneth, watched over by the tower of the Wallace Monument.

Fishing is divided into eight beats including Callander Town Water, Gart Estate, Cambusmore, Lanrick, Denston, Blair Drummond, Ochtertyre and Blue Bank. Opening day on the Teith, 1 February, often produces fish and these tend to be large salmon, with fish of up to 29 lb being taken over the years. Summer months see a run of grilse entering the river and autumn can also produce great sport.

Fishing on much of the Teith is readily available to members of the public, as is fishing on other tributaries. Fishing on the River Allan which rises on the northern slopes of the Ochil Hills and on its passage to the cathedral city of Dunblane, gathers in the waters from two first-class trout lochs, Lower and Upper Rhynd. The stream is managed by Allan Angling Association and day tickets are issued in Stirling and Bridge of Allan. The season extends from 15 March until 31 October and the Allan has runs of summer sea-trout and salmon during the autumn.

The last main tributary of the Forth is the Devon which stumbles into the tidal waters of the Firth upstream from Alloa. Headwaters have been trapped by a number of reservoirs and few migratory fish attempt to run the polluted lower waters of the river. However, upstream, the Devon is a delightful trout water, with some lovely pools and runs.

If the salmon and sea-trout going gets tough in the Stirling area, don't despair; apart from the huge Trossachs lochs there are many smaller trout waters where visiting anglers will find good fishing, readily available at reasonable prices; and an increasing number of recently developed put-and-take style fisheries. These are well managed, worth a visit and include North Third Fishery near Cambusbarron, Gartmore Dam by Alloa, Bowden Springs at Linlithgow and Loch Coulter near Bonnybridge.

Carron Valley Reservoir, owned by Central Regional Council, is one of the larger fisheries in the area; 965 acres in extent and stocked with good numbers of brown trout. Fishing is by fly only, from boats and there are twelve available for visiting anglers. Carron Valley can be stormy and an outboard motor is almost essential when fishing here. If you don't have one of your own, then the fishery can supply you with a reliable motor for the day.

The most productive trout fishery in the west is centred upon Lake of Menteith, one of central Scotland's best fisheries. The lake lies between the River Forth to the south, Venachar and the Trossachs to the north, Flanders Moss eastwards and the vast Loch Ard Forest to the west. Menteith covers an area of 652 acres and is expertly managed as a top-quality fishery. Fishing is by fly only and there are 22 boats available for anglers; the lake is not only busy with fisherpersons, for during the summer months a small vessel ferries visitors across the smooth waters to the island of Inchmaholme, where there are the ruins of an Augustinian monastery, established in 1283. In winter months, when the shallow lake freezes, other sportsmen gather and Menteith is a popular venue for curling.

The lake is regularly stocked with both brown and rainbow trout and some very large specimens are introduced each season which can weigh up to 15 lb. The average size of fish is more modest, 1 lb 8 oz, and fish are taken all over the lake, from margins to middle. The bays and long promontory on the south shore, along Cardross Moss, is a favoured fishing area but the resident manager will give visitors good advice concerning the 'drift of the moment' and which flies to be used on any particular day.

The 'auld grey city' of Edinburgh, Scotland's capital, may seem an unlikely fishing centre. Nevertheless, because of greatly improved road systems, not least of which is the Forth Road Bridge, some of Scotland's finest fisheries are within easy reach of the city centre. Indeed, a stone's throw from Princes Street, visiting anglers can find good trout fishing on the Water of Leith and the District Council have much improved this little river by controlling pollution and a vigorous restocking programme.

As a child, I first discovered trout in the Water of Leith, gazing over the bridge at Canonmills and over the years, as my angling interest grew, I explored the stream from Balerno on the skirts of the Pentland Hills down to Powderhall. Then, a single trout was a red-letter day. Now, decent baskets are frequently taken and there is some really splendid dry fly water.

Another much improved Lothian salmon stream is the River Almond, managed by the Cramond Angling Club, and this river is seeing increasing numbers of sea-trout returning to spawn, and even the odd salmon runs the river now. The association has its own hatchery and stocks the river regularly and, although busy, the Almond offers the chance of sport close to the city centre.

There are two Esks in the Lothians, Black and White Esk, but sadly, even in spite of improved sewage treatment, migratory fish are scarce, being mostly confined to the lower reaches of the South Esk. However, there are brown trout and they often oblige when offered a small dry fly. The best of the Lothian streams is the silver Tyne which rises near Crichton Castle at Pathhead in Midlothian. This is a narrow stream, often tree-lined and difficult to fish.

For the angler who perseveres and comes to know the water, then the Tyne can be superb. Brown trout abound and sea-trout run the river from June onwards. There are even a few salmon but few pass the falls at East Linton and they are rarely caught. Perhaps the most exciting aspect of Tyne fishing is the chance of a good sea-trout. They are best taken after dark and the thrill of playing a fresh-run three-pound sea-trout in such confined waters is all any angler could wish for.

Lothian Regional Council Department of Water and Drainage offer excellent trout fishing and most of the reservoirs in the area are available to visiting anglers. They are carefully stocked and managed and include Clubbiedean, Bonaly, Glencorse, Crosswood, Harperrig, Rosebery, Crosswood, Talla, Fruid, newly constructed Megget, Donolly, Hopes, Whiteadder. All have their own special character and charm. Fruid, Talla and Megget are large, often windswept waters, deep in the Moorfoot Hills south from Edinburgh. Hopes and Whiteadder lie high in the Lammermuirs, small, intimate waters, with small, intimate fish. The Pentland Hills reservoirs are almost within walking distance of Edinburgh and offer a wide variety of sport in lovely surroundings.

Near Linlithgow, birth place of Mary Queen of Scots, to the west of Edinburgh, there is a magnificent fishery at Linlithgow Loch. Fish can be dour but trout of up to 9 lb are taken and fish of between 3–5 lb are not uncommon. Beecraigs Loch nearby is also a super place to spend a day, trying to outwit the stocked rainbow trout. This little loch is pleasantly situated and produces upwards of 1,500 trout each season. Another top-quality fishery is Portmore Loch, south of Edinburgh, east of the road to Peebles, near the village of Eddleston. Some managed fisheries look it—Portmore doesn't. It is a lovely loch and the Moorfoot Hills line the east shore with Dundreich (622 m) dominating the skyline.

I first fished Portmore in the early 1960s and in those days Portmore had a well-deserved reputation for being one of the dourest waters in the land. It can also be a fiendishly windy place but in spite of everything Portmore always retains a high place in my angling affections. The loch is now properly controlled, managed and stocked and both boat and bank fishing are available for visitors. A fishing hut has been provided for shelter and a notice-board gives ample scope for anglers to leave behind comments on their day's sport. Each year up to 7,500 trout are caught and their average weight is in the order of 1 lb 8 oz. Fish of over 6 lb are frequently taken and the heaviest trout landed weighed a massive 9 lb.

But of all the Lothian waters, Gladhouse Reservoir is my favourite. Gladhouse covers an area of 400 acres and lies to the south of Edinburgh on the north slopes of the Moorfoots. It is a hill loch really, at an altitude of 900 ft and as such can often be windy. Nevertheless, it is an excellent trout loch and is regularly stocked. It is also an important nature reserve and breeding site for both resident and visiting birds. Have a look at the list of species noted in the fishing hut; it makes very impressive reading.

For as long as records have been kept, Gladhouse has produced between 2,000 and 3,000 trout each season and their average weight is about 12 oz, with a few fish each year of 3 lb or more. Trout rise and are caught all over the loch but the most productive areas are in the shallows and around the islands. One of my most enduring fishing memories concerns Gladhouse. It happened when Edinburgh Corporation controlled the reservoir and access to the fishing was by means of a 'secret ballot'. In theory, the names of all anglers seeking permission to fish on any particular day were placed in a hat and the first ones out were the lucky fishers. After several attempts and a word with a friend who worked with the Corporation, word finally arrived that we had managed to secure a booking. Some luck. Our day dawned wet, cold and windy but, undaunted, we launched the boat. Should have known better for within seconds we were being whisked down the loch at the speed of an express train.

We hit the south shore with the force of the Allied Army arriving on Normandy beaches and scrambled, shaken, to safety. My principal concern was how I was going to get the boat back to the mooring bay. Failure to do so, I was certain, would mean banning for life at the least and more probably being hung at the Tolbooth across from the Council Offices in High Street. After about an hour pondering the problem, I noticed the head and shoulders of a gardener, cutting a very high hedge and I called over to ask for his advice. I expected the man to climb down from the step ladders he was obviously standing on. Instead he just walked round and I was confronted by the most enormous man I have ever seen—and I'm no slouch at 6 feet 4 inches. He agreed to help row back and I shall always remember that frightful trip; an unforgettable flurry of flying oars and straining muscles, mostly mine. But I am still grateful for his help—he saved me from a fate worse than drowning at the hands of the City Fathers.

More sheltered Lothian waters may be found amongst the new fisheries recently established near Edinburgh. Morton Fishery and Selm Muir near Mid Calder; Loganlea by Penicuik; the Maltings Fishery at West Barns, Dunbar, and Markle Fishery by East Linton. Farmers and businessmen are converting ponds and pools into put-and-take fisheries and they all have an important part to play in meeting the increasing demand for good-quality sport.

It is often said that the best thing to come out of Edinburgh is the train to Glasgow. This of course depends very much upon where you were born, or live. Me, I come from Edinburgh and therefore always reverse the quip: the best thing to come out of Glasgow is the train for Edinburgh. There has always been friendly and not so friendly rivalry between Scotland's two major cities; and now, even I must admit that Glasgow is, as its motto declares, flourishing. The Glasgow Garden Festival has been a major success and with the Glasgow European City of Culture too, has Edinburgh City Fathers, scratching their whiskers, wondering what to do about it.

Even the River Clyde has come in for a good brush-up and such has been the improvement in the quality of Clyde water that salmon and sea-trout are again running this once famous salmon river; and in 1988 more than 300 salmon and even more sea-trout were counted over the weir at Blantyre.

The corpse of one salmon estimated as weighing 22 lb was recovered and fish are now spawning successfully in many of the Clyde's tributaries. A Clyde Fisheries Management Trust has been set up to control the letting of leases on parts of the river where there has been little angling interest for more than 100 years. One swallow doesn't make a summer, but it is wonderful to learn that the lower levels of this great Scottish river are beginning to recover from centuries of maltreatment and misuse.

However, because of the actions of poachers and unscrupulous fishermen, Clyde anglers applied in 1988 to the Secretary of State for Scotland for a Protection Order, to preserve and improve the quality of Clyde fishing. For above the erstwhile heavily polluted waters downstream, the Clyde has an outstanding reputation as a grayling fishery and there are also good stocks of brown trout.

The United Clyde Angling Protection Association controls most of the fishing along the 50 miles of Clyde between its source to the sea and all legal fishing methods are permitted on the river. The most scenically attractive part of the river is in the headwaters, around Elvanfoot, Crawford, Abington, Roberton and Lamington; but the best of the trout fishing is to be found below Carstairs in the deep pools by Lanark and Hazelbank where some very large trout lurk.

By mutual agreement, all salmon caught are being carefully returned to the water. Fish spawning upstream are far more important for the future of the Clyde than any lying gasping on the banks. Fishing on Clyde is easily accessible and readily available to visitors and if you are looking for sporting winter fishing, the Clyde grayling will more than test all your angling skills.

In the Campsie Hills, east of Glasgow and to the west by Greenock, anglers can find trout fishing on a number of small reservoirs and lochs, most of them managed and stocked by local angling associations where visitors are welcome, including Harelaw and Knocknaershill, Glenburn and the largest waters in the area, Loch Tom, Whinhill and Gryfe Reservoirs above Greenock. Better fishing may be found further south near Kilmarnock on Burnfoot and Craigendunton Reservoirs.

Some years ago I had the pleasure of fishing the River Ayr near Mauchline and although unsuccessful, enjoyed the experience very much indeed, in spite of cold, snow and rain. My host did manage to take one salmon, and we retired to the warmth and comfort of Poosie Nancy's pub by the bridge to regain feeling inside and out after our hours on the river.

The Ayr rises in the green Lowther Hills and flows westwards, reaching the sea in the old town, made famous through its association with Scotland's national bard, Robert Burns. Poaching has always been a problem on the Ayrshire salmon streams and no doubt was in the days of Rabbie Burns. Sadly, there are fewer fish about these days and the methods used by modern poachers included gassing the pools and the Ayr has often suffered in consequence.

A substantial barrier at Catrine prevents the upstream movement of fish so most angling is below this point and autumn months now bring most results. Pollution is another blight on the Ayr, with water from old mine workings entering the river. Much of the river is now in the hands of local angling clubs and, with the decline in salmon numbers, they often resort to stocking their waters with brown trout.

Sadly, the other principal Ayrshire salmon streams are similarly affected by the twin evils of pollution and poaching and the Garnock, which enters the sea in Irvine Bay and the Irvine itself suffer in consequence. The River Irvine Improvement Association has worked hard to restock its waters. Tragically, the poachers struck again recently when hundreds of fish were killed.

As consolation, there are a number of decent trout lochs in the area the best of which is probably Prestwick Reservoir; but even here the club has problems with poachers and have had to install an expensive warning system to protect their fishery. Prestwick Reservoir is stocked with both brown and rainbow trout and fish of over 3 lb are not infrequent. The average weight is a respectable 1 lb and all fishing is from the bank.

The Largs Angling Club, Ardrossan and Eglinton Angling Club, Munnoch Angling Club and Dalry Angling Club all offer visitors permits for fishing their waters and these include waters such as Muirhead and Camphill Reservoirs, Munnoch Reservoir, Caff, Knockendon and Collennan.

The largest Ayrshire water is Loch Doon and this used to receive salmon from the River Doon which flows westwards to reach the sea south of Ayr. Since the building of a 44-ft-high dam to impound the waters of the loch, salmon rarely enter and are even more rarely caught.

The river still manages to produce a few fish each year and there are probably far more taken, but not by the mouth and the river suffers considerably from the effects of pollution. Efforts are being made to improve water quality and fishing by the River Doon Improvement Association.

Loch Doon has large numbers of small trout and is a free fishery. From time to time monsters of over 10 lb are hooked but the smaller inhabitants are fun to catch. Furthermore, the Doon valley is a most attractive place to fish and the head of the loch is easily accessible via a narrow road that follows the north shoreline out into the hills.

The River Girvan has also had its troubles recently, being heavily polluted by toxic waters released from disused mine workings at Killochan. The headwaters are now impounded and much of the catchment area is afforested which, in my opinion, will have a damaging effect on water quality, making it more acid and less able to sustain parr and smolt life.

The lochs of the Carrick Forest are managed by the Forest Commission and they provide trout fishing on a number of their waters to the west of Loch Doon, including Bradon, Riecawr, Macterick and Linfern. The River Girvan flows north-west from Bradan past the beautiful village of Straiton, swinging south-west near Kirkmichael and thence through the old county of Kyle and Carrick to meet the sea at the small town of Girvan. Salmon and sea-trout fishing is widely available to members of the public through the angling clubs that manage the river and the Blairquhan Estate. Catches have been declining in recent years and not more than 100 salmon are taken each season. Water extraction and afforestation must have played a significant part in reducing salmon catches but the river has some nice pools, and in high water levels, there is always the chance of sport.

In 1988 prospects for the Girvan brightened substantially when coastal netting stations were bought out and estuary nets withdrawn. Some 70,000 salmon and 30,000 sea-trout alevins were raised in the Fishery Board hatchery and released into the river. Renegade rainbow trout were spotted in the river and as yet there is no indication as to where they might have escaped from. The Girvan has enough to contend with without having to cope with voracious immigrants and it is hoped that all the hard work being put into restoring it will eventually bear fruit for future generations of Ayrshire anglers.

There is a very good reservoir, Penwhapple, south of the Girvan on the road between Old Dailly and Barr and this water can produce more than 1,000 fish each season. It is regularly stocked and both boat and bank fishing is allowed. Further south, past Barrhill towards Newton Stewart there are a number of other waters, all of which offer good sport to visiting anglers: Ochiltree, Maberry, Dornal and the best loch in the area, Drumlamford, stocked each year with up to 3,000 brown trout which average 1 lb in weight.

These lochs supply the Duisk River which joins the River Stinchar at Pinwherry. The Stinchar is the best of the Ayrshire salmon streams and rises to the west of Loch Bradan in Balloch Plantation by Craiglure Lodge flowing 30 miles westwards to reach the sea at Ballantrae, the town made famous by Robert Louis Stevenson in his novel *The Master of Ballantrae*. Much of the headwaters have been trapped and leads to the Girvan and, like the Girvan, the Stinchar suffers from the effects of the massive programmes of afforestation that have covered more than 50 per cent of the area in recent years.

Fishing on the Stinchar is always in demand and many anglers return year after year, making it difficult for newcomers to obtain fishing at peak times; but the quality of sport makes it worth while inquiring to see if there might be a rod available. Colmonell Angling Club have fishing rights and this may be the best place to start your search.

Many of the pools are man-made and the Stinchar District Fishery Board stocks the headwaters with salmon eggs. The Stinchar has good runs of sea-trout which enter the system from May onwards and the best time to attack them is at night. They average between 1 lb and 4 lb but the heaviest sea-trout caught in recent years tipped the scales at 11 lb 8 oz.

Salmon make their main run later in the season with best sport being in September and October. The most productive stretch of the river is Knockdolian but much depends upon water levels, so pray for heavy rain, three days before your visit. 'Dear Lord, please may I be, for just once in my life, in the right place at the right time. Amen.'

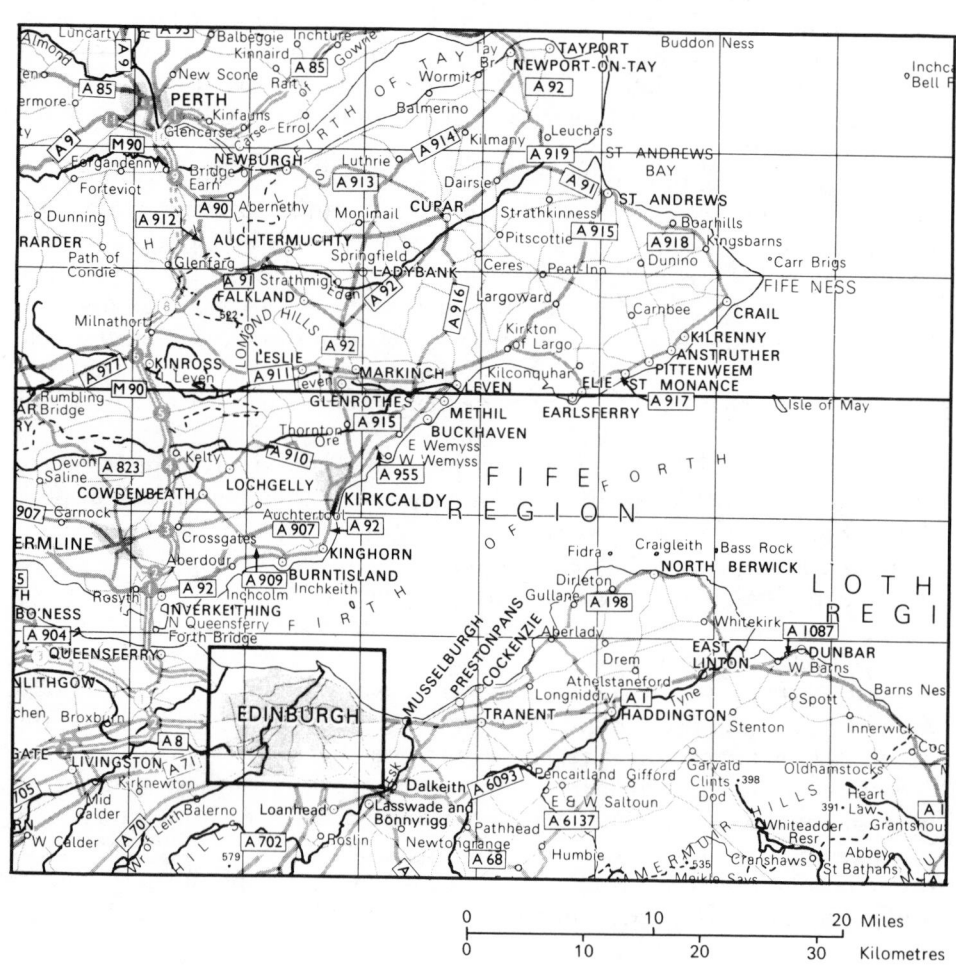

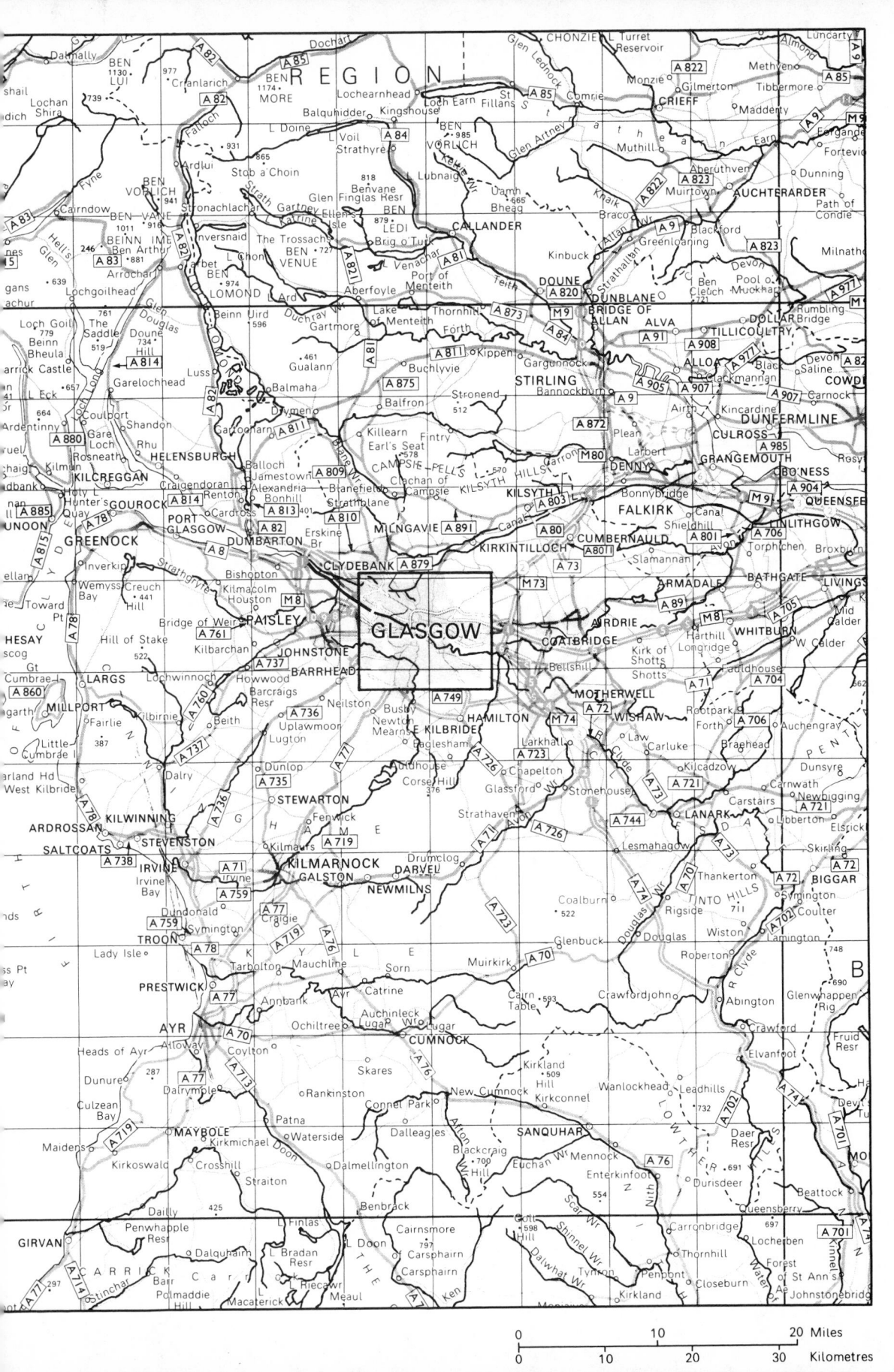

THE HEART OF SCOTLAND

FISHING DIRECTORY

LOCH LEVEN
The Manager,
Loch Leven Fisheries, The Pier, Kinross
(0577) 64212

RIVER LEVEN
River Leven Trust,
Sluice House, Loch Leven
(059284) 225

HARPERLEAS RESERVOIR
LOCH GLOW
Constable,
Jeweller, 39a High Street, Kirkcaldy
(0592) 60770

BALLO RESERVOIR
HALL RESERVOIR
GLENFARG RESERVOIR
Fife Regional Council,
Water Division Flemmington Road,
Glenrothes, Fife
(0592) 756541

ARNOT RESERVOIR
Mr M J G Tullis,
Arnot Tower, By Leslie, Fife
(059284) 222

LOCH ORE
Park Centre,
Lochore Meadows Country Park, Crosshill,
Nr Lochgelly, Fife
(0592) 860086

LOCHMILL LOCH
D MacLean,
Albert Bar, 109 High Street Newburgh,
Fife
(03374) 439

CAMERON RESERVOIR
St Andrews Angling Club,
Fishing Centre, Cameron Reservoir,
St Andrews
(033484) 236

UPPER CARRISTON RESERVOIR
J Caldwell,
Newsagent, Main Street, Methilhill, Leven,
Fife
(0592) 712215

CLATTO RESERVOIR
Crawford Priory Estate,
Cupar, Fife
(0334) 52678

STENHOUSE RESERVOIR
John McCracken,
Newsagent, East Porte Burntisland, Fife
(0592) 872292

CASTLEHILL RESERVOIRS
Boathouse,
Castlehill Reservoir, Glendevon Fife
(025981) 375

UPPER GLENDEVON RESERVOIR
LOWER GLENDEVON RESERVOIR
Fife Regional Council,
Water Division Flemmington Road,
Glenrothes, Fife
(0529) 756541

GLENQUEY RESERVOIR
Castle Campbell Hotel,
13 Bridge Street Dollar, Clackmannanshire
(02594) 2519

CRAIGLUSCAR RESERVOIR
Dunfermline Angling Club,
J Jamieson (Sec) 154 Wedderburn Street,
Dunfermline
(0383) 20442

LOCH FITTY
Game Fisheries Ltd,
Loch Fitty, Kingseat Dunfermline, Fife
(0383) 23162

RIVER ALLAN
RIVER FORTH
RIVER TEITH
RIVER GARTMORE
Messrs D Crockart,
Tackle Dealers 15 King Street, Stirling
(0786) 73443

LOCH ARD
Forest Hills Hotel,
Aberfoyle, Perthshire
(08777) 261
Post Office,
Kinlochard, Aberfoyle, Perthshire
(08777) 261

LOCH CHON
G MacNaile,
Frenich Farm, Aberfoyle, Perthshire
(087786) 243

LOCH KATRINE
LOCH ARKLET
Strathclyde Regional Council,
Water Dept, 419 Balmore Road, Glasgow
(041) 336 5333

LOCH VENACHAR
LOCH LUBNAIG
J Bayne,
Tackle Shop, Main Street, Callander,
Perthshire
(08777) 30218

LOCH VOIL
LOCH DOINE
Mr Ferguson,
Muirlaggan Farm, Balquhidder, Perthshire
(08774) 219

BALVAIG RIVER
Rosebank House Hotel,
Strathayre
(08774) 208

RIVER ALLAN
**McLeven Fishing Tackle and Sports
Shop,**
Bridge of Allan
(078683) 3530

RIVER DEVON
Scobbie Sports,
Primrose Street, Alloa
(0259) 722661
Hobby Shop,
New Row, Dunfermline
(0383) 722582

NORTH THIRD FISHERY
G Holdsworth,
Greathill, by Cambusbarron, Stirling
(0786) 71967

BOWDEN SPRINGS
W Martin,
Bowden Springs Fishery, Carriber,
Linlithgow
(0506) 847269

LINLITHGOW LOCH
J MacKay,
The Red Lion Inn, Linlithgow
(0506) 847269

BEECRAIGS LOCH
West Lothian District Council,
Beecraigs Country Park, Linlithgow
(0506) 844516

LOCH COULTER
LarbertandStenhousemuirAnglingClub,
Alex McArthur, Lynewood, 11 Bellsdyke
Road, Larbert
(0324) 2581

CARRON VALLEY RESERVOIR
The Director of Finance,
Central Regional Council, Viewforth,
Stirling
(0786) 3111

LAKE OF MENTEITH
Lake of Menteith Hotel,
Port of Menteith, Perthshire
(08775) 258

WATER OF LEITH
Lothian Regional Council,
Reception, George IV Bridge, Edinburgh
(031) 229 9292 Ext 2365

RIVER ALMOND
Cramond Angling Club,
Garden Centre, Cramond, Glebe Road,
Cramond, Edinburgh
River Almond Angling Association,
H Meikle, Sec, 23 Glen Terrace, Deans,
Livingston
(0506) 411813
Tackle Shop,
Roseburn, Edinburgh

RIVER ESK
The Sports Shop,
11 Newbiggin, Musselburgh
(031) 665 2671
Esk Valley Angling Association,
Mr K Burns (Sec), 53 Fernieside Crescent,
Edinburgh
(031) 664 4685

RIVER TYNE
East Lothian Angling Association,
J S Mair, Saddlers, 87 High Street,
Haddington
(062082) 2148

BONALY RESERVOIR
(Colinton)
Permission not required

CLUBBIEDEAN RESERVOIR
(Colinton)
GLENCORSE RESERVOIR
(Penicuik)
HARLAW RESERVOIR
(Balerno)
CROSSWOOD RESERVOIR
(West Calder)
HARPERRIG RESERVOIR
(Temple)
FRUID RESERVOIR
GLADHOUSE RESERVOIR
Lothian Regional Council,
Department of Water Supply Services,
Comiston Springs, 55 Buckstone Terrace,
Edinburgh
(031) 445 4141

MEGGET RESERVOIR
TALLA RESERVOIR
DONOLLY RESERVOIR
HOPES RESERVOIR
WHITEADDER RESERVOIR
Lothian Regional Council,
Department of Water Supply Services,
Alderston House, Haddington, East
Lothian
(062082) 2109

PORTMORE LOCH
At loch or from W McGeachie

LOGANLEA RESERVOIR
W McGeachie,
101 John Street, Penicuik
(0968) 74345

MORTON FISHERIES
Morton Fisheries,
Morton Reservoir, Mid-Calder
(0506) 88087

MALTINGS FISHERY
Maltings Fishery,
West Barns, Dunbar
(0368) 2244

SELM MUIR FISHERIES
W Mitchelhill,
Selm Muir Fisheries, Mid-Calder, West
Lothian
(0506) 882593

MARKLE FISHERIES
R Wallace,
Markle Fisheries, East Linton, East Lothian
(0602 860) 155

RIVER CLYDE
Permits widely available from tackle shops
in Glasgow and Lanarkshire

HARELAW RESERVOIR
KNOCKNAERSHILL RESERVOIR
P Graham,
12 Skye Road, Port Glasgow, Renfrewshire
(0475) 43143

GLENBURN RESERVOIR
MUIRHEAD RESERVOIR
CAMPHILL RESERVOIR
Lower Clyde Water Board,
19 Underwood Road, Paisley, Renfrewshire
(041) 887 5161

LOCH THOM
GRYFFE RESERVOIR
WHINHILL RESERVOIR
Findlay & Co,
23 West Stewart Street, Greenock,
Renfrewshire
(0475) 24056

BURNFOOT RESERVOIR
CRAIGENDUNTON RESERVOIR
Messrs McGuirick & Sons,
38 John Finnie Street, Kilmarnock,
Ayrshire
(0563) 25577

RIVER AYR
Director of Finance,
Kyle and Carrick District Council, Town
Buildings, Ayr
(0292) 269141
Gamesport,
60 Sandgate, Ayr
Mauchline Ballochmyle Angling Club,
J F McCall, Post Office, High Street,
Mauchline, Ayrshire

RIVER GARNOCK
CAAF RESERVOIR
Dalry Garnock Angling Club,
G King, 8 Peden Avenue, Dalry
Kilbirnie Angling Club
J Johnstone, 95 Dalry Road, Kilbirnie

RIVER GIRVAN
Carrick Angling Club,
J L Wilson, 1 Church Square, Girvan

RIVER IRVINE
Irvine and District Angling Club,
A Sim, Rugby Crescent, Irvine

PRESTWICK RESERVOIR
Red Lion Hotel,
Prestwick, Ayr
Prestwick Angling Club,
C Hendrie (Sec), 12 Glen Park Avenue,
Prestwick, Ayrshire
(0292) 70203

KNOCKENDON RESERVOIR
J M Currie,
Sports Goods, 32 High Street, Irvine,
Ayrshire

COLLENNAN RESERVOIR
Club Secretary,
1 Fairhaven Brassie, Troon, Ayrshire
(0292) 315466

LOCH DOON
Managed by Ayrshire Angling Association,
permits not required

DRUMLAMFORD LOCH
Head Keeper,
The Kennels, Barrhill, Girvan, Ayrshire
(046582) 256

PENWHAPPLE RESERVOIR
Reservoir Superintendent,
Penwhapple Reservoir, Girvan, Ayrshire
(Telephone bookings not accepted)

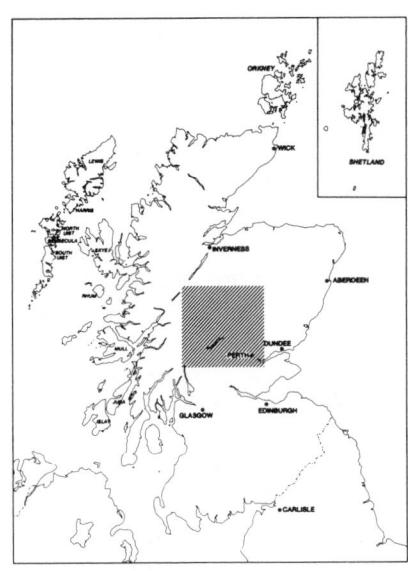

GATEWAY TO THE NORTH

Perthshire

When I was a boy, the journey from Edinburgh into Perthshire was a major adventure. It could take anything up to three hours, depending upon how long it took to cross the Firth of Forth at Queensferry. A trio of side-paddle steamers, *William Wallace*, *Robert the Bruce*, and *Queen Margaret*, ferried thousands of passengers and vehicles over the Forth to Fife; and in mid-summer they worked as hard across the narrow passage below the red spider-work of Forth Rail Bridge as ever their historical counterparts worked in days of old.

South Queensferry, in the old Scottish county of Linlithgowshire, is named after Margaret, the wife of Scottish King, Malcolm Canmore, slayer of Macbeth. Margaret was the daughter of Edgar Atheling, descended from Alfred the Great and the English-born Queen set about the task of anglicising southern Scotland which has continued to the present day. Perthshire and the Highlands remained, as always, a law unto themselves.

Perhaps it is the independent character of Perthshire people, as much as the glorious scenery of their county, that makes the lands beyond the Kingdom of Fife and Kinross such a special place. Perthshire has a foot in both Lowland and Highland camps with the Grampian Mountains north and west, and in the south and east, the Sidlaw and Ochil Hills. From the security of these vast wilderness areas, the inhabitants could safely observe the antics of their ambitious southern neighbours.

Perth, the 'fair city', celebrated in Sir Walter Scott's novel *The Fair Maid of Perth*, suffered greatly during the Scottish Religious Wars of the 17th century but survived to become the county town; reserved, polite and much given to matters financial, insurance and the industry of Scotland's 'water of life', whisky.

Perth is noted for its literary associations, particularly with regard to Scottish song. Caroline, Baroness Nairne, author of such well-known Scottish melodies as *The Land o' the Leal* and *Caller Herrin'* was a Perthshire lass, born at the Auld House of Gask and the French composer Georges Bizet wrote his opera *The Fair Maid of Perth*, loosely based upon Sir Walter's novel.

Nearby, Scone was the Pictish capital of the region during the 8th century. Scone was the coronation place for the old Kings of Scotland, famous for the Stone of Destiny, upon which monarchs were crowned, until stolen by Edward I in 1296 and taken to England to be set below the coronation chair in Westminster Abbey. The Scottish preacher John Knox did a lot of reforming round Tayside; which generally involved a great deal of burning and looting, all in the name of his personal God, and the old palace at Scone was one of the casualties of his reforming zeal.

Scone Palace, home of the Earl of Mansfield, was built around the ruins of the old Gowrie Castle and enlarged to its present glory during the 18th and 19th centuries. In doing so, care was taken to retain the room in which Charles II was crowned King of Britain in 1651, nine years before his more formal restoration to kingly authority. In order to preserve Mansfield's lordly peace and quiet, the Laird removed the local community, resettling them in the village now known as New Scone.

Some of Scotland's highest Munros, peaks above 3,000 ft, crowd the horizons: Ben Lawers, Ben More, Ben Lui and graceful Schiehallion. The valleys and hills are scattered with famous rivers and lochs: Tummel, Rannoch, Garry, Ericht, Isla, Almond and Earn. Scotland's highest and most extensive moorland plateau, Rannoch Moor, lies in Perthshire and remnants of the ancient pine woodlands that used to cover so much of Scotland, the Caledonian Forest, may still be seen.

Sir Walter Scott wrote in his book *The Fair Maid of Perth*, 'Amid all the provinces of Scotland, if an intelligent stranger were to describe the most varied and most beautiful, it is probable that he would name the county of Perth'; and often, when people ask me which is my favourite part of Scotland, I'm tempted to agree with the 'Wizard of the North', in spite of my love of the wild and desolate places of the far north.

I discovered Perthshire many years ago, whilst camping at Inver Park, near Dunkeld, as a boy scout. The Dunkeld bypass has long since obliterated our youthful camp site and I estimate that the new A9 road passes directly over the place where the Otter Patrol pitched their tent. But the same wonderful scent of wood-smoke and pine still drifts gently on the summer airs; and the same feeling of mounting excitement fills my heart when I survey the magnificent breadth of the sweetly flowing Tay.

I had my first encounter with Salar the leaper, upstream from Inver. Other boys had brought useful things to camp: extra blankets, books, games and playing cards. Me, I packed my first fishing rod, an old 12-foot greenheart, given as a present to my father and passed on to me because he did not fish. There was a steel spike in the butt and it took all my strength to cast a line; but it became a dear valued friend. The rod was about 50 years old when it fell into my hands and after a further ten years' action, including several new top sections, I had it whittled down into a delightful six-feet-long trout wand. Each of our four children were introduced to the mysteries of fly fishing using my old friend and he now takes pride of place, still cast-strung and fly-ready, retired on the wall of our sitting-room.

One evening, after yet another burnt-offering supper, I wandered up the river, casting at anything that moved without much success. For me, a normal state of affairs. Below where the new bridge crosses the Tay, there was a large, deep pool, where the river hesitated before rushing seawards past Dunkeld House Hotel. I had tied on a large Grouse and Claret and after several attempts, and much tree-climbing, managed to cast a long line out towards the middle of the stream. As the fly landed, there came a mighty swirl and my heart stopped beating as a huge fish rolled on the surface. I felt a mind-numbing tug and the reel began to scream. Moments later, the fly came loose and I fell on the bank, in utter despair. Thus are fishermen born. Back at camp, nobody believed me. Nor could they understand my excitement. But I will never forget as long as I live that first, utterly glorious moment.

The Tay is, in my opinion, the finest salmon river in Europe, in spite of the devastation caused by hydroelectric schemes and the depredation of stock by the activities of netting stations along the estuary and illegal drift netting at sea. The Tay seems almost indestructible and for centuries has given up its silver harvest of returning salmon; and it is this certainty of seemingly never-ending runs of fish that has possibly been responsible for declining numbers caught in recent years. The mistaken philosophy that Mother Nature will take care of all.

Nothing could be further from the truth, as has been seen so often in the past with other species, ruthlessly exploited for the pleasure of man. Between 40,000 and 50,000 salmon enter the system most years and the vast majority are caught by the nets. Rod and line anglers, of far more financial value to Perthshire's fragile economy, account for less than 10,000 and this figure has been declining steadily over the years. Yet netting continues and it is only very recently that any real action has been taken to control the annual net-slaughter and allow more fish to reach their traditional upstream spawning beds.

Even then, many of the old redds have been drowned by the hydro electric schemes and the Tay tributaries such as Garry, Tummel and Lyon, once famous for the quality and quantity of their salmon, have been devastated. I remember the River Garry in the old days, travelling by train from Inverness to Edinburgh. The river was everyone's conception of how a Highland stream should look. Fast-flowing waters, pressed between heather and rowan-covered banks breaking in endless urgency over old stones. An introduction and encouraging welcome to the fine fishing further north. Now the poor river is a monstrosity of a stream, bear-bedded and lifeless in summer, a derisory winter trickle, drained forever of its former splendour.

The River Tay draws its waters from a vast area of more than 2,800 square miles, flowing from Ben Lui in the west through dark, 500-ft-deep Loch Tay; fed by streams from the wild peaks of Black Mount in the north, tumbling along its 119-mile course, through Laidon, Rannoch, Dunalister and Tummel to the sea. The main tributaries are the Lochay, Dochart, Lyon, Tummel, Garry, Tilt, Isla, Ericht, Almond and Earn; plus a host of minor streams and burns along the way.

The best of the Tay salmon fishing is from where the Tummel enters near Logierait downstream to Perth. Which is not to decry the excellence of upstream beats between the Tummel and Loch Tay; but in any description of the Tay matters are relative and, although upstream beats such as Taymouth Castle, Bolfracks, Killiechassie, Cluny, Farleyer and Grandtully produce good numbers of fish, the middle and lower produce infinitely more. They are also infinitely more expensive to fish and even if one did have the wherewithal, it is almost impossible to obtain rods on the top beats because they are booked year after year by the same people. As a guide, fishing costs on the Tay vary from about £10 per day for a single rod for a single day's fishing on the upper river, to £9,000 for a week's let for four to five rods on a top beat at the prime time on the lower river.

Salmon fishing begins on 15 January when a gathering of hopefuls march behind a piper from the warmth of Kenmore Hotel to the river. A bottle of whisky is broken over the bows of a boat and battle commences. Always seemed to me to be a bit of waste of good cheer, but it seems to do the trick for opening day on the Tay usually produces a good number of salmon. Opening day in 1988 saw a fish of 8 lb 8 oz taken by a Kenmore Hotel guest and in the following days salmon of up to 18 lb were taken.

Most of the fish caught on Loch Tay are taken by trolling and the total number taken each season is in the order of 350. Guests at the Highland Lodges generally do well as do Ardeonaig Hotel anglers; Mr Raymond Jenetta had a magnificent 25-lb salmon on 26 January in 1988 and the fish took a red fluorescent Rapala lure. Local knowledge is essential if you are to have the best chance of sport on Loch Tay and money invested in the services of an experienced gillie is almost essential.

Recently, rainbow trout have escaped into Loch Tay and in June 1988 a fish of 12 lb was landed. Whilst this no doubt mightily pleased the angler on the end of the rod, concern is being expressed about the huge rainbow's eating habits. Certainly, it will be feeding on the large stocks of Arctic char that inhabit Loch Tay, and no doubt brown trout and infant salmon as well. Where there is one, there are bound to be others, for Loch Tay is an ideal rainbow trout larder and an excellent brown trout fishery in its own right.

Fresh-run salmon enter the Tay throughout the year and this, coupled with good water levels, makes the Tay one of the most attractive of all Scottish rivers; there is always the opportunity of catching sea-liced salmon, even in autumn months. However, Tay spring fishing has declined sadly over the years and autumn months now produce most sport.

Top beats, such as Islamouth, Meikleour, Cargill, Ballathie, Stanley, Scone and Redgorton account for most fish with Islamouth usually producing most, up to 1,000 fish each season. Cargill and, on the opposite bank, Ballathie, produce 600–700 salmon between them. Downstream at Almondmouth, the Stormant Angling Club rent fishings and club records for 1988 showed 51 salmon and 485 sea-trout caught.

The ten-year average for Lower Redgorton, fine autumn fly water, is 264 fish, most of which are taken in September. In the ten years to 1986, 252 salmon of over 20 lb have been caught on Lower Redgorton and there are 20 named pools on the lovely stretch of the river. The Upper Scone fishings are just as famous for the size and quality of salmon and a fish of 34 lb was caught in 1986. Upper Scone includes perhaps the most famous pool on the Tay, the legendary Pitlochrie Pool.

A fish to cheer the hearts of all spring anglers was taken in April 1988 by Blairgowrie angler Ian Davie. The sea-liced springer, a reminder of better, old, cold Tay fishing days and weighing 35 lb was caught in the Linn Pool. Mr Davie was spinning a red and gold Devon and completed his day with two other nice fish. Another fine springer was caught on 1 April by Edinburgh angler, Mr Jones, fishing a yellow-belly Devon in the Kindallachan Pool on Kinnaird. Could the capture of these fish mean better spring sport in future years?

The tributaries of the Tay can also provide less expensive, more readily available salmon fishing for visiting anglers. Dochart, by Killin at the west end of Loch Tay, fishes best in summer and autumn months; Lochay also receives late runs of salmon but the best of the upper Tay tributaries is the River Lyon, thirty miles long and flowing through the heart of Clan MacGregor country to reach parent Tay in the Appin of Doull near Comrie Castle.

The Lyon can be a first-class spring water. On a cold day in January, 1984, after wading through four-feet-deep snowdrifts, an Edinburgh angler, John Nevin, reached the banks of Peter's Pool. At 10 a.m., in the midst of a blizzard, he hooked, played and landed a magnificent 17-lb salmon. Not a bad way to start Orwell-ominous 1984. Nor for that matter 1983 when John Nevin caught a 19-lb fish or 1982 when he landed a 16-lb salmon. For three successive years the first fish taken from the river.

Waist deep in Tummel, Perthshire

But if braving the elements and breaking the ice is not for you, don't despair; when the first blink of spring sunlight eventually lures you waterside, the salmon of the Lyon will still be there, waiting to greet you. Apart from excellent game fishing, a walk up Glen Lyon is like making a journey through Scottish history; at Fortingall is the oldest tree in Europe, the 3,000-year-old yew tree in the churchyard; Pontius Pilate was reputed to have been born nearby at Balnacraig. Further up the glen are the remains of the forts of Fionn, King of Scotland in the 3rd century.

In the 7th century, Eonan, a priest from Iona, brought Christianity to Glen Lyon; and when the Black Death was advancing up the glen, Eonan, through prayer and devotion, halted its progress where Allt Bail a'Mhuilinn enters the main river. Parishioners were less fortunate in the 14th century when plague claimed the life of every inhabitant; there is a great stone in a field by the roadside marking their last resting place. But the blackest deed of all the black deeds that mar Scotland's story was the hunting and massacre of the landless Clan Gregor, the 'children of the mist', many of whom lived in Glen Lyon. In 1603 the Privy Council in Edinburgh passed an Act ordering 'the extermination of that wicked, unhappy and infamous race of lawless lymmaris, callit the MacGregour'. The men were hunted down like animals; women were branded on the forehead; children were transported to camps in the Lowlands and in Ireland, to serve as cattle boys.

In more recent times, others with less murderous intent have been captivated by the beauty of the glen. William Wordsworth and his sister Dorothy knew Glen Lyon; Alfred Lord Tennyson, Poet Laureate, found inspiration among the tree-clad banks of the river. Liberal Prime Minister William Gladstone often stayed in Glen Lyon and Baden Powell, hero of Mafeking and founder of the Boy Scout movement, tried his skill with rod and line in the fast-flowing waters. John Fisher, a senior Lyon gillie fished with Baden Powell and remembers him as being a 'courteous man, well mufflered against the cold and a fine caster'.

Of the best-known pools on the Lyon is Peter's Pool, named after Peter Dewar of the famous Perthshire distillers, who for several decades wrought terrible havoc amongst salmon here. Peter Dewar named many of the pools on the river, including Weaver's Pool where a 24-lb salmon was landed recently. The pool is near MacGregor's Leap, yet another fabled desperate Scottish jump in search of safety.

Downstream from Weaver's is the Platform Pool which produced a 19-lb salmon for Mr Roy in 1983; this is a spectacular gorge, where the help of a fellow angler spotting the fish from the high bank on the other side of the river can bring great results. However, don't be tempted to use the old wooden platform which gave the pool its name; it is unsafe and might give you a much closer look at the salmon than you had intended.

Another good pool on the river is Suspension Bridge Pool; turn left from the Fortingal Hotel and half a mile down the road park on the right. Go through the small iron gate and walk down to the river. Wading can be difficult in the shingly neck of the pool, but fish carefully down. The main lies are on the south bank, half way down, and just above the bridge, in mid-stream.

In spite of the impounding of its headwaters in Loch Lyon, the river still produces of its best in the early months of the season but, increasingly, fishes just as well at the back end. Catches of 13 fish in a day are still known but be warned, the river is much dependent upon good rainfall to produce its best sport. This is a classic, Highland river, tumbling through ragged, boulder-strewn corries one moment then opening out into gentle, deep pools the next. Countless small feeder burns cascade down from surrounding hills creating irresistible eddies and corners where good fish shelter. Some excellent quality wild brown trout also shelter here, with an average weight of 10 oz and trout of over 2 lb are caught most seasons.

Loch Lyon, at the head of the glen, also offers trout fishing, though the fish are more modest in size. A track opens up more than two miles of bank fishing along the north shore; and in the hills above is Loch an Diamh, where cattle were moved in old days to the rich, summer upland pastures. But it is hard to leave the charms of Lady Lyon, hurrying through the gentle glen amid the old pines of Caledonia, turning your fly invitingly round moss-covered, salmon-sheltering stones.

The waters of the Tummel and Garry are captured south of Killiecrankie in Faskally Reservoir and although the automatic fish-counter at the dam records upwards of 5,000 salmon ascending each year, few of these fish are ever caught. Below Faskally, Tummel produces some good sport but fish seem anxious to hurry northwards to spawning grounds in the River Tilt, deep in the mountains above Blair Atholl.

There is a well-known and much loved walk north from Blair Atholl, up Glen Tilt and over the watershed to White Bridge in Deeside. This is great news for hikers and also for trout fishermen because there are some lovely lochs along the way including Moraig, Valigan and the quaintly named Loch Loch. Always enquire first before setting off into the hills, for this is stalking country and in autumn months it could be dangerous to wander unannounced into the high glens and valleys. All these lochs are full of little wild brown trout which average three to the pound. Fish them for their wonderful remoteness, rather than in search for one for the glass case.

In less remote Blair Atholl fishing can be had in the Blair Walker Pond, a stocked loch in the castle grounds and on Loch Errochty. Pike also inhabit Errochty and keep the trout in order; this has the look of a 'reservoir' having been linked to the main Pitlochry hydro system, as does Loch Garry, another rather dour-looking loch whose waters are now passed by tunnel into Loch Ericht.

Faskally, by Pitlochry, is better known as a trout fishery and huge specimens, over 15 lb in weight, have been caught in its deep waters. Rarely salmon, although they are often seen splashing in the loch after climbing the salmon ladder. Pitlochry Angling Club and the Airdanair Hotel offer some fishing for visitors on the Tummel and as is the case with most of the Tay System, the best sport is now had during the autumn months.

The best salmon beat on the Tummel is Port na Craig at Pitlochry Dam and upwards of 150 salmon are taken during the season. Due to heavy demand for fishing Pitlochry Angling Club limits permits to three per day. The River Garry, above the dam towards Killiecrankie is only for agile anglers. There are spectacular falls, deep pools and good runs, but fishing them requires a fair degree of scrambling about.

Dalguise, between Ballinluig and Dunkeld on the Tay itself is more easily accessible and the fishing extends for a distance of one and a half miles. Boats and gillies may be booked with the fishing and, as always, the all important message is to book well in advance to avoid disappointment.

Other main tributaries of the Tay, Ericht and Isla, fished by the Blairgowrie Angling Association and Strathmore Angling Improvement Association, and Eden, which flows into the North Sea near St Andrews, offer visitors the chance of salmon and sea-trout fishing but since the advent of the hydroelectric schemes, salmon fishing has dwindled to almost no account, compared with heady bygone times; nevertheless, a salmon of 20 lb was taken from the Eden in 1985 so it is always worth a cast or two, or three, just in case there may be one for you.

The best of the Tay System waters is the River Earn which flows eastwards from Loch Earn past Crieff and Comrie to enter the Firth of Tay east of Perth. Here, also, a large-scale hydroelectric scheme has impounded a number of the most important Earn feeder streams: Lednock, Water of Ruchill, Water of May. The result of these schemes is a greatly restricted water flow and good spates are required to encourage fish upstream. Salmon fishing is best during autumn months when some large fish are taken.

The Earn is perhaps most famous as a sea-trout fishery and still gives great sport, particularly at night, despite the fact that east coast sea-trout runs seem to have been in decline for a number of years. Crieff Angling Association water produced a fine sea-trout weighing 7 lb 2 oz for Bill Fullard in July 1988. Of even greater interest is the capture of an 8-oz Tiger trout, a cross between a male American brook trout and a female brown trout. The fish was thought to have been the progeny of an escapee brook trout from Ochtertyre Loch, outside Crieff, which may have bred naturally with a brown trout in the burn that flows from the loch into the Earn.

Pitlochry is a good centre for brown trout fishing in Perthshire; a busy, bustling tourist town with something for everyone. Golf, pony trekking, swimming, music and drama at the Pitlochry Festival Theatre; excellent hotels and restaurants; shops, well stocked with traditional craft goods, superb tweeds and knitwear. A welcoming town with a happy atmosphere, attracting visitors from all over the world; and if after dinner you fancy a little exercise with some good trout fishing at the end of the climb, walk up to Loch a'Choirs, known locally as Ben Vrakie, above the town, well stocked with 8–10 oz brown trout.

The huge dam at Pitlochry, with its salmon ladder, also attracts visitors; each year, thousands of eager humans explore the vast structure inside, whilst thousands of equally eager salmon ascend the ladder to Loch Faskally, 'outside'. They meet, briefly, and peer inquisitively at one another through the thick glass of the viewing window set into the side of the ladder.

Northwards, at Killiecrankie, another less friendly meeting took place in

1689. Graham of Claverhouse and his ragged horde of Highlanders routed King William's well-disciplined army, led by General Sir Hugh Mackay of Scourie, sending them fleeing from the field of battle before a wild war-cry-screaming charge. Nearby is another Scottish leap, this time Soldiers leap, when a terrified Redcoat leapt the foaming Garry to escape from his claymore-rattling, kilted pursuers. The Highlanders' victory was short-lived. With their outstanding commander dead, killed in the fight, the rest of the army was routed a few weeks later when they attempted to capture the cathedral town of Dunkeld.

To the east of Dunkeld is Butterstone Loch, one of a group of three interconnected lochs close to the A923 Dunkeld to Blairgowrie road. Their setting is glorious, Perthshire at its finest, surrounded by forest-clad slopes and craggy heights. I 'found' Butterstone more than 30 years ago. As a boy, I had been walking in the hills to the north and had spent the night sleeping on a bed of heather by the shores of Loch Ordie. In the morning I picked up the track that follows Buckny Burn and made my way south. Eventually, I arrived at the road and saw Butterstone glistening in the early morning sun, a gentle breeze moving the rushes, sending tiny riplets chasing over calm waters. It was one of those moments that remain indelibly stamped on the mind forever.

In those days, trout fishing on Butterstone was controlled by the activities of a thriving pike population. Indeed, even today, controlling these voracious predators is an on-going, ever-present task. But Butterstone had been developed into a first-class fishery and the quality of both fish and management is very high indeed. This is due in a large measure to the enthusiasm and expertise of the fishery manager whose detailed knowledge of the loch and courtesy makes every visit a pleasure, fishless or not.

Good facilities have been provided for visiting anglers, without regimentation, and include a car park, picnic area, boathouse, fishing hut and well-maintained boats in a sheltered, accessible harbour. Butterstone covers an area of about 120 acres and has an average depth of six feet. The deepest part of the loch is in the middle where the depth is over 12 feet.

The loch holds a natural stock of brown trout and rainbow trout are introduced on a weekly basis throughout the season. Fishing is by fly only and there is a bag limit of six trout per rod. Three anglers per boat and the takeable minimum is six fish of at least 10 inches. The average weight on Butterstone is just over the 1 lb mark and on a reasonable day your efforts should be rewarded with at least one fish. However, limit baskets are frequent and fish of over 4 lb not uncommon. Larger fish of over 7 lb are also sometimes caught.

Trout rise and are caught all over the loch and the fishery manager is on hand to point you in that day's most productive direction. Reservoir lures such as Ace of Spades and Whisky Fly do well but if there is a good wind blowing, then you could do no better than mount these old Scottish angler's friends, Black Pennel, Grouse and Claret and Dunkeld.

More than 6,000 trout are caught each season and a few sample baskets from recent years will give you some indication of what to expect: six fish weighing 10 lb 13 oz; five fish weighing 7 lb 8 oz and four fish weighing 6 lb 8 oz. Results like these make Butterstone a popular venue, so book in advance. The scent of wood smoke, wind whispering through the trees, autumn heather and red-brilliant rowan; the sudden movement of a startled deer, wheeling osprey and the sound of rising trout; all these sights and sounds crowd my mind as I speed past Dunkeld on the A9. It's one of the places I really regret passing by. After fishing Butterstone, so will you.

There is so much fishing in the Pitlochry area that the only problem visitors will face is knowing where to begin. Apart from salmon fishing on Lower Tummel, Port na Craig Beat, River Tilt and Loch Tay, there are many first-class brown trout waters. You will find rainbow trout in Loch Bhac, Arctic char in Loch Garry and monster ferox in Tummel, Rannoch and Laidon.

Much of this sport is managed by the Pitlochry Angling Association, a well-organised, hard-working group, carefully managing and developing their fishing resources. It was largely due to their efforts and interest that a protection order was obtained for the Tummel/Garry Catchment Area. Therefore, no matter where you fish in the area, you must be in possession of a permit. This protection has now been extended to the rest of the Tay System and is to be much welcomed by anglers who value the quality of Perthshire fishing.

One of the Association's most popular waters is Loch Kinardochy, stocked with superb quality brown trout and a few years ago Clan Sandison visited the best of the Pitlochry Angling Association waters, Loch Bhac. It is certainly one of the most scenically attractive and, whilst you fish, any non-angling members of your party may laze in the shade of the woods or splash in the shallows—well away from where you are fishing, of course.

Bhac is a small water, covering an area of some 500 yds by 200 yds. It lies at an altitude of 1,000 ft and is stocked with brown and rainbow trout. There are three boats available and bank fishing is not allowed. The average weight of trout is in the order of 1 lb but fish of up to 7 lb have been taken and there is a bag limit of six fish per rod. This bag limit is often achieved so your efforts should be rewarded with at least a couple of nice fish.

Trout are caught all round the Bhac with no one area being substantially better than another. However, local anglers have their favourite drifts and if you wish to follow their example start with a drift from the mooring bay, directly over to the north-west shore where a small feeder burn enters. As the season advances, weed can become a problem, so use heavier breaking strain nylon. Far better that than risk a fish swimming off trailing your cast behind it.

The principal weed beds extend from the north end of the loch, eastwards to the mooring bay. Fish the edge of these weeds carefully; there are extensive growths of weed in the southern bay also and good fish lie there as well. Many Bhac anglers prefer to use reservoir-type lures but we found that the traditional patterns of Scottish loch flies worked just as well; but in calm conditions dry fly works well, so make sure that you arrive prepared for all weather conditions.

Like us, you will immediately fall in love with Loch Bhac but should non-fishing members of your of your party become bored, then they may always recourse to the flesh-pots of Pitlochry in order to keep themselves amused and entertained. Our lot are made of sterner stuff, brain-washed from birth into a love of fishing. A small price to pay for uncomplicated and unlimited angling holidays.

South of Bhac lie two of Scotland's best-known lochs, forever immortalised in the song, *The Road to the Isles*, 'Sure by Tummel and Loch Rannoch and Lochaber we will go. . . .' chanted out world-wide by thousands of expatriate Scottish throats, dry and not so dry. Anglers don't pass by with their cromachs, but linger awhile to pay their respects to the fine trout that inhabit these lovely lochs.

Tummel is seven miles long by up to one mile wide and very popular with visiting anglers due to its accessibility. Boats are available for hire and bank fishing can also produce good results. Take care wading, however, because in places the water deepens close to the shore. Trout average in the region of 8 oz but there are much larger fish in the depths. Surprisingly, few anglers bother to tackle them and they remain largely unseen, left to their own devices.

In the hills to the south of the Tummel, towards Aberfeldy, there are a number of good trout lochs of which my favourite is Lochan a'Chait, with its little offspring in a corrie above the north-east shore. For our first visit, Ann and I climbed up from Frenich Wood, on the south shore of Tummel, after obtaining permission from the owner who lives in Lick. This is a stiff, but rewarding walk across wonderful scenery and it is still my favourite approach. However, quarry works on the Aberfeldy side of the hill have seen a new road drive almost to the loch and this is passable by vehicles.

South from a'Chait lie Lochan Lairg Laoigh, below the steep crags of Creagan Loch; and west is Loch Derculich. Further towards Aberfeldy lies Loch Glassie and Loch Farleyer and eastwards between Meall a'Charra and Cregan Feadaire a number of tiny lochans all of which can produce sport.

Between the Tummel and Rannoch is a new water, Dunalister Reservoir, flooded when the hydro schemes began impounding the waters

Colin Leslie on Cargill Beat, River Tay

of Rannoch, Laidon and Ericht. Dunalister is a managed fishery which has mixed fortunes over the years and is now finding its trout place in the Scottish angling scene and provides first-class sport. This is more than can be said for it when I first fished it in 1965.

Our introduction to Dunalister came one cold April when we had taken a cottage with friends on the south shore. With snow still dressing surrounding hills and most intelligent anglers comfortably abed, Ann and I ventured out to see what we could see. Our expedition ended when I ran the boat aground on a sunken tree-stump in the middle of the shallow loch. After a bout of cold, wet heaving and cursing, we called it a day and retired hurt and fishless.

Our friends had more sense. They had made straight for the log fire in the Kinloch Rannoch Hotel. Smugly hunched over a large warming dram, they blushed when a local rushed in and announced, 'You will never guess what I have just seen! There are two idiots out in a boat on Dunalister and one of them is trying to fish from a tree stump in the middle of the loch!'

The Loch Rannoch Conservation Association now stocks Dunalister from their hatchery and in 1988 8,000 trout, reared from a local strain of fish, were released into the loch. The average weight of trout is over 2 lb and in 1987 a fish of 5 lb was caught. Dunalister is a much improved fishery and well worth a stop-over on the way to sample the delights of the waters that lie westwards. The most productive of these is Rannoch, guarded by the smooth slope of Schiehallion (1,083 m), marked on the first known map of Britain by Claudius Ptolemy, Egyptian geographer and astronomer. As you launch your boat on the clear waters of Rannoch today you may still see the remains of the vast pine forests that covered the area in Roman times. The Forestry Commission are making great efforts to preserve and restore these ancient Caledonian forests; the south shore, from Finnart to Bunrannoch, is lined with mature trees; silver birch, alder, juniper and rowan cover the hillside up to Cross Crag (747 m), Coire Caire and Meall Druidhe (627 m).

New forests have been planted along the north shore also, at Bridge of Ericht, Aulich Hill (355 m) and, at the eastern end of the loch, the Rannoch Lodge Estate dwellings nestle among slender birch, the white of the buildings contrasting with the silver and green of the surrounding forest. On a fine spring day, with wavelets dancing across the loch and wind sending trees swaying and nodding, Rannoch is one of the most lovely of all Scottish lochs and a perfect place to fish.

The local angling association offers day tickets to visiting anglers and, more important, good advice about the best areas to fish. Charges are very low and the money raised is used to improve the fishing; 4,000 half-pounders were released into Rannoch recently and whether boat or bank fishing a visit to the association is as important as the choice of fly and the work of the club deserves our fullest support.

Because of Rannoch's involvement in the hydroelectric scheme of things, variations in water levels can make fishing difficult at times. In dry years, such as 1983, the water level in the loch was 30 ft lower than usual; in fact, according to the old map in the Kinloch Rannoch Hotel, the level was very close to what it used to be in pre-hydro days. Nevertheless, good baskets are the rule, rather than the exception and there are few blank days: 27 trout weighing 16 lb; 84 trout weighing 39 lb for a visiting angling club. The average weight of Rannoch fish is about 10 oz but in recent years that average has been rising and each season sees a number of much heavier trout landed.

Loch Rannoch is famous for its monster ferox and in times past some very large fish have been hauled from out of its depths. In 1867 22 lb; 1904 21 lb; 1905 23 lb 8 oz; 1912 18 lb 8 oz and many more double figured glass-case specimens have been caught since then. It is interesting to note that many of these large fish can be taken whilst bank fishing and some of them come readily—well sort of readily—to standard pattern loch flies, rather than by the more traditional ferox-fishing method of deep trolling.

Bank fishing is excellent on Rannoch and there is a road down each side making access easy; but do be careful if wading because in some places, as on Tummel, the banks shelve quickly into deeper water. I prefer fishing Rannoch from a boat because it is a much easier way to get around such a large water; but hasten slowly for there are unexpected shallows, in unexpected places. Make sure that you have plenty of sheer-pins for the outboard motor. The Association boats are moored in a shallow bay near to the ugly power station at Ardlarach and, for your first drift, I suggest that you head up the loch towards Finnart Bay. Keep well clear of the little tower-topped island; the water here can be shallow and boulder strewn.

Begin your drift where the Allt Madaig enters and fish close to the shore; if you can't see the bottom then you are too far out. The bay shallows dangerously by Finnart Lodge, so 'weather' the point with care. Thereafter, drift eastwards along the shore, paying particular attention to where the feeder burns enter: Allt Camghouran, Dall and Allt na Bogair. And if by some mischance the fish are not rising, then so what! Beach the boat, sit in some bosky bower amidst the silver birch, and just watch the wonderful world of Rannoch going by.

If it is too windy to launch the boat on Rannoch, there are two alternative venues nearby where you will find good bank fishing: Lochs Finart and Monaghan, a short walk into the hills at the south end of Loch Rannoch. Both waters are well stocked with hard-fighting little fish which average 8 oz but I have had a fish of just under 2 lb from Finnart, so there are larger trout as well. Treat every rise with respect; and there should be plenty to practise on because baskets of ten or more fish are common on both lochs.

Northwards from Loch Rannoch is Loch Ericht, 15 miles long, crowded by Munros on either shore; Ben Alder (1,148 m), Meall Liath (911 m) and Meal Cruaidh (897 m). This remote loch is managed by the Bandeloch and Strathspey Angling Association and may be fished from either the Dalwhinnie end, close to the A9, or by walking in south, from the Rannoch end by Bridge of Ericht. The best of Ericht trout fishing is at the south end, particularly in the vicinity of Ben Alder Bay, below Prince Charlie's Cave. Bonnie Prince Charlie hid in a cave on the hill with six companions, during his flight from Culloden in 1746.

Brown trout are easier to catch and fish on Ericht average 8 oz, in large numbers. Remember, Ericht is a dangerous place to fish when the wind howls down the glen. If in doubt, never launch the boat and even then always remember to stay seated whilst fishing. There are huge trout in Ericht, but if you want a record breaker, you will have to troll for him. They lie deep and rarely rise to surface flies.

There are less windy waters in the hills around Ben Alder—Lochs, Pattack, a'Bhealaich, na h-Earba and Ardruigh. You just have to hike out to them. If you choose to do so, make sure that you contact the estate head keeper George Oswald first, for this is another of Scotland's renowned stag forests. The size of trout is in the order of 8 oz, with the odd fish of over 2 lb to keep your interest up.

At the north end of Ericht, across the busy A9, lies Loch Cuaich, closed for angling during the stalking season, and south of the A86 Kingussie/Spean Bridge road is Loch Laggan which is to be visited more for its scenic beauty than the quality of trout fishing for the fish are very dour and harder than normal to catch.

My most favourite Perthshire water is without doubt Loch Laidon and I was once accused by a fellow angler of misinforming him about what to expect on this magnificent loch. I asked what I had done wrong and he replied, 'Well, you said that baskets of 30–40 trout were common.' Good grief, I thought, the poor man has fished all day and caught nothing. Happily this was not the case. 'We fished Laidon last Wednesday and caught 50!'

Whilst nothing is as certain as the uncertainty of angling, Loch Laidon is less uncertain than most Scottish waters. You would have to be one of the world's great incompetents, or have an unimaginably bad day, or be very, very unlucky to return fishless from Laidon. Therefore, if you want to be assured of sport and a fine day's fishing, turn left at Garry Bridge, two miles north of Pitlochry on the old A9. Follow the winding, wooded B8019 westwards, 'the road to the Isles', past Queen's view; no, not 'unamused' Victoria, but a more earthy, Scottish Queen. Luckless Mary visited the rocky promontory in 1564 and was said to have been captivated by the view westwards over Loch Tummel. Drive past Dunalister and the shining waters of Rannoch. Five miles past the end of the loch, through the lands of the outlawed Clan Gregor, the road ends at Rannoch Station: a hotel, station, post office, a few scattered dwellings, and nothing else. This is the stepping-off point for a journey into one of Scotland's great wilderness areas, Rannoch Moor, the watery place; a desolate plateau, 1,000 ft above sea level, dotted with small lochs and lochans, unchanged in a thousand years, surrounded by mighty peaks.

Loch Laidon is a silver scar across the moor, carrying cold waters from Stop Ghabhar and Stob a'Choire Odhair, hurrying them through shallow Loch Buidhe, na Stainge and na h-Achlaise, Ba and Abhainn burn, into the west end of Laidon. The loch runs for a distance of nearly six miles across the moor before exiting via Garbh Ghaoir to Loch Eigheach and River Gaur to Rannoch.

Laidon is often used by canoeists who launch their craft at the Glencoe end and paddle across the moor to Rannoch Station, portering the vessels the short distance between the small lochs at the west end. Another famous Laidon journey was done some years ago, this time on ice-skates. During a hard winter, an intrepid skater from Glasgow made the return journey during the course of a single day. Three-quarters of a mile down the loch, from the west end, a long arm fingers northwards and this is considered to be one of the most productive fishing areas. The bay is two and a half miles long and scattered with small inlets, headlands, island and shallows. Take great care, fishing here. There are large, dangerous rocks, just below the surface. Row up, rather than using the outboard motor.

Further down the north shore is an equally productive bay guarded by a tree-clad island. Vegetation on Eilean Iubhair is ancestrally related to the woodland and scrub that used to cover most of the moor in days gone by. Due to the island's inaccessibility it has survived the depredations of both man and beast. Treat the island with care and respect for it is an important part of our national heritage. Treat the bay with respect too, because here also there are a number of underwater obstructions ready to catch the unwary.

Again, row in rather than motor. Over on the south shore is another fine bay, complete with its own two little islands and in the hills south-west, there are a number of delightful hill lochs where you will be assured of absolute peace and solitude.

Laidon is a deep loch, dropping to 140 ft in places so arrange your drift accordingly, close to the shore, with the bottom of the loch in sight. All round the loch are a multitude of inlets and points where you will catch fish; secluded, sandy beaches, ideal for a family picnic, summer sunbathing, a cool splash, a lazy hour in after-lunch sunlight.

On our last visit to Laidon, Ann and I found ourselves trying to fish in almost impossible conditions; the sun blazed down from a cloudless sky; not a breath zephyred the surface. So we abandoned ship and wandered in the hills. It was a marvellous few hours. We found *Scheuchaeria Palustris*, the Rannoch Rush, a six-petalled, yellow-green flowered plant of the bogs.

All that ends well

A dog fox sprang, startled from the reeds by a tumbling burn, looking accusingly as we disturbed his afternoon slumber. We found the pug marks of an otter; larks twittered interminably and curlew whistled down the wind. A never-to-be-forgotten afternoon.

We returned to Loch Laidon in the cool of the evening, and launching the boat, drifted into the bay east of Tigh na Cruaiche. When the great fish rose it hardly made a ripple on the surface; first the huge head, then long, never-ending back, dorsal fin, adipose fin, then massive coal-shovel shaped tail, all as though in slow motion.

Ann turned to look at me. We both tried to speak but words just wouldn't come. Eventually, in unison, we gasped, 'Did you see that?' It was the largest trout that I have ever seen and must have weighed at least 10 lb and it had risen to take small black fly being wafted over the surface in the light breeze.

So, when you fish Laidon, be ready. As you cast over yet another delightful little trout, be prepared. Perhaps, slowly making its way flywards may be that very same monster; jaws gaping in anticipation, making for the ever-ready glass case above your mantelpiece. Best of luck if it is.

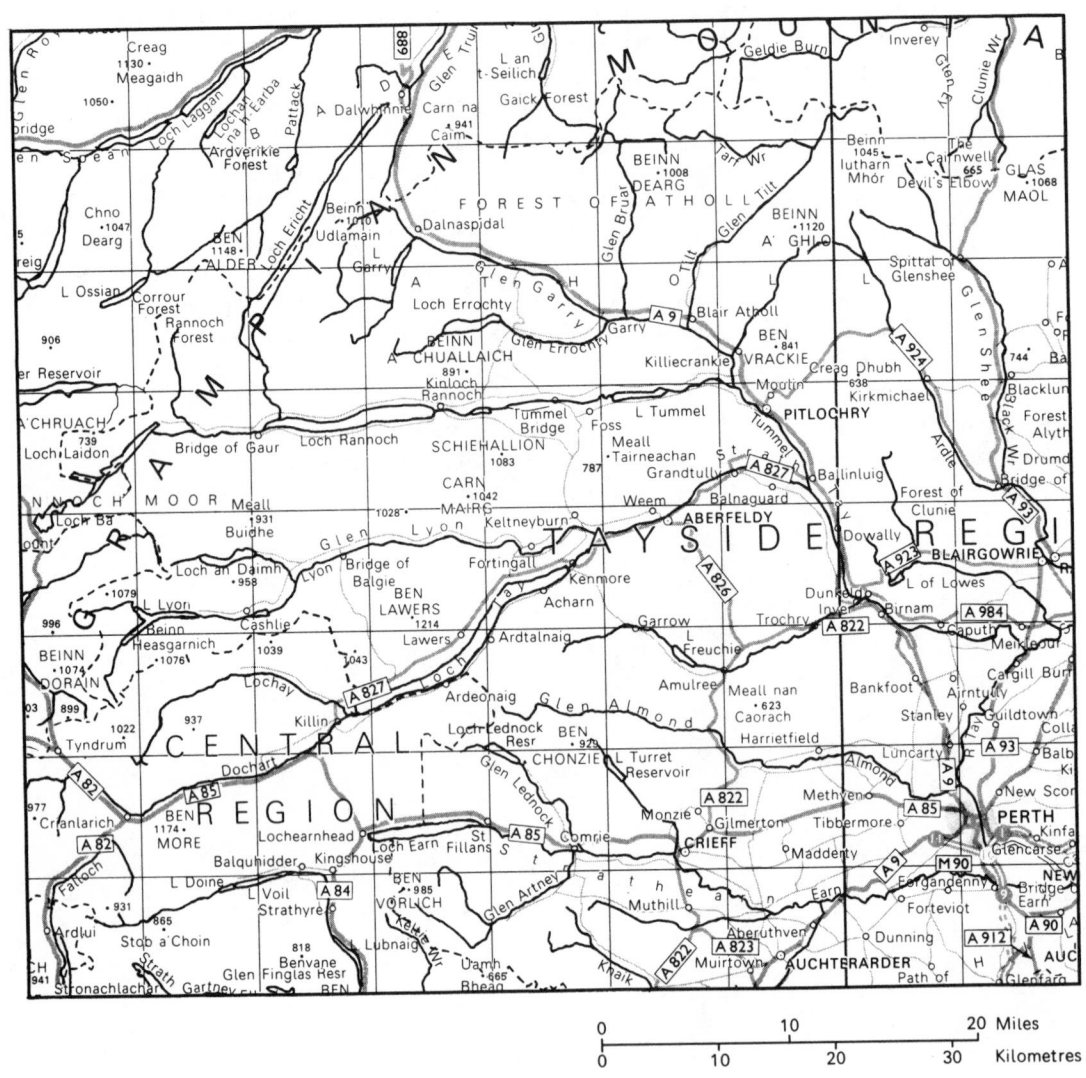

GATEWAY TO THE NORTH

FISHING DIRECTORY

RIVER TAY
Town Water
Director of Finance,
Perth District Council, Council Offices,
High Street, Perth
(0783) 21161

RIVER TAY
Dalguise
Perth & District Anglers Association,
J Alipski, 30 Lingay Court, Perth
(0783) 31766

RIVER TAY
Farleyer
Farleyer Estate,
Aberfeldy, Perthshire
(0887) 20540

RIVER TAY
Killiechassie
Killiechassie Estate,
Estate Office, Killiechassie, Aberfeldy,
Perthshire
(0887) 20496

RIVER TAY
Weem
Weem Hotel,
Weem, by Aberfeldy, Perthshire
(0887) 20381

RIVER TAY
Aberfeldy
Aberfeldy Angling Club,
The Secretary, 65 Moness Crescent,
Aberfeldy, Perthshire
(0887) 20488

RIVER TAY
Gradtully, Fyndynate, Cloichfoldich,
Edradymate and Dercluich Beats.
Renton Finlayson,
Estate Office, Aberfeldy, Perthshire
(0887) 20234

RIVER TAY
Grandtully
Grandtully Arms Hotel,
Grandtully, Perthshire
(08874) 207

RIVER TAY
Bankfoot
Hunter Lodge,
Bankfoot, Perthshire
(032484) 325

RIVER TAY
Kenmore
Kenmore Hotel,
Kenmore, Perthshire
(08873) 205

RIVER TAY
Ballinluig
Logierait Pine Lodges,
Ballinluig, Perthshire
(079682) 253

RIVER TAY
Logierait
Mrs J Grey,
Mill of Logierait, Pitlochry, Perthshire
(079682) 230

RIVER TAY
Ballathie
Estate Office,
Ballathie Farms, Balmains, Stanley,
Perthshire
(025083) 250

RIVER TAY
Glendelvine
Glendelvine Estate,
Estate Office, Glendelvine, Caputh,
Perthshire
(073871) 276

RIVER TAY
Murthly
Murthly & Strathbraan Estate,
Douglasfield, Murthly, Perthshire
(073871) 480

RIVER TAY
Newtyle
Mrs I Redford,
Miolimlea, Station Road, Errol, Perthshire
(08212) 276

RIVER TAY
Dunkeld
Dunkeld House Hotel,
Dunkeld, Perthshire
(03502) 593

RIVER TAY
Dunkeld
Dunkeld & Birnam Angling Association,
J Doig, 42 Willowbank, Birnam,
Perthshire

RIVER TAY
Dalguise
Mike Smith,
Burnside, Dalguise, Perthshire
(03502) 593

RIVER TAY
Kinnaird
Savills Limited,
12 Clerk Street, Brechin
(03562) 2187

RIVER TAY
Sketewan
John Garbutt,
Sketewan, by Grandtully, Perthshire
(079682) 207

RIVER TAY
Stanley
Tayside Hotel,
Stanley, Perthshire
(073828) 249

LOCH TAY
Ardeonaig Hotel,
by Killin, Perthshire
(05672) 249
Clachgaig Hotel,
Killin, Perthshire
(05672) 270
Killin Hotel,
Killin, Perthshire
(05672)
D & S Allan,
Tackle Dealers, Main Street, Killin,
Perthshire
(05672) 362
Loch Tay Highland Lodges,
Milton Morenish, by Killin, Perthshire
(05672) 323
Kenmore Hotel,
Kenmore, by Aberfeldy, Perthshire
(08873) 205
Loch Tay Guest House,
Croft-na-Caber, South Loch Road,
Kenmore, Perthshire
(08873) 236
Tigh-An-Loan Hotel,
Fearnan, Kenmore, Perthshire
(08873) 249
Ben Lawers Hotel,
Lawers, Aberfeldy, Perthshire
(05672) 436

RIVER DOCHART
Keepers House,
Auchlyne Estate, by Killin, Perthshire
(05762) 487
Portnellen Lodges,
Crianlarich, Perthshire
(08383) 284
D & S Allan,
Tackle Dealer, Main Street, Killin,
Perthshire
(05762) 362 ·
(05672)

RIVER LOCHY
D & S Allan,
Tackle Dealers, Main Street, Killin,
Perthshire
(05762) 362
05672

84

LOCH-NA-LARAIG
D & S Allan,
Tackle Dealers, Main Street, Killin,
Perthshire
(05672) 362

RIVER LYON
Finlayson & Hughes,
Estate Office, Aberfeldy, Perthshire
(0887) 29004
Fortingall Hotel,
Fortingall, Aberfeldy, Perthshire
(08873) 367   *£20.00 £5.00*
Gregor Cameron,
Keepers Cottage, Chesthill, Glen Lyon,
Perthshire
(08877) 216
~~**Mrs J Bickerton,**~~   *DONALD CAMPBELL*
Roroyere, Glen Lyon, Perthshire
(08876) 216   *£15.00.*
Coshieville Hotel,
Coshieville, Aberfeldy, Perthshire
(08873) 319

LOCH LYON
LOCH GIORRA
Invermearn Estate,
Glen Lyon, Perthshire
(08876) 244

LOCH GLENOULANDIE
Mr McAdam,
Aberfledy/Tummel Bridge Road,
Perthshire
(08873) 306

RIVER TUMMEL
Pitlochry Tourist Information Office,
22 Atholl Road, Pitlochry
(0796) 2215 or telephone Mr Gardiner
(0796) 2157 between 1730hrs and 1830hrs
Mrs Mohamed,
20 East Barnton Gardens, Edinburgh
(031) 336 1379
Airdnair Hotel,
160 Atholl Road, Pitlochry
(0796) 2266
Logierait Pine Lodges,
Ballinluig, Perthshire
(079682) 253

LOCH TUMMEL
Pitlochry Tourist Information Office,
22 Atholl Road, Pitlochry
(0796) 2215
Forestry Commission Exhibition Centre,
Queen's View, Loch Tummel,
Killiecrankie
(079687) 223
Port-an-Eilean Hotel,
Strathtummel, by Pitlochry
(08824) 233
Queen's View Hotel,
Strathtummel, by Pitlochry
(079687) 291

DUNALISTER LOCH
Mrs Stratton,
Lassentulloch House, Kinloch Rannoch,
Perthshire
(08822) 238
Dunalistair Hotel,
Kinloch Rannoch, Perthshire
(08822) 323
E Beattie,
2 Schiehallion Place, Kinloch Rannoch,
Perthshire
(08822) 261

LOCH RANNOCH
Dunalastair Hotel,
Kinloch Rannoch, Perthshire
(08822) 323
Bunrannoch Hotel,
Kinloch Rannoch, Perthshire
(08822) 367
The Country Store,
Kinloch Rannoch, Perthshire
(08822) 306
Moor of Rannoch Hotel,
Rannoch Station, Perthshire
(08823) 238

LOCH LAIDON
RIVER GAUR
LOCH EIGHEACH
LOCH DUBHLOCHAN
Moor of Rannoch Hotel,
Rannoch Station, Perthshire
(08823) 238

LOCH BHAC
LOCH KINARDOCHY
Airdanair Hotel,
Atholl Road, Pitlochry
(0796) 2266

LOCH EARN
J MacPhearson,
Rannoch, 4 Earn View, St Fillans
(076485) 219;
and also from the post office in
Lochearnhead and St Fillans

RIVER EARN
Crieff
W Cook Sons,
High Street, Crieff, Perthshire
(0764) 2081
A Boyd,
King St, Crieff, Perthshire
(0764) 2081

RIVER EARN
St Fillans
**St Fillans & Lochearn Angling
Association,**
J MacPherson, Rannoch, 4 Earn View, St
Fillans
(076485) 219

RIVER EARN
Bridge
Managed Estates,
18 Maxwell Place, Stirling
(0876) 62519
Mrs Lindsay,
Loanhead Farm, Aberuthven, Perthshire
(07646) 2687

RIVER EARN
Broomhill
David Black,
Hobby & Model Shop, New Row,
Dunfermline, Fife
(0383) 722582

RIVER EARN
Hilton
Perth & District Anglers Association,
J A Lipski, 30 Lingay Court, Perth
(0783) 31766

RIVER EARN
LOCH COWDEN
Comrie
The Royal Hotel,
Comrie, Perthshire
(07647) 200

LOCH TURRET
W Cook & Sons,
19 High Street, Crieff, Perthshire
(0764) 2081

MONZIEVAIRD LOCH
Mr Grout,
Octertyre House, Crieff, Perthshire
(0764) 3963

LOCH MONAGHAN
LOCH FINNART
J Brown,
The Garage, The Square, Kinloch
Rannoch, Perthshire
(08822) 331

RIVER GARRY
RIVER TILT
Atholl Estates,
Estate Office, Blair Atholl, Perthshire
(079681) 355
Atholl Angling Club,
The Corner House, Blair Atholl,
Perthshire
(079681) 246

LOCH FASKALLY
Pitlochry Tourist Information Office,
22 Atholl Road, Pitlochry
(0976) 2215

RIVER ISLA
Lower
DEAN WATER
J Crockart,
26-28 Allan Street, Blairgowrie
(0250) 2056
W Mitchell,
4 Mitchell Square, Blairgowrie
(0250) 3679

RIVER ERICHT
J Crockart,
26-28 Allan Street, Blairgowrie
(0250) 2056
Bridge of Cally Hotel,
Blairgowrie
(025086) 231

RIVER BRAAN
Amulree Hotel,
Amulree, by Dunkeld, Perthshire
(03505) 218

RIVER ARDLE
The Log Cabin Hotel,
Glen Derby, Strathardale, Perthshire
(025081) 288
Corrie Fodly Hotel,
Bridge of Cally, Perthshire
(028086) 236

LOCH MHARAICH
The Log Cabin Hotel,
Glen Derby, Strathardale, Perthshire
(035081) 288

BUTTERSTONE LOCH
The Bailiff,
Loch End Cottage, Butterstone, by
Dunkeld
(03504) 238

CARSBRECK LOCH
Blackford Farms,
Dunblane
(078682) 4000

CASTLEHILL RESERVOIR
The Boathouse,
Castlehill Reservoir, Muckhart
(025981) 357

CASTLEMAINS FISHERY
Mrs Bayne,
Castlemain Farm, Auchterarder,
Perthshire
(025981) 2475

SANDYKNOWES FISHERY
M A Brien,
Fishery Office, Sandyknowes Fishery,
Bridge of Earn
(0738) 813033

KINGSMYRE FISHERY
Mr Meldrum,
The Keepers House, Taymount Estate,
Stanley, Perthshire
(073882) 289

OLD ENGLAND LOCH
Ballathie Estate Office,
Stanley, Perthshire
(025083) 250

LOCH A'CHOIRS
D Seaton,
Gamekeepers House, Balsmund, Pitlochry
(0796) 2273

LOCH A'CHAIT
Major T W M Whitson,
Lick Foss, Strathtummel, Perthshire
(08824) 208

LOCH FARLEYER
The Farleyer Estate,
Aberfeldy, Perthshire
(0887) 20523

LOCH ERROCHTY
BLAIR WALKER POND
LOCH LOCH
Highland Guns and Tackle Shop,
Blair Atholl, Perthshire
(079681) 303

LOCH MORAIG
LOCH VALAGAN
Major W G Gordon,
Lude House, Blair Atholl, Perthshire
(079681) 240

LOCH GARRY
J Kennedy,
The Old School House, Dalnaspindal, by
Pitlochry
(079683) 202

LOCH ERICHT north
The Loch Ericht Hotel,
Dalnawhinnie, Inverness-shire
(05282) 257

LOCH ERICHT south
J Brown,
The Garage, Kinloch Rannoch, Perthshire
(08822) 331

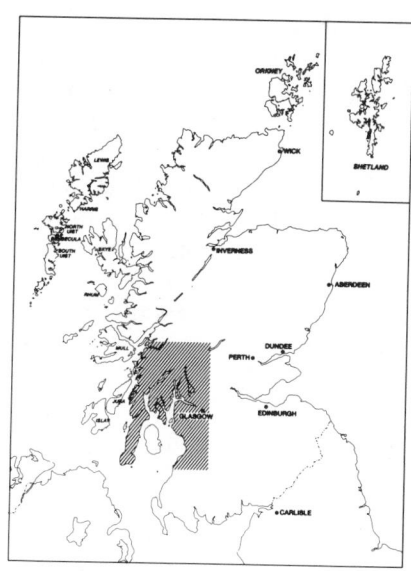

FJORD LANDS OF THE WEST

Lomond and Argyll

'Keep your elbow tucked in. Imagine that you are holding a book under your arm. Use the rod as a spring. Aim for the clouds, not the water. The wind will straighten out your cast. Good try. No, stand still, the flies are caught in your sweater. I'll get them out. Now, have another go.'

My beginner was a London media-man and we were fishing Loch Awe on a warm spring morning. Problem was that, like media men the world over, my embryonic Walton would not stop talking. I'm trying to explain the finer points of fly fishing and he's going on about what he said to Moshe Dayan. Eventually, I admitted defeat, retired to a safe distance, found a sheltered spot and dozed off. I was awakened an hour later by being slapped in the face with the tails of four freshly caught trout: 'Come on Bruce, I've got the fish. The bar's open. Let's go and celebrate. Did I ever tell you about the time General Gowan and I had to fight our way out? Well, we were pinned down by an ambush . . .'

My most enduring memory of this well-known personality was his response one morning when I pointed towards Ben Cruachan, the splendid mountain that guards the Pass of Brander at the north end of the loch, and suggested that he might like to try his hand at a little hill loch fishing. 'If anyone thinks that they are going to get me up Mount Kraken, then they are out of their tiny minds.' Whenever I see him on the small screen today, I smile secretly, remembering his garbled effort to pronounce 'Cruachan' the Clan Campbell war cry; but, to this day, in our family the Ben is still referred to as Mount Kraken.

When I first fished mighty Loch Awe, Argyllshire's jewel, you could guarantee a good basket of trout and it was the ideal place to introduce a novice to the art of fly fishing. The loch was full of willing trout, eager to please and they rose like gentlemen to the fly—almost regardless of how

89

expertly they were presented. Loch Awe was one of Scotland's most notable fisheries; famous for the quality of sport. Indeed, the all-time record brown trout was reputed to have been taken from Awe; a monster 39 lb 8 oz fish captured in 1866. Today, sceptics claim that the fish was a salmon. Spoil-sports! I'm sure it was a brown trout and sooner, rather than later, I propose to catch its great, great, great, great, great, great and then some, grandson, just to prove it.

More recent years have produced a steady flow of double figure specimen trout: 1973 15 lb 3 oz, 1975 13 lb, 1980 19 lb 8 oz. Fugitive rainbow trout, escapees from fish farms have now established themselves in Loch Awe and are breeding naturally and several of these graceful foreigners weighing over 10 lb have been landed. Awe also contains salmon, sea-trout, Arctic char, huge pike and no doubt several as yet unrecorded species in its dark, 300-ft depths.

To catch these monster ferox, bait a large hook with a half-pound brown trout and tow it, sunk at a depth of 15 to 20 feet, from a slowly moving boat. Fingers crossed, praying for action.

Loch Awe is a vast playground for the West of Scotland; with water ski-ing, sail-boarding, sailing boats and pleasure craft endlessly speed, tack, turn and gibe up and down the 26-mile length of the loch. Aweside has become increasingly popular with people from south of the Border; and I suppose, if you were condemned to year-long drudgery in Sheffield, then the prospect of escape to a Loch Aweside cottage, complete with your own mooring bay for the family power-cruiser, and free fishing, would seem like heaven.

But, sadly, not everyone plays the game fairly and fishing on the lovely, romantic Scottish loch has come under enormous pressure at the hands of a few people who could be better described as 'fishmongers' rather than anglers—the sort of people who are only interested in numbers and weight of fish caught and who are prepared to use any method to achieve what they consider to be their 'rights'. Worse, if they are approached by water bailiffs and asked to stop, the most likely outcome is that the bailiff gets, at least, a mouthful of abuse and frequently a dipping in the loch for his trouble.

In 1985 the Loch Awe Improvement Association was set up by all the owners of the shoreline, in an effort to prevent abuse of the loch and its environment. They issued 4,000 pamphlets locally and to Scottish angling clubs, calling for more care and consideration by the users of the loch. Nobody took much notice and the fishmongers fished on: six or seven rods each, tearing down trees and fences to make fires, leaving their litter scattered round the shores.

Consequently, the Association has applied to the Secretary of State for Scotland for a Protection Order under the 1976 Freshwater Fisheries Act; and, in my opinion, not a moment before time. In fact, this action should have been taken ten years ago, in order to preserve the quality of both the fishing and scenery of this magnificent fishery, an important part of our national heritage.

People have been fishing Loch Awe for thousands of years. Early settlers built their homes on artificial islands in the loch, *crannogs*, safe from attack, each with its prehistoric harbour to berth canoes and there are many *crannog* sites along the shores of Loch Awe but, to date, none have been properly investigated. Towards the end of the last century two boys found a cache of bronze spearheads, near Ford and, more recently, remarkably, visiting the same site, Mrs Marion Campbell discovered the famous Torran Hoard, now in the Scottish Museum of Antiquities in Edinburgh: a thickly-patinated green ring, bronze bracelet, armlet, knife, copper ore and three bronze axe-heads.

Until the Middle Ages, Argyll was almost a separate Kingdom within Scotland; indeed, some would claim that it remains so to this day. The early inhabitants of Argyll were a mixture of Irish, Scots, Lowlanders and visiting Vikings, the men of the bays. Norsemen paid frequent, less than kindly visits to these rocky, fjord-like shores which reminded them of distant homelands.

The raiders invented the concept of trade union rules, long before Tolpuddle and Keir Hardie: (1) The cook must be landed wherever possible, to prepare a hot meal; (2) Spoils of war were to be divided equally between crew members with the Captain taking an extra share, known as the boat's share—very much as is still done today in modern fishing vessels; (3) If the crew had to bail the boat more than three times a day then the contract of employment was null and void and crew members free to leave.

This reminds me a lot of some of the boats I have sailed in on Scottish trout lochs; one hand casting, the other bailing continuously. The Vikings would never have countenanced some of the leaking tubs in which I have risked my life. One should always be careful when afloat and nowhere more so than on Loch Awe. It can be a wild, dangerous place and to venture out in anything other than a sound boat is just asking for trouble.

I remember some years ago fishing with a friend, Tony Sykes from Glasgow. We had sailed all the way up from Ford at the south end to Innis Struie, opposite Kilmaha, where there is the site of a 12th-century chapel. This island is a noted fishing area and can be very productive. We arranged a drift towards the island and were inching our flies over the water, concentrating so hard that we failed to notice the wind rising. Suddenly alarmed, we decided to run for home and in starting the outboard motor, the propeller hit an unseen rock and the sheer pin snapped. 'You brought a spare pin?' I inquired without much hope of affirmative response.

I will never forget that nightmarish, exhausting, frightening row back

91

to Ford. We could have done with a couple of Vikings that day, to take a spell on the oars. That was the same day that we had cold curry sandwiches in what was laughingly called our picnic lunch. The place where we were staying adopted a policy of using the previous evening's left-overs as the basis of the following day's lunch. In fact, I'm sure that's why we didn't catch anything round the islands; because we threw the soggy bread overboard and I reckon that after one nibble every trout for miles around fled the area. It became very embarrassing. In the morning, 'Mine Host' would appear with the suspect picnic and wave us off lochwards. We would drive round the first corner and stop in the village shop and stock up. Each evening our host would ask, 'How was lunch, gentlemen?' I began to suspect that he knew our guilty secret and was really just having us on.

There are dozens of good fishing areas, all round the loch, from both boat and bank. In the north end, the shallows round Kilchurn and in the vicinity of the islands are productive drifts; the mouth of Teatle Water, Inistrynich, Eilean and t-Sagairt and Upper Sonachan on the south shore; and Ceann Mara, Annat Bay, Caillaig and Rubha nan Eun on the north shore. At the south end, on the north shore, try Liever Island, Innis Struie, Barr Phort and Kames Bay; from the south shore, Innis Sea-ramhach, Eredine, Fincharn and the shallows by Kilneuair are good fishing areas. As always, take care if bank fishing. There are areas where the bottom shelves very steeply and it is better to be safe rather than wet and sorry. We had one disaster at the south end of the loch where there is a deep lagoon, known as the Lodon, and the remains of an old wooden pier. We had parked there one wet morning with a full complement of families: six children, two wives and Tony and myself.

In an unexpected gesture of goodwill, and at great cost to valuable fishing time, Tony agreed to take the children for a trip round the bay before we got on with man's proper function in life, the removal of fish from their natural habitat. Excited 'wains' were packed afloat and Sykes started the engine. A cheery wave and off they went. We smiled benignly. But, as they returned to the jetty, Tony turned round to adjust the outboard motor and, to our horror, we saw his ample behind nudge his fishing rod overboard. It sank, almost in slow motion, without anyone aboard noticing. This particular rod was a classic of the rod-maker's craft. About 80 years old, a Hardy which had belonged to his grandfather. It was like breaking the news of a sudden death in the family and poor Sykes rushed back to the boat, searching in vain for the vanished rod. But Sykes was always a lucky tyke. A couple of weeks later, in a Glasgow bar, he eavesdropped on a conversation between two neighours. They were members of a Glasgow subaquatic club, planning a visit to Loch Awe. A deal was struck and the hunt was on. Aided by arc lights and a team of four divers, the rod was found, restored and is as good as new today.

Sykes tried to tell me that there was even a six-pound trout on the end, but I didn't buy that one.

The River Awe rushes seawards to Loch Etive through the dark Pass of Brander. Well, it used to, until in the early 1960s a 59-feet-high barrage was built across Shallows Pool as part of a hydroelectric scheme. The quality of fishing on the three-mile river was radically altered and the large salmon for which the Awe was justly famous soon disappeared.

Some huge salmon were taken prior to the Awe Barrage being built and the heaviest of these fish fell to the rod of A. W. Huntington and weighed 57 lb. The monster was caught on 26 July 1921 in Castledhu Pool. Mrs G. B. Huntington had a fish of 55 lb on 19 September 1927 in the Erract Pool and another marvellous salmon weighing 51 lb from Stepping Stones on 22 May 1930. I always knew that lady anglers were far more skilful than men.

Fishing on the Awe is in the hands of two syndicates and it is not generally available to casual visiting anglers. Inquire in advance and there is a chance that you might obtain a few days and if you don't mind fishing in full view of the thousands of tourists that drive the autobahn-like new road through the glen, then this is the place for you. Certainly, in spite of the depredations made by hydroelectricity works, the Awe still produces good numbers of fish each season and the river is divided into seven beats, from the barrage to Inverawe.

Before leaving the Pass of Brander, consider a visit to Inverawe Fisheries, one of the most well-known put-and-take trout fisheries in Scotland. Troubled in recent years by pollution, this excellent fishery is now back on form and continues to produce fine-quality brown and rainbow trout which often reach double figures in size. Because of its popularity, it is best to book your permit well in advance; and don't imagine that the fish give themselves up easily. The residents of this established fishery are just as difficult and exciting to catch as their wilder brethren in nearby Loch Awe.

Thousands of salmon are counted through the Awe barrage each year, heading for the safety of Loch Awe and the rivers Orchy and Lochy. Few are caught in the loch or the Lochy, but the Orchy can produce superb sport, given the right water levels. The Orchy is born amongst the wild hills to the south on Rannoch Moor as the Water of Tulla, between Loch Lyon and Loch Laidon, flowing south-west to meet Loch Tulla, west of the A82 Glasgow/Glencoe road.

Hundreds of tiny streams drain the distant peaks of Black Mount, Stob a'Bhruaich Leith (940 m), Meall nan Eun (926 m), Stob Coir'an Albannaich and Stob a'Choire Odhair. They gather in Lochan na h-Iuraiche, Lochan na Saobhaidhe and Loch Dochard and marry Tulla under Victoria Bridge by Forest Lodge. The River Orchy blossoms from Loch Tulla and strikes south, following the line of the tortuous B8074 through Glen Orchy to enter Loch Awe by the dramatically restored

Kilchurn Castle, ancient home of the Argyll Breadalbanes.

Dalmally Hotel offers fishing on the Orchy and day tickets are often available. Access to the other beats may be obtained via the estates and the river has some fine pools where notable salmon have been caught over the years: a fish of 35 lb from Black Duncan Pool in 1961. Evidence of other great salmon may be inspected in the Hotel and include salmon of 37 lb and the heaviest fish taken from the Orchy, a fine salmon weighing 42 lb caught in 1923.

Northwards from Loch Awe, the long finger of sea Loch Etive draws Atlantic salmon from the Firth of Lorne and Sound of Mull, enticing them through the narrows at Connel and eastwards up the loch. Both the north and south shores of Etive are lined with burns and streams, all of which attract greater or lesser runs of salmon and sea-trout. Along the north shore, Esragan, Cadderlle Burn, Abhainn Dalach and Allt Easach. Along the south shore, salmon and sea-trout may be found at Allt Nathais, Nant, Noe, Liver, Kinglass, Allt Ghiusachan and the streams eastwards. At the head of Loch Etive, the River Etive is the most productive stream but is not open to public fishing. At their best, the other streams that flow into Loch Etive, each produce about 50 salmon every season and numbers of sea-trout. The remote Kinglass River has some good pools although spawning grounds are limited and the river fishes best during autumn months.

Between Connel and Oban the Feochan is also a late salmon river, but is best known for its runs of sea-trout and there is also good sport with sea-trout on Loch Nell, the headwaters of the system where visitors can obtain permission to fish from the Oban and Lorne Angling Club. The angling club also have some good trout fishing in the Oban area and south towards Loch Awe. There are more than 20 lochs, all of which contain stocks of brown trout which vary in size from 8 oz up to much larger specimens of 3 lb and more. Loch Oude is the club's rainbow trout fishery and easily accessible, being close to the A816 Oban/Kilmelford road.

The Oude system is part of the Kilmelford hydroelectric scheme and the lower part of the river, below the loch, is used as a breeding station for salmon which are planted out in the river. There is no public salmon fishing on the river, being preserved by the owners for their own use.

Oban and Lorne Angling Club trout lochs offer a superb variety of sport to visiting anglers and permission to fish is readily available from David Graham's shop in Crombie Street, Oban.

There is something for everyone here; lochs where you can park almost by the waterside and others which will tax lungs and legs to reach. Of the latter, the group of waters to the east of the A816 near Kilmelford are my favourites. There are more than a dozen excellent waters scattered in the hills and corries of Cruach on Nid (289 m), Barr (235 m), Cruach Maolachy (378 m) and Feinn (236 m). Access is by hoof and you should take along a compass and map. If a mist comes down, finding your way can be difficult. Furthest out waters include a'Chaoruinn, Dubh-Bheag, a'Chreachan, Dubh Mor, Gully and Cruach Maoilachy.

The most remote of the club waters are the Soir Lochs, deep into the hills past Glen Feochan. Much of the water here has been trapped by viaducts, to be led unprotesting to feed the ever-hungry hydroelectric turbines milking Loch Nant. This is a spectacular place to fish and well worth the effort involved. Trout are not large and average three to the pound but the glorious solitude more than compensates for the lack of monster trout and these little fish rise well and fight hard.

The River Euchar, south from the Soir Loch has also suffered from the removal of headwater feeder stream to Loch Nant. What is left feeds into Loch Scammadale which lies some nine miles south from Oban. Scammadale is about two miles long by five hundred yards wide, often windy, and inhabited by salmon and sea-trout. With the loss of so much of the upstream spawning grounds the owners of the system have in recent years begun to restock the river, particularly with sea-trout fry and upwards of 30,000 salmon eggs. Fishing is readily available to visiting anglers, both in the river and on the loch where bank and boat fishing is allowed. The most productive area on the loch seems to be the north shore and sport is mainly with sea-trout. Baskets of three or four sea-trout can be taken during the course of a day but salmon are rarely caught in the loch.

The total catch for the season numbers about 50 salmon and 150 sea-trout throughout the system and some of the fishing is let in conjunction with self-catering properties. Fish enter the river from about April onwards but the best sport is not had until July. Remember, this is very much a spate river and in times of low water salmon and sea-trout find it hard to negotiate the falls between loch and sea. With plenty of rain, look out for some great sport.

Much of Argyll has been subjected to vast afforestation schemes and these have affected many of the salmon streams; forestry ploughing and planting has greatly lowered the water table and flash-flooding means that even after heavy, prolonged rain, the river systems empty quickly. More than 50 per cent of Cowal is completely afforested and the change in the landscape during the 30 years I have been visiting this part of Scotland is unbelievably dramatic.

South of Loch Awe, are the excellent hill lochs of the Ederline Estate, and these will appeal to anglers who like their fishing in open countryside. Great sport may be had with traditional Highland brown trout and one or two larger fish of over 2 lb. However, the Forestry Commission has tried to preserve trout fishing in the waters under its control and offers visiting anglers a number of fishing opportunities on forest lochs in and around Loch Awe and Lochgilphead. There are some good lochs in the forests near Ford: Cam, Eun, Dalach, a'Bhruic and Eireachan, all of which are stocked and contain brown trout averaging 8–10 oz, with larger fish in Cam.

Loch Avich, to the west of Loch Awe is not only afforested but also linked in to a hydroelectric scheme. On my last visit I thought that I had wandered onto a film set for an epic about the First World War; rows of stub-trees, lined, scarred, bare ground and if thousands of men had risen from trenches, rifle-bayoneted, I wouldn't have blinked an eye. Still, Avich has brown trout and they average 10 oz.

Of all the forest lochs, the best is still probably Coille Bharr, near Barnlusgan. When I first fished this loch, the size and quality of the trout was of the highest order and the average weight 1 lb 8 oz. Recently, the average has fallen and you are more likely to catch trout of 10 oz. The trees round the loch are a mixture of coniferous and broad-leaf, hugging the water's edge, so boat fishing only.

The Forestry Commission also owns Barnlusgan Loch which contains slightly smaller fish than Coille Bharr and several waters to the south of Loch Awe, including Linnhe, Losgunn, Buie, Blackmill, Bealach Gherran and Glashan, all available to visiting anglers. Loch Glashan is the head pond for yet another hydroelectric scheme, robbing the waters of Add and Tunns, diverting them into the much enlarged forest loch. A compensation flow keeps some water in the Add which flows through the vast forest to reach the sea at Isalandadd Bridge, by the Crinan Canal.

Salmon and sea-trout run the Add and the river is divided into three beats, Minard, Krinan and Poltalloch. Best fishing is in the autumn months and there are a number of good pools including Hardy's, Reed, Wood and Poacher's Pot and some 100 salmon are taken most seasons. Not so readily available to anglers are the waters of the Lochgilphead and District Angling Club who have fishing on seven lochs to the west of Cairnbann. Boats are reserved for the use of club members, bank fishing only for visitors.

The long leg of Mull of Kintyre runs south-west from Knapdale, enclosing sea Loch Fyne, dividing the island of Arran from the Inner Hebridean islands of Islay and Jura. The most productive salmon stream on the Mull of Kintyre is the little Barr River, but all fishing is preserved for the owners. Salmon fishing is offered on Lussa River and given good water levels, this system can give super sport. The owners of the river also operate a fish farm and about 50 salmon and 100 sea-trout are taken by anglers most seasons. Being in the right place at the right time is all-important.

A number of additional small spate river systems give Kintyre anglers good sport with salmon and sea-trout and are also available to visitors. Machrihanish, which enters the sea through the long, silver sands fringing Machrihanish Bay and the old links golf course; Strone, Breackerie and Conieglen Waters, entering the North Channel between Scotland and Ireland by Carskery Bay and Brunerican Bay at the southernmost tip of Kintyre.

The Kintyre Protection and Angling Club make their trout fishing available to the public and they have a number of waters including Tangy Loch, Lussa Loch, Auchalochy, Knockruan and Garasdale. For a special treat, sail westwards from Kintyre and visit the beautiful offshore island of Gigha. Mill Loch, the only fishing water in the island, is a well-stocked fishery where trout average 1 lb 8 oz.

Argyll is Campbell country, for centuries the most powerful of Scottish clans. The Campbells became Knights of Scotland in the 13th century and in 1445 Sir Duncan Campbell of Lochow was created Lord Campbell of Argyll. Archibald, the 2nd Earl, fell at Flodden in 1513 when the 'flower of Scotland' died with King James IV in a few hours of unimaginable carnage. Colin Campbell was made Hereditary Master of the Royal Household in Scotland and throughout history Campbells have played an important part in Scottish affairs, mostly in support of the established governments of the day.

Miles and miles of bugger-all. Tired feet in Torridon

One of the most famous of the clan was Sir Colin Campbell, Baron Clyde, born in Glasgow in 1792. During a long and distinguished military career, Colin Campbell served King and country throughout the world. He fought and survived the Peninsular War, being badly wounded twice; he was involved in the American War of 1814; served in Gibraltar, Barbados and fever-ridden Demarara; 1842 found him in China and 1848 in North India fighting the Sikhs. During the Crimean War, Sir Colin commanded the Highland Brigade, winning victory at the Battle of Alma and later organised the famous 'thin red line' at the Battle of Balaklava. He is reputed to have addressed his troops before the critical stage of the battle, when nothing other than the Highlanders stood between defeat or victory: 'Now men, remember there is no retreat from here. You must die where you stand.'

Gunboat Palmerston appointed Campbell to command the forces in India at the outbreak of the Mutiny in July 1857 and Sir Colin marched into history at the head of the force relieving the besieged town of Lucknow the following December. The grand old soldier ended his career as Field Marshall and died in 1863. He is buried in Westminster Abbey.

The Clan Campbell residence is Inveraray Castle, an imposing pile, close to the A83 Arrochar/Lochgilphead road, overlooking the waters of Loch Fyne. The old Campbell castle was extended and rebuilt by the 3rd Duke, much helped by the brilliant Scottish architects Roger Morris and William Adam. During the Second World War, the castle was used as a Combined Operations training base, training men in the skills of seaborne landings.

Other seaborne landings take place in the River Fyne, the most useful salmon stream in the area, but the quality of sport has been much reduced by the looting of the river's headwaters for hydroelectric schemes. Loch Sloy to the east and Loch Shira to the west were impounded in the mid-1950s to fuel the Clachan Power Station and fishing on the Fyne is largely governed by the station's generating needs. The heaviest fish taken from the Fyne weighed 34 lb 8 oz but catches have diminished seriously in recent years. The owners have instituted a restocking programme to improve matters and the best of Fyne fishing is now had during autumn months. South of Inverarachan, there are high falls, impassable to salmon, and below the falls the river is divided into four fishing beats.

There are a number of holding pools, upstream from the road bridge, including Ballingal's, Whirl, Clachan, Black Bridge, Strutt's, Cottage, Swing Bridge and Laraige and, given the right water levels, excellent sport may still be had. However, in recent years sea-trout fishing has improved and offers good sport from June onwards. Of even greater interest are reports in August 1988 of rainbow trout being caught in the tidal waters, superbly conditioned Scottish 'steel-heads', running the Fyne. These fish weighed up to 5 lb and fought furiously.

South from the mouth of the Fyne, the Kinglas River, another good little salmon and sea-trout stream, tumbles into Loch Fyne from the deep, dark glens between Ben Chorranach (885 m), Ben Ime (1,011 m) and Beinn an Fhidhleir (811 m), the Arrochar Alps. The river rises in Gleann Uanie and flows swiftly past the quaintly named croft of Abyssinia, crossing the old military road at Rest and Be Thankful near Butterbridge. Fishing is from below Butterbridge to the sea and day tickets are available to visiting anglers from the two owners, Ardkinglas and Cairndow Estates. Sea-trout are more prolific than salmon but upwards of 30 salmon are landed most years; depending upon water conditions.

Northwards across Loch Fyne, there are three salmon streams, the Aray, Shira and Douglas Waters, and permission to fish can be readily obtained from the Argyll Estate Office. Choosing the right time to attack is not so easy because all these rivers depend upon high water levels to give of their best. The Aray is best for salmon and the upper river, from Foal's Bridge, is let privately. Salmon run the river from May onwards and the best of the fishing is at the back end. Sea-trout don't seem to like what Aray has to offer and generally pass the river by and the extensive afforestation which has taken place in the glen is responsible for much flash-flooding in the river.

The Shira River has lost much of its power to the Glen Shira hydroelectric scheme and fishing now depends upon compensation flows. In its lower reaches the Shira is a tangled little stream to fish, crowded by trees and bushes in many places and the best sport is to be had on Dubh Loch, a substantial, deep holding water where returning salmon gather and rest before deciding what to do next. Spate water reminds them of their duty. Best results on Shira come in the autumn.

Douglas Water is a short stream which rises in Loch Dubh-ghlas, an afforested area between Loch Fyne and Loch Awe. It is barely three miles in length and much affected by flash-flooding. However, if you manage to be there at the right time, then there could be a salmon waiting for you in one of the small, shallow pools, the best of which is Roman Bridge.

South from Strachur, the A815 follows the shoreline of Loch Eck, six miles long and dropping to 140 ft in depth. Here again, a hydroelectric scheme holds back Eck from its swift course down the River Eachaig to the sea in Holy Loch. The source of the Eachaig lies in the hills and forests near Strachur and the system makes life difficult for itself by running south rather than north into Loch Fyne.

The conifer plantations that cover the hills surrounding Loch Eck make fishing on the main feeder stream, the River Cur, very much a matter of praying for rain. Even then, flash-flooding reduces the level of water in the river very quickly. Fishing on the Cur may be had from local farmers whilst Loch Eck is managed by the Dunoon and District Angling Association and the new owners of the River Eachaig, Salar Properties.

The Eachaig is now time-shared by Salar, but it is often possible to obtain weekly lets when owners do not wish to fish and the Eachaig is well known as one of Scotland's finest sea-trout streams. There are 35 named pools, consisting of deep holding water, pots, rocky gorges and long sweeping pools with gravel lies, all offering superb fly fishing. There is no longer any netting at the mouth of the river and this has brought about an immediate improvement in the numbers of salmon running the river. Upwards of 140 fish are taken and the autumn months provide best sport with salmon. In October 1984 one rod took eight salmon in a day and the largest fish caught recently weighed 20 lb.

The ten-year average for rod and line caught sea-trout, 1976–1985 was 276 fish; and this was during a period when netting was still carried out. The nets averaged 1,626 sea-trout. Therefore, under the new regimen, the future looks bright for this lovely river and if it is possible to obtain a week, then you should be assured of high-quality sport.

The Eachaig is renowned for its exceptionally large sea-trout and this is perhaps due to the genetic qualities and also the high post-spawning survival rate. Scale readings have shown that the big fish have spawned several times and there are records of spectacular catches in most years. In 1978, one rod had 26 sea-trout weighing 62 lb in one day. On another day that year, five sea-trout weighing 51 lb were landed, the heaviest being 14 lb. In August 1984, over the course of a week's fishing, an angler landed 80 sea-trout weighing 194 lb. The heaviest fish caught on the system have been taken in the estuary nets: in 1967 a 20-lb sea-trout and in 1974 a fish of 28 lb 8 oz.

Most anglers use light tackle when fishing the Eachaig and this can at times prove to be very 'interesting'; as Mr Mike Smith found out in 1985 when he hooked a large salmon in Ballochlye Pool. The fish took 55 minutes to land and weighed 19 lb 8 oz. Huge sea-trout are still regularly taken from the Eachaig and fish of over 10 lb are common.

To the west of the Eachaig is another good salmon and sea-trout stream, the River Ruel, for me, always associated with the stirring bagpipe tune *The Glendaruel Highlanders*. Sadly, if these Highlanders returned to their glen today, they would hardly recognise their land because so much of it has disappeared under forestry ploughing. This has greatly affected water flows in the river, as has the extraction of water from the feeder streams to supply a hydroelectric scheme at Loch Tarsan. Consequently, the Ruel is much dependent upon heavy rains to sustain its runs of salmon and sea-trout and is affected by flash-flooding caused by afforestation.

Salmon and sea-trout fishing is mostly private but some fishing is available to members of the public through the Glendaruel Hotel and in high water levels sport can be worth while. The river borders the A886 Colintraive/Strachur road and access is easy. Below the falls in the upper reaches, the river flows gently through farmlands to reach the sea at the head of Loch Riddon and the Kyles of Bute.

Loch fishing for trout in south Argyll is limited. There are still a few good hill lochs but many of the old waters have been impounded for the purpose of electricity generating or water supply systems and they seem to me to have a dismal, forbidding look. However, there is nothing dismal or forbidding about the 'Bonnie banks of Loch Lomond' and although Loch Lomond is a major water supply system for Glasgow and the west of Scotland, because of its vast size, there is little evidence of these works and fishing on this world-famous loch offers the angler the best of all things: salmon, sea-trout, ferox, brown trout, pike, perch and that beautiful species peculiar to Lomond, the powan, often referred to as freshwater herring.

Loch Lomond also plays host to thousands of visitors each year—tourists, sailors, climbers, hill walkers, campers, caravanners and just plain layabouts, looking for rest and peace; all flock to the lochside to enjoy the glorious scenery during warm summer days. Mighty Ben Lomond (974 m) towers over the east shore of the loch whilst the Arrochar Alps dominate the western horizon. Northwards lie the hills and mountains of Perthshire, crowned by Ben More (1,174 m), above the River Dochart, a principal feeder stream of Loch Tay.

Ben Lomond is one of the most popular Scottish Munros, easy to climb and visited each year by more than 3,000 walkers. The best approach is from the village of Rowardennan and the round trip takes about five hours, depending upon how often you pause to admire the view along the way. Never take chances with the weather because, for all its seeming simplicity, if you are caught in a sudden storm near the top it could be very dangerous indeed. I know, having been in such a position in November 1987. Not to be recommended.

There are two 'bibles' for Lomond anglers, Ian Wood's *Loch Lomond and its Salmon* and Bill McEwan's *Angling on Lomond*. On such a large water, prior knowledge of where the fish lie is essential if you are to have the best opportunity of sport. Both these books will tell you how, when and where. An alternative is to seek the services of a gillie. This gives the additional advantage of an experienced hand on the tiller of the boat, for Lomond can be as rough as the North Sea when the mood takes it. A few years ago, whilst staying at Rowardennan, we hired a boat and outboard at Balmaha on the eastern shoreline in order to make daily visits to the Island of Inchmurrin.

This was a long trip, lasting about an hour and, even in a light breeze, in reasonable weather, we had to take care with the choppy waves breaking through the islands which scatter the south end of the loch. I have only once experienced the full fury of Lomond and then, fortunately, I was in the company of a local angler who knew his way around. We spent the day covering the most likely drifts; well, to be truthful, I seemed always to end up managing the dapping rod, a favourite method of attracting shy Lomond salmon to the traditional wet fly patterns fished by the bow and stern rods. We saw a lot of fish; some even 'boiled' wickedly at the dap, but none of the brutes would take. In the evening the wind got up and we ran for Balmaha, arriving with as much water in the boat as there was outside.

In the early months of the season, most salmon are taken by trolling: cold, hard, frozen-finger work. Also, at times, as busy as Sauchiehall Street on a Saturday night, with boats jostling for the best routes. Care, courtesy and consideration are required to avoid accidents. April 1988 produced good sport with Balmaha boats taking a number of salmon, the heaviest of which weighed 16 lb. Balloch boats started catching fish in May and one boat arrived back in the evening with two splendid fish weighing 14 lb and 20 lb.

Loch Lomond fishes well for sea-trout and from February onwards runs of fish enter the loch from the River Leven until, by July, there are fish in most beats; 1988 produced some lovely fish, including three beauties for a Northampton angler, Mr Shane Miller, which weighed 3 lb 8 oz, 4 lb and 7 lb 10 oz. July is the peak month for Lomond fishing when fly fishing brings results and exciting sport. Salmon average 8 lb and sea-trout 2 lb 8 oz. In the early months, a good trolling beat is between Inchmurrin Island and the south-east shore. Start from Boturich Castle and motor north-east past Ross Priory and Gartochraggan Nature Reserve; keeping the boat in the right depth of water is vital and you should aim to be fishing in no more than eight feet of water. Any deeper and you are probably wasting your time.

Summer fly fishing drifts are best in the vicinity of the islands; along the north shore of Inchmoan and through the narrows between Inchmoan and Inchcruin. The Inchfad shoreline is another favoured drift as are the long drifts down either shore of Inchmurrin Island. As with trolling, depth is again critical and it is never bad policy to keep the bottom in sight.

The north end of Loch Lomond produces the best brown trout fishing, particularly out from Ardlui where the water is relatively shallow and Falloch River streams into Lomond.

Nevertheless, it is true to say that no matter where you stop along the shores, you will probably find rising fish and gravel banks to fish from; and, although Loch Lomondside can become very busy, if you are prepared to hike up the West Highland Way which runs up the east side, then within a few miles you will soon find yourself 'far from the madding crowd', alone with nature, at peace with the world. Excluding, of course, fish.

Less peaceful but more productive salmon and sea-trout fishing is to be found in some of the streams entering and leaving Loch Lomond, the best of which is the River Leven which carries the water of Lomond to the Firth of Clyde at Dumbarton. The river is fished by the Loch Lomond Angling Improvement Association and is usually very busy indeed, often with illegal fishers. The Leven produces good sport throughout its long season, from February until October, although the best of the fishing is generally in the autumn months. Spinning accounts for most fish taken and the river records upwards of 250 salmon and 400 sea-trout.

The River Endrick is one of the principal feeder streams of Loch Lomond and is very much a spate river. It rises in the Fintry Hills, flowing quickly through the magnificent Fintry Falls to the splendid series of pools and runs by Gartness. The Pot of Gartness is a difficult barrier for fish to pass and they need good water levels to make the passage upstream. Blane Water and the Endrick join hands downstream from the Pot in a famous pool known locally as Meetings Lynn. The best of Endrick salmon fishing is in this section of the river and fish of 20 lb plus are sometimes caught. The Endrick is also a notable sea-trout fishery with fine fish taken, particularly at night.

Two other Lomond streams are worthy of mention—the Fruin which rises in the hills above Helensburgh and enters the loch north of the village of Arden, opposite Inchmurrin Island. North from Fruin, the little river Luss is flung from the steep slopes of Beinn Eich (702 m) and Beinn Chaorach (713 m), cascading down the silent glen, passing under the busy A82 road and entering Lomond through the well-ordered calm of Ross Park. Both these rivers can produce sport with salmon and sea-trout from July onwards, provided that there is plenty of rain.

Discovering the delights and wonders of Argyll and Lomond can bring a lifetime's pleasure. Anglers, like the prey they hunt, once hooked, will find it hard to escape; these lovely hills, valleys and mountains will hold you enthralled. The diversity and high quality of salmon, sea-trout and brown trout fishing available throughout the area is outstanding. Even nicer is the fact that so much of it is available to visitors; and it won't cost the price of a small family saloon car to find rewarding, splendid sport.

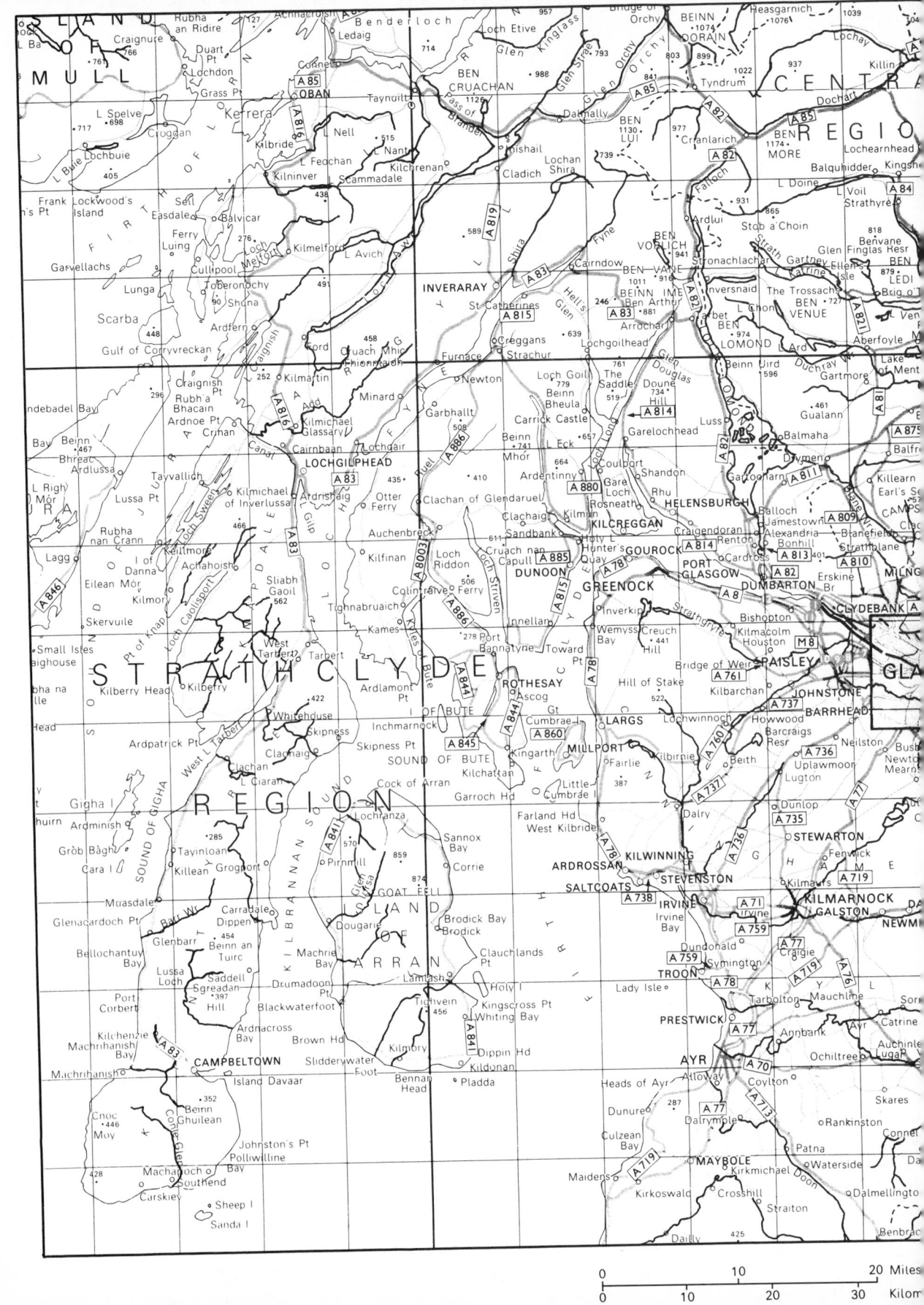

FJORD LANDS OF THE WEST

FISHING DIRECTORY

RIVER AWE
INVERAWE FISHERIES
Inverawe/Taynuilt Fisheries,
Argyll
(08662) 262

RIVER ORCHY
W A Church,
Croggan Crafts, Dalmally, Argyll
(08382) 201

LOCH AWE
Forestry Commission,
Loch Awe, Forest District, Whitegates,
Lochgilphead, Argyll
(08664) 211
Ford Hotel,
Ford, Argyll
(054681) 273
Portscnachan Hotel,
Dalmally, Argyll
(08663) 224
LOCH ETIVE AND STREAMS ON
NORTH
River Eragan
Cadderelle Burn
River Dolach
Allt Easach
STREAMS ON SOUTH SHORE
Allt Nathais
Nant
Noe
Liver
Kinglass
Allt Ghiusachan
Enquire at:
D Graham,
Tackle Dealer, 9–15 Crombie Street,
Oban
(0631) 62069

LOCH NELL
LOCH A'PHEARSAIN
LOCH OUDE
LOCH A'CHORUINN
LOCH DUBH BHEAG
LOCH A'CHREACHAN
LOCH DUBH MOR
THE GULLY LOCH
LOCHAN CRUACH MAOILACHY
LOCH A'MHINN
LOCH NA CURRAIGH
THE FEINN LOCHS
LOCH NA SAILM
LOCH A'CHEIGEIN
LOCH IASG
LOCH AN LOSGAINN
LOCH AN DAIMH
LOCH AN LOSGAINN BHEAG
SIOR LOCHS
LOCHAN AIRIGH SHAMHRALDH
LOCH A'BHARRAIN
LOCH OUDE SYSTEM
LOCH TULLA
LOCH DOCHARD
Oban & Lorn Angling Club,
D Graham, 9–15 Crombie Street, Oban

ENDERLINE LOCHS
The Enderline Estate,
Estate Office, Ford, Argyll
(054681) 273

LOCH CAM
EUN LOCH
LOCHAN DALACH
LOCHAN A'BHRUIC
LOCH EIREACHAIN
RIVER LEIVER
Post Office,
Ford, Lochgilphead, Argyll
(0546) 271

CAM LOCH
LOCH CLACHAIG
THE DUBH LOCH
LOCH NA FAOILINN
LOCH AN ADD
LOCH NA BRIC
Lochgilphead & District Angling Club,
H MacArthur, The Tackle Shop, Lochnell
Street, Lochgilphead, Argyll

LOCH GLASHAN
Lochgaird Hotel,
Lochgilphead, Argyll
(054682) 233

LOCH COILLE BHARR
LOCH BARNLUASGAN
LOCH LINNHE
LOCH LOSGUNN
LOCH BUIE
Chief Forester,
Knapdale Forest, Cairnbaan, Barnluasgan,
Lochgilphead, Argyll
(0546) 2304

LOCH AVICH
Chief Forester,
Forest Office, Dalavich, Taynuilt, Argyll
(08664) 258

LOCH DUBH MOR
GLENDUBH RESERVOIR
Chief Forester,
Forest Office, Barcaldine, Connel, Argyll
(063172) 203

THE HOSPITAL LOCHAN
Chief Forester,
Glencoe Forest, Ballachulish, Glencoe,
Argyll
(08552) 268

LOCH LUSSA
LOCH TANGY
LOCH AUCHALOCHY
LOCH KNOCKRUAN
LOCH GARASDALE
CONIE GLEN WATER
GLEN BREAKERIE WATER
**Kintyre Fish Protection and Angling
Club**
S Martin, Dunallister, Killkerran Road,
Campbeltown, Argyll

LOCH SCAMADLE
Mrs McCorkindale,
Glenann, Kilninver, Oban
(08526) 282

RIVER ADD
Poltalloch Estate Office,
Poltalloch, Argyll

RIVER ARAY
RIVER SHIRA
RIVER DOUGLAS
Argyll Estates Office,
Cherry Park, Inveraray
(0499) 2203

RIVER FYNE
RIVER KINGLAS
Ardkinglass Estate Office,
Cairndow, Argyll
(Cairndow) 217

RIVER EACHAIG
LOCH ECK
Dunoon & District Angling Club,
A H Young, 7 Blair Lane, Stewart Street,
Dunoon, Argyll
Salar Properties Ltd,
Lochloy House, Lochloy, Nairn
(0667) 55355

RIVER ADD
RIVER LUSSA
AND LUSSA FISH FARM
RIVER MACHRIHANISH
RIVER STONE
RIVER BREACHERIE
RIVER CONIEGLEN
Lochgilphead & District Angling Club,
Seven Lochs, west of Cairnbann
Kintyre Protection and Angling Club,
Including Tangy Loch, Lussa Loch,
Auchalochy, Knockruan, Garasdale Mill
Loch (Gigha)
A P MacGrory
Main Street, Campbeltown
(0586) 52132

RIVER CUR
RIVER FINNART
RIVER HASAN
LOCH TARSAN
LOCH LOSKIN
Whistlefield Hotel
Loch Eck, by Dunoon, Argyll
(0332) 553314

RIVER RUEL
Glendarvel Hotel,
Glendarvel

LOCH LOMOND AND
TRIBUTARIES
For Information and Permission Contact:
**Lomond and Angling Improvement
Association,**
29 St Vincent Place, Glasgow G1 2DT
(041) 221 0068

Boats May be Hired:
MacFarlane and Son,
Balmaha
(036 087) 214

107

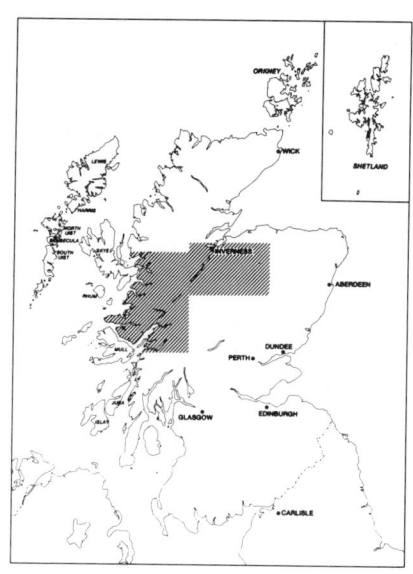

CAPITAL HIGHLANDS

Inverness, Aviemore and the Great Glen

The last battle fought on British soil was all over in half an hour. By just after midday on Wednesday, 16 April 1746, 1,500 men of Prince Charles Edward Stuart's army lay dead on Drumossie Moor, east of Inverness. The rest were fleeing in disarray or lying helpless, bleeding, broken, waiting for Cumberland's eager bayonets to end their misery. The brutality with which Government forces acted on that cold spring day, encouraged by their commander, the King's son, and his officers, slaughtering prisoners and wounded, burning many alive, leaves a dark, indelible stain on British history. Killing fields as devoid of humanity as any of modern times.

Long after the Young Pretender escaped to France, butcher Cumberland's brigades continued to ravage northern straths and glens, burning castles and crofts, raping defenceless women, murdering young and old, often only for barbaric amusement, killing all or any who stood in their way. Cattle, sheep, oxen and horses were stolen in thousands and sold to rapacious English and Lowland dealers who flocked north like scavenging vultures. Houses were stripped and valuables auctioned, spoils being divided among soldiers who were thus encouraged to continue their barbarity. Rebel or not, to be a Highlander was enough. Fear lived by every fireside. Terror reigned.

Guilty and innocent alike, without discrimination, were to feel the full wrath of a badly frightened Parliament and a thoughtless King. 'People must perish by sword and famine.' The strength of the northern clans and the dignity of the Highland way of life was to be destroyed forever.

I never walk or fish in Inverness-shire and Moray without thinking of these desperate, terrified, fleeing men. Men without hope, home or refuge; deserted by their own chiefs, whose outrageous arrogance and tyranny

109

had forced them, unwillingly, onto the field of slaughter. The area contains some of the most dramatic scenery in Scotland; magnificent mountains and secret straths, scarred by the knife-like stab of the Great Glen and monster-ridden Loch Ness. The empty wilderness lands of Knoydart, Morar, Moidart, Ardgour, Sunart, Ardnamurchan and Morven; the Great Ben, mighty Ben Nevis, guarding Fort William. Blue Monadliath Mountains and the huge thrust of snow-capped Cairngorms.

By the time he escaped from Scotland, Bonnie Prince Charlie knew this land better than most; spending months trekking through its vastness, always managing to stay one step ahead of his pursuers. The greatest manhunt ever launched in the British Isles failed to capture the histrionic, dilettante adventurer, helped along his way by an endless succession of simple men and women to whom the code of Highland hospitality and clan ties were sacrosanct—a living thing. The fugitive was rarely short of a meal, for the rivers, lochs and streams were full of salmon, sea-trout and brown trout; and, even today, less hotly pursued visitors will find a warm welcome waiting, from both fish and friendly people, always ready to greet game fishermen with a smile and point them in the right sporting direction.

The 1745 Rebellion was launched at the head of Loch Shiel, west from Fort William and the watchers on the shore must have viewed the Prince's approaching boat, as it rowed towards them up the loch, with mixed feelings. Most of the clansmen waiting to meet the Young Pretender were only there out of a sense of duty to their clan chiefs; many must have guessed, even then, the only way in which the mad adventure could end. But, on that cold autumn day, Cameron of Lochiel proclaimed King James VIII, the Royal Standard was raised and the gathered Highlanders managed a wild cheer. The die was cast.

Eleven months later, Charles Edward Stuart lay in the heather above Loch Shiel on the slopes of Fraoch-bheinn, an exhausted, half-starved fugitive. His loyal clansmen, scattered and broken, hunted like animals throughout the Highlands. I have never had much time for Carluccio, his family's pet name for Bonnie Prince Charlie, but as I stand by the monument at the head of Loch Shiel, my heart cries for these poor, long-dead Highlanders, who risked all, and lost all in the hopeless cause.

We last visited Loch Shiel on a warming spring morning, and with sunlight sparkling on the waters our boat bumped down the loch and the special magic of this dramatic Scottish loch quickly had us in its spell. Shiel is 17 miles long, a narrow ribbon of water, dropping to more than 400 ft deep by Meall nan Creag Leac and yet having irregular shallows and depths throughout its length; at the widest part there are areas in the middle where the depth of the water is little more than three to four feet. Seek local advice before setting out and hasten slowly, everywhere.

On either shore, mountains crowd the water's edge. The northern shoreline is trackless but there is a forestry road down the south shore, from Craigag to Ceanna Garbh, thankfully only open to pedestrian traffic, hoofing it. In these rough hills you will find grouse, ptarmigan, snow bunting, eagle and buzzard; wildcat, red deer, fox and mountain hare haunt the corries and glens; the last wolf to inhabit these desolate lands was shot by Cameron of Lochiel in 1680 and throughout the centuries fugitives from justice have sought Moidart and Sunnart as refuge.

Loch Shiel contains salmon and brown trout and some of the most exciting sea-trout fishing in the land and Shiel has always had a reputation for producing large fish. These silver-flanked, power-packed monsters could weigh as much as 14 lb and although there is less evidence of them today, sea-trout of great weight are still sometimes caught.

One of the problems facing visitors today is knowing where to fish; on such a vast water the services of an experienced gillie are almost essential but, sadly, these fine gentlemen are a fast-disappearing race. The Stage House Hotel at Glenfinnan, at the north end of the loch has solved this problem by producing a most detailed and informative map. This was prepared by Andrew Brooks, the proprietor of the inn, and Charles Cameron, a retired gillie who has fished Loch Shiel for more than 50 years. Armed with this map you may confidently set off, secure in the knowledge that you will be covering the best lies.

At the south end of Loch Sheil, information about the best places to fish is supplied by one of the most experienced and delightful personalities in the north, Fergus MacDonald of the Clanranald Hotel. Visiting anglers will benefit mightily by spending a few moments with Fergus. He is the secretary of the local angling club and a mine of information about fishing on Loch Shiel and the little River Shiel. Time well spent and often, the difference between a blank and a record day.

The river is always well booked in advance but it is sometimes possible to obtain fishing. Shiel is a slow-moving river, apart from Sea Pool, and salmon and sea-trout are caught throughout its three-mile journey to the sea. The principal pools are Boat Pool, Gullet, Ledges, Parapet, House Stage, Grassy Point, Cliff, Garrison, Captain's and Sea Pool. Main runs of sea-trout start towards the end of June and continue throughout July. Most fishing on the loch during early months is done by trolling, with up to three rods and the favoured lures are Golden Sprat, Kynoch Killer, Rapalla and Tobys; from the end of July until October, fish settle in the bays and then fly fishing brings good results; flies to use include Soldier Palmer, Watson's Fancy, Blue Charm, Peter Ross, Dunkeld, Woodcock and Yellow, Black Pennel, Grouse and Claret and Butchers. Dapping can also be productive, so you had better invest in a substantial roof-rack in order to transport all the fishing gear you are going to need.

Where you fish will depend upon the time of year and prevailing weather conditions; but you could do a lot worse than accept Charlie Cameron's advice; in early months, concentrate on the top end of the loch where fish tend to run straight up. Try East and West Perch, at the back of the island; Stag Horn Bay, by the two trees with the heather-covered rock in between; Sugar Lump Point, Guesachan Islands and Shelter Bay on the -south shore; on the north shore, inspect Boat Shed Bay, Salmon Bay, Black Bay and West and East Sandy Bays.

Later in the season, fish round Scamodale Point and into Black Rocks Bay near Eilean Mhic Dhomhnuill Dhuibh, then drift down to the old buildings by Gorstanvorran Bay and Point. Cross over to the north shore by Gaskan and fish down past the big tree into Gravel Bay by Gaskan House; this is an excellent fishing area and is known locally as The Rails.

As the long loch narrows at the south end, the River Polloch, a major tributary, enters from Loch Doilet which sometimes produces sea-trout and the occasional salmon. The loch is surrounded by forestry plantations and is reached by a narrow, twisting road that winds over Sunart from Strontian. Brown trout fishing on Doilet can be very good and this is a useful alternative fishing location where the wind howls down huge Loch Shiel.

Both Stage House Inn and Clanranald Hotels are well-established, comfortable fishing hotels. Indeed, when Bonnie Prince Charlie lay shivering in the hills that wild September night so long ago, the Stage House Inn had already been open for business for more than 60 years. There are good boats and outboard motors available for hire and visitors are always welcome. Although salmon and sea-trout fishing on Loch Shiel is not so good as in the 'old days', I still know of few more attractive places to fish.

North of Acharacle, at the south end of Loch Shiel, lie a further series of super hill lochs, approached from Ardmorlich on the A861 and these waters involve a hefty tramp up the steep slopes of the hills known as The Three Old Maids. They offer great sport in an amazingly beautiful setting and the best of these waters are Loch nam Paitean and Lochan na Craoibhe. The others all contain good stocks of fish and are an excellent venue for a healthy, invigorating week's fishing holiday, away from it all.

In the glen below, the little River Moidart is also worth a cast and fishing is sometimes available from the estate which has a very well furnished, six-bedroom, self-catering lodge, let with the fishing. Mrs Stewart at Kinlochmoidart House will supply details. The fast-flowing river is seven miles in length and given the right water conditions, good sport may be had with both salmon and sea-trout. July is the best time to launch your assault for sea-trout. Wait until September for salmon. Another attractive holiday base is on the privately owned island of Eilean Shona which guards the entrance to Loch Moidart. The island is two and a half miles long by one and a half miles wide and there are five lovely self-catering cottages, converted from old croft dwellings and a schoolhouse.

If you have a family who do not fish, then this us the place to park them whilst you get on with the job in hand. Eilean Shona is a natural haven for wildlife and plants of all kinds. Rhododendrons abound and there are 300 acres of woodlands to explore, with many of the trees being rare species imported in the last century by the first owner of the island, Captain Swinburne. There are magnificent, empty beaches near by, including the famous Singing Sands at Kentra Bay.

South from Loch Shiel and Acharacle lies Ardnamurchan, 'The Point of the Sea Otters' and most westerly point of mainland Britain. The dramatic lighthouse overlooking the wild Atlantic was built in 1845, taking three years to complete. The spherical mirrors were specially imported from Paris at a cost of £1,500.

A few years ago, the keeper was Jim Hardie who stayed there with his wife, Nan, old friends from Caithness. Therefore, it was with great pleasure that I read, a few years ago, that Her Majesty The Queen had visited Ardnamurchan. After climbing the 152 steps to the top of the lighthouse, Her Majesty stayed for tea. Knowing Nan Hardie, the tea provided would have been every bit as spectacular as the view from the top.

The Ardnamurchan Peninsula is scattered with good trout lochs, owned by the estate and fished from the Glenborrodale Hotel in the east and Kilchoan in the west. Loch Mudale is the largest water and occasional salmon and sea-trout are caught, running the little Achateny River from Port Ban and Ardtoe Island. Further out in the hills lie Locha a' Mhadaidh Riabhaich, na Cragie, nan Dearcag, an Ime and many more. Drag on the boots, obtain proper permission and attack.

The best of the salmon fishing in the area is to be found across Loch Sunart, in Morvern at Ardtornish. The Ardtornish Estate is in the south-west of the peninsula, and covers an area of some 60 square miles of hills, woodland, river and lochs, with a long coastline overlooking the Sound of Mull and Loch Linnhe. This area is noted for its marvellous variety of birds and flowers, as well as much of geological and historical interest, including two ruined medieval castles. There are connections with many famous people including Florence Nightingale, the Scottish soldier/statesman and writer John Buchan, and Poet Laureate Alfred Lord Tennyson. Apart from salmon, sea-trout and brown trout fishing, the estate has much to interest non-fishers: sailing, water sports, visits to the misty isle of Mull; walking and cycling on the estate's private roads and discovering the many rare shrubs and plants in the woodland garden of Ardtornish House. The largest of the estate waters is Loch Arienas out of which flows the River Aline, collecting in the streams of Allt Beitheach and Black Water along the way. They enter the sea by Loch Aline and at the head of the loch, Rannoch River, another little salmon and sea-trout stream, joins them.

Fishing on the River Aline and White Glen is divided into six beats: Bottom Beat, from the sea to George's Bridge; Middle Beat, from George's to New Road Bridge; Claggan Beat, from New Road Bridge to Old

All quiet on Loch Knockie, Inverness-shire

Claggan Bridge; Top Beat, from Old Claggan Bridge to Suspension Bridge; Acharn Beat, from Suspension Bridge to Baxter's Camp and Uillin Beat which is above Uillin Falls. Each beat is for two rods only and fishing is by fly. Salmon and sea-trout are sometimes caught in Loch Arienas and Doire nam Mart but these waters produce most sport with brown trout. Loch Ternait, a three-mile walk into the hills, is the best trout loch and there are a further 16 hill lochs on the estate, all of which will keep you busy and well fed on brightly marked, hard-fighting little fish.

Aline is very much a spate river and dependent upon good water levels for sport. Nevertheless, recent results have been good and the five-year average catch for salmon and grilse is about 60 fish. Best months for salmon fishing are July, August and September and the heaviest salmon taken from the Aline weighed 26 lb. The average weight is 5–6 lb. Sea-trout

114

figures are 170 per season with the most productive month being July. Fish of over 6 lb sometimes caught and an average weight of 1 lb. Brown trout catches for the same period average 450 trout per season; weighting about 8–10 oz with the odd fish of up to 4 lb 8 oz.

Another of Scotland's famous sea-trout fisheries lies a few miles west of Loch Shiel, along the Fort William/Mallaig route, romantic Loch Eilt, by the side of the 'Road to the Isles'. Wedged in a narrow glen between the majestic heights of Morar and Moidart, Loch Eilt is bordered on the north by the A830 Fort William/Mallaig road and on the south shore by the West Highland Railway line. Fishing is shared by two riparian owners, Inverailort Estate and Salar Properties Limited, a company that manages top-quality game fishing throughout Scotland on behalf of timeshare owners. Both proprietors have fishing available to the general public and weekly lets are often available, provided that you book well in advance.

If you think that it all sounds a bit public and overlooked, don't worry; out on the loch, when mighty sea-trout dash at the flies, the Third World War could be starting just around the corner and you wouldn't notice. Druim Fiaclach, Sgurr na Ba Glaise and Rois Bheinn in Moidart and Glas-charn, Creag Bhan and Creag Dubh in Morar tower over sparkling waters; trains and cars chug by, whilst you get on with the business in hand, tempting sea-trout to their doom.

Loch Eilt flows westwards to the sea by the River Ailort, mingling with the brackish waters of straggling, island-dotted Loch Ailort before hurrying out to the Sound of Arisaig. Salmon run the river and there are deep, clear pools between loch and sea where sea-liced salmon lurk behind lichen-covered boulders. A few hundred yards before river and loch meet, a wide extension of the stream, Lochan Dubh, offers perhaps the best sport on the River Ailort. A cottage overlooks the water and this is being renovated-for the use of Salar Properties fishing owners. Because of the nature of the Ailort and Lochan Dubh, worming is allowed and the run into the loch, and down the north shore is the most productive fishing area.

A few yards upstream is the famous 'Frying Pan' pool; a tiny hole in the middle of the river, nestling amidst tumbling waters, reached by a precarious stumble over wet rocks placed on wet planks. Hooking, playing and landing a fish from the pool requires skill, agility, nerve and, of course, the good luck for which all we anglers constantly pray. It must be said that Loch Eilt and the Ailort are not as productive as in days past. Even with netting at the mouth, in previous years, upwards of 1,500 sea-trout could be taken during a season; and some of these fish reached enormous proportions, the 'An Breac Mor An Earraich' (the big spring sea-trout) of angling mythology.

However, matters are being taken in hand and a comprehensive and vigorous programme of improvement is in progress. A modern, large-capacity hatchery and smolt rearing system is being installed and a patrol boat has been deployed on Loch Ailort to prevent illegal fishing.

Better still, under a long-standing agreement between the owners, there is no longer any netting in the estuary, from Glen Uig Bay to the North Channel of Eilean Shona, a distance round the coast of some 20 miles.

In recent years some spectacular baskets have been taken, of both salmon and sea-trout. In July 1983, Mr George Mutch and party had seven sea-trout weighing 54 lb and a salmon of 10 lb, all caught before breakfast from little Lochan Dubh; in October of the same year, Terry Rowantree and Colin Gibb, during the course of a day's fishing on loch and river, had five salmon weighing 47 lb 8 oz and 20 sea-trout weighing 56 lb 8 oz. In August 1985 a sea-trout of 7 lb 8 oz was caught and during 1986 several fish of over 5 lb were landed. There is a mystical tranquillity about fishing Loch Eilt, apart from when wrestling with furious sea-trout, that almost defies description. Although everything is easily accessible and clearly well managed, a sense of being away-from-it-all remains. I suppose that's part of the special magic that is fishing.

Along the 'Road to the Isles', past Glenfinnan and Loch Eilt, is sea Loch nan Uamh. A stone cairn by the side of the road marks the place where Bonnie Prince Charlie left his hapless followers to their terrible fate and hot-footed back to France and Mummy and Daddy. I often wonder how different things would have been if BPC had tramped round the Highlands with a fishing rod, rather than a bedraggled army of ill-equipped Gaelic-speaking Scots who would have much rather been attending to their own affairs anyway. Probably, a lot of heads would have remained a lot more firmly attached to a lot of shoulders; and untold misery and suffering would have been averted.

At the end of the road, near Mallaig, is Europe's deepest freshwater loch, Morar, and even here the ghosts of the Jacobites haunt you; for it was on one of the islands at the west end of the loch that Government forces finally caught up with that arch-schemer and rebel, Lord Lovat. The old man was found hiding in a tree-trunk and transported to London. There, his unrepentant head was struck from his unrepentant shoulders: the last public beheading to be carried out in Britain.

Loch Morar is nearly 12 miles long by one and a half miles wide at the west end, narrowing to half a mile in the east. The loch is separated by only a few hundred yards from the sea and plunges to a depth of over 1,000 ft between South Tarbet and Camus Lunge Bay. Apart from a five-mile stretch of road along the north shore as far as Bracorina, Loch Morar is trackless so the best way to explore is by boat, with a reliable outboard motor, spare fuel and life jackets because Morar can be a wild, windy, dangerous place.

But in all kinds of weather Loch Morar is dramatic. Mountains crowd the shore and at Kinlochmorar and Oban, at the head of the loch, lonely tracks wind off into some of the most remote and desolate areas of Scotland. Fishing on Loch Morar is for brown trout; although a few salmon and sea-trout enter the system and some are caught most seasons. Trout average 8–12 oz in weight but, as you would expect in such a huge water, much heavier fish are frequently caught. The largest trout taken weighed 15 lb 8 oz; 1980 produced a fish of 11 lb 8 oz and 1981, a trout weighing 7 lb 11 oz.

Your rewards will probably be somewhat more modest and expect a basket of perhaps half a dozen nice fish. In good weather conditions you will catch a lot more, so keep only the best. The most productive fishing areas are at the west end of the loch, in the vicinity of the islands. However, it is hard to resist the temptation to set off eastwards, into the hills, and great sport can also be had at the east end; particularly round the island near Camas Choimhieachain and Kinloch-morar Bay. Choose your flies carefully and I suggest that size 14s would be about right. All the standard patterns work well but you could do a lot worse than starting with Black Pennel, March Brown and Bloody Butcher. Fishing from the boat brings best results but if, because of high winds, you are confined to the bank, for goodness sake be careful—it's a long way down and in some areas the margins slope very quickly indeed. Watch out for a particularly strong 'tug'. Loch Morar, like Loch Ness, has its resident monster. She is called Morag and exactly which flies she prefers I can't say—just make sure that you have plenty backing on the reel and hold on tight.

The loch reaches the sea via one of Britain's shortest rivers: the River Morar is barely 600 yards old before it empties into the famous White Sands. Nevertheless, in decent conditions, it can produce good sport, particularly with sea-trout and a few salmon are taken most years, during summer months. There is a hydroelectric scheme and power station on the system and a fish pass allows salmon and sea-trout access to vast Loch Morar above, where they are relatively safe from grasping hands like mine.

If adverse weather conditions make Morar unfishable and you enjoy a little exercise, then have a look at the lochs to the north. There are more than a dozen lying between Mallaig and Tarbet and they all contain traditional Highland wild brown trout in the three-to-the-pound class, with one or two larger fish to keep you on your toes. The setting is really magnificent. From the heights of Cam a'Ghobhair (584 m), above lovely Loch Hireagoraidh, the view northwards and eastwards into Knoydart is a breathtaking vista of mountains, sea and sunlight; and the lands of the Rough Bounds contain the best salmon stream in the area, the River Inverie.

Inverie rises from Luinne Bheinn and Meall Buidhe and enters the sea to the east of Inverie Lodge. The fishing is let with the lodge and this 19th-century house occupies a superb position with spectacular views over Loch Nevis and out to the islands of Rhum and Skye. The estate has a number of other excellent self-catering cottages for rental, ideal for those seeking peace, seclusion and escape—apart, that is, from the 400 or so salmon that are taken from the river each year. Bad news, being a salmon.

Fort William, at the southern end of the Great Glen, lies amidst some of Scotland's grandest scenery, dominated by Britain's highest mountain, Ben Nevis, the Hill of Heaven. The first fort, built on the shores of Loch Linnhe, was erected by General George Monck in 1645, acting on the instructions of Oliver Cromwell, and was named Fort William 40 years later in honour of Britain's new Hanoverian king, William of Orange. To the north of the town are the ruins of Inverlochy Castle, destroyed during the Wars of Scottish Independence and the Covenanting Wars of the 17th century. The castle was built in 1260, by the Comyn family who first arrived in England as companions of another William—the Conqueror. The flat ground to the south-west of the castle was the site of one of the most notable battles in Scottish history when the great Montrose overthrew the convenanting army of Campbell of Argyll in 1645.

The route from Inverness to Fort William and Lochaber follows the north shore of Loch Ness, famous for its monster and a busy waterway; part of the Caledonian Canal which links North Sea and Atlantic through the Great Glen. The canal was cut by Thomas Telford and work began in 1803 and took 19 years to complete. There are 28 locks, including the series of eight locks near Banavie known as Neptune's Staircase. Midway down Loch Ness are the dramatic ruins of Castle Urquhart, a great 'monster' spotting site; and, at the south end, lies Fort Augustus, named after William Augustus, Duke of Cumberland who made his headquarters there after the Battle of Culloden in 1746. Fort Augustus was originally called Kilchumein, after a follower of St Columba and a Benedictine Abbey now occupies the site of Cumberland's original fort. In the cemetery is the grave of John Anderson, a carpenter friend of Scottish poet Robert Burns, immortalised in Burns's poem *John Anderson My Jo*.

The River Lochy flows south-west from Loch Lochy, the last of the Great Glen lochs, and is an excellent salmon fishery, one of the most attractive streams in Scotland. It runs for a distance of nine miles before entering the sea in Loch Linnhe by Fort William. There are more than 40 named pools and although the banks are mostly tree-lined, casting is easy, into clear waters from wide-open, stony shores and gravel banks.

Salmon enter the river from April onwards but the main runs do not appear until July or August, therefore, autumn sport is best and, given good water levels, catches of 40 fish during a week are not uncommon at the back end. Fishing is by fly only and because of the breadth of the stream, chest waders are a must. Some of the wider pools are often fished from a boat. Most of the river is let in advance. However, the Town Water, between the railway bridge and the sea, is available to visiting anglers and can produce upwards of 300 fish in a good year. Tickets may be obtained from The Rod and Gun Shop in Fort William.

The Rod and Gun Shop is the place to start for fishing expeditions in Lochaber. The staff are very well informed about all the local waters and offer the best possible service and advice to visiting anglers. They also factor a large number of streams and lochs in the area, including the rivers Nevis, Spean, Roy, Coe, Garry and Oich. The Nevis is about half a mile from the town centre and is a good spate salmon and sea-trout stream. It flows through Glen Nevis for a distance of seven miles and fishing is by fly only unless high water makes worming allowable. Permits are not issued until 9 a.m. on the day required, so be up early and waiting at the door for opening time to make certain of a ticket.

The River Spean is the most important tributary of the River Lochy and joins it just below its outfall from Loch Lochy, at Gairlochy and Mucomir. Spean Bridge was a commando training centre during the last war and much of the old woodlands in the area were burnt in the course of exercises. The bravery of the commando units during World War Two is commemorated by a memorial on the hill, where the A82 and little B8004 meet—three grey figures, battle-dressed, rifled and ready. This delightful little river has suffered much over the years from the damming of Loch Laggan and Loch Trieg, to provide water for the British Aluminium Company plant in Fort William, which has played havoc with runs of migratory fish, but good sport may still be had, dependent entirely upon water levels.

The Rod and Gun Shop issues day permits for the right bank, Beat A, and two rods are allowed each day. The river fishes from May until October and salmon of over 30 lb have been caught in recent years. Being in the right place at the right time helps. Fly fishing and spinning is permitted. Some of the river is mountain goat country, not for the elderly or for those who prefer more ordered calm. Be outside the Rod and Gun Shop at 9 a.m. to book a rod.

The River Roy marries Spean at Bunroy, south of Roybridge, and is a natural spate river, relying entirely upon rain in the hills to keep things moving. It flows Speanwards from the north, down a great glen, now the Glen Roy National Nature Reserve, famous for the Parallel Roads; for hundreds of years, these strange lines along the upper sides of the valley were thought to be man-made. More recent research has established that they are in fact the marks of receding ice, melting over the centuries, like prehistoric rings round a gigantic, geological bath.

The river can fish well and salmon and sea-trout arrive from July onwards. Because of the nature of the river, fly fishing is difficult and most fish are taken by either worming or spinning. If you appreciate wild country and a wild river, then you will instantly fall in love with little Roy. And if you like your trout fishing on the wilder side, then there is an excellent loch waiting, just outside Fort William itself, Lochan Lunn Da Bhra, or Lundavra as it is known locally. Lundavra lies in the heart of the Mamore Hills, to the south of town. Approach via the narrow, single track road that leaves Fort William near the mountain rescue post and follow up the course of the Alt na Lairige Moire burn to the southern shoulder of the Ben Nevis massif.

The loch is completely surrounded by mighty peaks rising to more than 900 m and because of the ease of access, Lundavra is all the more startling; being so close to Fort William and yet so wild and remote. The metalled surface of the road ends at the loch but a track continues through the inhospitable hills, down to the sea and Kinlochmore at the head of sea Loch Leven.

During the troubled time of the 1745 uprising this was an important link between Fort William and the south, giving access to some of the wildest areas of the Highlands. During these turbulent years thousands of cursing, sweating Government troops must have looked up at the bleak wilderness of range upon range of forbidding mountains and heartily cursed their luck and the truculent Highlanders who were responsible for them being there. Today, the hills are no less dramatic or hazardous and rarely a year goes by without some dreadful catastrophe occurring on their craggy, ice-covered wind-swept slopes. The Mamore Hills are no place for either the faint-hearted or ill-prepared.

Loch Lundavra is a haven of peace amidst the storm, offering first-class trout fishing at reasonable prices. It can be windy at times, but due to the protecting heights of Doire Ban (566 m), Beinn na Gucaig (616 m) and Meall a'Cleireach (535 m) to the south and west, and Mullach nan Coireainn (910 m) to the east, a sheltered spot can generally be found regardless of wind direction. The loch is one mile long by about 250 yds wide so the visiting angler quickly gets the 'feel' of it. There are two boats available and bank fishing is also allowed. More than a dozen small feeder burns cascade down from Sorn Gharb and Beinn na Gucaig from the north and these should be fished very carefully indeed.

At the eastern end of the loch, before it outlets into Alt na Lairige Moire, there is a small island and this is a much favoured fishing spot. It tends to become weedy as the season advances but good fish lie here so do have a few casts in the vicinity. The trout in Lundavra average about 12 oz and fight hard. Good baskets are taken throughout the season, with May and June producing best results. The heaviest fish taken in recent years weighed 8 lb and most years trout of between 3–5 lb are caught. Anglers may use their own outboards if they so wish and, with normal caution, should come to little harm throughout the loch. Lundavra is a well-managed fishery and is stocked from time to time; but it still retains all the charm of its magnificent setting and is an exciting place to fish.

The A82 Fort William/Inverness road runs alongside Loch Lochy and this ten-mile water has a reputation for being a dour, dismal place to fish. However, fishing is free and access is easy. So if you fancy a couple of hours fishing, to break the monotony of your journey, park by the shores and have a go. You might be surprised; Lochy has some really large brown trout and there is always the chance of a salmon or sea-trout. Trout of over 7 lb have been caught and both spinning and fly fishing are allowed. Good fishing areas are Letterfinlay Bay, midway up the loch on the A82 side, and at Kilfinnan Bay, in the north where the canal enters from Laggan Lochs and Clunes Bay and Bunarkaig, near the Mile Dorche and River Arkaig.

After Culloden, Government forces under the command of Grant of Knockando, arrived at Clunes and paid a less than friendly call on the home of Cameron of Clunes whose house stood by the banks of the river near Achnacarry. After setting fire to the house, 'he stripped Cameron's wife and some others naked as they came into the world, and deprived them of all means of subsistence except for five milk goats.' Grant continued up the glen and along the way met a Highlander, who had come to surrender his person and arms to a fellow Scot. Grant had him tied to a tree and shot.

Loch Arkaig is 12 miles long and a popular venue for trout fishers. A road runs close to the north shore, giving easy access and both boat and bank fishing is available. During recent years this lovely water has been very heavily fished and there are signs of 'strain'. Where once good sport was assured, now anglers have to work a lot harder for a decent basket. Perhaps part of the trouble is that all fishing methods are allowed and there are few restrictions on the activities of some less than scrupulous visitors.

Oich is the smallest of the Gren Glen lochs, four miles in length by up to 900 yards wide. The loch contains some superb brown trout and also good numbers of salmon and sea-trout. The largest fish caught on the loch was taken on 23 March 1907 and weighed 44 lb. The great fish was taken by the Duke of Portland and that day the Duke also had five salmon weighing 115 lb; 22 March 1913 was also a 'red-letter day' on Loch Oich for the Duke and his friend, Barker-Carr. They caught 19 fish weighing 267 lb from the loch and, during the week, a total of 83 salmon from Oich and the River Garry.

The Duke's gillie was the father of Jock McAskill, the recently retired Head Gillie of the Garry. Jock is no mean hand at landing salmon himself and had one of the best catches in recent years. At the age of 76 years young, one afternoon in 1985, Jock took three fish from the Estuary Beat: 10 lb, 18½ lb and a magnificent salmon of 31 lb 8 oz. The previous day he'd had a 14-lb fish and all were taken on an Abu spinner.

In the 1950s the waters of the Garry system were harnessed by a hydro-electric scheme and fishing has steadily declined since then. Compensation water provides artificial floods each week, when sport can be very good, but the great days of the Garry are a thing of the past. There are 26 pools on the river, below the dam from Loch Garry: Falls Pool, Otter Pool, Little Crooked, Big Crooked, Black Pool, Chest Pool, Iron Bridge, Mill Pool, Lower Falls Pool, Paul's Pool, Englishman Pool, Dog Pool, Shot

Pool, Redbrae Pool, Long Pool, Cairn Pool, Ceaggan Pool, Lundie Pool, Mandally Bridge Pool, Curling Pool, Castle Pool, Flag Pool, Bridge Pool, Carrie Pool, Slucie Pool, House Pool and River Mouth.

The fishing is let in two beats, three rods per beat, on a rotational system, and there are three and a half miles of double-banked fishing. The let also includes the use of two boats with outboard motors on Loch Oich—good news when water levels in the river are low. At the mouth of the river is an excellent fishing hut, complete with heating, light, grill and running water. Very welcome on cold spring mornings, when Garry can still produce the large salmon for which it is justly famous. The river drains a vast area and in the hills of Bunlionn, Glenquoich and Glen Garry, lie some of Scotland's most famous trout lochs. The centre of angling activity here is the Tomdoun Hotel, along the narrow road that edges westwards along the north shore of Loch Garry from the A87.

There has been a Coaching Inn at Tomdoun for more than a hundred years; Murray's Handbook in 1894 notes that 'carriages may be hired there' for the journey through Glen Shiel, past the Five Sisters of Kintail, on to Kyle of Lochalsh and Skye. Now, the road ends at the high dam on Loch Quoich where a tortuous track follows the scarred shore line on to desolate Kinloch Huron, The Lake of Hell. The rough bounds of Knoydart crowd the western horizon southwards, and over the ragged peaks of Gairich (940 m), Meall Coire nan Saobhaidh (824 m) and Ben Tee (904 m) lies Cameron country and Lochiel. The only road through the wilderness is the A87, linking Invergarry on Loch Oich to Glen Moriston, over Meall Dubh (789 m) in the north.

The area was opened up by General Wade. In seven years from 1725 he and a team of 500 sweating labourers completed more than 240 miles of road and 30 bridges throughout the Highlands. The land is full of sad and stirring tales. Near Invergarry, at Craig an Fhithich, The Rock of the Raven, lie the ruins of Invergarry Castle, ancient home of the MacDonnels of Glengarry; burned by Grant and his men after Culloden. The 200 soldiers involved in the destruction of Invergarry received 15 shillings each if they were privates, one pound for corporals, 30 shillings for sergeants and £11 5s for captains. Glengarry's belongings were auctioned to the highest bidder in order to produce the funds.

The area has the highest levels of rainfall in Britain with an annual average approaching monsoon proportions; good news for anglers but bad news for Bonnie Prince Charlie who spent a wet night in Coire nad Gall on Sgurr na Ciche above Loch Quoich, whilst fleeing westwards to the isles. BPC was surrounded by hordes of hunting red-coats, affectionately known as Tommy Lobster. Visitors today are surrounded by dozens of potential occupants for the angler's ever-ready glass case.

The British Record Brown Trout, a fish of over 20 lb was caught on Loch Quoich; John Sharp, an Ayrshire angler, had a trout of 16 lb in 1982 and in 1983 a fish of 12 lb was landed. Previous record trout have come

Tumbling streams in Stratherrick

from nearby Inchlaggan where a fish of 18 lb 2 oz was taken in 1965; and Loch Poulary has produced a number of trout of over 10 lb. So they are there; but you will have to troll, long and deep to tempt these monster ferox. Nevertheless, it is always possible to catch good baskets of 8–12 oz trout and, depending upon your ability, a reasonable day should see you home with half a dozen nice fish. Where to start is the problem and with so much water available it is wise to seek local advice.

Loch Garry is a deep water, falling to over 250 ft, so confine your activities to the margins. As a general rule, if you can't see the bottom then you are too far out. Fish the shallow east end, in the area of the island; then the section where Allt Ladaidh burn enters from Laddie Wood; and then westwards to where the Greenfield Burn enters.

On Inchlaggan, the most productive fishing area is along the line of the old river bed, prior to flooding. I know that this contradicts the general rule already stated, but that's fishing, full of contradictions. Also try the bays in the south-east corner. Inchlaggan holds good stocks of Arctic char. Fish for them half-way down the south shore, fingers crossed, in June.

Westwards from Inchlaggan, in the slow-flowing, flooded waters of the Upper River Garry, is where some of the best trout are caught. Fish of between 2–3 lb are taken most seasons and the areas to concentrate upon are the islands and, further upstream, at Allt a'Ghodbhainn, The Burn of the Blacksmith.

North from Glengarry, the A87 climbs Clach Criche and winds past shining Loch Loyne; a 'new' loch, created by damming the River Loyne. Loyne is full of small trout, the natural food of the voracious pike which rule the loch. Pike of over 40 lb have been reported and trout have a hard time staying alive in the long water.

At the foot of the hill, the A87 joins A887 and the two roads run westwards along the north shore of Loch Cluanie, another fine Scottish trout loch much altered by hydroelectric activities. In days past, Cluanie had the reputation of producing some of the best trout fishing in the north. Now, it is very much of matter of chance, although fish of over 7 lb are sometimes taken.

The waters of Loyne and Cluanie are directed down the River Moriston, to a power station at Ceannacroc, and then through an artificially created extension of the river at Dundreggan. Fishing on the river and in the hill lochs above Invermoriston is owned by the Glen Moriston Estate Company and at the time of writing, the estate is being sold. Therefore, if you intend to explore this area, contact the new owners to check what is available, and when. Invermoriston lies adjacent to the shores of Loch Ness, 37 miles north-east of Fort William and 27 miles south-west of Inverness. It looks south over Loch Ness to the grey hills of Monadhliath while the Five Sisters of Kintail dominate the western skyline. To the east and north are the hills and forests of Glen Affric and Glenurquhart and all around, peace and tranquillity.

Except, that, is, when it comes to fishing. The River Moriston is a noted salmon stream and even in spite of the hydroscheme, upwards of 200 salmon are taken most seasons. Moriston fish, like their cousins on the Garry, are noted for their weight and salmon of over 20 lb are not uncommon. The season starts on 15 January and although spring fishing can be cold, hard work, the fish are generally of the highest quality. Spinning accounts for most fish and the best sport is had on the Lower River.

Dundreggan Reservoir, through which the Moriston flows, is an excellent trout water where the average weight is in the order of 1 lb and recently a fish of 7 lb 4 oz was landed. Best results on Dundreggan come from boat fishing and the most productive areas are along the north-west shore and in the western end of the loch. But, for me, the real gems of Invermoriston are the trout-filled hill lochs. In spite of being so close to civilisation, they are sufficiently remote to give the angler complete privacy; and it isn't necessary to be a mountain goat to reach them. Indeed, if your car has a high wheel-base, then it is possible to drive most of the way on the estate roads.

The road starts a few miles west of Invermoriston at Bhlaraidh, where, incidentally, there just happens to be a herd of wild goats, secretive beasties who live in the Coille forest and neighbouring hills. With reasonable care, you should find this road passable. If in doubt, start off from the end of the tarmac road behind the Invermoriston Hotel. A steepish walk but the best point of access for those who do not want to risk their car exhaust system. The hill lochs vary in size from Loch ma Stac which is one mile long by quarter of a mile wide, to tiny Loch na Feannaig, a few acres in extent. All are stocked and the average weight of fish is 12 oz; but ma Stac and Loch Liath have much heavier trout. Apart from Stac, where there is a good boat, all the other waters are fished from the bank. Loch a'Chrathaich, to the east of Stac, has the reputation of holding the largest fish and trout of up to 6 lb have been taken there. The best fishing area on a'Chrathaich is at the southern end where the feeder burn enters on the west shore and also at the outlet burn, near to the small island.

Over Carn Loch a'Bhothain hill lies beautiful Lochan Ruighe Dhuibh, a superb water and exciting to fish. The east and north shore is best and this small loch can often provide welcome shelter on a windy day. Whilst it is never possible to be certain, an average day on these lochs should send you home with a nice basket of about a dozen trout averaging 8 oz with the chance of a 2 lb. This depends upon which loch you choose, skill, or, in my case, luck. Not everyone enjoys a ten-mile tramp over the hills in search of sport; indeed, there are many who, for health reasons, could not consider such an expedition. For them, Loch Ness is an ideal place to fish; easily accessible, always the chance of a salmon and fine sport with wild brown trout and, if the wind is howling down the loch, then, as an alternative, less wild fishing can often be arranged on the River Oich.

The River Oich is about six miles long and joins Loch Ness with Loch Oich. The Garry fish hurry through in the spring and it is often possible to tempt one whilst they rest on their journey in the pleasant pools. It is less easy to find the brutes on vast Loch Ness and the best way to try is to employ the services of a local gillie, such as Bill Davidson at Modsairidh. Bill grew up on the shores of Loch Ness and knows the famous loch in all its moods; from flat calm to raging turmoil. No one could pretend that Loch Ness is the salmon angler's dream, from the point of view of numbers caught, but most seasons produce about 400 salmon and, from May onwards, sea-trout also run the loch.

Trolling is the most productive method of salmon fishing and few fish are taken on the fly. Two spinning rods are placed, port and starboard in the stern and the boat slowly manoeuvred over known lies. Anglers wait, expectant, baited breath, until a fish strikes. The fish keep close to the shore, often no more than 20 yards out, and during spring months, they run straight up the 24½-mile length of the loch to Fort Augustus. Summer and autumn fishing is best in the vicinity of Castle Urquhart Bay, Dores Bay, Lochend and Foyers, on the remote east shore.

The River Ness flows for six busy miles from the loch to the Moray Firth, passing through the Highland capital, Inverness. Salmon anglers are busy also and the river produces good sport with upwards of 1,000 salmon caught each season. Most of the early fish run the river without pause, anxious to reach Moriston, Oich and Garry. Summer and autumn fishing is preferable and although the best beats are generally well booked in advance, fishing is available on the Inverness Angling Club waters. A fully prepared angler, chest-wadered and rod-clutched, striding through the busy town is an unremarkable sight and, on a summer evening, it is a great pleasure to stroll along the river banks, watching expert casters fishing the wide river.

It is also a great pleasure to see fish running the river and one day a few years ago I was accosted by a tourist, convinced that he had just spotted the Loch Ness monster in the river. In fact, it was a very large Ness salmon, surging upstream, dorsal and tail fins out of the water, like great sails. I estimated that the salmon must have weighed at least 30 lb, probably more; but in spite of my reassurance, the visitor rushed off for his camera, determined that Nessie was on the move.

The most productive Ness beats, Dochfour, Laggan, Ness Castle and Ness-side are above the islands, favourite haunt of courting couples. The pools are best fished from a boat. Sea-trout also appear from June onwards and for the visiting angler in search of easily accessible, good salmon fishing, the Ness can be the answer. Perhaps a bit public but, when you have a 15-lb sea-liced salmon on the end of your line, who cares anyway?

Northwards from Inverness, in the beautiful hills and glens of Glen Affric and Strathfarrar, Lovat country, are a number of streams and lochs the most famous of which is the River Beauly. The Beauly starts its life in Loch Affric, flowing through narrow Loch Beinn a'Mheadhoin, known locally as Beannacharain, and the whole system has been incorporated into a vast hydroelectric scheme with dams and power stations at Loch Mullardoch, Beannacharain, Fasnakyle, Strathfarrar, Culligran, Aigs and Kilmorack. The river changes its name along the course of its journey to the sea, beginning as the Affric, then the Glass and is only called Beauly during the last few miles. The Farrar is the principal tributary, rising from distant Loch Monar and although numbers of salmon caught are not as many as in pre-hydroelectric days, some excellent catches are still taken, particularly below Kilmorack Dam, where the river is divided into three beats: Falls, Home and Dounie, with such famous pools as Cruives, Groams and Minister's.

Details of fishing on the Beauly system waters may be obtained from the Lovat Estates office in Beauly and there is no netting at the mouth of the river. As with so many of our northern salmon rivers, spring runs have virtually disappeared and the best sport is had during summer and autumn months. It's warmer too. Willie Gunn's and Waddington's do most damage and fish average about 8 lb in weight. There are larger specimens and Mr Hamilton, fishing the Beauly in July 1988 had a fine fish of 19 lb and Robert Phillips had a fish of 17 lb from Piles Pool on the Association Water. Good runs of sea-trout also bless the Beauly, and Downies Beat which includes the excellent Piles Pool, is the most productive water. Catches have varied enormously over the years; 1986 produced only 91, whilst 1987 managed over 500. Salmon are also taken in the beat and most years see 50–60 fish landed.

Trout fishing on the large, impounded headwater lochs is excellent and a good base from which to attack is the Glen Affric Hotel near Cannich, which also offers salmon fishing to guests. The principal waters are Affric, Mullardoch, Beannacharain and Monar and all can be very wild and windy. Don't forget the drogue, to keep the boat side-ways on to the drift; wear a flotation jacket and remain seated whilst fishing. The average weight of trout in these lochs is in the order of 8 oz but there are good numbers of much heavier trout; fish of over 10 lb are often taken, mostly by trolling and this is good glass-case country. Concentrate your efforts in the shallows, paying particular attention to where feeder streams enter. Even if you don't catch a record breaker, you will find plenty to keep you amused and busy, for weeks on end.

Strathnairn and Stratherrick lie to the south of the silver-blue ribbon on Loch Ness, cradled gently between the bristling peaks of Glen Albyn and the majestic mountains of Monadhliath. Silent, desolate lands, knifed by General Wade's narrow track, wind northwards from Laggan, through Corrieyairack, by Carn Leac (883 m), Gairbeinn (895 m) and Creag Mhor (764 m).

East of Corrieyairack is Creag Dubh (789 m), the mountain which gave Clan Macpherson their war cry. After Culloden, Ewen Macpherson, the clan chief, hid for almost nine years in a cave on the hill. In spite of having a price of £1,000 on his head, clansmen protected him until he escaped to France in 1755. Macpherson was almost captured one night when visiting friends near Loch Ness. A party of soldiers had arrived unexpectedly, demanding the right to search the house and Macpherson threw on an old plaid and rushed out, offering to hold the captain of the guard's horse. The moment the soldiers entered the house, Ewen quickly mounted and cantered off, back to his 'cage' on Creag Dubh. Macpherson died in Dunkirk in 1756, disillusioned and broken by ill-health.

Few now travel the little road that marries General Wade's old way from Inverness to the Atlantic. It still fingers the shore of Loch Ness, winding through tree-clad slopes to Foyers, then climbing by Glenlia into Stratherrick; on to one of the most stunning views in the north, at the head of Gleann nan Eun, overlooking island-scattered Loch Tarf. Range after range of mountains crowd the horizon; Kintail, green-dressed, aristocratic dames, elegantly inviting you in; mighty Ben Nevis; the hills of Inverwick, Inchnacardoch and Drundreggan, north of Loch Ness; Fort Augustus, crouched by the Caledonian Canal, guarding the south end of long, leaden waters.

North-east lie heavily wooded hills, pierced by the crags of Beinn a'Bhachaidh (554 m) and in the midst of this forest, set on a rocky plateau, is Knockie Lodge, one of Scotland's most comfortable country hotels; the perfect place to escape from the pressures of everyday life. And if you happen to be an angler, then Knockie Lodge offers good trout fishing on nearby Loch Knockie, peaceful, serene and full of fine-quality fish. Knockie trout are not easy to catch—what trout are?—but given a reasonable degree of ability, and the luck all we anglers put our trust in, then you should arrive home in the evening with your fair share. Fish average 10–12 oz, rarely more than 1 lb, but they fight spectacularly and give a good account of themselves.

Bank fishing is allowed, although best results come for the boat; and the best place to get at them is in the vicinity of the little islands. Inch round, alert and concentrating. That's the way to catch trout. If things prove dour, then the bird-life that bustles round Knockie should brighten even the dullest day: mallard, teal, redshank, oyster-catchers and, if you are lucky, the pleasure of fishing in company with rare Slavonian grebes. Black-eyed wrens blink in surrounding woods; the air is full of the sound of lark and lapwing—and the happy sound of rising trout. To the west of Knockie Lodge, a brisk after-dinner walk distant, is another good trout water, Loch nan Lann, well worth a cast or two or three or four; and, near by, is the Pike Loch, a sad name for a super little water that holds some really fine wild brown trout. Out in the hills, below the cairns of Beinn a'Bhacaidh, at the end of a heart-bursting tramp, is yet another delightful loch, little Lochan Mam-chuil.

Highland gillies are competitive, always anxious that their gentlemen should catch most fish. One evening, in the Whitebridge Hotel, a few miles up Stratherrick from Knockie, the youngest gillie, a mere lad of 55 years, rushed into the bar and announced that his gentleman caught a salmon on Loch Ness that was six feet in length. The senior gillie put down his dram and looked up, 'That's nothing to what my gentleman caught today. He hooked an old Inverness-shire County Council lamppost in Loch Mhor. And the light was still on.'

'Rubbish!' cried the youngster and several other incredulous listeners.

'Rubbish it is not,' replied the old gillie, 'but if you will take about four feet off the length of your salmon, I might just be persuaded to put out the light on my lamp.'

Similar tales may still be heard today in this comfortable old fishing inn, nestling in Stratherrick and the owners, Donald and Margaret Campbell are always ready to instill in you the will and wisdom to emulate such great feats.

For hundreds of years, travellers have rested at Whitebridge. However, one who did not stop was Prince Charles Edward Stuart, fleeing from Culloden. He paused at Gorthleck House, to impart news of the disaster. Not surprisingly lights were out and Gorthleck shuttered. Not the time for tea and pleasantries. BPC shouted in vain and cantered off into history.

Whitebridge Inn is a traditional fishing hotel; no Hilton, but well furnished and welcoming. In the public bar there is evidence of past glories: a glass case bursting with two fish caught in June 1922 by T.M.A.; modest, was T.M.A. One weighs 5 lb 8 oz, the other 4 lb. Another case displays a trout of 3 lb, enigmatically captioned, 'Caught in the River'. The rivers are one of the delights of fishing from Whitebridge, rushing Highland streams with a new pleasure and delight round every corner. Waterfalls, pots, pools and glides, waiting for your carefully presented fly. Fechlin, Cumlack and Foyers—splendid fun in splendid surroundings.

The River Nairn rises amongst these hills and the Nairn Angling Association holds salmon and sea-trout fishing rights over about eight miles of water, as well as useful beat up-stream from Whitebridge. Reaching some of the pools is hazardous, but most of the river is easily accessible and there are many good holding pools where salmon lie, hopefully waiting just for you. Donald Campbell of the Whitebridge Hotel is a keen angler and he can arrange salmon, sea-trout and brown trout fishing on most of the rivers and lochs in the area, including Loch Knockie and nam Lamm, as well as salmon fishing on Loch Ness. One of the most attractive waters is little Loch Killin, high in the hills, at the end of a narrow, nightmare road that twists up Feehlin Glen. A burn tumbles down the hill, collecting together cold streams from Carn a'Choire, Meallan

Odhar and Meall nan Ruadhag.

It is fine stalking country, owned by red deer, wildcat, grouse and eagle. Wheatear flit ahead, white rumps flashing in the sun and the road eventually exhausts itself at the head of Loch Killin, by a grassy turning place. Years of floods have washed sand and silt from the mountains to form a wide sandbank flanked by rich, green grass. The perfect place for a picnic. Trout in Killin are great fighters, although they average only 8 oz in weight. But there is the added attraction of the possibility of catching Arctic char; Killin is 300 m above sea level and hosts a decent stock of these prehistoric relatives of our more common brown trout.

The largest water in Stratherrick is Loch Mhor, formed when the hydroelectric scheme was built at Foyers. Lochs Farraline and Garbh were joined by rising waters that now feed the hungry turbines down the hill on the shores of Loch Ness. Fishing can be difficult when water is being extracted but excellent sport may still be had, particularly in old Loch Garbh, the southern section. Drift across the bay at Western Aberchalder on a quiet summer evening, rod poised, ready for action. Trout average about 10 oz, but there are larger ones lurking in the depths. Donald Campbell told me of one trout that had fallen foul of an otter in 1988. Even with a sizeable chunk neatly sliced from its side, the fish still weighed 8 lb. So treat every rise with respect, you never know your luck.

Down from Aberchalder is another lovely bay, by Migovie, below the wooded slopes of Choire Riabhaich and Carn na Glaice Moire. Slip in and catch them unawares. The south bay can also produce results, round the point where Iron Age men built their settlements more than 4,000 years ago.

The channel between the two sections of Loch Mhor can be navigated, with care. I remember a time when I stood on the bridge over the rapids and a hunting owl ghosted by on silent wings. Mallard bustled downy broods, line astern, into the safety of weedy shallows; sunlight sparkled on spring waters; rowan, silver birch, beech and sycamore nodded in the gentle breeze. Rising trout dimpled the surface of the loch. What angler could ask for more?

The valley of Strathnairn and Stratherrick is a secret land; infrequently visited. Mainstream life seems to pass by, roaring up and down the A9 between the flesh-pots of Aviemore and the old world charm of Inverness. We discovered Strathnairn a few years ago, one sharp spring, when we stayed in a cottage overlooking Loch Ruthven, north-east from Knockie and Whitebridge. The younger children, Jean and Charles, were introduced to the delights of hill walking and we took them, stumbling and protesting, up Stac Gorm and Craig Ruthven, then, the following day, tackled Stac na Cathaig (447 m) to the north.

The next day was spent monster-gazing on the shores of Loch Ness near Dores. Jean's face was bright with expectation, certain that the mythical beast would bob up any moment to say hello, and Charlie, glued to binoculars, was tense with excitement. Every movement, every shadow on the surface of the loch was examined in minute detail. They get you that way, monsters. After a cold hour on the banks of Ness, we walked through the woods in Strath Dores, from An Tor, down to Lochend. Through a proper wood, swaying with ancient beech and oak, alive with bright-eyed blue tits and finch, carpeted with last year's russet, fallen leaves, urgent with the sound of the swiftly flowing river. It is undoubtedly one of the most attractive woodland walks in Scotland.

Thomas Pennant, that dour Welsh observer of things Highland passed this way in 1769. 'In many parts,' he noted, 'we were immersed in woods; in others, they opened and gave a view of the sides of vast mountains soaring above. The wild animals that possessed this picturesque scene were stags and roes, black game and grouse; and, on the summits, white hares and ptarmigans. Foxes are so numerous and voracious that the farmers are sometimes forced to house their sheep, as is done in France, for fear of the wolves.'

The view that Pennant enjoyed has changed little over the years; it is still a lovely valley, lorded over by golden eagle and buzzard, summer-carpeted with wild flowers, autumn-policed by red deer from heathered crags. A narrow road gives access from East Croachy on the B851 west to the B862, winding past Loch Ruthven and Dalcrombie, down to the crystal-clear waters of Loch Duntelchaig and Loch Ashie. Both waters are used to supply Inverness and fishing is free; but, prior to fishing, you are required to call at the Water Department in the city, to sign a declaration that you will not pollute the waters. Bank fishing only, and hard work. The water is so clear that the slightest error in casting sends shy trout scurrying to the safety of deeper waters. Stalk them, muttering your favourite fishing prayer. Duntelchaig trout are numerous and small, which does not mean that they give themselves up easily, but that there is good stock in the loch. Ashie has larger trout and fish of over 2 lb are taken most seasons. But they are much harder to catch so look out for blank days. If you do connect on Ashie, it will be worth the catching.

My favourite water in this area, Loch a'Choire, is tucked away in the hills above Loch Ruthven, surrounded by the heights of Creag Dhearg and Stac na Cathaig. This is a deep, cold loch, home of Arctic char and some circumspect, cautious wild brown trout. There are boats available for visiting anglers and the loch is carefully managed and preserved by Ash and Kay Humfrey who live in a cottage at Balvoulin at the start of the track through the forest to the loch. Loch Ruthven is the most popular of the Strathnairn waters, two and a quarter miles long by half a mile wide. Over most of its area the loch is rarely deeper than 10 ft but below Stac Gorm it drops to more than 40 ft. The average weight of trout is 12 oz with a few fish each season of 5 lb or more and fishing is from boats only.

Cairngorm calm. Loch Pityoulish

The bad news is that outboard motors are not allowed. So pack a strong friend. Ruthven can be a very windy place to fish.

Of all the storms that rage over the Cairngorm Mountains, none rages more furiously than the storm of conflicting human interests. Conservationists, ornithologists, botanists, geologists, Nature Conservancy Council, Highlands and Islands Development Board, Highland Regional Council, District Councils, National Trust for Scotland, Royal Society for the Protection of Birds, Forestry Commission, private forestry companies and mountaineering clubs. Ski-ing interests, canoe clubs, windsurfers and sailing boat clubs, riding schools, salmon fishers, trout anglers, estates, heritage societies, hotels, guest houses and B&Bs, restaurants, fish and chip shops, old Uncle Tom Cobley and all are, endlessly locked in bitter dispute, bickering and squabbling for their bit of the action.

Few other areas in Scotland demonstrate as clearly the complete lack of any co-ordinated, land use policy. Everything, it seems to me, is up for grabs. If you have the money or can persuade one of the local or national Government agencies to back you, Caledonia is available for apparently unrestricted exploitation. Nightmare buildings mushroom and disfigure beautiful Highland villages; narrow roads are packed with ever-increasing numbers of vehicles; litter and rubbish mar valleys and hills. It is now as easy to reach and walk the high tops, couresty of chair-lifts, as it is to stroll down Glasgow's Sauchiehall Street on a Saturday night, and often just as crowded. Industrial and tourist projects are welcomed with open arms almost regardless of their impact upon the environment. Promise the prospect of a few jobs and the public coffers open. Thousands of acres of Scottish hillside and moorland disappear every year under taxpayer-funded mass-afforestation and the Government proudly announces its intention to encourage and finance even more.

In spite of the commercialisation of Speyside's glorious landscape, once described by Lord Fraser of Allander as 'the merchandise', it is still possible to find peace and quiet in the foothills of the Cairngorms; and one of the best places to do so is from a boat in the middle of one of the excellent trout lochs in the vicinity of Grantown and Boat of Garten. Loch Pityoulish is such a place. It lies to the east of the B970 Nethy Bridge/Coylumbridge road, flanked by Craiggowrie (686 m), Creagan Gorm (732 m) and Meall a'Bhuachaille (810 m). This deep loch is fed by cold mountain streams, gathered together in a tiny lochan by Druimintoul Lodge, and emptying into the Spey by Pityoulish Farm.

Pityoulish is half a mile long by up to three-quarters of a mile wide, tree-lined and contains a number of large trout, guarded by a smaller number of very large pike. Do not expect to catch a lot but any you do manage to hook should be good fish. The boat is moored close to the outlet burn at the north end of the loch and you should concentrate your efforts round the margins. The outlet burn bustles the waters of Pityoulish into the mighty Spey, one of the world's finest salmon rivers, always busy, but offering readily available, good fishing for all. An angler's paradise.

Speyside has always been busy. In 1645, Cameron of Lochiel noted 'Morray lands, quhare all men take their prey'. Horses, cattle, sheep, crops, goods and chattels, hard cash and anything else not actually nailed down was likely to be taken away by raiders. The rich lands of Morayshire were an irresistible magnet to predators. Particularly the impoverished clans from the west who paid frequent, less than friendly, calls on their more prosperous neighbours in search of free meals. Visitors arrive today with less greedy intent. Holiday-makers, and anglers from all over the world descend upon the Spey Valley, winter, spring, summer and autumn; seeking peace, solitude and respite from the slings and arrows of hum-drum late-20th-century life. Lovely Lady Spey soothes them with all-embracing charm and sends them home refreshed and renewed.

The old Pictish Kingdom of Moravia covered a vast area, stretching northwards across the Ness as far as Beauly Firth, westwards to Lochaber lands and south over Cairngorm into Atholl. Forests and hills were full of wildlife: red deer, grouse, partridge, blackcock, ptarmigan, mountain hare, wildcat, and otter. Rivers were loud with sound of splashing salmon, lochs stippled with rising trout. Self-styled sportsmen, such as Colonel Thomas Thornton from Yorkshire in 1786 and Charles St John, resident in Morayshire during the latter years of the 19th century, and hordes of tedd-clad Victorian and Edwardian emulators, soon put paid to that bucolic scene. Osprey were blasted to extinction; otters and wildcat shot or trapped; rivers and lochs were ruthlessly netted and nothing that flew in the air or haunted the high hills or swam in the cool waters of Spey escaped their murderous intent.

It takes a long time for wildlife to recover from such ungentle ministrations and it is only in comparatively recent years that Speyside is recovering; thanks largely to the efforts of conservationist organisations and concerned local people. They all deserve our fullest support, praise and encouragement.

The fast-flowing Spey, 89 miles from source to mouth, draining an area of 1,300 square miles, is usually well lined with busy anglers all chasing the King of Fish, Salmo the leaper. Begin your search in Grantown-on-Spey, Scotland's earliest 'new town', planned by Sir Ludovic Grant in 1765 when he offered feus and long leases to those 'sufficiently recommended and attested as to Character and Ability'. Halfway down the High Street is the centre of all things angling on Speyside, Grant Mortimer's fishing tackle shop. Apart from arranging fishing on Speyside waters, Mortimer's will give you all the advice you need regarding the best method to use to catch them; they also hire tackle and can arrange gillies and instruction. I recently sent a retired businessman to Mortimer's, a man of advancing years who had never fished before in his life, tackle-less and hardly knowing one end of a rod from the other. He was greeted with great courtesy, kitted out and sent off with an experienced gillie to the Spey, where he caught his first salmon. Unmatched courtesy and service.

Much of the Spey is outwith the normal angler's reach, not because of any lack of casting ability, but rather because of cost. Prime fishing of the Spey can cost an arm and a leg and prices on the best waters can cost as much as a small family saloon. These beats, downstream from Grantown, are Castle Grant, Tulchan, Ballindalloch, Pitcroy, Knockando, Laggan, Carron, Wester Elchies, Aberlour, Easter Elchies, Arndilly, Rothes, Aikenway, Delfur, Orton and Gordon Castle. Having said which, the Association waters produce upwards of 500 salmon each season and issue more than 10,000 visitor's permits; and with most of the netting now stopped in the estuary, these numbers should increase. Catches of sea-trout are also good with more than 1,000 fish most seasons. When salmon are dour, then, during summer months, sport with sea-trout more than compensates and there are few more exciting sounds than the surge of sea-trout moving upstream on a warm, bat-flicked, pine-scented night.

The Strathspey Angling Association has seven miles of the main river and twelve miles on a good tributary, the Dulnain. Abernethy Angling Association has six miles of river, near Boat of Garten, and the Badenoch Angling Association has further fishing on the upper river which can also produce good results, particularly at the back end. The river rises amongst the high peaks of Corrieyairack and flows snow-cold down the moutains into Spey Dam, a trout fishery of some repute although much marred by unsightly electricity pylons. At Spey Dam, water is diverted westwards, through Laggan to Lochy, for the aluminium works in Lochaber, the main flow continuing towards Newtonmore where the Spey marries the Truim, made famous by John Inglis Hall in his delightful book, *Fishing a Highland Stream*.

In the upper reaches, Loch Insh and Loch Alvie, pike infest the stream and in spite of periodic attempts to root Jack out, this freshwater shark survives and thrives. A number of important feeder burns join the river along its fast-flowing course: Calder, Tromie, Feshie, Druie, Nethy, Dulnain and Avon, an important spawning stream, which can produce more than 700 salmon each year.

Over the years Spey has produced some notable fish, few more so than the salmon caught by Duncan Grant, shoemaker of Aberlour in 1812. The fish took twelve hours to land and weighed a massive 54 lb and a blow by blow account of the battle is given by Thomas Tod Stoddart, Border angler and author. Another fine specimen was caught more recently by Mr Ronnie Faulkner and weighed 41 lb 8 oz. Hooked in Dewsies Hole, the salmon was eventually landed 'way downstream at Green Bank.

Because most anglers come to Speyside to fish for salmon, few bother to fish for the superb brown trout that are waiting for attention in a number of attractive lochs. Two of my favourites are Vaa and Dallas, both well-managed fisheries, regularly stocked with brown and rainbow trout. Whilst others jostle for the chance of elusive salmon on Spey, wander off into the woods and cast a line on Vaa. This lovely loch lies to the north of Aviemore, east of the A9 and although the sound of passing traffic sometimes filters through, you are in a private world, surrounded by tall, sweet-resin-smelling pines, sparkling with glancing beams of sunlight, loud with the song of woodland birds.

To the west of Vaa, across the old A9, lie the ruins of a Pictish hill fort, Avielochan, covered by a wide tangle of juniper. The outlines are still discernible and no doubt these ancient Scots found plenty of sport in the loch-larder on their doorstep. Vaa covers an area of 35 acres and the water is crystal-clear. Ancient trees give welcome shelter from high winds and fish rise well to surface flies. Trout average 1 lb in weight, with a few of up to 4 lb and fish are caught all over the loch with no one place being really any better than another. Cast with confidence.

When you have done with Vaa, pay a visit to its neighbour, Dallas, approached from Boat of Garten along a bumpy, pot-holed forest and farm track. Drive this road slowly with due regard for the sanctity of your exhaust system. Dallas is much smaller than Vaa, about eight acres in extent, and it is possible to drive your car almost to the lochside. The boat is moored at the north end and is a well-found, wooden vessel; a proper loch boat which will take three in comfort, two fishing, one minding the oars and muttering appropriate incantations.

Craiggowrie (686 m), Creagan Gorm (732 m) and Meal a'Bhuachaille (810 m) rise west, snow-sprinkled in June. The sound of lake water lapping reed-fringed shores and the anxious squawk of busy birds amongst the rushes, calms the most troubled spirits. Let the bustle of Speyside pass by and enjoy the pleasures of this delightful Highland glen.

Loch Morlich, south from Dallas, used to be a similar haven of tranquility. Now, it is very busy indeed, visited each year by thousands of holidaymakers; as is Loch Garten, famous for its own, resident anglers, the Garten osprey. But before leaving Speyside let's visit a less frequented water, Lochindorb, seven miles north-west from Grantown on desolate Dava Moor, unseen from the A939 Grantown/Nairn road. The name means 'loch of trouble'; but not for anglers, for Lochindorb is the ideal place to introduce beginners to the gentle art of fly fishing; or to restore one's own angling self-confidence.

It would be a poor day if this lovely Highland water sent you home empty-handed. Even the biggest duffers in the world, and I include myself in that luckless brigade, should catch their fair share. Lochindorb is full of small, brightly marked, wild brown trout averaging just under 8 oz which give great sport and even on a bad day you should manage a brace or two for breakfast, fried, dressed in oatmeal, a meal fit for a king. There are larger trout in Lochindorb, so treat every rise with caution and respect. In 1987, Mr Anderson, a Glasgow angler did so and landed a magnificent fish of 6 lb 13 oz for his trouble; and there are signs that the average weight is increasing with greater numbers of 8–12-oz fish being caught each year.

Fish rise and are taken all over the loch and no one place is very much better than another. Lochindorb is shallow, so it is possible to catch fish as easily in the middle as it is amongst the shallows. If I have a preference, then it is down the east shoreline, particularly between castle and lodge; but the west bank, from Terriemore Farm south to the feeder burn which enters before a 'fishy' promontory can be just as good. The loch is two miles long by up to three-quarters of a mile wide and, because of its exposed position on the moor, can be windy. Nevertheless, even in a strong wind trout still rise and these little fish give a good account of themselves. Perfect gentlemen at all times.

Lochindorb gained the 'trouble' reputation because of its association with the great and mighty. Or rather the great and nasty, dependent upon your point of view and who happened to be listening at the time. An important castle stood on a small, man-made island at the north-east end. In Scotland where there was a castle, there was generally trouble. The 'Hammer of the Scots', Edward I, paid a less than social call in 1303, whilst putting down yet another rebellion of his unwilling, surrogate subjects. After doing the death and disaster bit he relaxed at Lochindorb, no doubt catching a few trout, enjoying the view, and before departing south he left instructions for the old keep to be enlarged to the status of castle. In due course, the castle on the island became the property of one of Scotland's most infamous villains, Alasdair Mor Mac an Righ, or 'Big Alasdair' to his new friends; remembered in history as the Wolf of Badenoch, natural son of King Robert. Big Alasdair was regarded as a monster. Which is saying something, given the lawless state of 14th-century Scotland.

Having married the Countess of Ross, for her rich lands, rather than for her rich beauty, Alasdair deserted her when he discovered that the lady's family had excluded said rich lands from the marriage agreement. The Countess appealed to the Bishop of Ross and Moray, seeking compensation, and the prelate made the mistake of finding in the Countess's favour. The Wolf responded by stealing large chunks of the Bishop's lands and the Bishop promptly excommunicated him. Clearly, Big Alasdair thought, the Bishop wasn't getting the message and had to be re-educated; so the Wolf paid a late-night call on the towns of Forres and Elgin, doing what he knew and enjoyed best, burning, raping and pillaging; including the destruction of one of Scotland's most beautiful places of worship, Elgin Cathedral.

The affair was eventually patched up with Big Alasdair on his knees, doing penance at the front door of The Church of the Blackfriars in Perth. But the Countess never got her money, or her husband, for Badenoch preferred his mistress who bore him five, lusty sons. Alasdair died in 1394, not much mourned, after losing a game of chess with the Devil at another of his lairs, Ruthven Castle, on the banks of the River Spey near Kingussie.

The ruins of Lochindorb Castle still crowd the tangled undergrowth of the small island and I never cast a fly by the shore without thinking of the wild, self-seeking Wolf, sitting in the great hall with his cronies, plotting his revenge on the Bishop of Moray.

Plotting the downfall of trout is less taxing and damaging, at least to human life and limb, or should be. One autumn day, Ann and I were fishing Lochindorb when the wind rose suddenly to gale force. Flinging both rods to Ann, I grabbed the oars and began fighting to row across the wind, back to the mooring bay. With lines trailing astern, as we bumped and tossed towards the mooring bay, two fish grabbed our flies, one to each cast. In a tangle of lines and hot cursing, anxious not to lose the fish, rods were passed from hand to hand and, in the heat of the moment, the boat grounded in shallow water and tilted sideways.

I slid out, backwards, in slow motion, clutching a rod, and found myself sitting waist-deep in freezing water. Wet is wet. So I dragged the boat ashore and, dripping, reeled in. Firmly attached to a size 14 Silver Butcher was a good trout of about 1 lb. Nothing on the other rod. 'Thank you dear,' said my dry wife, leaping nimbly ashore. 'Let me have my rod and I'll land it.' Momentarily, I considered a bit of pillaging myself; but even Big Alasdair would never have got away with that from Ann, Wolf or not.

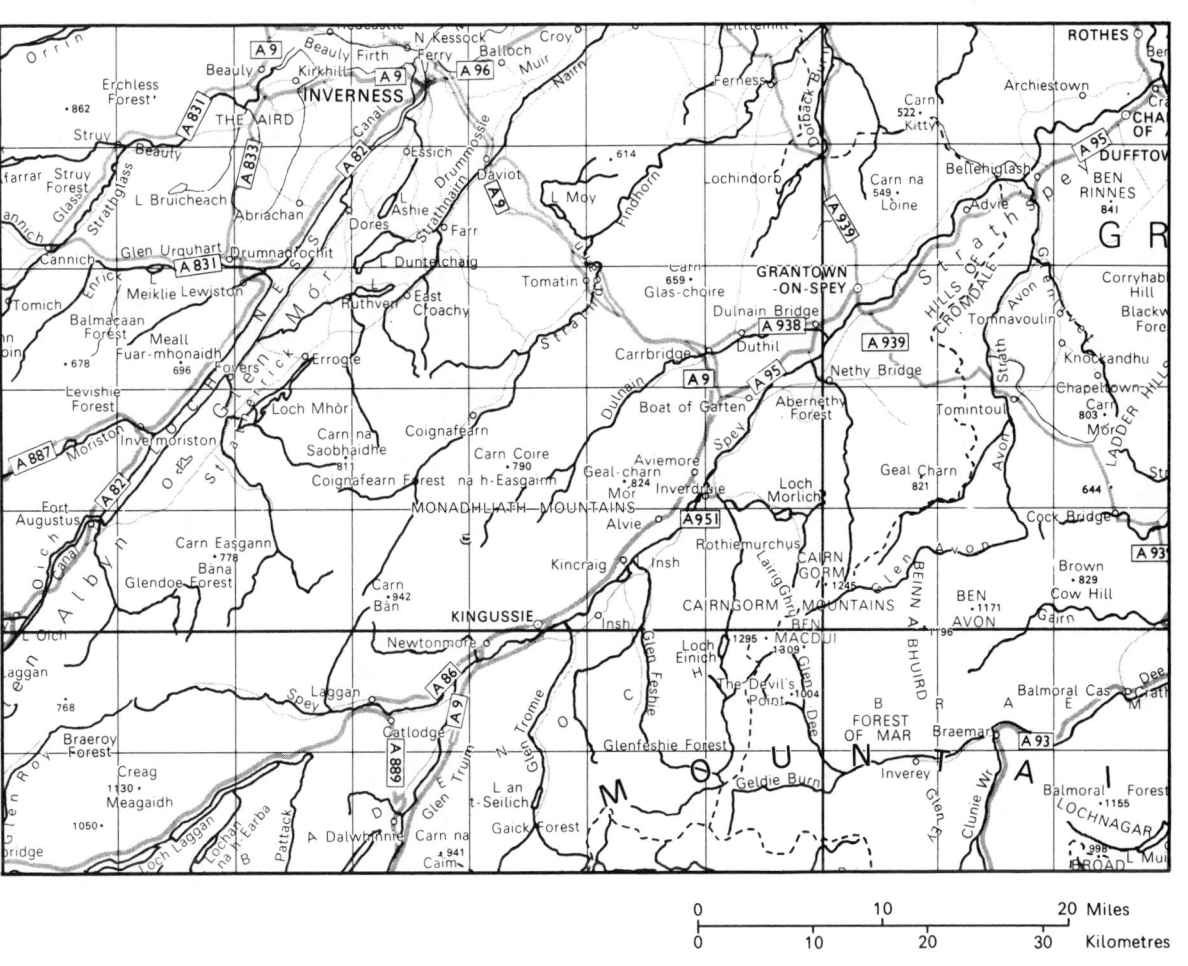

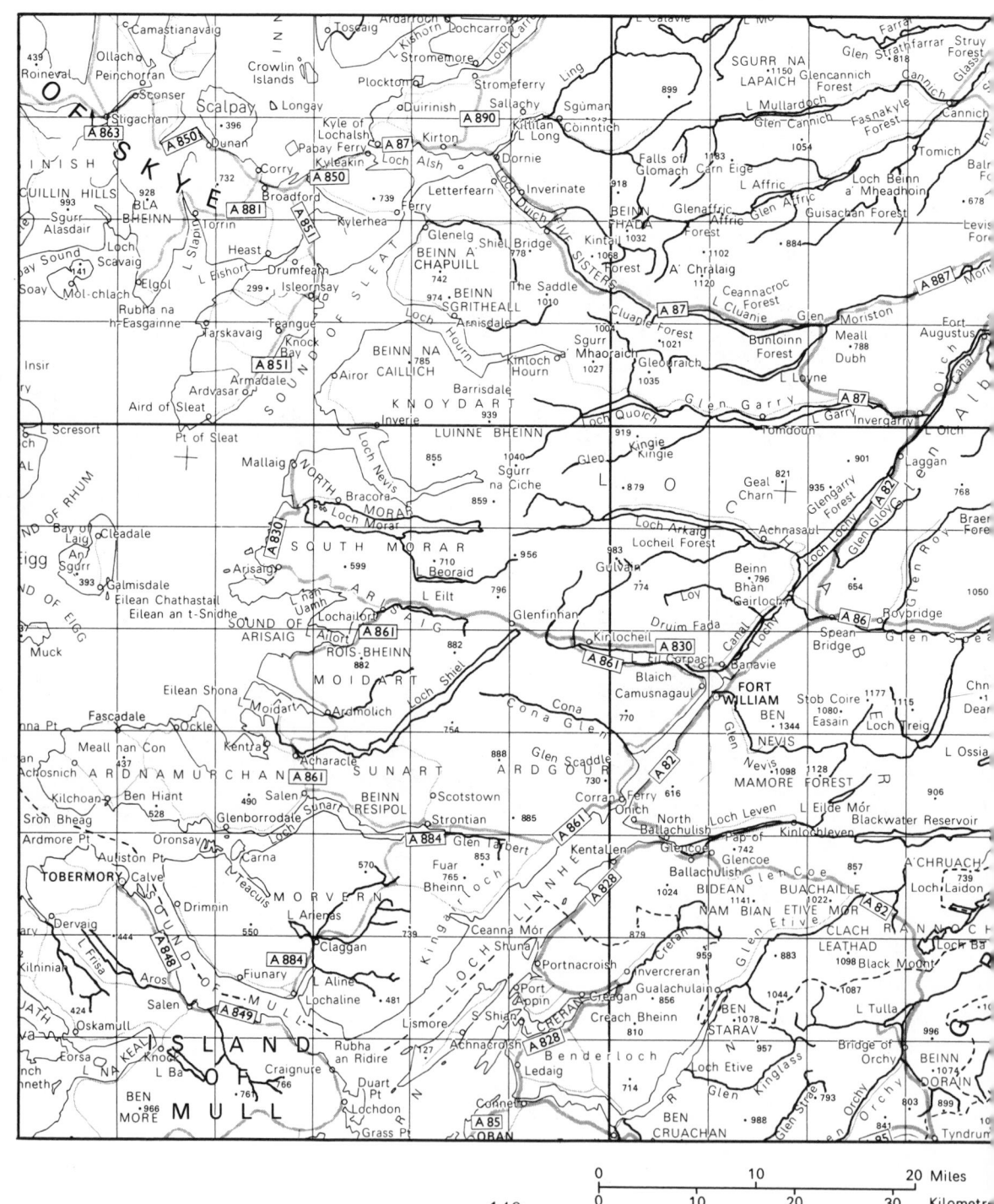

CAPITAL HIGHLANDS

FISHING DIRECTORY

SALMON AND SEA TROUT
RIVER SPEY
Tulchan Estate Enquiries to:
The Factor,
Tulchan Estate Office, Advie, Grantown on
Spey
(0479) 200

GRANTOWN AND CARRBRIDGE
Seven miles of main river and twelve miles
of River Dulnain
**Strathspey Angling Association
Secretary,**
Grant Mortimer, Tackle Dealer, High
Street, Grantown on Spey
(0479) 2684

BOAT OF GARTEN
Six miles of main river
Abernethy Angling Association,
The Boat Hotel, Boat of Garten
(047983) 258

KINGUSSIE
SPEY RIVER
SPEY DAM
Badenloch Angling Association,
Mr Jock Dallas, Jeweller, High Street,
Kingussie
(05402) 229

RIVER SPEY
RIVER FESHIE
INSCH LOCH
Invereshie House Hotel,
Kincraig, by Kingussie, Inverness-shire
(05404) 332

RIVER SPEY
RIVER TRUIM
Silverfjord Hotel,
Kingussie, Inverness-shire
(05402) 292

RIVER SPEY
FESHIE LOCHS
The Osprey Fishing School,
The Fishing Centre, Aviemore Centre,
Aviemore, Inverness-shire
(0479) 2684

RIVER SPEY
RIVER CALDER
LOCH ERICHT
LOCH LAGGAN
LOCH CRIACH
Mains Hotel,
Main Street, Newtonmore, Inverness-shire
(05403) 206

BROWN TROUT
LOCH PITYOULISH
Osprey Fishing School,
Aviemore Centre, Aviemore, Inverness-
shire
(0479) 810767

AVIELOCHAN LOCH
LOCH VAA
LOCH DALLAS
G C Mortimer,
Fishing Tackle Shop, 61 High Street,
Grantown on Spey, Morayshire
(0479) 2684
Mrs M McCook,
Avielochan, Aviemore, Inverness-shire
(0479) 810450

LOCH MORLICH
Camp Warden,
Forest Information Office, Glenmare, by
Aviemore, Inverness-shire
(047986) 271

LOCH ALVIE
Alvie Estate,
Estate Office, Kincraig, Kingussie,
Inverness-shire
(05404) 255

INVERDRUIE FISHERIES
Inverdruie Fishery,
Rothiemurchus, Aviemore, Inverness-shire
(0479) 810703

SPEY DAM
A McDonald,
6 Gergask Avenue, Laggan, Newtonmore,
Inverness-shire
Badenloch Angling Association,
39 Burnside Avenue, Aviemore, Inverness-shire
(0479) 810798

LOCH LOCHIRDLARB
J Scott,
Head Keeper, Lochindarb Lodge,
Glenferness, Nairn
(03095) 270

LOCH VAA
LOCH DALLAS
LOCH AVIELOCHAN
LOCHINBARB
MORLICH
MHAR
PITYOULISH
Craigaird Hotel,
Boat of Garten, Inverness-shire
(047983) 206

LOCH GARTEN
AVIELOCHAN
LOCH VAA
Nethy Bridge Hotel,
Nethy Bridge, Inverness-shire
(047982) 203

LOCH ERICHT
LOCH LAGGAR
LOCH GUAICH
Mains Hotel,
Newtonmore, Inverness-shire
(05403) 206

*SALMON AND SEA TROUT
FISHING*
RIVER LOCHY
RIVER NEVIS
RIVER SPEAN
RIVER ROY
RIVER COE
RIVER GARRY
River Oich
LOCH GARRY
LOCH OICH
The Rod and Gun Shop,
18 High Street, Fort William, Inverness-shire
(0397) 2656

RIVER CONA
RIVER SCADDLE
Ardgour Hotel,
Fort William, Inverness-shire
(08555) 225

RIVER MORRISTON
LOCH NESS
Glenmoriston Estates Office,
Glenmoriston, Inverness-shire
(0320) 51202

RIVER BEAULY
Lovat Estates Office,
Beauly

RIVER NAIRN
Clava Lodge Hotel,
Culloden Moor, Inverness
(0463) 790228

UPPER RIVER NAIRN
Whitebridge Hotel,
Stratherrick, Gorthleck, Inverness-shire
(04563) 226

BROWN TROUT
LOCH LUNDAVRA
(Lochan Lunn Da Bhra)
Mrs MacCallum,
Lundavra Farm, Fort William, Inverness-shire
(0397) 2582

LOCH LOCHY
Fishing is free

LOCH ARKAIG
The Rod and Gun Shop,
Fort William, Inverness-shire
(0397) 2656

HOSPITAL LOCH
J Alabaster,
Scarrybreac Guest House, Glencoe,
Argyllshire
(08552) 225

CHURCH LOCH
COTTAGE LOCH
Ardgour Hotel,
Ardgour, Fort William, Inverness-shire
(08555) 225

LOCH QUOICH
INCHLAGGAN
LOCH POULARY
Tomdoun Hotel,
Invergarry, Inverness-shire
(08092) 230

LOCH BLAIR
The Rod and Gun Shop,
Fort William, Inverness-shire
(0397) 2656

UPPER RIVER GARRY
Garry Gualach Ltd,
Invergarry, Inverness-shire
(08092) 230

LOCH LOYNE
Cluanie Hotel,
Glenmoriston, Inverness-shire
(0320) 40238

LOCH CLUANIE
Duncan Stoddart,
Stalkers Cottage, Cluarie Lodge,
Invergarry, Inverness-shire
(0320) 40208

DUNDREGGAN RESERVOIR
LOCH NESS
LOCH ACHTRIACHTAN
Glenmoriston Estate Office,
Glenmoriston, Inverness-shire
(0320) 51202

GLENMORISTON
HILL LOCHS
LOCH MA STAC
LOCH NA FEANNAIG
LOCH LIATH
LOCH A'CHRATHAICH
CARN LOCH A'BHOTHAIN
LOCHAN RUIGHE DHUIBH
Glenmoriston Estate Office,
Glenmoriston, Inverness-shire
(0320) 51202

LOCH AFFRIC
LOCH AFFRIC HILL
LOCHS INCLUDING
MULLARDOCH
BENAVEN
MONAR
Glen Affric Hotel,
Carrnich, Inverness-shire
(04565) 214

LOCH KNOCKIE
LOCH NAN LANN
PIKE LOCH
LOCHAN MAM-CHUIL
LOCH KILLIN
Whitebridge Hotel,
Stratherrick, Gorthleck, Inverness-shire
(04563) 226

LOCH MHOR
LOCH FAVALINE
LOCH GARBH
LOCH BRAN
The Foyers Hotel,
Foyers, Inverness-shire
(04563) 216

LOCH RUTHVEN
Estate Office,
Brin Estate, Flichty, Inverness-shire
(08083) 211

LOCH A'CHOIRE
Ash Humfrey,
Balvoulin, Flichity, Inverness
(08083) 283

LOCH DALCROMBIE
LOCH DUNTELCHAIG
LOCH ASHIE
Fishing is free but you are required to call
at the Water Dept in Inverness for permit

DOCHFOUR
Dochfour Estate Office,
Dochfour, Inverness
(046386) 218

RIVER FECHLIN
LOCH NESS
Whitebridge Hotel,
Stratherrick, Gorthleck, Inverness-shire
(04563) 226

SALMON AND SEA TROUT
LOCH DOILET
Ben View Hotel,
Strontian, Sunart, Inverness-shire
(0967) 2333

RIVER POLLOCH
RIVER MOIDART
Mrs Stewart,
Kinlochmoidart House, Kinlochmoidart
(096785) 609

LOCH MUDLE
Ardnamurchan Estate,
Glenmore Cottage, Glenborrodale, Salen,
Inverness-shire
(09724) 263

WHITEGLEN
RIVER ALINE
ALLT BEITHEACH
BLACK WATER
RANNOCH RIVER
Ardtornish Estate,
Estate Office, Morvern, Oban, Argyll
(096784) 288

LOCH EILT
Salar Properties Ltd,
Lochlory House, Nairn
(0667) 55355
Lochailort Inn,
Lochailort, Inverness-shire
(06877) 208

RIVER AILORT
Lochailort Inn, Lochailort, Inverness-shire
(06877) 208

BROWN TROUT
LOCH DOILET
Ben View Hotel,
Strontian, Sunart, Inverness-shire
(0967) 2333

LOCH SHIEL
Johnston-Mann,
Creel Fishing Facilities, Creel Cottage,
Acharacle, Argyll
(096785) 281
The Rod & Gun Shop,
Fort William, Inverness-shire
(0397) 2656

LOCH NAN PAITEAN
LOCHAR NA CROABHE
Mrs Bley,
West Lodge, Kinlochmoidart, Loch Ailart,
Inverness-shire
(096785) 218

LOCHAR A'MHUILLINN
LOCH NA CAILLICH
LOCHAN MEALL A'MHADAIDH
and others
ARDNAMURCHAN HILL LOCHS
LOCH MUDLE
LOCHAN A'MHADAIDH RIABHAICH
LOCH NA CRAGIE
LOCH NAN DEARCAG
LOCH AN IME
and many more
Ardnamurchan Estate,
Glenmore Cottage, Glenborrodale, Salen,
Inverness-shire
(09724) 263

ARDTORNISH ESTATE WATERS
LOCH ARIENAS
LOCH DOIRE NAM MART
CROSBEN BLACK LOCHS
Archtarnish Estate,
Estate Office, Morvern, Oban, Argyll
(096784) 288

LOCH TEARSNAIT
LOCH NAN CLAH
LOCH UISGE
CAOL LOCHAR
LOCH MORAR
Morar Hotel,
Morar, Mallaig, Inverness-shire
(0687) 2237
The Superintendant,
Altan Loin, Morar, Mallaig, Inverness-
shire
(0687) 2237

RIVER INVERIE
Knoydart Peninsula Ltd,
Knoydart Estate, Mallaig, Inverness-shire
(0687) 2331

LOCH SHEIL
Fergie Macdonald,
Clanranald Hotel, Acharacle
(098785) 662
The Creel Fishing Facilities Co,
Creel Cottage, Acharacle, Argyll
(096785) 281
Strontian Angling Club,
Argyll
The Stage House Inn,
Glenfinnan, Inverness-shire
(039783) 246

MORAR HILL LOCHS
LOCH AN NOSTARIE
LOCH EIREAGORAIDH
LOCHAN A'MHEADHOIN
LOCH A'GHOBAICH
and others
Permission not required

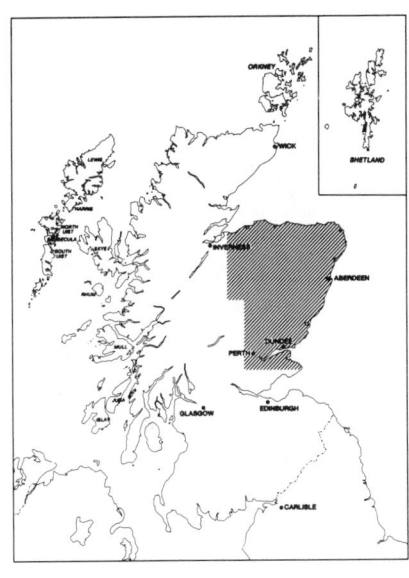

MORAVIA

AND

NORTH-EAST

Morayshire, Aberdeen and Angus

A few years ago, I belatedly discovered one of Britain's most beautiful salmon and trout streams, the Aberdeenshire Don. Of course, I had heard stories about the quality of salmon fishing and the Don's monster brown trout but never really believed them. After all, what could possibly compare with my beloved Tweed or give such splendid sport as our remote northern hill loch? To me, and to thousands of my fellow anglers, Aberdeenshire is synonymous with exclusive salmon fishing—a belief, I suspect, for reasons now clear, that Don anglers have carefully nurtured. The Don is most certainly an excellent salmon river but it is also one of the most lovely trout streams that I have ever seen.

Aberdeenshire has always played an important part in Scotland's story and the Howe of Alford is no exception. The Gordon District Tourist Board has mapped out a Castle Trail for non-fishing visitors—there are such people—and this is centred upon the little village of Alford. The route takes you to some of Scotland's most dramatic castles, a few in ruins, most well-preserved and open to the public. Fyvie Castle, now in the ownership of the National Trust, is a masterpiece of Scottish baronial architecture and the oldest part dates from the 13th century. Five great towers rise as a memorial to the five lairds: Preston, Meldrum, Seaton, Gordon and Leith; and one of the finest features is a splendid wheel stair.

Nearby, at Methlic, is Haddo House, home of the Earls and Marquesses of Aberdeen. It was designed by William Adam and built in 1732 and played host to Queen Victoria when she visited her Prime Minister, the 4th Earl of Aberdeen. Today, it is a cultural centre, with an outstanding Choral Society—the public concerts given at Haddo are a feature of Aberdeenshire life. There are seven other castles along the way: 15th-century Tolquhon, now in ruins; Castle Fraser, with its famous

147

eavesdropping device, known as the 'Laird's Lug'; Craigievar, with its magnificent plaster ceilings, home of the Forbes family; 13th-century ruined Kildrummy, close by the excellent hotel that bears its name; Corgarff and Huntly. There is a Transport and Railway Museum and narrow-gauge railway at Alford, craft workshops, country parks, a farming museum and formal gardens at Pitmedden; pre-historic stone circles, standing stones and hill forts; distilleries, a bird sanctuary at the Sands of Forvie Nature Reserve and a Fishing Heritage Trail all along the coast. Golf, swimming, ski-ing, hill walking, surfing, petanque, bowling, orienteering and pony trekking. Plenty for the family to do, whilst you tackle the Don.

Over the years Don fishing has been much affected by pollution but, recently, great strides have been taken in controlling the activities of industrial concerns along the banks and the river is improving year by year. Even better news is the fact that there is no longer any netting at the mouth of the river and returning salmon have freedom of access at all times.

There are more than 60 riparian owners and much of the Don fishing is readily available to visiting anglers. Nor does it cost an arm and a leg to fish for salmon. Gordon District Council, Aberdeen, and District Angling Association and a number of hotels all offer fishing to visitors: Kintore Arms Hotel, Kildrummy Castle Hotel, Forbes Arms Hotel and Grant Arms Hotel; and fishing is often available by the day, rather than by the usual weekly lets.

The River Don rises amidst the wilderness of the Grampian Mountains, from the Well of Don on Little Geal Charn (710 m); dashing past Lagganauld, narrowly missing the Avon on its busy way north-westwards to Speyside. Feith Bhait, Allt nan Aighean, Allt Reppachie, Allt Tuileach and Meoir Veannaich mingle and meet at Delnadamph Lodge where the collected streams are named Don. But unlike its famous Aberdeenshire neighbour, the Dee, the Don is not really a spate river and good water flows are sustained throughout most of the year. After leaving the hills, the Don becomes a well-behaved, almost pastoral stream, flowing through well-tended agricultural land, bordered by rich fields. In farming parlance, in Aberdeenshire, it is said that 'A mile o' Don's worth twa o' Dee' and the river is slow-moving, unlike the Dee's often frenzied bustle.

Amongst the best of the Don fishing is the Castle Forbes Water in the Howe of Alford. The fishing extends for nearly nine miles, double bank, from Bandley, downstream to Glenton. There are more than 30 named salmon pools and an endless delight of trout water. The Estate Office is clearly signposted, to the north of the village of Whitehouse, on the left of the B992 road to Insch. Approach from Aberdeen along the A944 or from Ballater via the B9119 and A980.

Although spring and autumn fishing is well booked in advance, during June, July and August the casual angler should find at least trout fishing available and probably salmon fishing but, as always, it pays to plan ahead and book in advance. Although gillies are not available on the Forbes Castle Waters, the Estate Office will provide you with all the information you need and most of the pools and lies are obvious. On our last visit, Ann and I left the Estate Office and drove north to Oakbank, near Castle Forbes. We stood on the old bridge, watching Don's clear waters hurrying seawards. Leaving the bridge, we followed an estate road through woodlands of Scots pine, beech, sycamore and elm to the footbridge at Craigport. Whilst Ann fished by the bridge, I wandered upstream to have a look at the Dam pool. In fact, I had a much closer look than I had anticipated, nearly drowning in the process.

Dam Pool is classic dry fly water; deep, clear, slow moving, alive with insect life, bordered by high trees on the north bank, trout-stalking water. Walking along the bank, I noticed a fish rise behind me and went back to have a cast at him. The number of times I have done so over the years, and never caught the brutes, you would have thought that I would have learned my lesson. The moment my fly landed, an enormous trout rushed out from under a rock ledge and grabbed—mightily. I saw him coming but still got such a shock at the size of the fish and the strength of his 'take' that I took an involuntary step and performed a neat forward-roll, right into the pool. Fully equipped in waders, fishing jacket and tackle bag, under I went. In such circumstances, you are advised to remain calm and let the air trapped in your waders and clothes take you to the surface; then you paddle shorewards, on your back. In reality, what you do is panic. Strange thoughts flashed through my mind as I struggled under water. 'Well, this is it, wonder what it will be like?' I opened my eyes and noticed fronds of green weed moving in the current. Eventually, I managed to struggle upright and, fortunately, being six feet four inches tall, my head was just above the water. The rod was still firmly grasped and the furious fish still tearing line from the reel. Then I remembered the £400 worth of cameras in my fishing bag. The rod was unceremoniously heaved shorewards. I staggered out onto the bank and the only damage done was to my dented dignity. But I lost the fish. In almost 40 years fishing I have never done anything so stupid.

Needless to say my explanation—being pulled into the river by a huge trout—was greeted with hoots of derision from Clan Sandison: 'Where did you say the hip flask was, Dad?' 'Not safe to let you out alone . . . . Get your eyes tested, Father.' Sympathy was noticeable by its absence. The revered personage's near-demise passed unnoticed and unremarked. That's the last blood knot I tie for that lot.

But it was a very large trout, one for the glass case, if I had landed him. They are still there. A trout, 4 lb 12 oz, was landed in 1987 and in 1985 a fish of 7 lb 12 oz was caught. Each season, depending upon how many trout anglers fish the Castle Forbes Water, up to 500 fish are taken and the minimum takeable size is 10 inches.

After my morning dip, we fished Upper and Lower Auchreddachie in the afternoon, catching some lovely, silvery, pink-fleshed trout and we also saw several salmon splashing their way upstream. The Forbes Estate fishing offers something for everyone: superb brown trout fishing and fine sport with salmon. The heaviest salmon taken during 1988 was a grand fish weighing 17 lb 8 oz and each season the best produces an average of over 100 fish, in spite of often being very lightly fished. Downstream from Castle Forbes is another fine stretch of water, the Monymusk Fishing, centred on the village of Monymusk, just off the B993 Kemnay/Huntly road. In 1078 Malcolm Canmore rested at Monymusk while on his way north to quell yet another uprising in Moravia. Using his spear, he marked on the ground an outline of the church he would build if granted victory over the rebels.

A better known pattern is still regularly traced on the ground today, by thousands of feet throughout the world, commemorating this delightful Strathdon village—the Scottish country dance, 'Monymusk'. The village was substantially rebuilt at the beginning of the 19th century and even today motor cars and the trappings of modern life seem out of place amid the old-world charm of the grey-stoned buildings. One of Scotland's most important religious relics came from The House of Monymusk, the ancestral home of the Grants since 1712—the Monymusk Reliquary, a 7th-century casket reputed to contain a bone of St Columba. The casket was carried at the Battle of Bannockburn in 1314, inspiring the army of Robert the Bruce, and can still be seen in Queen Street, Edinburgh, at the Scottish Museum of Antiquities.

The quality of game fishing on the Monymusk water reflects the level of care with which it is managed and preserved and there are few better, more readily accessible, salmon and trout waters anywhere in Scotland. The Monymusk fishings extend for a distance of almost 15 miles and are managed by Colin Hart of the Grant Arms Hotel. Colin is an experienced angler who has fished throughout Britain and as far afield as New Zealand and Australia, so guests at the Grant Arms are assured of expert advice. Most seasons, upwards of 200 salmon are landed, with the upper beats producing the best early season sport; beats 6, 7, and 8 are best during autumn months and the heaviest fish caught recently weighed 24 lb; during two memorable days in spring 1986, Grant Arms anglers took 36 sea-liced, fresh fish. One of the Grant Arms regulars, Mr MacGregor, had 11 fish weighing 97 lb in 1987 and the average weight of salmon caught is in the order of 8 lb.

But, as well as excellent salmon fishing, Monymusk also offers superb sport for brown trout as recent catches show. Mr Wilmore, a Cambridge angler, took 45 trout weighing 55 lb during the course of a two-day visit; Messrs Moulet, Buchard and Louvernnier, visitors from France, had spectacular dry fly fishing during three days in May 1985 catching 115 trout. Their bag included of 3 lb 8 oz, 3 lb 1 oz and several of over 2 lb. All but the 'specimen' fish were returned to the water.

The Monymusk trout fishing is challenging dry fly water, most of the best baskets being taken by experienced anglers; but we mere mortals can try and emulate their skill. After all, once on the water, our flies will look just as tempting to trout as any cast by latter-day Izaak Waltons; and we can always pray. Without question, however, the patterns to use are March Brown and Greenwell's Glory. These two good friends of fishermen account for most of the large trout caught and the best time to use them is during May, June and July, early morning and late evening. Stalk your fish, watch and wait; do not be too quick about wading. Use the cover of reeds and rushes along the river bank; keep every finger crossed. What angler does not need is fair share of luck?

A possible exception is Mike Edwards, from Glasgow, who has fished at Monymusk for many years. Dr Edwards rarely has a blank day and his knowledge of the river is second to none. During the recent visit, Dr Edwards had seven trout weighing 11 lb 12 oz, including a fine fish of 3 lb 10 oz; on another cold, blustery day he landed three trout weighing 6 lb 12 oz; and then, to complete his entertainment, a fine grilse of 5 lb 2 oz. Ann and I failed to match that performance but we spent a glorious day fishing from Slatestone to Holly Bush Pot. The wood by the river, bordering the south bank, is magnificent, beautifully planned and laid out —not regimented rows of conifers that blanket out all light and life. This most perfect of woods was planted by Lord Cullen in 1719 and is known as Paradise Wood. We parked our car near to the old mill and walked through a dappled day of sunlight and shadow, amidst ancient oak and beech. I do not think that the composer Frederick Delius was a fisherman, but when he wrote his haunting melody 'Walk to the Paradise Garden', surely he must have had Monymusk in mind.

For insects, the upper reaches of the river Ythan are another type of Paradise Garden, but for the anglers, it makes fishing the narrow stream very difficult indeed. My son, Blair and I, had an evening on the river a few years back, in the vicinity of Methlick and found it to be hard going. The river was alive with sea-trout smolts and the air alive with midges. Both were feeding voraciously, the young sea-trout upon anything that moved on the water, the midges mostly upon us.

The Ythan used to have the reputation of being Scotland's finest sea-trout fishery and it rises 40 miles west from its estuary, in the schoolmaster's garden at Wells of Ythan. It winds its way eastwards through the countryside, entering the North Sea some 14 miles north from Aberdeen. Salmon also run the river and in recent years more are being caught, particularly during autumn when fish average about 12 lb. But the main interest here is sea-trout and the best place to catch them is in the long, finger-like estuary that runs from Kirkton of Logie Buchan to Foveran Links and the Sands of Forvie Nature Reserve.

The estuary forms an area of nearly a quarter of a mile across by three miles long and at ebb tide the water reduces to the size of a medium-sized river. In high water fishing is from boats and the Ythan is a very popular fishing venue for locals and visitors alike. So be prepared for company, lots of it. Just the place for gregarious anglers. Local angling associations control much of the Ythan fishing and consequently it is readily available to the public. For newcomers, local advice and a good knowledge of tide tables is essential and you will find that this information is supplied when you book your ticket. When fishing the brackish waters of the estuary, the most productive flies are Dunkeld, Grey Monkey, Priest, Peter Ross, Teal, Blue and Silver, and Butcher's various. Salmon and sea-trout will also respond to lures, such as Sutherland Special, Krill, Toby's and Mepps. July is probably the best month to attack Ythan sea-trout and the average weight of fish is about 2 lb. Much heavier fish are sometimes caught, with superb specimens of up to 10 lb and heavier taken. If you fail in your efforts, retire to the Udny Arms Hotel for refuge. I did, and fed on sea-trout the easy way, straight from the sea to the hotel kitchens; and what a marvellous meal it was.

North from the splendours of the Ythan Estuary fishings, the River Ugie is a less well known salmon and sea-trout system that can also provide excellent sport and is not so populous with anglers. Not so populous with fish either but very respectable nevertheless. In a good year 150 salmon and grilse may be caught and more than 1,000 sea-trout and finnock. The Ugie is made up of two streams. North Ugie rises almost on the north coast, near New Aberdour, then wends south-east through Strichen and Fetterangus before joining its brother, South Ugie which rises from Maud to this meeting near Strawberry Bank and Buthlaw. The river flows sluggish, reluctantly, to the sea, entering just north of the fishing port of Peterhead between the town hospital and the golf links.

Fishing on the river is available to visiting anglers and the local tackle shops in Peterhead, Dick's Sports or Robertson Sports, will keep you right and point you in the correct direction. The best fishing times are between July and September. July for sea-trout, autumn for salmon and there are a number of good pools on the river of which the best are Flats, Scotts, Pot Sunken, Meadows and Cruvies.

If salmon and sea-trout on Ythan and Ugie prove unresponsive, make for Rattray Head and Loch of Strathbeg, one of the least known yet most delightful lochs in north-east. Loch of Strathbeg lies at the heart of one of Scotland's most important nature reserves. The land was first leased by the Royal Society for the Protection of Birds in 1972 and the reserve now covers an area of 2,300 acres. Before 1700 Strathbeg formed the estuary of the Burn of Rattray; this estuary was gradually blocked by sand until, in the early 18th century, a huge storm completely closed the outlet, thus forming the present loch. This 550 acres of water lies midway between Fraserburgh and Peterhead, close to the village of Crimond, separated from the North Sea by the narrow Black Bar.

Access is easy; approach from the A952, turning east at North Mosstown towards Old Rattray; and approach with confidence, the light of battle shining in your eyes, for here is trout fishing of the highest quality. Although overlooked by gaunt radio masts and an abandoned war-time airfield, Strathbeg still magically creates a feeling of remoteness. Short-eared owls quarter the marshlands in search of prey whilst swallows and terns dip and splash, feeding among prolific hatches of flies—and rising trout. In winter thousands of wildfowl cover the surface: Arctic greylag geese and pink-footed geese and vast flocks of Icelandic whooper swans. There are hundreds of diving ducks: tufted, pochard and goldeneye. Mallard, wigeon, merganser and goosander abound and more than 186 bird species have been recorded. Strathbeg is also a botantist's delight of pondweed and stonewort, reed-grass and yellow iris. Meadowsweet, angelica, marsh valerian, tufted vetch, butterfly and marsh orchid flourish at the west end of the loch while the dunes, heartsease, bird's-foot trefoil, eyebright and grass of Parnassus thrive.

The boundaries of the loch are shared by two ancient Aberdeenshire parishes, Rattray and Lonmay, both scattered with relics and tales of the north's turbulent past. The clock on the steeple of Crimond church bears the inscription 'the hour is coming' and at the south end of the loch lie the ruins of St Mary's Chapel, founded in AD 911. My elder son Blair and his wife Barbara took us to Loch of Strathbeg recently and we instantly fell under its spell. During the course of a memorable day we fished the loch, studied the bird and plant life and wandered among the miles of deserted sand dunes.

Strathbeg was stocked with Loch Leven trout 12 years ago and these fish now breed naturally. They rise well to the fly and Robert Wilson of the Fraserburgh Angling Club told me that during July in 1986, 26 club rods had 40 fish averaging 12oz with a heaviest fish of 2lb. The loch is two and a half miles long by up to half a mile wide with an average depth of between three to six feet. High winds tend to churn up the bottom, discolouring the water but Strathbeg fishes best in a good breeze. Consequently, a drouge is essential and an outboard motor even nicer. But you will have to take along your own motor because there are none available for hire.

Fish rise and are caught throughout the length and breadth of the loch but the south end is probably most productive. Nevertheless, we caught good fish on a drift down the east shore, past the Angling Club mooring bay, housed in the remains of an old RAF building. Local anglers tend to use a slow-sinking line, stripping back quickly, but we found that the traditional 'in front of the boat' technique to be just as effective. Arrive prepared for both. Flies that do damage include Cinnamon and Gold, Black spider, Soldier Palmer and Whickham's Fancy. We also have sport on Ke-He, Silver Butcher and Dunkeld; size 14 and 16 dressings. There are only six boats on the loch, five of which are available to visitors, so Strathbeg never becomes crowded. Because of the importance of the margins as a wildlife habitat bank fishing is not allowed. Nor are anglers allowed to land on any of the islands. Most of the anglers I know are just as interested in what is above the water as what is below. Show me an angler and I will show you an enthusiastic lover of wildlife. Loch of Strathbeg will satisfy every need.

The River Deveron almost holds the record for the heaviest salmon caught in Britain. In 1924, Mrs Morrison caught a fish of 61 lb, just 3 lb lighter that the fish caught on the Tay in 1922 by Miss Georgina Ballantine. Proving yet again that ladies are far more skilful anglers than we poor men. Nevertheless, Col H. E. Scott did his best for us on the Deveron a few years earlier, in 1920, and managed to land a salmon of 56 lb.

The Deveron has always been famous for the size of its salmon and large numbers of fish weighing over 40 lb have been taken through the years. Big fish are still taken but the days of 40-lb-plus fish seem to have gone forever. However, salmon of over 20 lb are still caught: Jim Robertson had a 23-lb salmon from Avochie in April 1988; the same month, Dr G. Mackay had a salmon of 18 lb from Bridge Pool on Bridge of Marnoch Beat and Brian Catto landed a 20-lb fish from Castle Beat at Rothiemay. So the Deveron is alive and kicking, still producing excellent sport throughout its long February until October season.

The Deveron blossoms from the hills north of Strathdon, near Cabrach 'the place of antlers', collecting in the streams from Meikle Firbriggs, Dead Wife's Hillock, Hill of Three Stanes, Sand Hill and Blairlick Hill. A few miles north, at Inverharrock, Deveron is joined by Black Water and then flows on through farmlands to greet the little rivers Bogie and Isla near Huntly and Idoch Water at Turriff. The Deveron is a spate river: no water, no fish; so it is very much a question of being in the right place at the right time, usually dripping wet. If, however, you do get it right, then rewards can be great, not only with salmon but also with sea-trout for Deveron has good runs of these fine sporting fish with as many as 5,000 entering the system each season.

Some of these sea-trout rival their west coast brethren in size and in 1969 Mr W. B. Sheret landed a fish of 18 lb and sea-trout of over 5 lb are caught most seasons. The Deveron produces upwards of 1,500 salmon and 2,000 sea-trout each year and the river is divided into more than 40 beats. Much of the best Deveron fishing is booked every year by regular tenants, but excellent sport is still available for visitors and newcomers to the river.

The Sports Shop in Huntly and local hotels have permits for visitors and a number of estates may have vacancies at short notice. For instance, Huntly Lodge Fishings, from the south bank of the river, have three-quarters of a mile of the right bank which contains 13 named pools and this beat produces about 60 salmon each season. It also has the added attraction of having a comfortable fishing lodge, right by the waterside, available for the use of tenants. Similarly, the Mayen Beat has three-quarters of a mile, single bank fishing and three-quarters of a mile double bank fishing with eight named salmon and sea-trout pools. The ten-year average for this beat is 64 salmon and 56 sea-trout. Salmon average 10 lb 4 oz, sea-trout 3 lb 6 oz. Heaviest salmon in recent years weighed 28 lb, heaviest sea-trout 7 lb 12 oz and the heaviest brown trout 5 lb. Here also, excellent self-catering accommodation is provided in a modern Scandinavian bungalow, fully furnished by Habitat.

Bognie, Frendraught & Mountblairy Estates may be able to offer sport during spring months, when salmon are not so great in numbers but certainly great in quality and there are three beats, and also two fully equipped and modernised holiday cottages to let with the fishings. In 1987 the Mountblairy Water produced a salmon of 25 lb.

A few miles north of Loch of Strathbeg, in Fraserburgh Bay, Philorth Water meets the sea, and this little stream can give very good sport with sea-trout. The stream rises to the south of Fraserburgh from the gentle slopes of Waughton Hill, topped by ruined Hunter's Lodge and the White Horse. It flows serenely amidst rich farmlands past Rathen and Cairbulg Castle. The Pet Shop in town issues tickets, and, in the right conditions, you may find great sport here.

As well as Loch of Strathbeg, the north-east has other, equally as good, brown trout waters. A useful place to find out about them in detail is to call on Mr Sommers, in Thistle Street, Aberdeen. This is the north-east's premier fishing tackle shop and centre of Aberdeenshire angling knowledge. Sommers issue tickets for Loriston Loch, which is easily accessible and only four miles south of the city. Loriston is stocked with both brown and rainbow and fishing is from the bank only. There is a bag limit of six fish per rod per day and trout of over 2 lb are sometimes caught.

Along the Moray coast are a few excellent trout lochs, such as Loch of the Blairs, two miles south of Forres, off the A940. Boat fishing only and a bag limit of six fish. Angling effort is divided into two sessions: 8 a.m. until 5 p.m. and then 5 p.m. until dusk. Milbuies is another good water, four miles south of Elgin, off the A941; and there are also a growing number of commercial, put-and-take fisheries in the area, such as Mill of Artloch Trout Farm, near Huntly and Loch Na Bo, near Khanbryde; Sommers Tackle Shop in Aberdeen will help you make bookings.

The River Lossie, wedged between its more famous neighbours Spey and Findhorn, is a productive little spate salmon and sea-trout stream where fishing is readily available to visiting anglers. Best sport is had from July onwards and of course, action is very much dependent upon water levels. The Lossie rises from The Seven Sisters Springs in the hills around Glen Trevie, 35 miles south-west of Elgin. As it gathers momentum it also gathers in the streams of Clashgour, Lochans Burn, Burn of Corrhatnich and, at Bliarnha, the Glenlatterach streams. A dam has impounded the waters of Glenlatterach, forming a useful trout fishery in the reservoir above; but be warned, the trout do not give themselves up easily and Glen Latterach Reservoir has a reputation for being dour.

From its junction with Glenlatterach, the Lossie becomes a slow-moving, wandering river, as though unsure about what to do with itself or where it should finally enter the sea. It wends drunkenly past Elgin and finally turns north and enters the Moray Firth by the fishing town of Lossiemouth and Branderburgh. The Lossie has recently benefited greatly from improvements carried out to sewage treatment works in the Elgin area; much of the effluent is now pumped directly to the sea, rather than the river. Agricultural drainage works in the vicinity of Loch Spynie have also helped the river and the local angling association expend a considerable amount of their time, energy and money maintaining the Lossie. Which is good news for anglers because most seasons upwards of 150 salmon are landed and also several hundred sea-trout. Elgin and District Angling Association controls the productive Beach Fishings and all the fishing upstream to the confluence of Lossie and Leanoch Burn. Above the junction, Kellas Estate own the fishings and the upper river is controlled by the Dallas Angling Association which has a four-mile stretch up to the junction with Auchness Burn.

The Dallas Angling Association also have trout fishing on remote Loch Dallas which lies at an altitude of 1,000 ft. This is a wonderful place to cast a fly and the scenery is outstanding with, on a good day, reasonable numbers of bright trout which average 8 oz in weight. West from Lossiemouth is the River Findhorn, one of the north's most productive and attractive salmon streams. I fell in love with Findhorn many years ago, in 1955, when I first fished its swift-flowing, clear waters above Tomatin. If I remember correctly it was when the Royal Highland Show came to Inverness for the last time before taking up permanent residence at Ingliston, just outside Edinburgh.

A friend had invited my father for a day's salmon fishing and I was tagged along also, to have a go at Findhorn brown trout. Nothing in angling is as certain as the uncertainty of salmon fishing. The two men flogged and thrashed the river mightily but caught nothing. I had a basket of six lovely brown trout, the largest of which weighed 2 lb 2 oz, and good sport all day. My next brush with the river came in 1967, when they advertised for a new General Manager for Findhorn Fisheries. Several hundred applications were received and, although I was amongst the leaders, I didn't get the job. A recently retired Lieutenant and Territorial Army Captain, no matter how enthusiastic, was obviously not what they were looking for.

The Findhorn reaches the sea amidst the wonderful sands of Culbin, the only true sand desert in Britain. The Forestry Commission have been hard at work for several decades, planting trees to stabilise the shifting sands. Always puzzles me, why people can't leave things alone; what's so wrong with having a mini-desert in the north? I suppose the people of Findhorn wouldn't agree with me for there have been three villages of that name on the site. The first was overtaken by the sea and the second lies buried under the Culbin Sands. In days past, Findhorn was an important trading port, importing continental wines, silks and tapestries and exporting beef,

The River Findhorn at Drynachan

grain, malt, hides and salmon. Now, Findhorn is a holiday village and most of the boats that grace the harbour are pleasure, rather than working vessels.

Forres is the principal industrial and commercial centre today, busy for 2,000 years when it was marked on Roman maps as Varris. Shakespeare opens his tragedy *Macbeth* in Forres Castle, long since demolished; and, five miles west of town close to the A96 at Hardmuir, is MacBeth's Hillock, the site of our hero's meeting with the three witches on the 'blasted heath'. Between Macbeth's Hillock and Forres stands lovely Brodie Castle, built in the 15th century and modernised during the 18th and 19th centuries. The castle is owned by the National Trust for Scotland and contains a marvellous collection of French furniture, English, Continental and Chinese porcelain, and a major collection of paintings.

Forres and Findhorn have plenty to interest any non-fishermen in your party and if you are faced with the problem of mixing top-quality salmon fishing with sand-castles, buckets and spades and good shops, then this is the place to go. Also some fine golf courses near by, particularly at Nairn. Horse riding, water sports, plenty to do for them all. For more serious water sports, head for the tackle shop in Forres where visitors' tickets are issued for the Forres Angling Association Water which extends from the estuary to four miles upstream. Anglers must be resident in the Forres area. Most of the rest of the river is leased out to tenants by various estates, and is generally booked year after year by the same people.

Nevertheless, it is often possible to pick a week's sport and the key to success is to contact the estate well in advance. You also have to have the wherewithal to pay the fee and Findhorn fishing, on the best beats in prime time, will cost in the order of £300 (plus VAT) per rod (1988 charges) and estates prefer to let their fishings as a minimum two-rod beat. If that figure seems fearsome, believe me it is a lot less wicked than prime time on Tay, Spey, Tweed or Dee and, in my opinion, represents good value for money. Save up. It will all seem worth it in the end, and you will have exclusive use of the fishing.

The Findhorn rises in the Monadhliath mountains and the principal spawning areas lie in the hills above Tomatin. Downstream from Dulsie the river flows through a 20-mile-long, steep-sided, rocky gorge, by Randolph's Leap, named after the mighty jump of a clansman fleeing from his pursuers. Great jumpers, Highlanders, for there are many such 'leaps' throughout the north. Good sport on the Findhorn depends very much on hard winters in the hills. As snow melts on the heights, fresh water is released into the river, encouraging fish in from the Moray Firth. From July onwards, until the end of the season in September, sport depends upon autumn rains; most years, they appear and autumn fishing is now the most productive time of the season on Findhorn.

Much of the best of the Findhorn fishing is mountain goat country and, particularly in the gorge, anglers should beware of sudden floods which can raise water levels to a dangerous height very quickly. Forestry operations in the hills have exacerbated this problem and Findhorn now suffers greatly from the effects of flash-flooding. The Drynachan Beat, owned by Cawdor Estate, is one of the most accessible stretches of the river and weekly lets are sometimes available. The estate has a good self-catering cottage, Gardener's Cottage, near to Drynachan Lodge and this is a super base for a fishing holiday from which you can walk to the main beats. Fishing is divided into three beats and the five-year average for Drynachan is 100 salmon each season. Most of the fish are caught in September, although June fishing can also be very rewarding, given good water levels.

Findhorn salmon average 10 lb in weight with fish of 20 lb or more taken most seasons. The Association Water, owned by Moray Estates, is the most readily available to visitors and there are times when these beats are the best on the river. As always, it is all a question of being in the right place at the right time. Work at it. The Findhorn is well worth the effort.

The most famous Aberdeenshire river, indeed, perhaps the most famous European salmon stream, is glorious, Royal Dee, whose best-loved patron is HM Queen Mum. Ninety miles of sheer delight, designed by Gods for the pleasure of man. Sadly, obtaining access to this haven is very difficult and the best fishing is jealously guarded, booked year after year in advance; so there is little opportunity for mere mortals to cast their flies on Dee's lovely breast. Nevertheless, there is no harm in trying and from time to time there are cancellations; contact the various estates that own the river and inquire. Costs vary, depending upon where you fish, but can range from £10 per day right up to £8,000 per week, including accommodation, for five rods. Start saving now.

Banchory Lodge Hotel, Crathes Castle Hotel, Invery House, Ardoe House Hotel, Raemoir Hotel, Bell Ingram in Perth, MacSport and Petlett Administration in Banchory will help you in your search for Dee fishing; the dream of every aspiring salmon angler. Aboyne 'the place of the rippling stream' is one of the principal angling centres along the river. This attractive Deeside village was created a Royal Burgh in 1676 and, apart from its spectacular fishing, close by is one of Aberdeenshire's most spectacular castles, the graceful tower of Craigievar, completed in 1626 and largely unchanged since then.

Upstream, the village of Ballater was popularised by Queen Victoria and Prince Albert when they purchased the Balmoral Estate. In order to preserve Royal peace and quiet, Victoria arranged that the railway line from Aberdeen should go no further than Ballater and the proposed railway line was converted into a road. At the end of this road lies Braemar, famous for its Highland Games. Braemar is a recent invention, formed in 1870 by joining together the hamlets of Auchendryne and Castleton. Braemar Castle, standing by the banks of the sweetly flowing river, was originally built in the 14th century but did not survive the turbulent middle-ages of Scottish history. The present castle was built in the latter years of the 17th century, prior to the ill-fated 1715 Jacobite Rebellion that began when the Old Pretender's standard was raised on the Braes of Mar.

Knowing where and when to fish the Dee can save you money and the possibility of disappointment; for there is little point of paying considerable sums if the main runs of salmon have already passed on. The Dee opens for business on 1 February and in these early days, the lower river fishes best, below Banchory, up until about mid-April. From Banchory up to Ballater, middle Dee, fishes best from March until May and the Upper Dee, from then until the end of June.

The Dee is, above all, a spring river and unlike most Scottish salmon streams where spring fishing is almost a thing of the past, the Dee is in top form during the first part of the year. Hard winter snows melt clear waters from the Cairngorms, drawing fish quickly upstream; and after the temperature of the water rises, spates hurry fish straight through the lower river to middle beats. However, fresh fish are caught throughout the year and the river produces upwards of 8,000 salmon each season, averaging 9 lb in weight. Some very large salmon have been caught in years past, the heaviest being 56 lb, or 57 lb 8 oz, depending upon which report you read, caught in Oct 1886 by gillie J. Gordon on Ardoe Water. In 1917 a fish of 52 lb was taken from the Park beat and a number of 40-lb-plus fish have been landed in recent years.

Opening day on the Dee can often be splendid and in 1988 produced fish of up to 23 lb; Potarch, fished from Invery House, landed 16 on 1 February and eight the following day. Aboyne had 11, with a salmon of 25 lb and at Dinnet a fish of 27 lb was caught by John Green from Lincolnshire. But the best salmon landed was a truly magnificent fish of 30 lb 8 oz caught by local angler James Lyndal. First week catches ranged from 20–40 salmon throughout the river and the Dee really lived up to its reputation of being the finest spring river in the land.

The Silver Dee rises in the Cairngorms, from distant Well of Dee and plunges down the Lairig Ghru, collecting in Gharbh Choire Burn to join the Geldie Burn at Whitebridge. In its upper reaches, the Dee flows through one of Scotland's finest stalking estates, past Mar Lodge; built in the late 19th century by Queen Victoria for the Duke of Fife and HRH Princess Louise, daughter of King Edward VII. The ballroom at Mar is adorned with 3,000 stags' heads and Mar Lodge is one of Europe's premier sporting estates.

Upstream from Mar is the Linn of Dee, the only substantial obstacle throughout the length of the river for returning salmon. The Linn is a narrow, deep gorge, through which the water roars in a foam-fringed torrent. Salmon congregate in great numbers, waiting to leap the falls and this is a popular outing for tourists who stand bewitched as Salmo, the leaper, lives up to his name. Another well-known Dee leaper was Caird Young, although his was but a single jump. Above the bridge at Potarch, when the river is low, the stream is confined between craggy rocks, 15 feet across. Caird leapt across to escape from pursuers, hot for revenge because Caird had murdered their chief.

As the river flows eastwards, it gathers in a number of important tributaries, all of which add to the even flow of Dee's crystal waters. There are 45 beats and perhaps the best known is Cairnton, where Arthur Wood developed his greased line method of fishing. A. H. Wood had the lease of Cairnton from 1913 until 1934 and during that time landed 3,490 salmon from the beat.

Everything about the Dee pleases and delights the senses: the scent of pine needles and wood smoke, constantly charmed by the sound of mountain waters hurrying seawards; the surge and splash of salmon, sea-liced and Greenland-silver, returning to the place of their birth. Hopefully, along the way, there may be one or two for you.

Brown trout fishing is available in some of the tributaries of the River Dee and the Invercauld Estate issues day tickets for fishing on the Clunie Burn, by Braemar and the Gairn Burn by Ballater. Other useful salmon, sea-trout and brown trout fishing may be found by visitors on the River Feugh, Fiddich, Turriff Burn, Muckle Burn near Forres and the Boyne Burn by Portsoy; Chabet Water and Cnocglass Waters, near Tomintoul, have brown trout fishing and no permit is required to fish these delightful hill streams.

Loch fishing south of the River Dee is limited but of a high quality. Some of it is also at a high altitude. For instance, Lochs Vrotachan, Nan Eun and Shechernich, the latter two being about 2,000 ft above sea level. These lochs are close to the Spittal of Glenshee so you can cheat a bit and save your legs by hitching a lift on the chair-lift.

The largest thing about fishing here are the mountains of Mar and this is an absolutely glorious place to fish, where you are surrounded by dramatic scenery and good numbers of 8-oz trout. Shechernich, known locally as Loch Beanie, has much large trout and fish of up to 3 lb are sometimes caught. However, there is no chair-lift to help you on your way, so if you wish to experience the delights of Beanie, it's hoofing-it time.

Loch Saugh is more accessible though none the less rewarding to fish. Controlled by the Brechin Angling Association, Saugh is well managed and regularly stocked. Brown trout average 10 oz with the occasional fish of up to 2 lb. Bank fishing only. Even more accessible is Fasque Lake, west of Laurencekirk, man-made in the 18th century, close to Fasque House, the ancestral home of the Gladstone family. The house dates from 1809 and was the home of William Ewart Gladstone, four times Prime Minister, of whom Queen Victoria complained, 'He addresses me like a public meeting.' This lovely house is open to members of the public. Even nicer for anglers is Fasque Lake which is surrounded by mature woodlands and is a haven for wildlife. It is also a haven for some very nice brown trout and their average weight is in the order of 1 lb with fish of between 3 lb and 5 lb often caught. Dry fly fishing, particularly on warm summer evenings, when insects hum and whirl above, can be very productive and Fasque Lake in its idyllic setting is well worth a visit. Book in advance.

North-east from Fasque and Stonehaven is the village of Muchalls, where my parents lived before the last war and close by are Cowie and Carron Waters, both fished by the Stonehaven Angling Association which issues day tickets to visitors. Cowie rises on the slopes of Monluth Hill and winds its way through Fetteresso Forest, crossing the A975 Stonehaven/Crathes road near Rickarton House; continuing to Stonehaven Bay, passing under the Glenury Viaduct.

Given the right conditions, Cowie can be a really splendid sea-trout water. Fish run the river from June onwards and in the autumn months there is always the chance of salmon as well. Sister Carron is a shorter stream rising from Cold Well by the Hill of Trusto, entering the sea at the south end of Stonehaven Bay. In the late 1970s a fish pass was built on the Carron but local reports seem to indicate that migratory fish are reluctant to use it. However, the Carron does give good sport with brown trout.

The Angling Association requires that all juniors are supervised by an adult and this makes good sense, given the ease with which accidents can happen. However, in my case, remembering my junior years, I seem to recall that it was often the other way about; pulling off stuck waders, retrieving ill-judged casts, carrying everything. It was a hard life, but small price to pay for a quick car-borne trip to the river. Never really did trust buses.

Southwards, a fan of streams in the Drumtochty Forest feed the enigmatic River Bervie; Burn of Luchray, Burn of Duglermy, West Burn of Builg, East Burn of Builg and Mavie Burn. The Bervie flows eastwards to Bridge of Mondynes where it slips under the A94 Stonehaven/Laurencekirk road and then swings south and east in a long meander to the sea at Inverbervie. The river's exit into Bervie Bay can sometimes become blocked by a build-up of sand and gravel and diggers have to be called in to clear a passage for returning fish. There is also evidence of poaching but in recent years much greater efforts have been made to control this most virulent form of angling disease.

There are records of a huge salmon being taken from this little river before the last war, when the Town Provost of Inverbervie, Mr Burnett, is reported to have landed a salmon of 50 lb; and as recently as 1985 a salmon of 32 lb was caught. But don't raise your hopes too high. You are more likely to catch sea-trout, for there are good summer runs and salmon don't appear in any real numbers until autmn.

Inverbervie is famous as being the birth-place of another great lover of water, but salt water. The designer of the tea-clipper *Cutty Sark*, Hercules

Linton was born in Inverbervie; the little town also saw the first linen spinning machine in Scotland, set to work in 1788. Set to work today on the river and try and tempt the Bervie sea-trout. Joseph Johnstone & Sons in Montrose or J Mowat in Laurencekirk will give you permission to do so. Joseph Johnston & Sons also have good salmon and sea-trout fishing on the River North Esk, an excellent and productive salmon stream that rises in deep in the Grampian Mountains. North Esk is born out of the Waters of Mark and Lee, two highland streams that feed in winter snows from the high tops.

The Mark flows northwards between Black Hill of Mark (774 m) and Easter Balloch (834 m) and swings south-east by Craigichael and Little Hill, tumbling over the waterfalls and gorge of Craig of Doune and Balnamoon's Cave, past Queen's Well, joining the Water of Lee at Invermark Castle.

The Lee has even more turbulent beginnings, collecting in a spider-web of streams from the slopes of Bently Roads (841 m), Green Hill (870 m), White Hill (850 m) and Muckle Cairn. They rush northwards to Falls of Unich and into the cold depths of Loch Lee. Loch Lee has been impounded to provide water for Kincardine and Stonehaven and is a good trout loch, also with a reputation for producing some fine Arctic char which can weigh up to 2 lb. Brown trout average 8–10 oz with heavier fish of over 4 lb sometimes caught. Lee is a wild, windy place and it is always advisable to telephone, prior to arriving, to see if it is possible to launch the boat. The estate also prefers anglers to make a booking by post, well in advance of fishing. Take along a reliable outboard motor and a drogue. Concentrate your efforts in the shallows, particularly at the west where Water of Lee enters.

From Loch Lee, almost to the Bourn of Loups, the river flows through magnificent countryside, over a series of lovely falls and Glen Esk is a popular place with visitors who come to enjoy the peace and solitude of its heather-covered slopes. Access is easy with a good minor road paralleling the north bank of the river and estate roads following the south bank, from Dalbog almost to Invermark Castle.

Eastwards from the Loups, the North Esk becomes much more orderly, sweeping past Edzell to Inchbrae where it gathers in West Water and North Water Bridge, near where Luther Water joins the flow. The North Esk glides under the A937 at Marykirk, dashes by Craigo and enters the sea under the A92 between Montrose and St Cyrus over Charleton and Kinnaber Links. Because of the nature of the upper river, most salmon are taken by either spinning or on the worm. The pools are deep and often dangerous, so if you are new to this part of the Esk, take great care; even better, take along a gillie. The best known pools are Jack London's Run, The Pot, Major, Kitbog, Coffin and Holly Tree.

Much of the North Esk is booked in advance, through the estates, but Johnston's offer salmon and sea-trout fishing on the Canterland and

Safely in the net on the North Esk

Gallery Beats on the lower river which are excellent waters. Johnston's also offer day tickets for sea-trout and brown trout fishing on the stretch between Lower Northwater Bridge to Denmouth of Morphie; the Craigo Beat is in the hands of the Montrose Angling Club and they also sometimes have day tickets available to visiting anglers.

As always, success depends very much upon water levels; but when conditions are right then look out for great sport. In March 1988, six salmon were taken by Glasgow angler, Gordon Aikman, from Balmakewan Beat, all on Devon minnows. Below Morphine Dyke, with more than 15 fish caught on opening day, 15 February, and 42 for the first week of the season, including a splendid fish of 18 lb.

South from the source of the North Esk, above the infant River South Esk, below the sheer crags and corries of Green Hill and Ben Tirran, lie two of Angus's most remote and beautiful trout lochs, Brandy and Wharral. Brandy is approached via a well-tramped hikers' path which starts behind the welcoming doors of the Ogilvy Arms Hotel. If you enjoy a decent walk with your fishing, then Brandy is for you. This delightful little loch lies at an altitude of almost 2,000 ft, in the echoing, horse-shoe corrie below the summit of Green Hill.

There is bank fishing only on Brandy, with fish that average 8 oz, but fight well. The water is crystal-clear and the south shore, where wading is easy, is perhaps the most productive area of the loch. Carrying the waders up the hill is not so easy, so if you have decided that discretion is the better part of valour, fish the east and west shores from terra firma: the water deepens quickly.

Wharral is attacked from Wheen, where a track leaves the B956 and climbs steeply uphill along the west side of Adielinn Forest. It will make you catch your breath a bit, but the rewards at the top are outstanding. Not only from the point of view of lovely trout, but also because of the splendour of the panoramic view from the top. Wharral is similar in size and shape to Brandy, slightly smaller, but also cupped in a dramatic corrie below the sheer Crags of Loch Wharral.

For a really splendid day out, visit both lochs, climbing Ben Tirran and Green Hill along the way. There is a good path and provided that you take proper account of the weather, then the only thing that should come to any harm are fish. Remember to tell someone where you are going and when you will be back. I suggest that you start the expedition by walking to Wharral. That way, you can plan your descent to coincide with opening time at the Ogilvy Arms. A splendid way to end a splendid day. The most notable salmon river in Angus is without doubt the South Esk and this excellent river has its source high amongst the braes of Angus in the land of the Five Glens: Prosen, Clova, Ogil, Lethnot and Esk. This is Ogilvy country. In 1432, Sir Wallace Ogilvy, treasurer of Scotland, was granted permission by James I to fortify his Tower of Eroly, the site of the present-day Castle of Airlie. The original structure was utterly destroyed in 1640 during the Covenanting Wars by Lord Lorne, Marquess of Argyll. It is said that such was Lorne's fury against the Ogilvies, that he physically helped to tear down the castle himself. Perhaps he should have spared himself the effort, for, after nearly quarter of a century supporting, variously, both Covenanter and Royalist causes, he was found guilty of treason and beheaded in Edinburgh on 2 May 1661.

The South Esk rises from the heart of the Caledonian National Nature Reserve; here there are more than 60 peaks of more than 600 m and this is fine climbing and walking country. The principal feeder stream is Burn of

Gowal, flowing down ragged gullies from Cairn Bannoch (1,012 m) and Broad Cairn (998 m), into a deep, dark glen, through new woodlands to meet White Water near Acharn and Glendoll Lodge.

Glen Clova tames the stream and the flow slows to walking pace as it meanders and twists past Inchdowrie, Wheen and Rottal, where Willie Hanton, one of the most respected and best loved gillies on the South Esk used to spend his childhood holidays. Leaving the calm of Glen Clova, the river hurries through Elly and Crossbog Pools to meet Prosen Water, below Cortachy Castle. After the steep gorges of Inshewan, the river becomes gentle once more and flows seaward by Brechin to House of Dun and the vast, tide-washed, Montrose Basin.

Montrose has a long, often violent place in Scotland's story. The Vikings paid vicious visits in the 10th century and in the 12th century, William the Lion, King of Scotland, built a castle there. Edward I of England, the Hammer of the Scots, captured it in 1296 and a year later, Sir William Wallace, my childhood hero, destroyed it during his fight for Scottish independence. During the great days of the herring fishings in the 18th and 19th centuries, Montrose flourished and today the town owes much of its prosperity to the activities of the North Sea oil industry. Other activities, dearer to the hearts of anglers, take place in the river and although much of the best fishing, such as the famous Kinnaird Beat, is securely booked years in advance, it is still possible for visiting anglers to find sport.

The Justinhaugh Hotel has the Lower Justinhaugh Beats and this fishes well in the spring and also during the summer when there are excellent runs of sea-trout. Kirriemur Angling Club has about seven miles of salmon, sea-trout and brown trout fishing available, although visitors must be sponsored by a club member. The Ogilvy Arms Hotel has two beats in Glen Clova, each three miles long and East Kintrochat Fishings are sometimes available through Savills in Brechin. The East Kintrochat Beat is an attractive stretch of the river, two miles upstream from Brechin and is double-bank fishing extending to almost one mile in length. This is let as a three-rod beat and fishing is restricted to fly only except during the month of April when spinning is allowed.

The dam at Kinnaird restricts the passage of fish until April but once over the pass salmon move upstream and may be caught in Kintrochat waters throughout April and May. June and July see the arrival of sea-trout and these fine sporting fish average 3 lb in weight, with many heavier fish being taken each season, both during the day and at night. Autumn brings the best of the salmon fishing.

Trout fishing in Angus and the Dundee area is well worth your attention and my favourite water is the Loch of Lintrathen, an excellent, well-managed fishery which offers visiting anglers fine sport in lovely surroundings. The loch covers an area of 445 acres and is one and a half miles long by three-quarters of a mile wide; open woods of larch, spruce and pine line the shore and the shallow margins of the loch attract a wide variety of water fowl. An osprey regularly fishes Lintrathen and high above Knock of Formal, hang-gliding-man swoops and turns in the strong thermals like some prehistoric raptor.

The name Lintrathen means 'rapids of the river' (Linn-an-t-Abhainn) and the rapids in question is Reekie Linn on the River Isla. Close to the Bridge of Craigisla, west of the loch on the B954, the river is forced through a narrow wooded gorge; the water plunges over a great waterfall and spray hangs like smoke over the whirlpool and cavern of the Black Dubh. A mile or so further downstream are the equally impressive race and waterfall of the Slug of Auchrannie.

The loch is managed by the Lintrathen Angling Club which has some 300 members. There is a comfortable fishing hut, good toilets, a boathouse and boat-repair workshops and the facilities provided are amongst the best I have seen in Scotland. The club has 12 first-class boats and also supplies well-maintained outboard motors. Two or three rods are allowed in each boat and single anglers are not permitted. No, I don't mean that you have to produce either wife or marriage certificate before fishing, but for safety reasons there must always be at least two anglers in the boat. The other rules are simple: fly only, no trolling, no bank fishing and no fishing from an anchored boat. In my opinion, all is as it should be.

The average weight of Lintrathen trout is in the order of 12 oz although most seasons produce fish of up to 3 lb. There are two good spawning burns and the fish are wild brown trout of a native strain since the only restocking that takes place is with fish reared in the Club's own hatchery. The main inlet burn is the Melgan, between Balnakeilly Wood and Boghall; the Scottish Wildfowl Trust have a reserve here and the water in this bay is shallow, providing good fishing.

From Boghall, along the Sa'mill Bank fishing is also productive. However, Sharp's Bay, in the south-west corner can also offer great sport and another good drift is down the east shoreline. On our most recent visit, my wife and I had the pleasure of fishing in company with Sandy Forgan, a Lintrathen expert. Ann struck a blow for female supremacy by catching three lovely, golden trout and Sandy had two. If I had caught two more, I would have had a brace. At times, life can be cruel.

North from Lintrathen and feeding it via Meglam Water are two further trout lochs worthy of mention. Blackwater Reservoir wasn't there when we first travelled the glen in the early 1960s and this now offers reasonable fishing. We were staying in a cottage owned by a friend of my father and after a few days found our way through the forest to Loch Shandra, on the west side of Cairn Hill. We caught some nice trout, including fish of over 1 lb in weight. Today, the average size is somewhat less but it is still worth a visit because of its lovely setting.

More accessible sport with brown trout can be found north of Dundee, one of Scotland's oldest Royal Burghs. The town was captured by the army of Henry VIII of England, during his 'Rough Wooing' in 1547. The Duke of Montrose burned Dundee in 1647 and shortly afterwards, General Monck performed a similar act. The last time Dundee played unwilling host to invaders was in 1745, when the Highland army of Bonnie Prince Charlie occupied the town for nearly a year. Dundee survived and grew into one of Scotland's most prosperous cities, its fortune based upon jute, jam, journalism, fishing and shipbuilding. Recently, one of its best-known vessels returned to its birth-place: the *Terra Nova*, in which Sir Ernest Shackleton sailed in search of the North-West Passage.

Sail upon less dangerous waters by courtesy of the Monikie Angling Club; on Monikie Reservoir and Crombie Reservoir, both excellent trout fisheries. Monikie lies within the Monikie Country park and there are two

Concentration—how to catch trout

waters, both available to visiting anglers. Trout average 12 oz and there is a generous bag limit of 12 fish per boat. Crombie lies to the north of Carnoustie and is also within a well-laid-out country park and wildlife sanctuary.

Fortunately, the fine quality trout are not included in the sanctuary designation and this long, narrow water can give great sport, particularly in the vicinity of the large island at the western end of the reservoir. Boat fishing only on Crombie and a deposit is asked for when booking. Return the key for the boat and your deposit is also returned.

Monk Myre Loch, close to Cupar Angus is another excellent little loch covering an area of 14 acres and containing trout of up to 3 lb; but the best of the trout fishing in this vicinity is to be found in Rescobie, one of Scotland's least-known and best-managed fisheries. Up to 1,000 rainbow trout are introduced each season, as well as good numbers of brown trout and fishing is readily available to visitors.

Rescobie lies to the east of Forfar and is managed by a hard-working association formed nearly 20 years ago. The association is a non-profit-making body; all revenue is used to improve and develop the fishery. There is a car park, landing stage, boathouse, first-class boats and good facilities for disabled anglers. Few lochs in Scotland can boast such consistently good sport. The average weight of rainbow trout is 1 lb 5 oz whilst brown trout average 1 lb 8 oz. Fish of over 6 lb are often caught and the loch superintendent, Jack Yule, is an expert angler, determined to maintain the highest possible standards.

Fish rise and are caught all over the loch. However, in the evening, trout tend to seek shallow waters and in the early months of the season Church Bay, at the west end of the loch, and Condor, at the east end, probably produce best results. The south shore is known as Green Bank and is the best bank fishing area. But, there again, many will tell you that Drimmie Bay and Drimmie Shallows on the north shore is where 'the action' is. Try them all and make up your own mind. Rescobie covers an area of 200 acres and is one mile long by about half a mile wide. Although Rescobie is easily accessible, it is rarely crowded and there is plenty of room for all. Bank fishing is possible round most of the shoreline and there are seven boats available. The loch is a haven for wildlife, both above and below the waters. Look into the west bay, out from the boathouse. There are the outlines of one of Scotland's few remaining crannogs, artificial islands, built during the Iron Age, almost 5,000 years ago.

In the surrounding hills is ample evidence of days past. Kemps Castle, overlooking the loch is another Iron Age fort; whilst at Battledykes, to the north-west of Rescobie, there is the site of a huge Roman camp, believed to have been large enough to accommodate 26,000 soldiers. As you watch the mist gathering among the weeds on warm summer evenings, spare a thought for these long-gone legionnaires, cursing over the steep Angus hills, dreaming of Mediterranean sun and their far-off home.

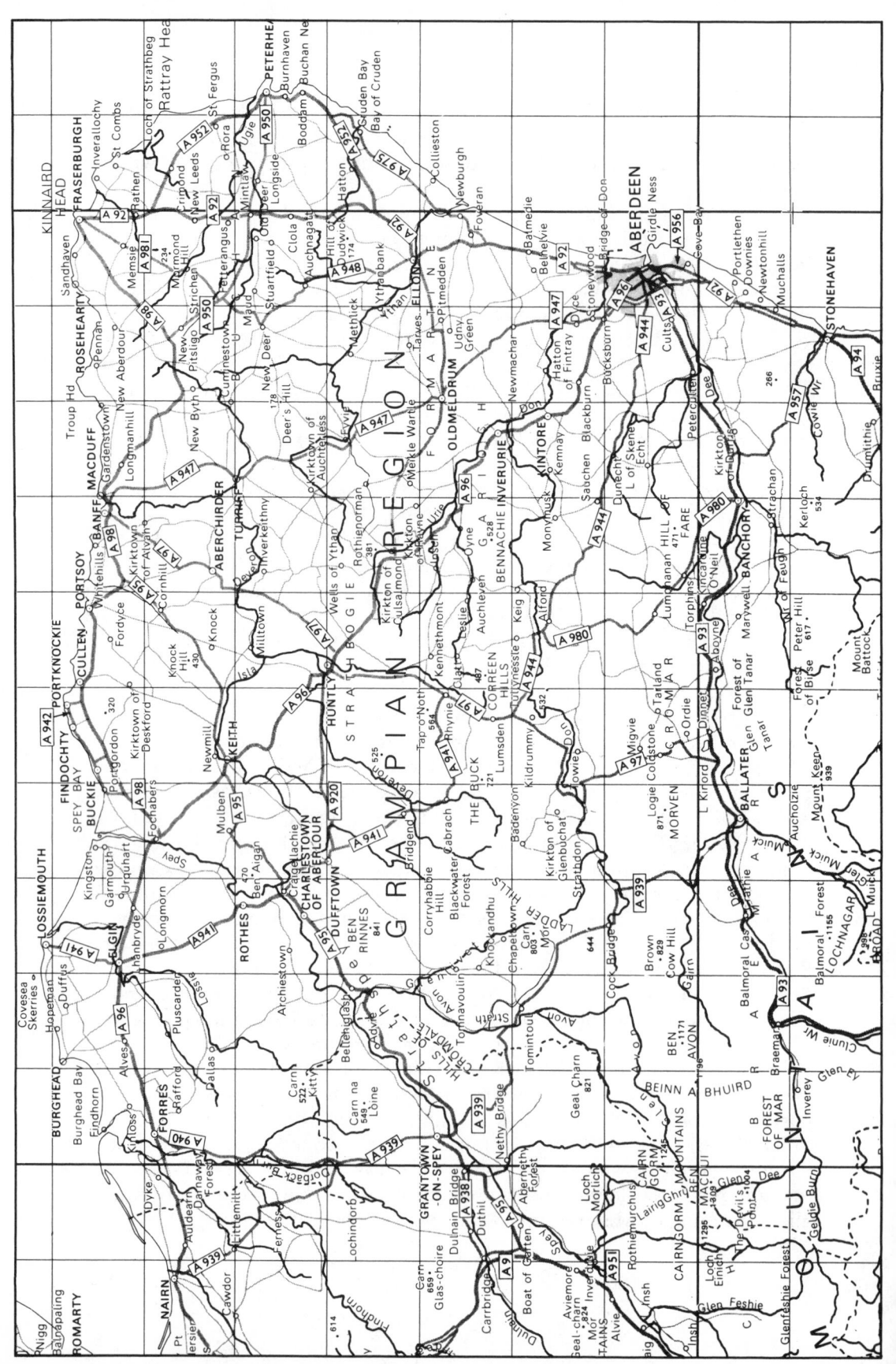

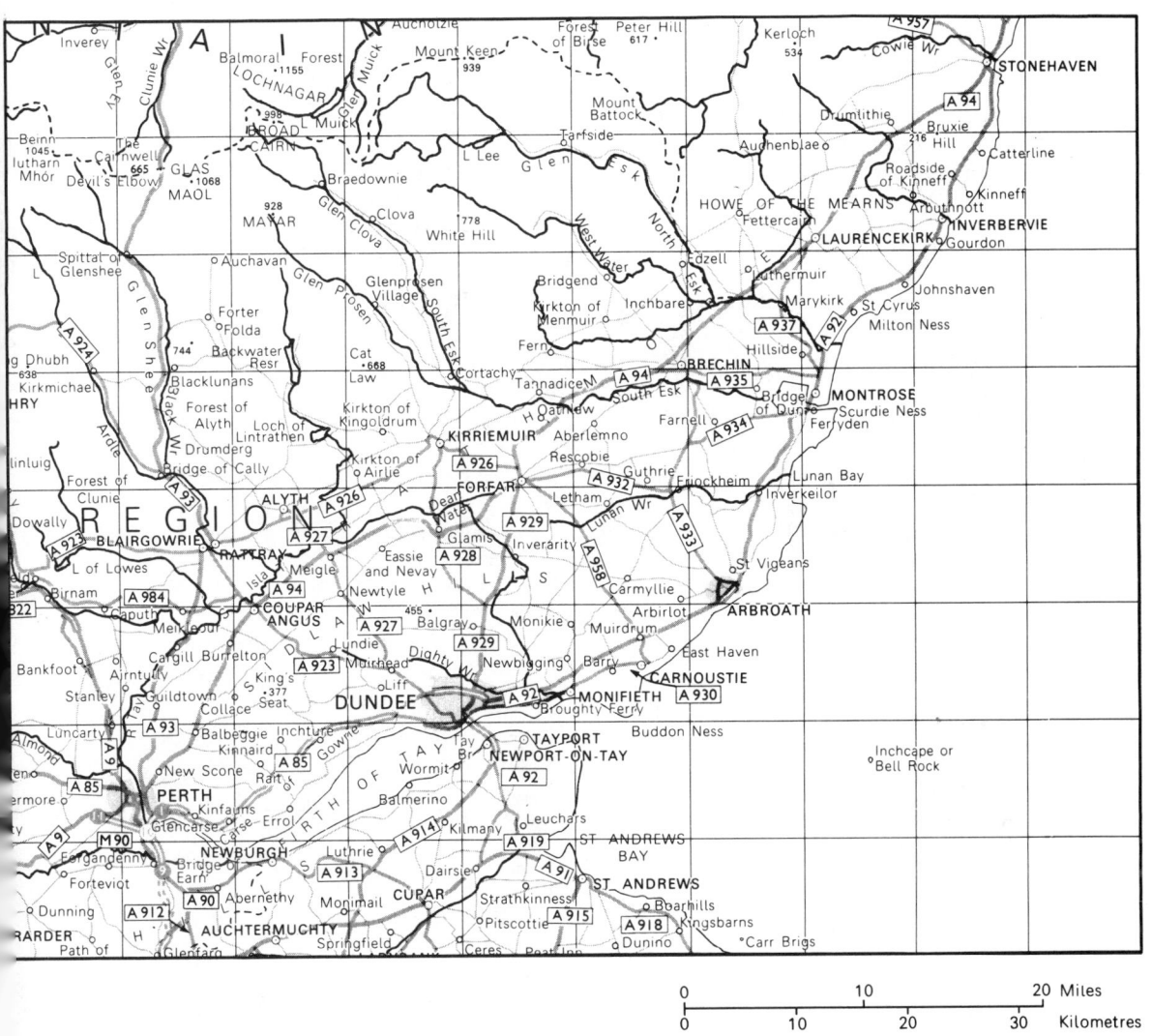

MORAVIA AND NORTH-EAST

FISHING DIRECTORY

SALMON, SEA TROUT AND BROWN TROUT FISHING
RIVER DON
MONYMUSK WATERS
Grant Arms Hotel,
Monymusk, Aberdeenshire
(04677) 226

KILDRUMMY WATERS
Kildrummy Fishings,
Hillary, Achnavenie, Kildrummy, Alford,
Aberdeenshire
(03365) 208

KEMNAY WATERS
F J and S L Milton,
Kemnay House, Kemnay, Aberdeenshire
(0467) 42220

STRATHDON WATERS
Colquhannie Hotel,
Strathdon, Aberdeenshire
(09752) 210

STRATHDON WATERS
Glenkirdie Arms Hotel,
Glenkirdie, Strathdon, Aberdeenshire
(097530) 288

KINTORE WATERS
Kintore Arms Inn,
Kintore, Aberdeenshire
(0467) 32216

ALFORD WATERS
The Forbes Estate,
Estate Office, Whitehouse, Alford
(0336) 2524

INVERURIE WATERS
J Duncan,
4 West High Street, Inverurie,
Aberdeenshire
(0467) 21363

RIVER BERVIE
W Davidson,
26 Provost Robson Drive, Lawrencekirk
(05617) 8140

RIVER COWIE
RIVER CARRON
Davids Sports Shop,
31 Market Square, Stonehaven

RIVER BOGIE
RIVER DEVERON
RIVER ISLA
Clerk of Fishings,
27 Duke Street, Huntly
(0466) 2291

RIVER DEVERON
Banff
Jay Tee Sports Shop,
Low Street, Banff
(02612) 5821
County Hotel,
High Street, Banff
(02612) 5353

Huntly
G Manson,
Sports Shop, Gordon Street, Huntly
(0466) 2482

Rothiemay
Forbes Arms Hotel,
Rothiemay, Huntly
(046681) 248

Turriff
Turriff Angling Association,
J Masson, The Cress, 6 Castle Street,
Turriff
(0888) 62428

RIVER FIDDICH
E & O Smith,
The Square, Dufftown
(Dufftown) 20358

RIVER UGIE
G Milne,
Newsagent, 3 Ugie Road, Peterhead
Robertson Sport,
1–3 Kirk Street, Peterhead
(0779) 72584

RIVER URIE
P McPherson,
Ironmonger, 45 Market Place, Inverurie
(0467) 21363

RIVER YTHAN
Ellon
Buchan Hotel,
Ellon, Aberdeenshire
(0358) 20208

Fyvie
Fyvie Angling Association,
G A Joss, Clydesdale Bank, Fyvie, Turiff
(06516) 233

RIVER LOSSIE
Elgin and District Angling Association,
The Tackle Shop, High Street, Elgin

RIVER FEUCH
Feuchside Inn,
Banchory
(033045) 225

RIVER LIVET
Richmond Arms Hotel,
Tomintoul
(08074) 209

MUCKLE BURN
Tackle Shop,
97D High Street, Forres
(0309) 72923

RIVER YTHAN
Methlick Waters
Haddo House Angling Association,
Kirton, Methlick, Ellon, Aberdeenshire

RIVER DEE
Braemar
Inverauld Arms Hotel,
Braemar
(03383) 605
Countrywear,
32 High Street, Ballater

Banchory
Banchory Lodge Hotel,
Banchory
(03302) 2625
MacSport,
High Street, Banchory
(03302) 3022

Blairs
Ardoe House Hotel,
Blairs, Aberdeen
(0224) 867355
James Thorburn,
Aboyne Business Centre, Old School,
Aboyne
(0339) 2347

TURRIFF BURN
MUCKLE BURN
BOYNE BURN
CHALET WATER
CROCGLASS
No permit required for these streams

RIVER FINDHORN
J Mitchell,
Tackle Shop, High Street, Forres
(0309) 72936
Cawdor Estate Office,
Cawdor, Nairn
The Factor,
Moray Estates Development Co, Forres

CLUNIE BURN
GAIRN BURN
Invercauld Arms,
Braemar
(03383) 605

PHILORTH WATER
Fraserburgh Angling Club,
G S Clark, 40 Cross Street, Fraserburgh
(03462) 4427

ANGUS AND NORTH – EAST FISHING DIRECTORY

LOCH DALLAS
P McKenzie,
79 High Street, Forres, Morayshire
(03092) 2111

LOCH MHIC LEOID
Strathspey Estate Office,
Grantown on Spey, Morayshire
(0479) 2529

TYNET TROUT FISHERY
The Manager,
Tynet Trout Fishery, Buckie, Banffshire
(05427) 295

BISHOPMILL TROUT FISHERY
The Manager,
Bishopmill Fisheries, Spynie Churchyard
Road, Elgin, Morayshire
(0343) 3875

GLEN LATTERACH RESERVOIR
Grampian Regional Council,
Water Services Dept, Grampian Road,
Elgin, Morayshire
(0343) 3361

LOCH-NA-BO
Kirloch,
Gardener's Cottage, Loch-Na-Bo,
Lharbryde, Elgin, Morayshire
(034384) 2214

MILLBUIES LOCHS
Dept of Recreation,
Moray District Council, 30/32 High Street,
Elgin, Morayshire
(0343) 45121 Ext 31
The Warden,
Millbuies Lochs, Elgin, Morayshire
(034386) 234

LOCH OF THE BLAIRS
Department of Recreation,
Moray District Council, 30/32 High Street,
Elgin
(0343) 45121 Ext 31
G Lilley,
79D High Street, Forres, Morayshire
(0309) 72936

LOCH OF STRATHBEG
Brown and McRae,
Anderson House, 9–11 Firthside Street,
Fraserburgh, Aberdeenshire
(03462) 4761

THE RED LOCH
G S Clark,
40 Cross Street, Fraserburgh,
Aberdeenshire
(03462) 4427

LORISTON LOCH
J Somers and Sons,
40 Thistle Street, Aberdeen
(0224) 50910

LOCH BEANIE
(Loch Shechernich)
Estate Office,
Invercauld Estate, Braemar, by Ballater,
Aberdeenshire
(03383) 224

LOCH NAN EUN
LOCH VROTACHAN
Invercauld Estate,
Braemar by Ballater, Aberdeenshire
(03383) 224

MILL OF ARTLOCH
Trout Farm
Mr Sommers Fishing Tackle,
Thistle Street, Aberdeen

FASQUE LAKE
Peter Gladstone,
Fasque, Fettercairn, Lawrencekirk,
Kincardineshire
(05614) 201

LOCH SAUGH
Drumtochy Arms Hotel,
Auchenblae, Kincardineshire
(05612) 210

LOCH LEE
Fred Taylor,
Invermark Estate Office, Glenesk, Angus
(03567) 208

LOCH BRANDY
LOCH WHARRAL
The Factor,
Airlie Estate Office, Cartachy, Kirriemuir,
Angus
(05754) 222

CROMBIE RESERVOIR
MONIKIE RESERVOIR
Monikie Angling Club,
Club Secretary, 30 Charleston Drive,
Dundee
(038235) 300

MONK MYRE LOCH
David Simpson,
Post Office, Cupar, Angus
(08282) 329

RESCOBIE LOCH
**Rescobie Loch Development
Association,**
Jack Yule, The Bailiff, South Lodge,
Reswallie, Forfar, Angus
(030781) 384

LOCH OF LINTRATHEN
Water Services Dept,
Ward Road, Dundee
(0382) 21164

BLACKWATER RESERVOIR
LOCH SHANDRA
Glenisla Hotel,
Glenisla, Angus
(057582) 223

LOCH DEAR
Mrs A Henderson,
364 Blackness Road, Dundee
(0382) 68062

DEN OF OGIE RESERVOIR
Canmore Angling Club,
Forfar

*SALMON AND SEA TROUT AND
BROWN TROUT*
NORTH ESK
Links Hotel,
Montrose, Angus
(0674) 72288
J Johnston and Sons Ltd,
3 America Street, Montrose
(0674) 72666

SOUTH ESK
Kirriemuir Angling Club,
13 Clara Road, Kirriemuir, Angus
(0575) 3456

LUNAN
Arbroath Angling Club,
Cycle and Tackle Centre, High Street,
Arbroath
(0241) 73467

RIVER ISLA & DEAN
**Strathmore Angling Improvement
Association,**
Mr A Henderson, 364 Blackness Road,
Dundee
(0382) 68062

RIVER ERICHT
Mr J Rattray,
Craighall, Blairgowrie
(0250) 2678

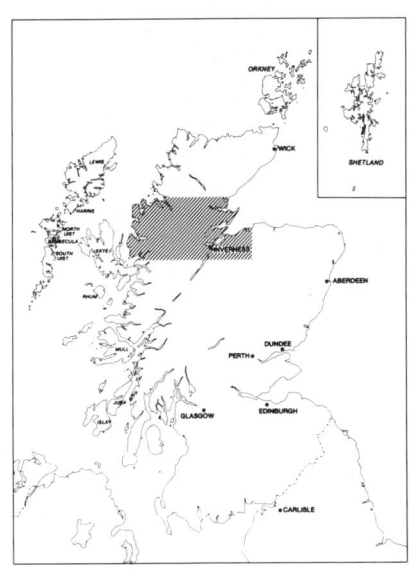

COIGACH,

LOVAT

AND AFFRIC

West and East Ross-shire

From Muir of Ord, north of Inverness, follow the road to Ullapool; past the Falls of Rogie, along the A835 by grey, windswept Loch Garvie. Ullapool was built by the British Fishery Society in 1788 to exploit the ever-growing demand for herring, then the main food for slaves in the plantations of the West Indies. But due to the wild, rocky nature of the coastline and unpredictability of arrival of herring, Ullapool never gained the same stature as Wick or the east coast centres along the Moray Firth. Nevertheless, even today Ullapool boasts a sizeable fishing fleet and plays host to many foreign vessels hunting the rich waters of the eastern Atlantic for prey and profit. Ullapool is the gateway to the Coigach of Ross, a fifth part of the Cromarties. In Roman times, Ptolemy noted that it was inhabited by the Carini tribe. In days of Norse domination the north of Scotland was known as the Province of Cat; hence Caithness, the eastern part, and Sutherland, the southern section. Hardy people still stalk the hills and moorlands of Coigach and Inverpolly, but with different ambitions, for Coigach is a wilderness of delight for climber, hill walker, naturalist and game fisherman. There are easily accessible roadside lochs, full of brown trout and one famous for the quality of its sea-trout fishing. Spate streams, such as the Ullapool and Polly, host salmon and offer an endless array of delightful hill waters, remote, distant and serene.

Accommodation in the area is easy to find and ranges from good hotels to welcoming bed and breakfast establishments. My wife Ann and I prefer the freedom of self-catering and recently found a prize bungalow overlooking the Summer Isles near Achiltibuie. There are many more, beautifully positioned, but it is always advisable to book well in advance because the area is very popular with discerning visitors.

Coigach offers all things to all people. There are magnificent, challenging mountains such as Ben More Coigach, Sgurr An Fhidhlier, Cul Mor and Cul Beag; and that most dramatic of all northern peaks, little Stac Polly, one of the most easily climbed and best loved Scottish mountains. The view from Stac Polly is magnificent. South and westwards, across the sparkling Summer Isles, the horizon is lined by dramatic peaks; the Cuillin of Skye, Harris and Lewis, the heather isles of the Outer Hebrides, and mighty An Tealach above Destitution Road in the Fosherfield Forest. Northwards, Cul Mor, Cul Beag, Suilven and the vast bulk of Ben More Assynt.

Good game fishing is everywhere and, like a long, silver chain, Lochs Lurgainn, Bad a'Ghaill and Osgaig grace the narrow valley between Coigach and Inverpolly. Lurgainn is four miles long by half a mile wide. Bad a'Ghaill is about two miles long by a mile wide with Oscaig of similar size and shape. The lochs are linked together and, in theory, it is possible to catch sea-trout in Lurgainn and Bad a'Ghaill but few are ever seen.

The Green Loch is a small loch between Lurgainn and Bad a'Ghaill and in high water levels a boat may be hauled over the bar in order to get afloat. A small, trout-filled stream joins Bad a'Ghaill to Oscaig and the system exits at the west end of the loch, down the rocky River Garvie to the sea.

In spite of their proximity to civilisation, none of these waters is heavily fished. It is the exception, rather than the rule, to see any boats out and to see more than one boat would be extraordinary. Therefore, it is difficult to be accurate regarding what you are likely to catch. However, one thing is certain, Lurgainn and Bad a'Ghaill are typical Highland trout lochs, packed with large stocks of 8-oz trout and large baskets are the rule. But there are much larger fish lurking in the depths. The trouble is that no one really bothers to spend time looking for them. I mean trolling for ferox; even more so, using traditional wet-fly methods to tempt the 3–4 lb fish that undoubtedly feed in the shallow waters, close to the shore. The barman from the Royal Hotel, Ullapool, fishing on Lurgainn, found one in 1986, a super brown trout of 5 lb 12 oz.

Matters are a lot simpler on Loch Osgaig, and this fine water is perhaps one of the best yet least known sea-trout fisheries in the north. Osgaig is the most westerly of the waters lying adjacent to the road from Drumrunie on the A835 and the loch is one and a quarter miles long by up to three-quarters of a mile wide. Sea-trout make the journey from sea to loch with ease and fish run the short river from late June, the main runs coming in July when good sport may be had, boat fishing from Summer Isles Hotel boats. The north end of Osgaig fishes best and you should arrange your drifts accordingly. Another good place to try is in the tree-lined south bay and along the south-west shoreline. Remember, sea-trout tend to roam so it is often a case of going to them, rather than waiting for them to come to you. If you do find the shoals, look out for action, for sea-trout of up to 7 lb are taken most seasons.

178

The River Garvie drains Oscaig through Loch Garvie, a hesitation on its short journey to the sea in Garvie Bay. Loch Garvie is a weedy pond, difficult to fish and from the bank only; but rewards for effort can be spectacular and given the right conditions Garvie can produce outstanding sport. Even on a bad fishing day, this is a perfect place to take the family. Just over the small hill to the north of the loch, at the mouth of the river, is one of Scotland's classic beaches: a promise of undisturbed peace and solitude. Picnic time. Shining white sands washed by green, foam-flecked waves, rolling across Enard Bay from the Atlantic. Suilven crowds the northern horizon whilst Stac Polly, seen end on, looks almost unassailable.

North of this line of lochs lies the Inverpolly National Nature Reserve, covering more than 40 square miles. An area where you may walk all day without meeting another soul; where you will share the lonely solitude of a remote lochan with red-throated diver or otter; a place of secret corries and corners, raven and red deer. Where a sudden storm can sweep down making even the best prepared shrink. Where the shimmering heat of a blistering summer day can lull you to drowsy sleep, on a tree-fringed, soft, sandy shore.

At the heart of Inverpolly lies that Ross-shire jewel, lovely Loch Sionascaig. Two square miles of shimmering water, enclosed by shores that meander in and out round bay and headland for a distance of more than 16 miles. I can tell you the facts and record the names, but what I can't do is properly describe the sheer beauty of Sionascaig. Go there and find out for yourself is what I mean. The loch can't be seen from the road but park at the quarry at grid reference 094151. Across the road from the parking place a track leads down to the lochside and the walk is an easy ten minutes. Longer if you are lugging an outboard motor. Sionascaig can be a wild and windy place and what might start out as a calm summer morning can very quickly change into an uncontrollable storm.

An outboard motor is essential. As, I would suggest, are floatation jackets in case of emergencies. Carefully secure the outboard motor. Tie it in. Tie in oars also. And don't forget to make provision for our little Highland friends, the midges. Even this paradise has its quota and they can attack in Exocet-like swarms with ferocious determination. Be prepared.

Sionascaig contains huge ferox, brown trout and char; and from time to time there have been efforts to make it accessible to salmon, from the Polly River which drains from the loch at the south-west. Local feeling has it that the next record-breaking British brown trout lurks somewhere in the depths and certainly fish of more than 16 lb have been caught over the years. Best fishing areas are in the shallow waters round the margins and in the vicinity of the islands. Landing on the islands is not permitted since they are important nesting sites for birds. Nevertheless, don't be too surprised should you see a stag swimming towards one of them. They graze on the islands and obviously haven't read the small print on the permit.

If you are limited for time and perhaps have only a single day, I suggest you start by inching round the largest island, Eilean Mor. Then try the smaller island, adjacent to it. Next, enter the large bay on the east side of the loch and carefully fish round, paying particular attention to where the feeder burns enter near the Sheiling. Take great care and keep a close look out for underwater boulders. Also take spare sheer pins for the engine. Just in case.

During service for Queen and country, in the late 1950s, I used to lead, with unerring accuracy, convoys of vehicles through rebel-infested mountains in Southern Arabia. This does not, however, qualify me for map reading in the north of Scotland. Ann does it all. Just because once, well, perhaps twice, I made slight errors of judgment.

I am told by Clan Sandison, unkindly, that trail blazing, if left to me, would mean spending most of the day going round in ever-decreasing circles getting nowhere: other that is, than you know where, and would they want that? Which is why I found myself one morning, resting in Inverpolly, near Sionascaig, whilst Ann planned our route ahead. The objective was one of our favourite lochs, Doire na h-Airbhe, between Sionascaig and the northern slopes of Stac Polly. Earlier that morning we had parked the car near Loch Dail, the lower of the Polly Lochs, and, gallant to the last, Ann on my back, forded the little river and set off, eastwards, up the hill.

No matter how experienced you are, or think you are, never take chances in the hills. Always make sure that someone knows where you are going and when you expect to return. Be well shod, warmly clad and carry spare clothing. Also have a compass and map, and know how to use them. Spring sunlight warmed my back as I followed Ann down into Gleann na Gaoithe, The Glen of the Wind, by a small stream, tumbling over rocks and boulders. This is the outlet burn from the loch and with renewed confidence and quickening step we followed it up the valley.

Loch na h-Airbhe is one mile long by a quarter of a mile wide; the name means 'loch of the oak grove' and along the south shore trees cluster unexpectedly, providing welcome shelter when cold winds blow. However, that morning, the weather was perfect and our first action upon arrival was to cool off with a splash in the loch.

The west end of the loch produces an endless flow of small, well-shaped trout and here wading is safe and easy; it is possible to cast a fly far out into the loch; relatively speaking, given my casting ability. As you progress eastwards, however, the water deepens and the bank becomes much steeper. Soon, rather than later, it is 'mountain goat' time and you find yourself casting from high above the loch.

Look out for great action; after that first swirl, when, by the time you have decided that it really was a fish, it has gone. Concentrate, because all the way along this steep bank is good fishing from the start of the first

180

The Loch of the Night.

bay, round to the hazel tree. We had constant sport here and kept three good fish, each weighing just under 1 lb. Landing them was difficult and a long-handled net would have been a great asset. Otherwise, get your partner to hold on to your heels whilst you dreep down. Important not to have fallen out with said partner first. Otherwise, you could have a closer look at the fish than you expected.

The east end of Doire na h-Airbhe is easier to fish and every bit as exciting. You will find a shelf of rock, over shallow water, and excellent trout lie here. Eastwards again, the hillside is tree-clad and idyllic. We had lunch there, and lazed and slept in afternoon sun. When we wakened, two wasted fishing hours later, it was time to head for home. For variety, that day, we walked round the north shore and stopped for a few casts in an

181

unnamed lochan on the hill. Here again, trout rose readily to the fly, hard-fighting and averaging about three to the pound. The walk back to the Polly Lochs was hard and typically Ross-shire: wet, soggy and tiring.

This time we arrived at Upper Polly and followed down the steep bank to where it flows out into the next lower water. It is possible to cross dry-shod here, although it involves some minor mountaineering, over fences and across a narrow 'suspect' bridge. We made it safely and walked through the evening woods, arriving at the car just before the midges. A monument to excellent planning.

It is always hard to stop talking about na h-Airbhe because, like being there, you wish the day would go on forever. As I write, looking southwards from my window over Loch Watten and wild Caithness moors, the call of the 'loch of the oak grove' is always there, tempting and pleasurable. Something to look forward to with a wonderful sense of anticipation.

The Polly River, which drains out of Sionascaig and na h-Airbhe crosses the twisting Aird of Coigach road from Badnagyle to Lochinver where the estate has established a large salmon hatchery. Salmon fishing on this little river is, like most west coast streams, very much dependent upon water levels. Whilst good brown trout inhabit the stream above the hatchery, including the chain of three deep, dour lochs at its head, most sport with salmon is from the hatchery down to the sea at Enard Bay. Access is from the road that runs out to Inverpolly Lodge, on the headland of Rubha Phollaidh, and the slow-moving stream can produce excellent sport. Fishing is preserved for the Estate but it is always worth inquiring to see if a rod might be available. Backing up is the best method of fooling Polly salmon and when a fish does take, playing it in the narrow confines of the stream requires considerable skill.

In days past, the Polly was famous for another type of fishing, just as rewarding though much colder, wetter work: pearl fishing. So if all else fails you could try your hand in order to raise funds for future fishing expeditions. Never know your luck and over the years this lovely river has produced some magnificent pearls—and some magnificent salmon.

Westwards from Oscaig lie Achnahaird and Achiltibuie and the desolate, remote moorlands of Rubha Mor, a trackless land sprinkled with more than 20 delightful trout lochs. Most have lots of small fish; but some contain trout of over 2 lb. Find out for yourself by walking and fishing which are which. It is worth the effort for this is the stuff from which fishing dreams are made. Leave the car at Achnahaird and forget the world for a day.

There are also two substantial roadside waters for the less adventurous, Raa and Vatachan and both hold excellent trout, along with a large supply of more traditional Highland brownies. Because of their exposed position these lochs become very windy but do not let this fact deter you too much since bank fishing is just as productive as is fishing from a boat.

The roadside lochs are enjoyable and exciting to fish but best of all, in my opinion, are the hill lochs. Whilst you may not find an occupant for the ever-ready glass case above the mantel, you will find something just as rewarding: the special pleasure of catching breakfast, won after hard exercise and welcome rest. The most dramatic of Coigach hill lochs is Lochan Tuath, a blue sheet below the massive bulk of Sgurr an Fhidhleir. A less taxing, although just as rewarding day out can be made to the group of lochs to the north-east of the Summer Isles Hotel. After an invigorating tramp of about one hour you will reach Lochan Sgeireach, where the trout will happily rise to meet you. East of Sgeireach lie three further small waters all worth a visit and a cast: Lochans Leacach, Fada and Ballach.

We have had some glorious days in Coigach and if you have to arrange your fishing holidays round the needs of non-fishing members, or are blessed with little ones, then this area has something for everyone. There are safe beaches for the bucket-and-spade brigade, the delights of Ullapool for wet days and plenty to keep every member happy whilst you get on with man's proper function in life: the removal of fish from their natural habitat. And after a day out in the hills, or an afternoon wrestling with sea-trout on Oscaig, what better way to end than with a visit to the food-famous Summer Isles Hotel? Or with a quiet pint in the little pub at Altandhu? Or, better still, stock up from the sea-food shop in the village and retire to your cottage for a meal to remember.

Coigach and Inverpolly offer all that makes fishing important to me: solitude, scenery, bird-song and silence, apart that is, from the happy sound of rising trout. The size of fish and numbers caught are unimportant compared to that. Keanchulish House sits at the mouth of the twin rivers, Runie and Kanaird. The system produces good numbers of salmon and sea-trout and fishing is in the hands of Keanchulish and Langwell Estates. Kanaird is the better of the two streams, rising from Rappach with a series of lochs and lochans at the head of Strath nan Lon, between Cromalt Hills and Rhidorroch Forest.

The little River Runie is made of sterner stuff, gathering its waters from the streams and lochs of Ben More Coigach to the west and scree-covered Cul Beag north. The two rivers meet in the Junction Pool, perhaps the best pool on the river, and then sparkle seawards to Loch Kanaird and Isle Martin, The Holy Isle of Coigach.

Considerable effort has been sustained during recent years on agricultural improvement works at Keanchulish and some years ago I was involved with the drainage of one of the deep peat plateaus north of the river. A small pumping station was then in operation, because of the level nature of the surrounding land, in order to keep things dry and in good order for growing vegetables. Salmon didn't seem to mind too much and I remember seeing several great runs of fish into the system. One afternoon, as we crossed the bridge over the river, I noticed a salmon, beached on a sandbank in the middle of the stream. I waded over the river and examined the fish. As far as I could see, there was nothing amiss, so I carefully picked the fish up and held it, head upstream, until it shot off. However, after an initial surge, the fish turned back and swam by me, seawards. It turned and rushed upstream once, heading straight for the same shingle bank, and arrived back at my feet. This was repeated several times before the salmon, a bright, silver, sea-liced bar, got its direction right and disappeared leaving watching seagulls disconsolate and dinner-less.

Fishing on these rivers is reserved but rods are sometimes available and it is always worth inquiring. The Ullapool River is more available to visiting anglers and can provide sport, given good water levels. Although rocky in nature, there are a number of good holding pools and fishing is divided into three beats, with the middle beat producing best results.

Highland Coastal Estates let fishing on the Ullapool River, and also have a number of really excellent cottages and lodges for rental in Glen Achall. Fishing is included, on Loch Achall, River Rhidorroch and Loch an Daimh and a number of good hill lochs. The scenery is superb and these properties are ideal for a family party wishing to escape the pressures of everyday life and find a few moments of absolute peace in the wilds.

Closer to civilisation, in the hills above Ullapool, are a series of trout lochs readily available to visiting anglers and known as the Dam Lochs. The road up leaves the A835 seven miles north from town and, as we say in the north, 'you can't miss it'. This time, however, it is true because the road up follows the line the hydro-pipes, down to the power station on the banks of the Kanaird River. Drive this way with great care. The road is very narrow and very steep. Coming back down is even nicer and you should take great care. The Dam Lochs used to be three separate waters, now joined together and there are fine trout to be caught. The variations in water levels makes things difficult at times, but this is still a pleasant place to spend a few hours fishing.

Less easy to get to but in much more dramatic surroundings, are the Leckmelm Hill lochs, four miles south from Ullapool, along the north shore of Loch Broom. A track climbs Strath Nimhe, from north-east of Tir Aluinn Hotel and this gives moderately easy access to the hill. However, once 'up' that is only the start. To reach the Leckmelm lochs, you have to leave the track and take to the heather. A hard, uphill slog north.

Why bother? Because, quite simply, these lochs are splendid. Not only in the quality of their fish but also in the quality of their setting; remote, secret, inviting and exciting. Classic Scottish hill lochs. There are about 15 waters here, close together and you may spend the day walking and fishing many of them. Some have really excellent trout; others more modest fish. The pleasure of fishing here lies in wondering what is going to come next: penny plain or three pound foolish. At the end of the day, stagger back down the hill to the Leckmelm holiday cottages, a group of comfortable self-catering chalets, complete with central heating, open fires and colour TV. There is lots for non-fishers to do as well: pony trekking, boating, golf and water sports. But for me the call of the hills and the fine fish of these delightful little lochs is always foremost. Rest weary feet and plot the following day's assault.

The River Broom, at the head of sea-loch Broom by Inverlael, used to be a good salmon stream but in recent years a hydroelectric scheme has robbed the river of all but compensation flow. Salmon and sea-trout still run the river, arriving about July and, with good water levels, some sport may be had. It all depends upon being in the right place at the right time. The famous Corrieshalloch Gorge and Measach Falls bar the way for returning fish, who head south up Abhainn Cuileig in search of Loch a'Bhraoin.

In the hills to the south of the River Broom are a number of lochs, all offering good sport in magnificent surroundings. But you have to work hard to experience their special magic. Tracks lead out from Auchlunachan and access is also possible from the road that skirts the south shore of Loch Broom. You may also approach from Dundonnell and Strath Beag, where a track leads out of Creag a'Chadha, and round Beinn nam Ban to Alt na h-Airbhe, where the ferry from Ullapool lands.

But the most dramatic view here is of An Teallach (1,065 m), a mighty intimidating shriek daring you on, dominating Strathnasheallag Forest. Dundonnell River hurries down Strath Beag to Little Loch Broom and fishing on this stream is available from either the Estate Office or the comfortable Dundonnell Hotel. Arrive after heavy rain, in the autumn and look out for action. The river holds salmon and sea-trout in reasonable numbers then.

South from An Teallach, in the heart of the Fisherfield Forest, is the Fionn Loch; where, even on a bad day, you will almost certainly catch fish; where rawest recruits to the gentle art will find sport; where the world's greatest duffers end their day convinced that they are 'complete anglers', worthy descendants of the father of angling, Izaac Walton.

Scotland's most famous basket of brown trout was caught on Fionn on 12 April 1851. Osgood Mackenzie, in his book, *A Hundred Years in the Highlands*, describes the event: 'There were four beauties lying side by side on the table of the small drinking room, and they turned the scales at 51 lb. The total weight of the 12 fish caught that 12 day of April by trolling was 87 lb 12 oz.'

Another record catch from Fionn was made by Mr F. C. McGrady fishing Fionn in June and July 1912, taking a total of 3,625 trout weighing 1,410 lb. Fifteen of these fish weighed more than 3 lb, the largest being 8 lb 4 oz. Mr McGrady noted that all small trout—under six inches—were thrown back. Goodness knows what Mr McGrady wanted with all these fish. If he was trying to reduce the overall population, in order to leave more food for remaining fish, thus increasing their size, he did a good job;

Fionn Loch, 'The White Loch'. Gairloch gem

but I find it impossible to consider this 'sport', even if carried out in the interests of fishery management, which it was not, otherwise he would not have thrown the little ones back.

Fionn lies between Little Loch Broom and Loch Maree, an area 15 miles long by 12 miles wide. Thirty-five mountains, 18 of which rise to over 3,000 ft crowd the Fisherfield and Letterewe forests; crowned by graceful Slioch (984 m), the Spear, overlooking Loch Maree in the south and An Teallach north.

The 'bright loch' is six miles long by up to one and a half miles wide and falls to a depth of 150 ft near Carnmore Bothy. Draining westwards down Little Gruinard river, Fionn reaches the sea in Gruinard Bay, guarded by infamous Gruinard Island, used for anthrax experiments during the last war, recently decontaminated. Eastwards, Fionn is dominated by magnificent peaks; Ben Lair (861 m), the Mountain of the Mare; A'Mhaighdean (936 m), the Maiden; Meall Mheinnidh (731 m), the Grassy Hill and Beinn a'Chaisgein Mor (857 m) the Forbidding Mountain. The only forbidding aspect of Fionn, however, is getting there. On foot, it is a walk of more than six miles. We travelled out in a bone-shaking Land-Rover, but even then it is a long journey. Worth every rattle and lurch, for Fionn is one of Scotland's special places, offering everything that is best in fishing; solitude, silence, wild empty hills, a circling eagle and the exciting sound of rising trout.

In 1963, one happy angler took 21 fish weighing 63 lb, the heaviest being 11 lb and even today, with trolling banned, most seasons produce trout of over 5 lb and salmon and sea-trout also enter Fionn by way of the Little Gruinard River; but few anglers fish for them, preferring to concentrate upon their smaller, more accommodating cousins. Nevertheless, when we last fished Fionn, we saw a good salmon rise, close to the shore in Old Boathouse Bay and several records were broken as we quickly changed to larger flies.

The bay at the north end, split by the promontory of Aird Dhubh, offers good sport and another favourite area is in the shelter of Eilean Fraoch. But perhaps the most productive drift is down the south shore, from New Boathouse Bay, scattered with huge, underwater rocks, shallows and sudden deep pots. Take care and hasten slowly to avoid accidents.

Our day on Fionn proved the point about the quality of fishing. It was not just a bad day. It was appalling. The wind howled, and we sat, rain-soaked and frozen, with gritted teeth and determined not to give in. When we were finally forced ashore, there were 12 fish in the boat. My wife Ann caught six, our fishing partner, John Corbin caught six. I caught the rest. After all, I suppose, even great duffers have their off days.

The principal salmon streams in the area are the Gruinard and Little Gruinard Rivers, which flow down from the vastness of Fisherfield entering the sea through a semi-circle of golden sands. Park the family safely and head for the hills. Gruinard is the best of these two streams and also has good runs of sea-trout; beginning life in Loch na Sealga, below An Teallach, collecting in streams from Loch Ghiubhsechain, Beinn Dearg, Mor Bad an Ducharaich, an Eich Dhuibh and Gaineamhaich along the way.

There are more than 30 pools and runs throughout the system and the river is divided into three beats. Best sport is from July onwards but the river has a reputation for producing good sport with large sea-trout early on in the season, although runs have declined in recent years. A good track follows the south bank of the river all the way to Loch na Sealga, where there is a boathouse and boat. If you wish to explore and fish further into the hills, follow the track along the north shore of Sealga, by the west shoulder of Sgurr Ruadh. One of the most dramatic walks in Ross-shire. Good trout fishing along the way.

Little Gruinard enters the sea a mile or so south from the main river and, like its more notable neighbour, you need good water levels for decent sport. Apart from the obvious pools, in high water levels you may catch fish throughout the system as it tumbles down from Fionn in search of Gruinard Bay. Recently, the Estate has done much to improve the track that edges the south bank of the river and it is now possible to drive right out to Fionn in relative comfort.

To the west of Gruinard is the Rubha Mor Peninsula and this is approached by the little road from Laide in the north, which leaves the A832 close to the ruined Chapel of Sand, built by St Columba in the 7th century. The road leads out to Mellon Udrigle and Opinan. On the other side of the peninsula, another convenient road winds along the shore of Loch Ewe from Aultbea to Mellon Charles and this is traditional Highland crofting country, much influenced by the Royal Navy during the two world wars.

During the Great War, the Tenth Cruiser Squadron was based in Loch Ewe and used it as a coaling station and even today the Royal Navy has a considerable presence. So do brown trout and they are all waiting for your carefully presented fly. A minor road runs across the moors from near Achgarve to Slaggan and this gives easy access to the lovely lochs and lochans in the vicinity of Beinn Dearg Mhor. Reaching the furthest out waters, at Greenstone Point, is not quite so easy. Hiking time, but marvellous sport at the end of the trek.

One of Scotland's most famous sea-trout systems enters Loch Ewe by the little village of Poolewe at the head of the long sea loch. For decades anglers have made the pilgrimage north to fish the River Ewe and the outstanding waters of lovely Loch Maree. The river used to produce good numbers of salmon but catches have declined. However, what has been lost to the River Ewe seems to have been gained at the top of the system, in the Kinlochewe River and its tributaries and in recent years, particularly

1987, excellent sport was had, especially during autumn months.

However, the star attraction here is Loch Maree itself; running like a silver scar below Slioch, the spear, north and the majestic hills of Beinn Eighe National Reserve to the south. For many centuries, pilgrims other than anglers visited the loch; to sail over to Eilean Ma-Ruibhe, a tiny island off the north shore. There is an old tree-trunk on the island, by the 'well of wishing' and struck into the bare trunk are hundreds of coins—offerings of pilgrims, who wished and then left their token of payment.

The island is reputed to have been the home of the monk who gave Loch Maree its name, Maol Rubha, The Red Priest, who is buried in the churchyard of Applecross, south over Torridon. The island is endowed with magic qualities and was supposed to provide a cure for insanity. The patient knelt before the altar, drank some of the water from the well and left his coin in the bark of the tree. The madman was then rowed a few times round the island, dunked three times in the loch and all was well. Or supposed to be. I have seen anglers to this day, fishless and despondent, rowing quietly round the saintly island, deep in prayer, wishing all the time.

There are two old stones on the island, each marked with a cross, the burial place of a Viking Prince and his intended bride. To test her lover's faith the young woman pretended to be dead and had herself rowed out to meet her Prince's returning longship. Before the truth of the matter was exposed, the grief-stricken man stabbed himself to death. The unhappy couple were buried side by side on the island.

Sea-trout fishing on Loch Maree is a less dangerous affair and the ten-year average catch for this splendid water is over 1,000 fish per season. Best fishing has traditionally always been in the hands of the Loch Maree Hotel and sea-trout run the river to the loch from mid-June onwards with the most productive time being late July and August. There are ten beats, Back of Islands, Fool's Rock and Pig's Bay, Weedy Bay, Gruide, Hotel, North Shore, Ash Island, Coree, Isle Maree and Steamer Channel.

In 1988 the Loch Maree Hotel fishings were offered for the first time on a syndication scheme, involving 12 prime weeks; with a right to purchase fishing for a week for a period of 21 years. However, the hotel has retained some rights for guests and both Sheildaig Lodge and Flowerdale House have boats; as does the Kinlochewe Hotel at the south end of Maree. Trick is to book well in advance because Maree is a much sought after fishery and always busy.

Gairloch is the centre of tourist and commercial activity in this part of Ross-shire and during summer months it is a busy, bustling village. Thousands of visitors flock to the famous Inverewe Gardens, begun in 1865 by Osgood Mackenzie, now containing some 2,500 species of plants gathered from around the world. Seaton Gordon, stationed at Aultbea during the Great War, recalls 'seeing a mimosa tree in full bloom at

Christmas and eucalyptus trees as high as the well-grown Scots firs which surrounded them'.

Children play on Gairloch's shining sands or splash in clear waters, warmed by the Gulf Stream. There are excellent restaurants, hotels, museums, craft centres, golf courses, pony trekking, sailboarding and Highland safaris. Indeed, something for everyone.

But the shores of the Short Loch were not always so peaceful. Famine and eviction during the 19th century brought ruin and disaster to the north. When Lowland granaries were full, Highlanders starved. People went barefoot, clothed in meal bags, while Free Church ministers appealed in vain to Edinburgh and London for help. Lord Napier, leading a Royal Commission in 1882, reported: 'a state of misery, or wrong-doing, and of patent long-suffering, without parallel in the history of our country.' The open-air pulpit of the Free Presbyterian Church is a reminder of these sad times, when sheep were preferred to people, when young and old alike laboured for Destitution Boards or accepted the blandishments of Emigration Societies and took ship for the Colonies. Packed abroad with £1, a bible, a blessing and not much else. Today, a new wind of hope is blowing throughout the Highlands and the sympathetic development of Gairloch as a major tourist centre is evidence of respect for the past and confidence in the future.

For the visiting angler, Gairloch is an ideal place to set up camp. The local angling club offers trout fishing on more than 20 hill lochs, lying between Loch Maree and the sea. Getting out to the best of them involves a hard walk but it is worth the effort and you will be rewarded with some of the grandest views in Scotland along your way; and, if you are lucky, baskets of excellent quality wild brown trout.

The association also has fishing on Loch Bad an Sgalaig, to the south of the A832, and this water contains pike, introduced in Victorian times. It also contains some good brown trout and in 1986 produced a basket of five fish weighing 6 lb. A German visitor recently had a pike of 20 lb one day and three brown trout weighing 3 lb 8 oz the next. Further on from Bad an Sgalaig, by the shores of Am Feur Loch, is a hut and parking place. A track crosses the outlet stream and this leads south, to some of the finest fishing in the north. Takes about two and a half hours' hike to reach it, but what better way to start a holiday than with a good long walk? Brush away office cobwebs and set off for a magnificent, silent land, where mighty peaks sparkle in summer sunlight and golden eagles wheel and glide over a landscape that has remained unchanged for thousands of years.

Your destination is Loch na h-Oidhche, the 'loch of the night', in the heart of the Flowerdale Forest. It lies at an altitude of 1,450 ft and there is a good track all the way. Na h-Oidhche is one and a half miles long by about half a mile wide. The clear waters drop to a depth of over 100 ft and the best fishing areas are close to the shore. If you can't see the bottom, you are too far out.

The north bay and along the west shore is perhaps the most productive. Tiny rivulets cascade down from Baosbheinn, 'the wizard's mountain' and fish gather to feed on flies and grubs washed from the hill. The south bay is also shallow and can provide great sport, particularly between the small island and the far bank. Take care, however, for there are several large underwater boulders ready to catch the unwary outboard. Keep a sharp lookout and never start the outboard motor until you are well clear of the margins. This is especially true at the north end, so row out, cautiously, then start the motor.

Loch na h-Oidhche trout are perfectly matched and all weigh in the order of 12oz. As an example of what to expect, a recent party of four anglers, spending three days fishing, returned with a basket of 50 fish, all trout being almost identical in shape and size; but these wild brown trout fight furiously and what they may lack in size they more than make up for in spirit.

Flies that do most damage include these good friends: Soldier Palmer, Black Pennel, Greenwell's Glory, Peter Ross, Grouse and Claret and Zulus. Weather conditions will dictate the size. Indeed, weather conditions will dictate whether or not you fish at all because this can be a violent, stormy place. The wind rushes down the loch, funnelled between the mountains with astonishing force, building up waves that would look respectable in the Pentland Firth, let alone a Highland trout loch. So, if in doubt, don't launch the boat. Stay safely ashore and fish the lee side. You will not have to cast far to be amongst them because the bottom shelves very steeply and wading is neither necessary nor advisable.

At the south end of Loch na h-Oidhche, sheltered by Beinn an Eoin, 'the mountain of the birds', stands Poca Buidhe and the yellow stone. The hollow beneath this huge granite boulder provided overnight shelter for anglers in days gone by. The long walk to the 'loch of the night' leaves little time for fishing, unless you camp out. Furthermore, best fishing times are early morning or late evening, so anglers used to rest at Poca Buidhe, waiting for the right moment to attack.

Today, there is less uncomfortable accommodation and a good bothy is sometimes available for an overnight stay. Civilisation is ten miles distant, at Gairloch, so you have to carry everything you need with you. But, once installed, you are alone amidst a mountain and moorland wilderness. Southward, lies Beinn Alligin, 'the mountain of beauty' and Sgurr Mhorr, 'the great rocky peak', Beinn Dearg, 'the red mountain' and Carn na Feola, 'the hill of the flesh'.

On a calm morning in 1986, accompanied by our two dogs, a large, boisterous golden retriever and a hardy Yorkshire terrier, my wife Ann and I left the bothy and followed the track southwards to explore the

191

waters between Beinn an Eoin and mighty Liathac, 'the grey one'. The track ends a few hundred yards from Poca Buidhe and from there on the going is rough, very rough.

South of na h-Oidhche lies Gorm Loch Fada and Gorm Loch na Beinne. They contain excellent brown trout and fish of up to 3 lb have been caught here. Na Beinne is my favourite: promontories, fishy corners, sandy bays, interesting weed beds. These lochs fish best during the day, so the ideal plan is to fish them in daylight hours, then return in the evening to do battle with na h-Oidhche trout. But the most startling aspect of fishing here is the sudden shock of your first glimpse of Ruadh-stac Mor (1,012 m), Sail Mhor (984 m) and the famous Triple Buttress of A'Choinneach Mhor. Be assured, as you are gazing, mouth-wide in astonishment at these magnificent peaks, that is when the 3 lb trout will grab the fly. That's what happened to me. I lost the fish but will never lose the memory of that stunning view.

We walked south from Loch na Beinne, across wide granite pavements, and onto the moor. An hour later we reached the shores of Lochan Carn na Feola, below the eastern peak of Beinn Dearg. The ordnance survey map shows only one loch but in fact there are two sections, quite separate. After a few, fruitless casts, we tramped on, aiming for Loch nan Cabar which nestles between Beinn Dearg and Sail Mhor, and fished it for an hour. It was full of little trout, well marked and eager to rise. One or two harder tugs indicated, perhaps, something larger in the depths but we returned all the fish, to fight another bay. Just being there was enough.

The march back to civilisation was 'something else'. After a meal at the bothy, we loaded the boat and set north down Loch na h-Oidhche. The loch of the night turned nasty, halfway home; huge waves building up, driven by rising wind. As we neared the mooring bay, at breakneck speed, I cut the outboard and leapt into the shallows to avoid being driven onto the rocks. Tired, wet but safe, we secured the boat, then set off on the last leg of our journey. The miles slipped by, almost unnoticed. All Scotland seemed to be laid out before us. The mountains of Assynt shimmered north; Suilven, Ben More, Canisp and Quinag. Westwards over the broken waters of the Minch, haze-blue Heather Isles. If getting away from it all is important to you, then drag on the hiking boots and head for Poca Buidhe. You will not be disappointed.

Less taxing fishing is offered by the National Trust for Scotland who have five lochs in the Poolewe area, available for visitors. Fly fishing only, some with boats, all offering sport. The largest of these lochs, shared with the Creag Mor Hotel, is Kernsary and the last time I spoke to the hotel there were ambitious plans afoot to restock Kernsary. Kernsary is approached from Poolewe, along the same road used to reach Fionn. Cross the River Ewe and follow the track eastwards. There is a forest gate over the outlet stream and then, as you climb past the woodlands, the loch lies sparkling below; a wild, straggling water of long bays and inlets with magnificent views westwards to sea-Loch Ewe. As we passed, last summer, a graceful hind drank from the outlet stream, belly-deep in yellow flag and sweet meadow grass; surrounded by clumps of purple heather, backed by the vivid, silver-blue of the loch. An unforgettable moment.

Between Loch Ewe and Loch Gairloch is another peninsula, scattered with a number of delightful trout lochs, some distant and some easily accessible. Twin roads fringe either side of the moorlands and a track from Midtown on the north shore winds its way north-west to a small, sandy bay at Camas Mor, passing Loch Ceann a'Charnaic and Loch an Draing on the way. Few people make the journey and, to the east, there is another lovely beach, by Meall Glac a'Bheithe.

Gairloch's best salmon stream is the Kerry River, flowing from Bad an Sgalaig and entering the sea just south of Charlestown. The A832 road runs close to the north bank and fishing on this spate stream can sometimes be arranged through the Creag Mor Hotel or the local angling club. The character of the river has been much affected by the building of a hydroelectric scheme and the damming of the loch. Compensation water from the dam helps to maintain a reasonable flow in the river but nothing can repair the damage done to this once lovely glen by rampant hydro works. Salmon run the Kerry from July onwards. Best sport is had in autumn months and the Kerry fishes into October with about 40–50 salmon taken each season. There are 15 pools and they may be fished using a light, single-handed rod. Stalking salmon time and great sport in the right conditions.

If you turn west, over the River Kerry, the tortuous B8056 directs you to Redpoint, by Badachro River and the hill lochs of Shieldaig. Salmon run the Badachro and about 30 fish are taken each year, mostly from the loch, which also offers good sport with brown trout. And in the hills to the south of the Shieldaig Lodge Hotel lie Diamonds, Spectacles, Aeroplanes and Faires; the names of a group of classic trout waters, easily accessible and fished from the hotel.

Further out into the wild of the Shieldaig Forest are another dozen waters, all containing trout which vary in size from three-to-the-pound right up to monster ferox. The hotel is situated on the shores of a sea loch and over a post-dinner coffee you may watch eider ducks rooting among the seaweed-fringed margins; or wander through evening woodlands, followed by the sound of cuckoo and finch. This is good relaxing country, never too crowded, always restful and welcoming.

The small village of Torridon crouches by the shore of Upper Loch Torridon, glowered over by one of Scotland's most photographed mountains, Liathach, 'the grey one'. Climbers outnumber gamefishers here and hundreds of heavily booted walkers head for the high corries throughout the year. The Torridon Hotel offers fishing on a number of

North face of 'The Grey One', Torridon

excellent waters, including the Rivers Balgy, Torridon, Loch Damh and Loch an Iasgaich. The rivers are all very much spate streams and often the best sport is to be had in the lochs, particularly Loch Damh which has good runs of sea-trout.

There are three other salmon streams in the Torridon area but they are almost entirely preserved and not available to members of the public: Kishorn, Carron and Shieldaig. Don't worry too much. Wrap up warmly and head for the hills; Torridon and Glenshieldaig have fine trout fishing. All you need is proper permission, strong lungs, legs and willpower.

The A896 leads south from Shieldaig to Kishorn and Loch Carron. Much more interesting is the little minor road that twists round the coast

194

to Applecross Bay, still one of the most remote and inaccessible places in Scotland. Applecross is famous as one of the most important Scottish religious centres, the workplace of Maol Rubha who was born in the year AD 640 and died on the Black Isles on 21 April AD 721. He established the church at Applecross in AD 672 and is buried there, the grave being marked by two rounded stones, placed east and west. Tradition has it that those leaving Applecross on a dangerous or difficult journey would carry a little earth from Moal Rubh's grave and that this protected them from danger and ensured their safe return. There is an adventure school near the village, close to the banks of the river which rises from the grim fastness of Carn Dearg and the cold waters of Loch Coire Attadale.

Salmon and sea-trout run the river and over the years considerable work has been done to improve lies and pools. Fishing is available to visitors and it is divided into half days, from 8 a.m. until 2 p.m. and from 2 p.m. until 10 p.m. There are good runs of fish and, dependent upon water levels, upwards of 70 salmon and sea-trout can be taken.

South from the village, the landscape is dotted with dozens of little trout lochs, all involving heavy breathing to reach. There is really no easy way in, which is what makes this remote part of Ross-shire such a pleasure to fish. Nor is there any easy way out. Grit your teeth and check the brakes on the car. Then tackle nightmare Bealach na Ba, the pass of the cattle, dropping 2,000 from Meal Gorm to the sea at Tornapress. A gripping journey and on a clear day, unforgettable. In bad weather, downright dangerous. To rest and recover from your ordeal, stop off at Attadale. Mrs MacPherson at the Lodge has some good self-catering cottages and, even better news, some excellent trout fishing available for guests on the hill lochs to the south of the village. After the wilds of Applecross, you will find reaching these waters an easy amble. Good fish in them too.

The firth lands of Easter Ross are a complete contrast to the vast wilderness of Coigach, Flowerdale and Applecross. A wide, fertile plain, rich farmlands, spread with fine sheep and cattle and fast-growing crops. The Black Isle gained its name because when the rest of Ross-shire was snow-covered in the grip of winter, this gentle peninsula always seemed to escape the worst of the weather.

Wresting a living in the east of the county, throughout the turbulent years of early Scottish history, was less traumatic than in Wester Ross; and still is today. Communications are better and facilities for visitors well organised and widespread. The earliest tourists to the land of the Picts, the Romans, stopped on the south shore of the Moray Firth leaving the northern tribes to their own devices. Consequently, Pictish culture flourished and evidence of their culture is evident throughout the north; hill forts, settlements, brochs and beautifully carved stones.

The Vikings were made of sterner stuff and displaced the Pictish traditions and it is from out of their domination of the northlands that present-day Ross-shire evolved. The dreadful Highland Clearances devastated Ross-shire during the 18th and 19th centuries, when people were evicted to make way for sheep and the brutality with which they were carried out is still remembered today. Sir John Lockhart-Ross inherited the vast Balnagowan Estate in 1762 and the first lowland sheep-farmer, Thomas Geddes, arrived in 1782. From then until 1860 evictions and clearances were ruthlessly carried out, culminating in the 'massacre of the Rosses' in 1854.

The only creatures forcibly removed from Easter Ross today are fish; and even that has become increasingly difficult due to the massive hydroelectric programme begun in 1954 to harness the waters of the Conon, the principal East Ross salmon river. No less than nine dams hold back the waters of the Conon and its tributaries, directing the stream through six power stations before releasing them into the sea. Huge reservoirs have been created in the hills and once superb salmon and sea-trout systems have been reduced, sometimes to a state of fishless 'senility'. Nevertheless, the Conon has survived and each season provides good sport on a number of beats, most of which are available to visiting anglers. As always, seek a booking well in advance because Conon fishing is much in demand.

The best pools on Conon include such famous names as Bridge Pool, near the village of Conon Bridge, Slaggan, Brander, Little Junction and Top Box, Greenbank, Rushing Pool, Ferry Stream, Kettle, Plock and Junction Pool. Below Torr Achilty Damm is the Coul beat, with some excellent holding pools: Deer Fence, New Pool and Clachuil.

Spring fishing on Conon, as in so many of our Scottish rivers, is very much a thing of the past. A few fish are taken, but it is hard, cold work. There is a good run of summer grilse and they appear in June, but autumn fishing now produces most consistent results. One of the best fish taken in recent years was a 24-lb salmon from Rushing Pool and double-figure fish are taken each season. Summer grilse fishing can be spectacular and last season some of the beats produced upwards of 40 fish for a week's work. Lower Brahan's catch return for 1987 was 134; Middle Brahan 357 and Upper Brahan 145.

The Bran and Orrin tributaries produce few fish but the Black Water can give great sport. The Upper River is owned by the Achonachie Angling Club and visitors' tickets are readily available. Visitors and club members took 84 salmon during 1987 and 53 fish from the club's Conon water. But perhaps the best of the club's fishing is for sea-trout in the estuary, which produced 1,574 fish during 1987. Marvellous sport.

The Alness is the other main East Ross salmon stream and fishing is available to visiting anglers through the Novar Estate and the Alness Angling Club. Estate beats are well booked in advance but the club water

Home sweet home—wilds of Ross-shire

can be excellent; 1987 saw 127 salmon landed and, even nicer, 340 sea-trout. This was down on the previous year when 168 salmon and 447 sea-trout were taken. For visiting anglers, this represents value-for-money, quality sport, and is to be highly recommended. Launch your attack for sea-trout in July and August; wait until September for salmon. Pray for rain, all the time.

East Ross trout fishing has not the same diversity as over in Wester Ross but there are many delightful accessible and remote hill lochs where the visitor will find peace and quiet and good sport. East Lodge Hotel in Strathconon has a number of waters and the Fairburn Estate sometimes has rods available on Orrin Reservoir.

The new reservoirs also provide sport; Loch Luichart, Loch Meig, Loch Garvie, Achonachie and Achilty. Most contain small fish, in the order of

8–12 oz but from time to time they produce larger surprises with fish of 4 lb and heavier being taken. And to the north of Contin is the first 'put-and-take' fishery in the north, Loch an Eich Bhain, better known as the Tarive Lochs, regularly stocked with both brown and rainbow trout.

The saddest aspect about fishing in Ross-shire is leaving. There is never enough time to do proper justice to all the waters available. Which, it seems to me, is an excellent excuse for returning, again and again, for a lifetime's pleasure. Ross-shire is like that.

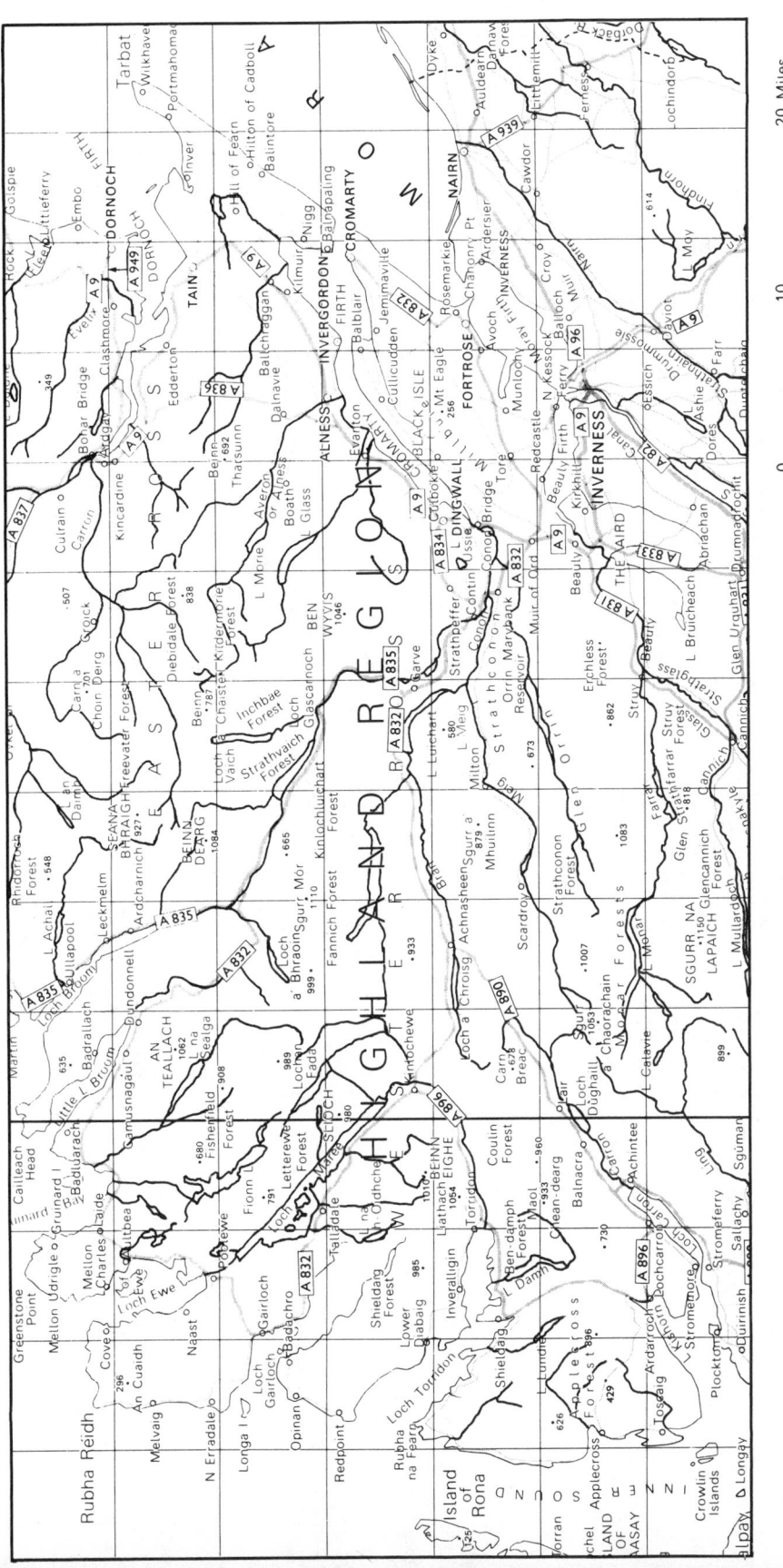

COIGACH, LOVAT AND AFFRIC

FISHING DIRECTORY

SALMON AND SEA TROUT
RIVER GARVIE
LOCH GARVIE
Mrs A McLeod,
No 2 New Houses, Strathpolly
(05714) 314

LOCH OSGAIG
Summer Isles Hotel,
Achiltibuie, Ullapool, Ross-shire
(085482) 282

RIVER POLLY
Inverpolly Estate Office,
Inverpolly, Ullapool, Ross-shire
(05714) 252

RIVER RUNIE
RIVER KANAIRD
RIVER ULLAPOOL
Highland Coastal Estates,
Coulmore, Kessock, Inverness
(046373) 212

BROWN TROUT
INVERPOLLY FISHINGS
LOCH SIONASGAIG
Mrs A McLeod,
No 2 New Houses, Strathpolly
(05714) 214
Inverpolly Estate Office,
Inverpolly, Ullapool
(05714) 252

LOCH NA H'AIRGHE
POLLY LOCHS
LOCH BAD A'GHAILL
LOCH OSGAIG
Inverpolly Estate Office,
Inverpolly, Ullapool
(05714) 252

LOCH LURGAINN
Royal Hotel,
Ullapool, Ross-shire
(0854) 2181

LOCH RAA
LOCH VATACHAN
Summer Isles Hotel,
Achiltibuie, Ullapool, Ross-shire
(085482) 282

RUHBA MOR LOCHS
COIGACH LOCHS
LOCHAN TUATH
LOCHAN SGEIREACH
Mrs J Longstaff,
Baden, Tarbat, Achiltibuie
(085482) 225

LOCHAN LEACACH
LOCHAN FADA
LOCHAN BALLACH
LOCHAN DAIMPH
LOCH ACHALL
and other Hill Lochs
Highland Coastal Estates,
Coulmore, Kessock, Inverness
(046373) 212

DAM LOCHS
Frigate Shop,
Argyll Street, Ullapool, Ross-shire
(0854) 2488

LECKMELM HILL LOCHS
Leckmelm Holiday Enterprises,
Lochmelm, Ullapool, Ross-shire
(0854) 2471

GAIRLOCH FISHING DIRECTORY

BROWN TROUT FISHINGS
THE FAIRY LOCH
SPECTACLES
THE AEROPLANE LOCH
THE DIAMOND LOCH
LOCH BAD NA H-ACHLAISE
LOCHAN SGEIREACH
LOCH BAD A'CHROTHA
LOCH NA H'OIDHCHE
LOCH BRAIGH HORRISDALE
LOCH A'BHEALAICH
LOCH GAINEAMHACH
LOCH FADA
LOCH CLAIR
LOCHAN NAM BREAC ODHAR
LOCH AIRIGH VILLEIM
Sheildaig Lodge Hotel,
Badachro, Gairloch, Ross-shire
(044583) 250

LOCH A'BHAID-LUACHRAICH
LOCH GHUIRAGARSTIDH
LOCH KERNSARY
LOCH NA BA CAOILE
LOCH AN DAILTHEAN
Inverewe Visitors Centre,
Poolewe, Ross-shire
(044586) 229

FIONN LOCH
Creag Mor Hotel,
Gairloch, Ross-shire
(0445) 2068

LOCH MAREE
GAIRLOCH ANGLING CLUB
WATERS
Twenty Hill lochs between Loch Maree and
the sea
LOCH BAD AN SGALAIG
Lochmaree Hotel,
Loch Maree, Achnasheen, Ross-shire
(044589) 200

LOCH DUBH
LOCHAN NAM BREAC
LOCH FEUR
LOCH COIRE NA H-AIRIGH
The Wildcat Stores,
Gairloch, Ross-shire
(0445) 2242

LOCH GARBAIG
BLACK LADY LOCH
Craig Mor Hotel,
Gairloch, Ross-shire
(044586) 229

BROWN TROUT
LOCH FANNICH
LOCH GARVE
Strathgarve Lodge Hotel,
Garve, Ross-shire
(09974) 204

LOCH GLASCARNOCH
Aultguish Inn,
Aultguish, Garve, Ross-shire
(09975) 254

LOCH BEANNACHARAIN
LOCH MEIG
S W Tough MBE,
East Lodge Hotel, Strathconon, Ross-shire
(09977) 222
M Burr,
The Tackle Shop, Cromarty Buildings,
Strathpeffer
(09972) 561

LOCH BHAD GHAIREAMHAICH
LOCH AN ALTAIN BHEITHE
LOCH AN EILEIN
LOCH CUL
S W Tough MBE,
East Lodge Hotel, Strathconon, Ross-shire
(09977) 222

ORRIN RESERVOIR
The Fairbairn Estate Office,
Muir of Ord, Ross-shire
(09973) 273

LOCH LUICHART
Jas Shanks & Sons,
Tulloch Street, Dingwall, Ross-shire
(0349) 2346

LOCH ACHONACHIE
M Burr,
The Tackle Shop, Cromarty Buildings,
Strathpeffer, Ross-shire
(09972) 561

LOCH ACHILTY
Craigdarroch Hotel,
Contin, Ross-shire
(09972) 561
Achilty Hotel,
Contin, Ross-shire
(09972) 355

SALMON AND SEA TROUT
RIVER CONON
RIVER BRAN
RIVER ORRIN
Achonachie Angling Club,
D McLay (Secretary), Conon Bridge Post
Office
(0349) 61201

BLACK WATER
Craigdarroch Lodge Hotel,
Contin, Strathpeffer
(0977) 21265
Strathgarve Lodge Hotel,
Garve, Ross-shire
(09974) 204
Achonachie Angling Club,
D McLay (Secretary), Conon Bridge Post
Office
(0349) 61201

RIVER ALNESS
Alness Angling Club,
J Paterson, Ironmonger, High Street,
Alness
(0349) 882286
Novar Estates,
Novar, Evanton, Ross-shire
(0349) 830208

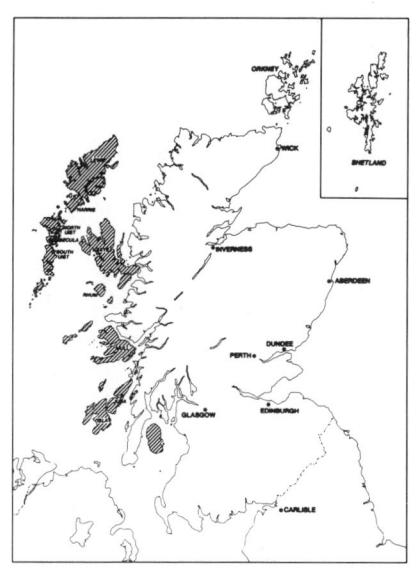

THE PLEASURE ISLES

Inner and Outer Hebrides

Escape time. Over the sea to Skye, most romantic of all Hebridean Isles. Linked forever with Bonnie Prince Charlie and Flora MacDonald. Most people imagine the prince, kilted and handsome, being rowed from mainland Scotland by a group of swarthy Highlanders to safety in the 'misty isle'. In fact, the prince was fleeing east from the Outer Hebrides, having narrowly eluded capture in Benbecula. Victorians wallowed in the concept of Flora, selflessly risking her all to help the Young Pretender escape from his relentless pursuers. Nothing could be further from the truth because Flora MacDonald had little time for either the Jacobites or their lost cause. Her real reason for helping Charles was probably more practical: with the prince gone, soldiers would leave and people could get on with their normal lives.

Escaping from Skye today is just as hard, although for different reasons. The beauty of the scenery and gentle charm of the people make it hard to leave. Indeed, increasing numbers just stay. After a few, brief weeks' holiday, they succumb to the spell of the isles' 'sweet airs, that give delight and hurt not' and remain forever. Skye has some of Scotland's greatest scenery; the magical Cuillins, a flurry of Munros, all over 3,000 ft with Sgurr Alasdair towering above the clear waters of Loch Coruisk; the green lands of Storr, Staffin and Trotternish ridge; Portree, the bustling business and commercial centre. Portree derives its name from the Gaelic Port-Ruighe, King's Harbour; James V used Portree as a base for his expedition to quell the might of the Lords of the Isles in 1540.

Visit Skye today and try and quell the might of its salmon, sea-trout and brown trout. Salmon run the little rivers which all depend upon the heavy rains to produce good sport but when it comes to rainfall, Skye often has more than its fair share. Good news for anglers, not so good for general visitors. The principal salmon streams available to anglers are the Rivers Snizort and Ose, both excellent in their own right, given decent water levels. Salmon average 7 lb with the occasional larger fish of up to 16 lb and the ten-year average for Snizort is an impressive 180 fish. Most are taken in August and September but sea-trout run the streams from July onwards and, particularly on the Ose, often give much better sport than their larger cousins.

The River Lealt has some salmon and sea-trout fishing available to the public, on the north bank, below the falls; and River Brogaig fishes well in spate conditions for sea-trout and brown trout. As does the Kilmartin River, near Staffin, and also Kilmaluag. Visitors may also find good spate river salmon fishing on the Rivers Conon and Rha, up to the falls, with excellent brown trout on the Upper River.

Trout fishing is available on the island in a number of waters, both remote and accessible. Lochs Connan, Duagraich and Ravag are fished from Ullinsh Lodge Hotel and at Isle Ornsay, Hotel Eilean Iarmain has three trout lochs for guests. To the north of Portree, the local angling association has some delightful fishing on the hill lochs of north Skye including: Lochs Cuithir, Cleap, Cleat, Leum na Luirginn, Fada, Haco, Langaig, Droighinn, Sneosdal and Loch Mealt which contains Arctic char; and the gamekeeper at Staffin will direct you to Loch Corcasgil which has trout averaging 1 lb in weight, and its neighbour, Loch Dubhar-Sgoth which has smaller but equally exciting fish.

The best trout fishing on Skye is to be found in the Storr Lochs, a group of three interlinked waters formed by the construction of an 11 m-high dam. Water from Storr is directed via an 856 m long tunnel to the power station at the foot of high cliffs in Bearreraig Bay. Each morning, the resident engineer makes the descent of the cliff in a specially constructed, one-man railway, the only one of its kind in Britain.

The Storr Lochs are managed by Portree Angling Association and both boat and bank fishing are allowed. Most seasons produce good numbers of fish which are of a high quality and the heaviest trout taken from Storr weighed 12 lb. Fish of over 3 lb are caught frequently and the average weight is in the order of 12 oz.

Skye is perhaps not the first place that would spring to mind when considering a fishing holiday, but in view of the superb scenery and the host of attractions for any non-fishing members of your party, then it is worth considering, particularly in the autumn months when sea-trout and salmon fishing on the delightful spate rivers is at its best. However, be warned, the Skye midges are generally at their best then as well. Take along a few pints of repellant, or a huge, well-filled briar pipe.

The Island of Mull has a coastline of more than 300 miles in length; wonderful beaches, hidden glens, glorious Ben Mor (970 m) and the tiny Island of Iona, chosen in 563 AD by St Columba as the base from which to launch his attack on the minds and hearts of heathen Picts and Scots. Tobermory is the principal town, famous for the sunken Spanish treasure ship, *Florida* which lies in the deep waters of the bay. In the deep waters of loch and river, other Mull treasures abound, salmon, sea-trout and brown trout. There are six salmon and sea-trout streams: Coladoir, Lussa, Forsa, Aros, Ba and Bellart and much is available to members of the public. Island estates and the Tobermory Angling Club issue day and weekly tickets; but as always, it is best to plan ahead and book in advance.

The Aros flows eastwards to enter the Sound of Mull near Salen and on its way collects in the waters of a tributary, the Ledmore River which drains Loch Frisa. Frisa is the largest Mull water, five miles long by up to half a mile in breadth. Although mostly regarded as a brown trout fishery, salmon and sea-trout also reach Frisa so there is always the chance of surprising one along the shores of this 200 ft-deep loch. The heaviest salmon taken from the Aros system was caught in 1911 and weighed 45 lb 'Be thou also ready.'

Loch Ba and the River Ba is preserved by the owners but fishing is available on the Lussa through the Forestry Commission. The Lussa flows into the Firth of Lorn and apart from the lower pools which are long and deep, much of the little stream is rocky and fast flowing. In good water levels almost every pot and hole can hold fish and most fish run the river during June and July. Plan your visit accordingly.

The Forsa is a most attractive stream which fishes well from June onwards, when sea-trout arrive in numbers. Salmon appear about the end of July and the river has more than 30 noted pools. Fishing on the Forsa is sometimes available through the tackle shop in Tobermory which has two beats which rotate daily. They also may be able to arrange fishing on the Lower Bellart and offer boats on Loch Sguabain for salmon and sea-trout fishing.

One of the most exciting Mull waters is Loch Assopol at Fionnphort, on the road to Iona. The loch has excellent runs of salmon, sea-trout and a good stock of native brown trout. Fishing is available to members of the public and James McKeand at Scoor House also offers comfortable accommodation. Assopol brown trout average 8 oz, sea-trout 2 lb and salmon 7 lb. Migratory fish depend upon high July tides to reach the loch so fishing before then is for brown trout only. Not too bad a prospect when you consider that the heaviest trout taken from Assopol in recent years weighed 7 lb 8 oz. Furthermore, Loch Poit na h-I and Little Loch Arm to the east of Bunessan also provides good sport with brown trout. Makes you puff a bit, getting up to Arm, but you might well return in the evening with perfect fish which can weigh up to 2 lb.

The Tobermory Angling Association manages the fishing on the Mishnish Lochs, Mull's most productive brown trout waters and stock Mishnish regularly. Trout average 10 oz but most seasons produce much larger fish which often weigh over 3 lb. Both boat and bank fishing is readily available. The association offers fishing on Loch na Gualine Duibhe, reputed to be dour but always the odd chance of wandering sea-trout; and rainbow trout are stocked in Aros Lake, one mile south of Tobermory.

Islay is one of the most beautiful of all Hebridean islands and is proud of its title 'Queen of the Hebrides'. It is easily accessible via a regular car ferry service from Kennacraig on the Kintyre Peninsula, operated by the Hebrides work-horse, Caledonian McBrayne Ferries. In times past, Islay was the principal seat of the MacDonald Lords of the Isles and in the 14th century the clan were so powerful that they even concluded treaties with France, against the interests of mainland Scotland. New clan chiefs were proclaimed on a little island in Loch Finlaggan where the ruins of their castle may still be seen.

Finlaggan today resounds to the sounds of rising trout, rather than clan war-cries, and fish average a modest 8 oz; but plenty of them. There are two principal administrators of all things trout angling: the Bridge End Estate, which offers fishing on a number of excellent waters such as Ardnave, Ardnahoe, Finlaggan and Skerrols; and the wonderful Islay Estate hill lochs, lying amidst wild moorlands, haunt of golden eagle and merlin. For naturalist and ornithologist, Islay is a paradise and over 250 species of birds have been recorded on the island. The rare chough is present, as are two-thirds of the world population of barnacle geese during winter and spring. Much to the anger of local farmers who complain constantly about the damage these birds cause to their grasslands.

The Port Askaig Shop is the other place to go in order to obtain trout fishing. Visitors' tickets are issued for a number of waters, including Lochs Lossit, nan Cadhan, Fada, Leathann, and Allan. Containing good numbers of brown trout which average 8 oz with fish of up to 3 lb taken occasionally, particularly on Leathann.

The largest and most productive of the Islay waters is Loch Gorm, to the west of Bridgend and visitors may obtain permission to fish from the estate office. Gorm contains trout which average 12 oz and they have a reputation of fighting like fish twice their weight. The shoreline meanders in and out round countless bays and headlands and fish may be caught anywhere in the loch. So might the propeller of the outboard motor, because Gorm is scattered with underwater rocks, ready to catch the unwary, so take along spare sheer-pins and hasten about your business slowly.

At the south end of Islay is the Oa peninsula, one of the most attractive and historically interesting areas on the island. The Oa has been inhabited for almost 5,000 years, from the time of Iron Age man; his burial chambers and forts remain, grey memorials to man's endeavour. Less comforting are the ruined crofts which scatter moorlands and hillsides, grim reminders of the terrible times of Highland Clearances when many clan chiefs brutally evicted their tenants to make way for Lowland and English sheep farmers.

The Oa coastline is magnificent, with cliffs rearing 180 m above foam-fringed Atlantic waves. There are five good brown trout lochs here, to the west of Port Ellen: Kinnabus, nan Gillean, Lower and Upper Glenastle and Ard Achadh. All are easily accessible and to the north of Port Ellen, amongst the hills of Kildalton, are many more: Leorin, Beinne Brice, Sholum, Uigeadail, Leathann an Sgorra, Dearag an Sgorra and Beinn Uraraidh. These, however, are in compass, map and hiking boot country, some of the most remote waters on the island.

Salmon and sea-trout fishing on Islay is not so easy to come by, with the best of it, on the River Laggan, being booked, year after year by the same tenants. The Sorn, which rises from Loch Finlaggan, is preserved but it is worth noting that there is a record of a salmon being taken from the loch. Only one. Caught in 1930 by Scottish comedian and singer, Harry Lauder, of *I Belong to Glasgow* and *Keep Right on to the End of the Road* fame.

Choose to visit Islay for its dramatic scenery, magnificent beaches and fine trout fishing; for the golfer, there is the beautiful 18-hole links course at Machrie; for sunbathing and sand-castles, seven miles of golden sands at Loch Indaal; and, if that is not enough, then make a tour of some of the island's famous whisky distilleries. Guaranteed to brighten even dullest spirits.

Literary spirits haunt Islay's neighbour, lovely Jura. George Orwell wrote *1984* there whilst staying at Kinuachdrach, at the north end of the island. The world nearly lost his masterpiece because Orwell almost drowned in the infamous Corryvrechan whirlpools, in the tide-race between Jura and Argyll. Corryvrechan has been declared unnavigable by the Royal Navy and at flood-tide the waters roar through at speeds in excess of eight knots.

Jura is perhaps the least visited of all the Hebridean islands and as such holds great charm for lovers of wild and remote places. The island derives its name from the Gaelic word meaning deer and Jura is renowned for the high quality of its stalking. There are only a few miles of road, starting at the pier by Feolin Ferry and running south to Brosdale and then northwards up the east coast, ending at Lussagiven. The rest of the island is virtually trackless and the only way in is by foot, or by sailing into skerrie-strewn Loch Tarbert. The southern part of Jura is dominated by a mountain ridge known collectively as 'The Paps of Jura'. The three main peaks are Beinn a'Chaolais (734 m), Beinn an Oir (784 m) and Beinn Shiantaidh (755 m).

Most of the fishing on Jura is preserved by the owners for their own use but, outwith the stalking season (autumn) it is sometimes possible to obtain permission to fish the many trout lochs scattered throughout the island. Be prepared for some hard tramping to reach them and never venture out into the hills without being properly clad and leaving a note about where you are going and when you expect to return.

The Lussa River is available to visitors for salmon and sea-trout fishing, linked with some really super self-catering cottages, by the banks of the river and on the seashore at Killchianaig. Northwards from Ardlussa, the road degenerates into little more than a track; west lie wonderful open moorlands, specked blue and silver with tiny lochs and lochans. The Lussa is a spate river and salmon don't arrive in any numbers until well into July; even then, a high tide is required to encourage them upstream. Consequently, Lussa fishing is best booked at the time, depending upon the state of the river, rather than booked in advance. Guests in the estate cottages have first rights of fishing.

At the head of the Lussa is an excellent loch, known simply as Fishing Loch. It has a dam and supplies the little community with water but even in times of drought, sea-trout can be caught here and offer great sport when the river is sulking. Salmon in the Lussa system average 6lb in weight, with the odd larger fish of over 10lb; sea-trout average 2lb but most seasons produce fish of over 5lb.

Apart from the excellent quality of sport with salmon and sea-trout, Ardlussa Estate also offers brown trout fishing on five hill lochs, both distant and remote, all of which provide a pleasant alternative to wrestling with Mr Salar; but, perhaps above all, being on Jura is enough, almost regardless of numbers of fish caught. Jura is a special place. Go there and you will understand exactly why.

One of my earliest and enduring childhood holiday memories was a visit to the 'sleeping warrior' island of Arran, the most southerly of the Hebridean isles. We stayed in a cottage at Lavencorrach, at the south of the island, and spent a glorious two weeks wandering in the hills or splashing in the warm waters of the Sound of Pladda. Sadly, most of the lands where my brother and I used to roam are now covered in forests and it is hard to recognise the places we loved. But the memory is indelibly stamped on my mind; and in the case of my brother, on his foot. One morning he was feeding a calf called Miranda, when I jumped down to help. The startled beast stamped hard on Ian's foot and the mark of its tiny hoof remains there to this day.

Goat Fell (847 m), is Arran's highest peak and the surrounding mountains are much used by the climbing fraternity: Beinn Tarsuinn (825 m), Caisteal Abhail (834 m), Cir Mhor (798 m) and Mullach Buidhe (819 m). The island is scattered with relics of ancient man, chambered tombs, stone circles, brochs and duns. Arran was a frequent port of call for those sea-wolves the Vikings and tradition has it that Robert the Bruce was inspired by his spider in the caves at Drumadoon. Others would have you believe that this momentous event took place on mainland Scotland.

Brodick is the principal place of business on Arran and in its time the old castle has been much knocked about by such famous visitors as King Edward of England, 'Hammer of the Scots' and the soldiers of Oliver

Cromwell, before the islanders got their act together and murdered every single one. Brodick Castle is now a wonderful cultural and horticultural monument; the castle contains an outstanding display of paintings, furniture and porcelain whilst the gardens, begun in 1710, have the finest show of rhododendrons in Britain.

Trout fishing on Arran is not of any great worth. The few lochs on the island are remote and involve a long hard walk to reach. Loch Tanna is the largest water and it lies locked between the heights of Beinn Tarsuinn and Beinn Bharrain. The fish are of poor quality, small, dark and white fleshed. Arran is best known for its sea-trout and salmon fishing, in that order. One of the first angling books I ever read was by Moray MacLaren and I thrilled to his description of sea-trout fishing on Arran. Although sport may not be as spectacular today, when the rains bring the burns and streams to life, sea-trout are still there, waiting for your carefully presented fly.

Machrie Water is one of the best streams and it is in Gleann ant-suidhe, by the B880 road known as The String, that crosses the middle of Arran from the west to east; depending upon which way you are travelling; coming the other way it would of course then be east to west. Fishing on Machrie is from the bridge below where Garbh Allt burn enters down to the main road, the A841 which circles the island. The river is divided into three beats and these are let through the estate office in far-off Aberfeldy; fish Machrie in between July and October. Preferably, in the rain.

Forsa Water, north from Machrie, is also a useful sea-trout and salmon stream and it includes Loch Torsa, an extension of the river about three miles upstream from Dougaire Lodge. Fishing may sometimes be obtained by inquiring at the lodge and sea-trout of up to 7 lb have been caught in the Torsa during recent years.

Arran burns of note include Glen Croy Burn, which provides good sport in spate conditions and is readily available to visitors who may obtain permission at the tourist office in Brodick. The most productive burn is Sliddery Water and its tributary, Allt Duilleachry. When conditions are right, both these waters will produce sea-trout and some salmon. As always, it is just a case of being there at the right time. Only four rods a day are allowed and tickets may be purchased from Sliddery Post Office.

What Arran may lack in the way of numbers of trout lochs and salmon rivers it more than makes up for in the high quality of its sea-trout fishing in the small streams and burns. Like Islay, Arran is a superb place for a really relaxing family/fishing holiday where everyone will find plenty to do amidst lovely scenery. And if you should meet someone on the beach with the mark of a calf's hoof stamped on his foot, tell him that I'm still very, very sorry.

The Small Isles of the Inner Hebrides are some of the most splendid places in the world to laze away hot summer days. Each has its own distinctive charm and character and some also have the added attraction of good trout fishing. Colonsay is one of the largest islands and is eight miles long by three miles wide. The climate is warm and there are semi-tropical gardens at Colonsay House.

There are wonderful walks on cliffs and moorlands, sandy beaches, lily-filled ponds generally more sunshine hours than anywhere else in Scotland, other than the island of Tiree. The island goats are said to be descended from animals that survived the wreck of a Spanish galleon after the disaster of the Armada, and otters are often seen, playing in the surf. More than 150 species of birds have been recorded on Colonsay, from wren to golden eagle and there are some 500 species of plants, including such rarities as Sea Samphire, Marsh Helleborine and the very rare Spiranthes Romanzoffiana Orchid, first found on Colonsay in 1930.

There are three trout lochs on the island, all of which offer good sport: Fada, an Sgoltaire and Tuirmain. An Sgoltaire has the best fish, which average 1 lb in weight. Apart from Fada, fishing is from the bank only. The island has a number of comfortable self-catering cottages for visitors, and a good hotel. There is also an 18-hole golf course, surfing, bathing and sea-gliding. Above all, peace, perfect peace.

Just as beautiful is the island of Tiree, 'the land below the waves'. Tiree is flat and often windswept, four hours by boat from Oban. Nevertheless, the little isle holds the record for having more hours of sunshine than anywhere else in Scotland. There are two trout lochs on Tiree, Loch a'Phuill and Loch Bhassapol, both of which are private, but visitors' tickets are sometimes issued on Bhassapol. Expect brown trout averaging 1 lb with the odd fish of up to 4 lb and, if you are lucky, a few sea-trout.

Westwards across the broken waters of the Minch lie the long islands of the Outer Hebrides, 'the heather isles'; or as my son Blair used to say, 'the utter he-brides'. There are five main islands, Lewis, Harris, North Uist, Benbecula, South Uist and Barra. Far out into the Atlantic, even further westwards are the rocky pinnacles of St Kilda and scattered amongst the main group are hundreds of smaller isles.

For me, the Hebrides are a life-long love; offering peace, seclusion, magnificent scenery and some of Scotland's most outstanding and easily accessible game fishing. There are brown trout lochs in their hundreds; salmon streams of outstanding quality; sea-trout waters, both fresh and Atlantic-brackish, where tide-fresh fish rush from amongst brown, green and red-rust weeds to grab your flies. Everything an angler could ever desire may be found in plenty. Roadside waters, teeming with eager small trout. Distant moorland lochs, silent and still, where monster fish lie. A constant delight with something new round every corner, a pleasure over every hill. Even better, the vast majority of this fishing, particularly brown trout, is readily available to visiting fishermen and paying for it is unlikely to break your bank.

Lewis is the largest of the Outer Hebridean islands and has a population of over 26,000. The principal industry is weaving the world-famous Harris tweed and Stornoway is the main centre. Stornoway was probably first established as a Viking base and from the 8th century until 1263 AD the Hebrides were ruled by Norway. Alexander, 26-year-old King of Scotland destroyed the Viking's power at the Battle of Largs.

The best of Lewis salmon fishing is to be found on the Grimersta River. But not by casual visitors. Grimersta fishing is preserved and controlled by a syndicate of anglers, rarely available to visitors during peak times, from June onwards. The Grimersta rises in Loch Langavat, largest of the Lewis freshwater lochs, where fishing is shared by a number of neighbouring estates. There are four other main lochs on the system—Airigh na h-Airde, Kirraval, Faoghail Charrasan and Faoghail an Tuim.

Recently, the estate has offered spring salmon, sea-trout and brown trout fishing to visitors. Whilst this can be very much a matter of chance, there are runs of early fish and spring salmon of up to 19 lb have been taken in the past; but returns are widely variable. Spring months in 1986 produced about 100 salmon; 1987 produced less than 10. Nevertheless, it is encouraging to note that this once exclusive river has, to a certain extent, been opened up and if you wish the thrill of casting into some of Grimersta's legendary pools, such as Bridge, Captain's Long and Battery, why not take the chance? At the very worst you will find excellent sport with brown trout which are in good condition from May onwards.

Almost as good as Grimersta is the Blackwater System on the Garynahine Estate. The estate consists of 12,500 acres and offers salmon and sea-trout fishing on the Blackwater River which is divided into three beats, fished from the bank and from boats. The average weight of salmon is in the order of 7 lb but fish of up to 18 lb have been taken and sea-trout average 11 lb 8 oz. There are dozens of trout lochs on the estate and a loch near the lodge has been stocked with rainbow trout of up to 5 lb. At the time of writing, the estate is up for sale, so details about what, if any, sport is available for visiting anglers is not known. Salmon runs have been declining in recent years and, as is the case throughout Harris and Lewis, more fish are probably taken by poachers than by legal anglers. It always has been that way on the islands and always will be.

Soval occasionally offers fishing on its 38,000 acre estate, linked with excellent accommodation in Soval Lodge. The estate is let for trout fishing during May and June; for salmon and sea-trout fishing and grouse shooting from mid-August through until October. The principal fishery is the River Laxy, three and a half miles long with six named pools, flowing from Loch Trealaval down to Loch Valtos and from there to the sea. Most salmon are caught in Loch Valtos and the pools near the loch and access to the fishing is easy. Water flow is controlled by dams from both lochs and flood water thus 'saved up' for rainless days.

211

Apart from fine sport with salmon and sea-trout, the estate also has first-class brown trout fishing and there are good boats on twelve of the best waters. The heaviest salmon taken from the Laxy was caught in 1933 and weighed 33 lb 8 oz. The man on the business end of the rod was Richard D'Oyly Carte, and he no doubt had little difficulty in finding a good tune to whistle to celebrate his famous victory.

Uig Lodge on the west coast of Lewis offers fishing on the Fhorsa and Loch Slacavat system, which can be one of the finest salmon and sea-trout fisheries on the island. Netting rights are not exercised (at least, not by the owners) and fish run the river from June onwards until the end of the season in October. Boats are provided on Slacavat where there are many well-known salmon lies and the short Fhorsa river has good holding pools, and at Uig it is sometimes possible to catch salmon in the sea, regardless of the state of the river. Uig Lodge also has brown trout fishing on more than 50 lochs, both remote and accessible, and sea-trout and salmon fishing can sometimes be arranged on neighbouring Red River and Loch Raonasgail.

North Eishken Estate makes some of its fishing available to visitors as does the Stornoway Trust which has the fishings on the River Creed which flows into Stornoway Harbour. Creed has five miles of fishing and there are some good pools: Bend, Sheriff, Bridge, Peatstack, Falls, Long and Junction. This attractive stream has good runs of sea-trout and there is also a boat available on Loch Clachan.

Brown trout fishing on the island, apart from the estates already mentioned is free of charge, and there are so many that it would take years to explore them all properly. Some of the better known and most productive waters may be found adjacent to the Pentland Road which runs across Lewis from Carloway to near Stornoway and the East and West Arnish lochs are also excellent waters.

The Sports Shop in North Beach Street is the place to head for to obtain specific information on Lewis lochs and a good fishing centre is the Claitair Hotel at Shieldinish. Mr Anderton, the owner, is a keen angler and will direct guests to the best waters. You will also be greatly helped in your search for brown trout fishing on Lewis by my own book *Trout Lochs of Scotland* which details many more, and by the fishing directory and map at the end of this chapter.

Harris is much more mountainous than Lewis and apart from a few outstandingly good fisheries, Harris trout tend to be smaller than the fish in Lewis. The principal exception is Amhuinnsuidhe, which is quite splendid and offers some of the best salmon and sea-trout fishing in Europe. Unfortunately, prices are high and availability very limited. Nevertheless, if you can put together a party of up to 15 guests and rake up sufficient funds, then you will most probably experience outstanding sport. Accommodation is also of a very high standard. Amhuinnsuidhe Castle has been completely refurbished and yet retains all the charm of an established sporting lodge.

Amhuinnsuidhe take about 253 salmon and 600 sea-trout each season with the most productive month for salmon being August and for sea-trout, July. Fly fishing only, in pampered luxury. Allow about £9,000 for 15 people, with ten rods fishing; thankfully, VAT inclusive.

Horsacleit Lodge, three miles south from Tarbert along the A859, is not so grand as Amhuinnsuidhe but in many ways much more personal and attractive. The lodge is situated close to the shore of House Loch with spectacular views to East Loch Tarbert and the Shiant Isles. It is close to fine deserted beaches, warmed by the waters of the Gulf Stream.

Fishing is by fly only, six days a week, and there is a resident gillie available to give guests advice on flies, tackle and techniques. There are two salmon lochs and a good holding pool on the little Horsacleit River and all this fishing is within walking distance of the house. Sea-trout may be encountered in lochs Grosebay and Collam, two or three miles away and in Loch Drinishader, two miles distant, there are brown trout of a very high quality, pink fleshed, silvery and fighting fit.

At the south end of Harris, Borve Lodge Estate has loch fishing for salmon, sea-trout and brown trout and the Rodel Hotel at Leverburgh also offers sport with salmon and sea-trout to their guests. Good water levels are all-important to ensure the best sport. Hit a long dry summer and fishing can be non-existent. If you are unlucky, head for the hills, booted and trout-rodded. The wild brown trout of Harris and Lewis will not let you down.

On our first visit to the Uists and Benbecula, we sailed from Uig on the Isle of Skye, across the turbulent waters of the Minch; behind us, a distant prospect of snow-capped Cuillins, westwards, the gentle hills of the Uists. Lochmaddy on North Uist was our arrival point; a small cluster of houses round a sheltered, island-strewn bay.

Even the most careful examination of the ordnance survey map cannot prepare you for the sudden shock of North Uist and the vast number of freshwater lochs. Nearly a third of the island is covered by water and, around every corner, blue lochs sparkle in Hebridean sunlight. Almost no matter where you stop, within minutes you can be fishing. Tiny roadside lochans beckon; a walk over the moors tempts you ever onwards, from one gem to another. Many of the lochs are such a wild scatter that on the same loch there seems to be an endless number of different lochs. For instance, the shoreline of Loch Sadavay meanders in and out round headland and bay for a distance of 50 miles. There are hundreds of little islands, reputed to number one for each day of the year, and many are adorned with their own small lochs.

One of the most exciting North Uist lochs, and my favourite, is Loch na Geireann. Situated in the north of the island, it lies close to the road and, like its neighbours Scadavy and Fada, the shoreline of Geireann is crooked and wandering. There are several islands and on one of them neolithic pottery remains have been found; indeed excavations yielded up so much, it is possible that the kilns on the island supplied most of North Uist with prehistoric crockery.

For the angler, nan Geireann offers the very best of all worlds: excellent quality brown trout, hard-fighting sea-trout and silvery, sea-liced salmon, found throughout the loch; Following the outlet burn down to the shining white sands, after the sea has retreated. A mile distant, the burn enters a beautiful sea pool; clear, crystal water, surging through a gap in the rocks, bringing marvellous salmon and sea-trout that shatter the silence with their mighty leaping. If I were given but one place to fish, then I would most probably choose the Geireann sea-pools.

Evening Drift on Geireann Mill, North Uist

214

If you decide to follow my footsteps, do so with great caution and preferably in company with a local angler. There are dangerous, shifting, sands along the way. Otherwise, keep to the grass margins of the bay. A longer, but safer approach. This is where the great raptors soar and there is every chance of seeing a golden eagle. Listen for the rusty-engined cough of corncrake; red-necked phalarope nest in the Balranald Nature Reserve near by. Whooper swans carefully watch your efforts on the loch; intently concentrating heron haughtily ignore your presence; flights of wild fowl whisk by; red-shank, curlew, plover and gulls cry and sing all day long.

Newton Estate lies to the north of Lochmaddy and is owned by the Department of Agriculture and Fisheries for Scotland. The estate has dozens of small, un-named lochs and lochans where you may wander all day without meeting another soul. Buzzard, eagle and peregrine nest here and the landscape is an unending vista of moorland, light and water.

Three lochs on the estate deserve your particular attention because they contain much larger trout than the rest, although you will have to work a lot harder to catch them. They are Loch an Armuinn, Deadman's Loch and Loch an Duin. There is an Iron Age ruin on a narrow promontory at the south-west corner of this interlinked chain of lochs; indeed there are more than one hundred such Duns throughout North Uist, sited in easily defensible locations, on small islands or narrow peninsulas.

A good road leaves Lochmaddy and runs in a half circle round the top of the island; within easy reach of this most convenient road are dozens of fine sea-trout and brown trout waters; sea-pools between Griminish and Valley Island, Loch nan Clachan, Loch Eaval, Vausary, Dusary and Trosavat; sea-pools at Claddach Kyles and Kirkbost and many many more.

The principal salmon system on North Uist is Loch Skealter, close to Lochmaddy. Until recently the loch was used as a salmon farming site but this enterprise has now ended and fish are now returning to Skealter in ever-increasing numbers. Skealter is linked westwards by a narrow stream to Loch na Garbh-abhainn Ard and fish may also be caught there; but local knowledge is essential in order to find the best lies and this is readily available from Ian MacIlwraith, the owner of the hotel. On the south of North Uist, along the trackless, ragged shore of Loch Eport, there are numerous bays, crowded with sea-trout during the summer and autumn months: Roisinish, Oban Sponish and Tota Hunder. Reaching them involves a long tiring walk from the A867, winding your way across the moor, round Scadavy, Deorval and Hunder. An easier way in is by sea, but remember, even these sheltered waters can turn nasty, so wear a life jacket at all times.

South again from Loch Eport, a little road runs eastwards to North Uist's highest peak, Eaval (347 m), guarding lovely Loch Obisary, the best of the brown trout waters where the fish are of superlative quality. On the way, examine in detail some of the lochs on your left. Sea-trout run these waters as well and offer great sport; if you can find them. Start your search in Oban nam Fiadh and Loch na Ceithir-Eileana. Fingers crossed.

Southwards now, over the North Ford, to Benbecula 'the hill of the ford', a flat, moorland landscape is dominated by Rueval, the only hill on the island. Here, in a shallow cave in June 1746, Bonnie Prince Charlie anxiously waited for Flora MacDonald. Flora's step-father, Captain Hugh MacDonald, was guarding the South Ford and it was he who supplied the necessary travel documents which allowed the prince to escape, dressed as Flora MacDonald's maid, Betty Burke. Flora MacDonald was arrested the following month by that most relentless, brutal pursuer of the prince, Captain Ferguson of HMS *Furnace*. Imprisoned in the Tower of London, Flora was released in 1747 under the Act of Indemnity and three years later married Alan MacDonald of Kingsburgh. Dr Johnson, that great Highland traveller, met Flora MacDonald in 1773 by which time Flora was 50 years old but still a considerable presence: 'We were entertained at Kingsburgh with the usual hospitality by Mr MacDonald and his lady Flora MacDonald, a name that will be mentioned in history; and if courage and fidelity are virtues, mentioned with honour.'

Until surprisingly recent times Benbecula was isolated from its neighbours by the shifting sands of North and South Fords, a dangerous passage which claimed many lives over the years. In 1943 a causeway was built over South Ford, still known as O'Regan's bridge in honour of the priest who was most active in encouraging its construction. A further 17 years had to pass before Benbecula was linked to North Uist; in 1960 HM Queen Mother opened the route over the North Ford and the link was completed. Benbecula's economy was further stimulated by the establishment of Ministry of Defence operations at Balivanach and of the three principal Outer Hebridean islands, Benbecula shows the greatest signs of change.

But, in the Hebrides, change is very much a 'relative' word; in spite of all the increased activity and rocket galore, Benbecula still retains its distinctive charm and offers both holiday-makers and game fishermen hours of pleasure and enjoyment. Benbecula lochs are managed by the South Uist Angling Club and most are easily accessible. Some involve a stiff pledge over the wet moors, but don't be put off from trying some of the more remote waters. In many you will find sea-trout, lurking in brackish bays, in all excellent brown trout which vary in size from a few ounces up to fish of 3 lb and more.

One of the many fine roadside waters is East Loch Olavat, near Balivanach; follow the peat track down to the island-scattered east bay and you will find first-class bank fishing. There are other Loch Olavats, which can be confusing, and the best of them is to the west of the A865 and south of the little road that leads out to Griminish. The trout here are of particularly good quality and may be caught as well from the bank as from a boat.

At Market Stance a track opens up a vast area of moorland and water eastwards, with something for everyone. The first loch to the right of the track is Loch Ba Una, full of bright little fish; the ideal place for a family picnic, with a shallow, sandy shore where even the littlest of anglers can practise their act in safety. Further eastwards are yet more delightful waters and at the end of the road is my favourite Benbecula water, Loch Scarilode, a long walk, but worth every step of the way and I defy anyone to show me a more beautiful place to spend a day.

For a less taxing expedition, or a few casts after dinner, try the Caravan Loch, near Balivanach; so called because of the caravans parked nearby. We stayed in one on our first visit in 1977 and very comfortable it was too. Less comfortable is trying to tempt the inhabitants of Caravan Loch which holds some very large trout indeed.

It is impossible to leave Benbecula without directing you to another of my favourite waters, Loch Ba Alasdair, a series of interconnected waters at the end of the road from Craigstrome to Uskavagh. You can't see them from the road but a ten-minute walk over the small hills on your left brings you the main body of water. Ba Alasdair is on several levels. The main loch is brackish and hosts large numbers of sea-trout; particularly at Oban nan Fursanan. Above this is Bluebell Loch, its islands summer-ablaze with wild flowers. Close to these two waters are many other, smaller ponds and pools. One of them has some monster trout. Find out for yourself which. Half the fun of fishing.

O'Regan's Bridge crosses the clear, green waters of Loch Bee, an outstanding fishery with beautiful brown trout, and leads to South Uist, Clanranald country; deserted beaches washed by endless Atlantic breakers, backed by the springtime riot of colour that are the machair lands. Hecla, Ben Corodale, Beinn Mhor and Stulaval line the eastern horizon; eagles wheel and soar from their sharp crags; past Loch Druidibeg, an important nature reserve, home of greylag, white-fronted and barnacle geese; black and red-throated divers, whooper swans and otters.

The centre of angling activity on South Uist is Lochboisdale, at the southermost tip of the island where most fishing visitors stay at the Lochboisdale Hotel, famous for the enormous bar, one of the longest in Britain. It was necessary during the days of the whaling industry when Lochboisdale could become instantly crowded by thirsty crews of returning ships. Pride of place in the bar is a photograph of a more recent and more famous vessel, SS *Politician*, the cargo ship that sank containing several thousands of cases of whisky, immortalised in Compton MacKenzie's classic book *Whisky Galore*.

Game fishing on South Uist is amongst some of the best, yet least known in Europe. The Machair lochs of the western sea-board contain brown trout of great quality and they provide wonderful sport throughout the season, from April onwards. These are classic waters, lime-rich, shallow

A good day's work for Edinburgh anglers David Smart and Phillip Reid

and full of splendid fish and, as well as the Machair lochs, there are more than 80 available waters to visiting anglers. The most productive include: East Loch Bee, Grogarry, Stilligarry, Altabrugh, the Ollays, Upper Bornish and Upper Kildonan; but others, such as Toronish, Dun na Cille, Teanga, Chlachain and Airigh Ard are also first-class fisheries in their own right.

The average weight on the top lochs varies between 14oz on Kildonan to 2lb 6oz on West Ollay. Grogarry and Stilligarry produce trout of over 3lb and even larger fish are taken from East Loch Bee; but size of fish is almost irrelevant, because their quality and strength is quite remarkable. An 11-lb wild brown trout from the Machair lochs fights as well as a 5-lb fish from any lowland put-and-take pond.

Fishing is controlled by the estate and managed by the Lochboisdale Hotel and South Uist Angling Club. There are less than 40 club members and they managed to take upwards of 500 brown trout each season, averaging 12oz, 100 sea-trout with fish up to 7lb and good numbers of

218

salmon of up to 12 lb 8 oz in weight. There are three main loch systems for sea-trout and salmon and these are Roag, Fada, Schoolhouse and Castle; Kildonan and Mill; Bharp Loch and sea-pools. Fishing is divided into nine beats and each beat has its own boat. Sea-trout and salmon arrive at the beginning of July and run the systems until the end of the season in October.

If I was asked to select the most inviting, all-season fishing location in Scotland, then it would probably be South Uist. Often, during long, dark, fishless winter months, I lie abed, planning how and where I would spend my fishing if the constant need to earn a crust did not get in the way. Far into the night I envisage my delight: May and June on the Machair lochs, July wandering distant moorlands, exploring remote hills lochs of South Uist and magnificent Barra; August and September, courteously greeting sea-liced sea-trout and salmon. Of such are angling dreams made.

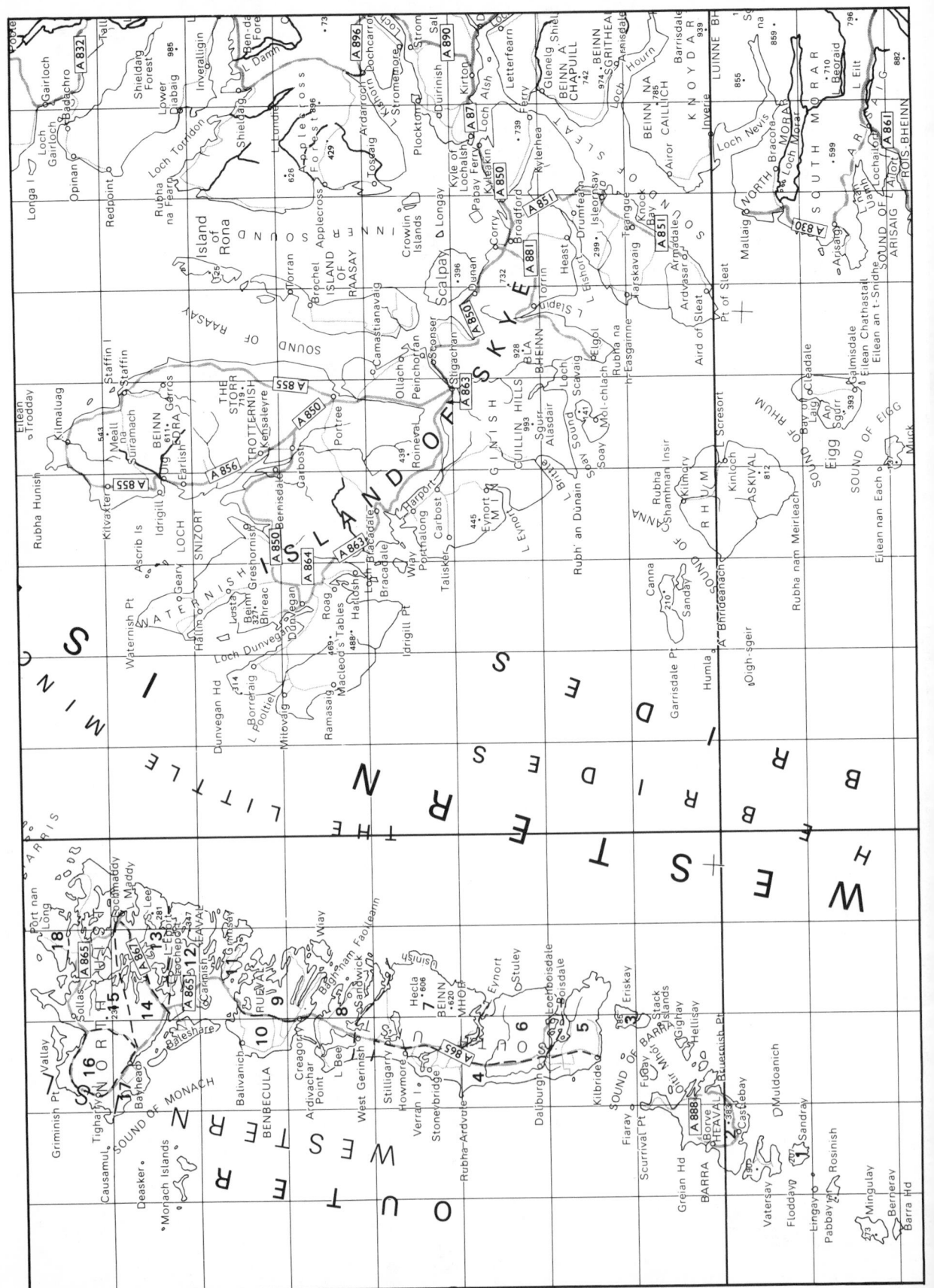

Meall nan Con
437
Pt of Ardnamurchan
Achosnich
A R D N A M U R C H A N
A 861
Kentra
Acharacle
S U N A
Rubha Mór
Cairns of Coll
Eilean Mór
Sorisdale
Kilchoan
Ben Hiant
528
490
Salen
BEINN RESIPOL
Sron Bheag
Glenborrodale
Loch Sunart
Ardmore Pt
Oronsay
Auliston Pt
Carna
570
Ballyhaugh
104
Arinagour
C O L L
TOBERMORY
Calve
Loch Teacuis
M O R V E R N
Acha
Eatharna
Caliach Pt
Drimnin
L Arienas
Gunna
Soa
Crossapol Bay
Calgary Bay
Calgary
Dervaig
444
550
Claggan
Urvaig
Gunna Sound
Caoles
A 848
ugh Skerries
119
T I R E E
342
Kilninian
L Frisa
A 884
Balevullin
Gott
Soa
Bay
Scarinish
Aros
Fiunary
L Aline
Middleton
Treshnish Isles
L T U A T H
424
Salen
A 849
Lochaline
481
Hynish Bay
Rinn Thorbhais
Balemartine
Gometra
155
Oskamull
Balephuil Bay
141
Hynish
Ulva
Dutchman's Cap
Little Colonsay
Inch Kenneth
Eorsa
L NA KEAL
Knock
L Ba
I S L A N D
O F
M U L L
Craignure
766
Rubha an Ridire
Duart Pt
Staffa
761
BEN MORE
966
Lochdon
Grass P
519
Skerryvore
Eilean Annraidh
L Spelve
698
717
Iona
100
Sound of Iona
LOCH SCRIDAIN
Croggan
A 849
Lochbuie
Fionnphort
Bunessan
376
Carsaig
L Buie
405
Soa Island
R o s s o f M u l l
Eilean a' Chalmain
Frank Lockwood's Island
Malcolm's Pt
Seil
Easdale
Rubh' Ardalanish
Torran Rocks
F I R T H O F L O R N
Ferry
Luing
West Reef
Garvellachs

Dubh Artach
Gulf of Corryvreckan
Kiloran Bay
143
Rubh a' Geodha
A 870
An Rubha
Kiloran
A 871
Glendebadel Bay
296
COLONSAY
Scalasaig
A 869
Staosnaig
1
Garvard
Corpach Bay
Beinn Bhreac
467
Ardlussa
Dubh Eilean
Oronsay
Shian Bay
Eilean nan Ron
L Righ Mór
2
Tayvallich
J U R A
Lussa Pt
Rubh' an t-Sàilein
Rubha nan Crann
L Tarbert
Post Rocks
Rubha a' Mhàil
Lagg
3
Sgarbh Breac
364
I of Danna
Nave I
Ardnave Pt
Beinn 'an Oir
784
Eilean Mór
Ardnave
Bunnahabhainn
PAPS OF JURA
A 846
Kilmory
An Clachan
Gortantaoid
1
Skervuile
L Gruinart
SOUND OF ISLAY
Jura Forest
Sanaigmore
2
Port Askaig
Feolin Ferry
561
Pt of Knap
Loch Caolisport
Gruinart
L Finlaggan
Small Isles
Saligo Bay
Ballygrant
4
Craighouse
Coul Pt
L Gorm
S T R
Kilchoman
A 846
Rubha na Tràille
Machir Bay
Bridgend
Brosdale I
Kilberry Head
Kilchiaran
3
Bruichladdich
McArthur's Head
L Indaal
Bowmore
Rinns of Islay
232
Port Charlotte
I S L A Y
Beinn Bheigeir
491
Ardpatrick Pt
Laggan Point
5
A 847
Ardtalla
Faing
4
Claggain Bay
Orsay
Portnahaven
Ardmore Pt
Rinns Pt
LAGGAN BAY
Gigha I
347
Eilean a' Chuirn
Rubha Mór
A 846
SOUND OF GIGHA
Ardminish
Lagavulin
Ardbeg
THE OA
Port Ellen
Gròb Bàgh
Lower Killevan
Texa
Cara I
202
Mull of Oa
Rubha nan Leacan
Muasdale
Glenacardoch Pt
10 20 Miles
10 20 30 Kilometres

Skipness
Inchmarnock
Cum
A 845
Claonaig
Skipness Pt
Kingarth
SOUND OF BUTE
Kilchattan
Cock of Arran
Garroch Hd
G I O N
Lochranza
Farland West
KILBRANNAN SOUND
A 841
570
Sannox Bay
859
Pirnmill
Corrie
874
Glen Iorsa
GOAT FELL
I S L A N D
O F
A R R A N
Dougarie
Brodick Bay
Brodick
Machrie Bay
Clauchlands Pt
Lamlash
Drumadoon Pt
Holy I
Blackwaterfoot
Tighvein
456
Kingscross Pt
Whiting Bay
Brown Hd
A 841
Kilmory
Dippin Hd
Slidderywater Foot
Kildonan
Davaar
Bennan Head
Pladda

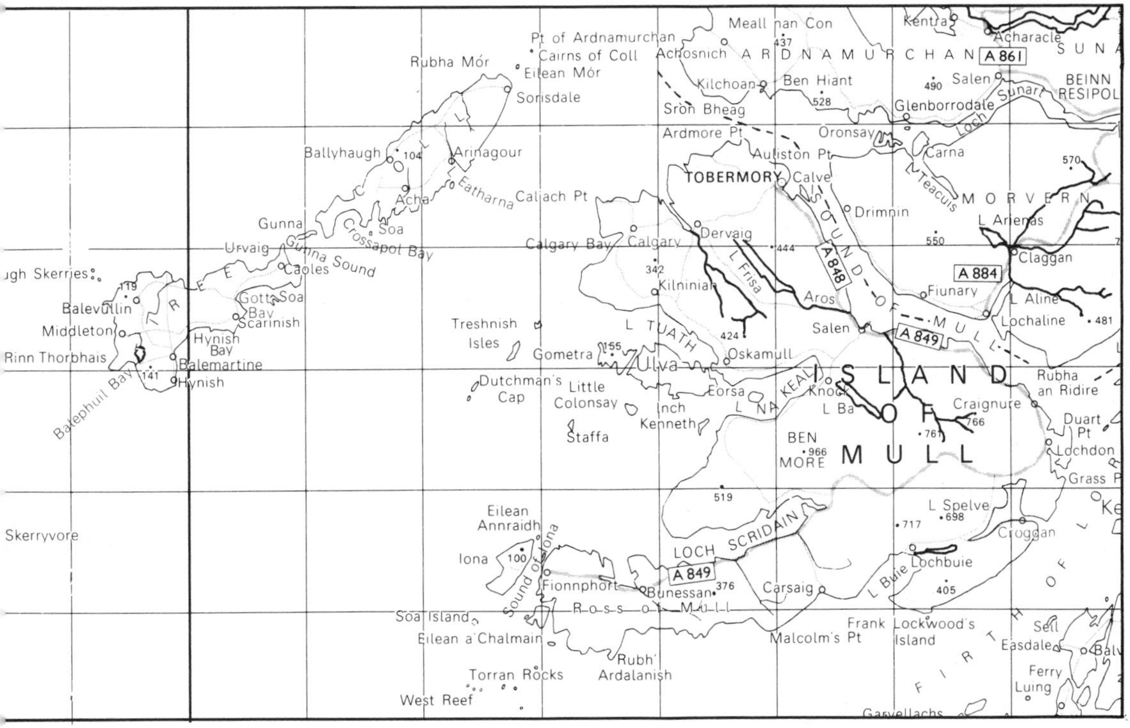

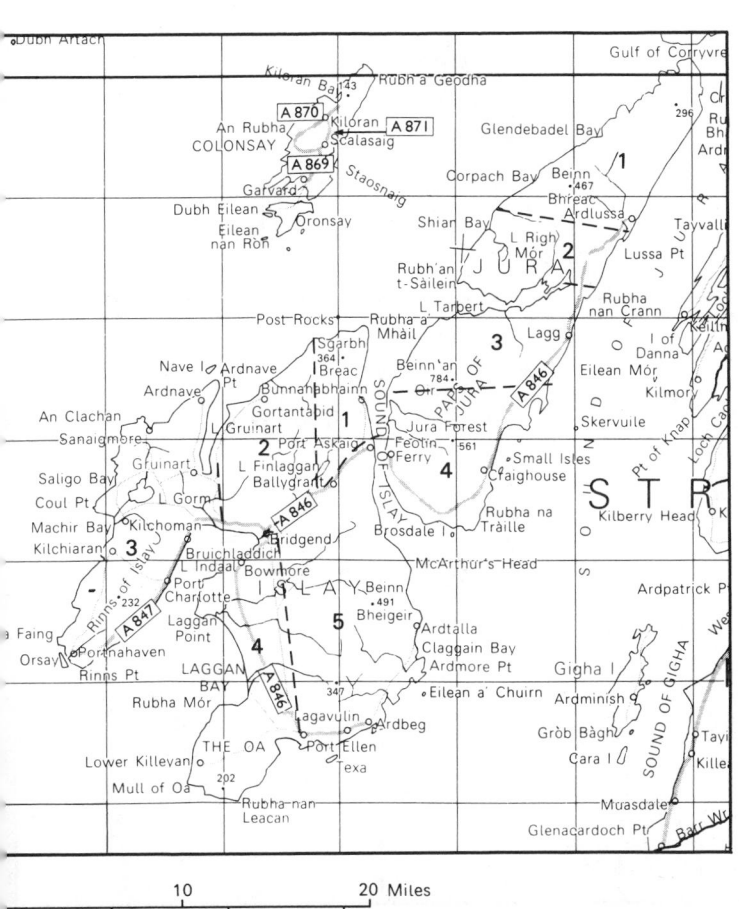

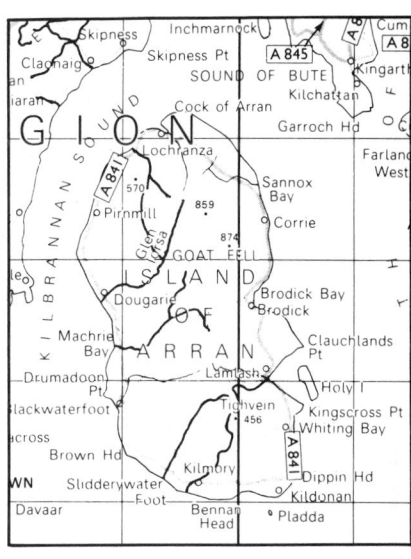

BUTT OF LEWIS

THE MINCH

Rubha Rèidh

Greenstone Point
Mellon Udrigle
Mellon Charles
Loch Ewe
Cove
An Cuaidh
Naast
Loch
Gairloch
Badachro
Opinan
A 832

LEWIS

Lionel
Eoropie
Port of Ness
Skigersta
Ness
68
67
Cellan Head
North Tolsta
Tolsta Head
Borve
Stadhe
Muirneag 249
Gress
Back
65
66
BROAD BAY
Triumpan Head
Portnaguran
Tong
A 866
Shulishader
Melbost
Garrabost
Knock
Bayble
54
EYE PENINSULA
Chicken Head

Barvas
Arnol
Bragar
Shawbost
Garynin
A 858
62
61
64
63
Benn
Mholach 292
Newmarket
A 857
STORNOWAY
A 859
Coll
Gress
Bernera
Breasclete
Callanish
Callafirst
Carloway
Doune Carloway
58
59
60
57
56
Achmore
Crossbost
Leurbost
Keose
Laxay
Balallan
Arivruaich
52
53
Gravir
Cromore
Marvig
Kershader
Eishken
38
37
Kebock Head
Lemreway
36
35
34
33
32
31

Shiant Islands

Sound of Shiant

THE LITTLE MINCH

Fladda-chùain
Rubha Hunish
Eilean Trodday
Kilmaluag

Garynahine
Uig
Bosta
Miavaig
Timsgarry
Enaclete
Callanish
Garynahine
Loch
Roag
West Loch Roag
E Loch Roag
Gallan Hd
Aird Brenish
Mealasta I
44
45
46
47
48
49
50
51
55
Ardvourlie
Loch
Langavat
Loch Resort
Forest of Harris
Meavaig
799
Benn Mhor
467
572
Crionag
Seaforth
Seaforth I
Scalpay
Kinloch
Grosebay
CLISHAM
Tarbert
W Loch Tarbert
E Loch Tarbert
Carnach
334
506
Renish Point
26
25
24
23
22
21
20
27

Flannan Isles

HEBRIDES

ISLANDS

OUTER HEBRIDES

Scarp 308
Gasker
Hushinish
Hushinish Pt
Amhuinnsuidhe
Govig
308
Taransay
679 MOR
TIRGA
39
40
41
42
43
43-74
Suainaval
Brenish
Toe Hd
Shillay
196
Pabbay
Boreray
385
Berneray
Sound of Pabbay
Port nan Long
19
18
A 865
Sollas
Vallay
Tigharry
Griminish Pt
Causamul
Haskeir I
16
17

Taransay
267
Tarransay
Glorigs
Kyles
Scalpay
Ensay
Killegray
Rodel
Leverburgh
Northton
365
A 859
SOUND OF HARRIS
460
Fhoslay
Ensay

Haskeir I

THE PLEASURE ISLES

FISHING DIRECTORY

LOCH COROUSIK
LOCH CREITHEACH
LOCH NA SGUABAIDH
Mr MacKinnon,
Strathaird Estate, Strathaird, Skye

RIVER BROADFORD
Broadford Hotel,
Broadford, Skye
(04712) 205

RIVER SNIZORT
RIVER OSE
Skeabost House Hotel,
Skeabost Bridge, Skye
(047032) 202
Ullinish Lodge Hotel,
Struan, Skye
(047072) 214

RIVER LEALT
KILMARTIN RIVER
KILMALUAG
RIVER CONON
N.O.S.C.A.,
Masonic Buildings, Portree, Skye
(0478) 2933

RIVER RHA
Sligachan Hotel,
Skye
(047852) 204

RIVER SLIGACHAN
LOCH CONNAN
LOCH DUAGRAICH
LOCH RAVAG
Ullinish Lodge Hotel,
Struan, Skye
(047072) 214

LOCH AN IASGAICH
LOCH DUBH
LOCH BARAVAIG
Ferann Gilean Isamain Hotel An E-Eilean,
Sgitheanach, Skye
(04713) 226

LOCH CUITHIR
LOCH CLEAP
LOCH LEUM NA LUIRGINN
LOCH FADA
LOCH HACO
LOCH LANGAIG
LOCH DROIGHINN
LOCH SNEOSDAL
LOCH MEALT
LOCH CORGASGIL
LOCH DUBHAR – SGOTH
N.O.S.C.A.,
Masonic Buildings, Portree, Skye
(0478) 2933

MULL FISHING DIRECTORY

RIVER COLADOIR
RIVER LUSSA
RIVER AROS
RIVER BELLART
RIVER FORSA
Tackle and Boots,
Main Street, Tobermory, Isle of Mull
(0688) 2336

RIVER BA
Private

LOCH FRISA
LOCH SGUABAIN
Tackle and Boots,
Main Street, Tobermory, Mull
(0688) 2336

LOCH ASSAPOLL
LOCH ARM
James McKeand,
Scoor House, Bunessan, Mull
(06817) 297

MINISH LOCHS
LOCH NA GUALINE DUBHE
AROS LAKE
Tackle and Boots,
Main Street, Tobermory, Mull
(0688) 2336

LOCH AN TORR
ARDNAVE LOCH
MULL HILL LOCHS
W R Fairbairns,
Cuinlodge, Dervaig, Mull
(06884) 275

LOCH AN EILEIN
LOCH AN EILEON
LOCH AIR DEGLAIS
LOCH AN T-SIDHEIN
LOCH A'GHCGANNAIN
LOCH BEARNAGH
LOCH NA DAIRIDH
LOCH FUARON
LOCH AN E-SIDHEIN
Tackle and Boots,
Main Street, Tobermory, Mull
(0688) 2336

ISLAY FISHING DIRECTORY

For Permission to Fish Waters In
Areas 1, 2 and 3 and north 5 contact:
Brian Wiles,
Islay House, Bridgend, Islay, Argyll
(049681) 293
Mrs K McPhee,
The Port Askaig Shop,
Port Askaig, Islay, Argyll
(049684) 633

For Permission to Fish Water In
Sections 4 and 5, Write to:
Mr V Montgomery,
Kinebus Farm, The Oa, Port Ellen, Islay
(0496) 2366

JURA FISHING DIRECTORY

Information on all fishing on Jura may be
obtained by contacting:
Mr C Fletcher,
Ardlussa Estate, Ardlussa, Jura
(049682) 323

JURA
Loch na Sgorra
Loch na Conaire
Loch nan Eilean
Loch Gasl-bheinn
Loch a Bhurra
Loch Doire na h-Achlaise
Loch a'Gheoidh

Loch Carn nan Gillean
Loch Fada Ben Garrisdale
Lochan Tana
Loch nan Bu
Loch nan Caorach
Lochain Bheag a'Bhaile-dhoire
Loch a'Chinn Ghairbh
Loch Lochadarach a'Chruaidh-ghlinn
Lochan Barr Bhealaich
Loch Nighean Aillein
Dubh Loch
Loch Cathar nan Eun
Loch Shiffin

Loch a'Bhalaich
Loch an t-Sithein Tarsuinn
Loch Fad'a Chruib
Loch Mor Bealach na h-Imriche
Loch Lochdarach Airigh Nualaidh
Loch Airigh Nualaidh
Loch Fada Cúl a'Chriub
Loch an Tuim Vaine
Loch an Aoinidh Dhuibh
Loch a' Mhile
Loch Righ Mor
Loch Righ Meadhonach
Loch na Caime
Loch Righ Beag
Loch La'Gharbh-uisge
Fòrr an Lochain
Loch a'Mhuilinn
Loch na Pearàich
Loch Braigh a'Choire
Lochan a' Tana

Loch Tarbert
Loch Sgitheig
Loch Losguinn
Loch Maol an t-sornaich
Loch Mhic-a-phi
Loch anAircill
Loch na Fudarlaich Beag
Loch Lesgamaill
Loch nan Breac
Loch na Cloiche
Lochanan Tana
Loch an Oir
Loch a'Chnuic Bhric
Loch an t-Siob

Lochan Gleann Astaile
Loch'a Bhaile Mhargaidh
Loch a Mhuilinn
Lochan nan Caorach

ISLAY
Ardnahoe Loch
Loch nam Ban
Dubh Loch
Loch Mhurchaidh
Loch Smigedail
Loch Giùr-bheinn
Loch an Dhubhaich
Loch Staoisha
Loch Airigh nan Caisteal
Loch Finlaggan

Loch Skerrols
Loch Sibhinn
Loch Dro!say
Loch Cam
Loch Leathan
Loch nan Caorach
Loch a'Chaoruim
Loch Carn nan Gall
Loch Broach
Loch an Leinibh
Loch a'Chlaidheimh
Loch a'Bhealaich Aird
Loch a'Chnuic Bhric
Loch a'Mhàla
Loch a'Churragan

Ardnave Loch
Loch Laingeadail Beag
Loch Laingeadail
Loch na Làthaich
Loch Arish
Loch an Fhir Mhor
Feur Lochain
Loch Ruime
Loch Corr
Loch Gorm
Loch Clach a'Bhuaile
Loch Gearach
Loch Conailbhe
Loch a'Bhogaidh

Loch Tallant
(River Laggan)
Grunnd Loch
Lochan na Nigheadaireachd
Loch Airigh Dhaibhaidh
Loch Tallant
Loch Dhomhnaill
Loch Dubh
Loch Eanin
Loch Eighinn
Loch Eidhinn
Loch nan Gabhar
Loch Muchairt
Glenastle Loch
Lower Glenastle Loch
Loch nan Gillean
Loch Kinnabus
Loch na Beinne
Loch Indaal
Loch Larnan
Lochan Sholum

225

Loch na Beinne Brice
Leorin Lochs
Loch Laoim
Loch nan Diol
Loch Carn a'Mhaoil
Loch nan Clach
Loch Uigeudial
Loch Leathann an Sgorra
Loch Deary an Sgorra
Loch Beinn Uraraidh
Loch nam Breac
Loch a'Mhuilinn-ghaoithe
Loch Allallaidh
Lochan Dubh
Loch Leatham

Loch Fada
Loch Bharadail
Loch Lossit
Loch Ballygrant
Loch nan Cadhan
Loch Allan

COLONSAY
Loch an Sgoltaire
Loch Fada
Dubh Loch
Loch Cholla
Loch Breac
Lochan an Laoigh Bháin

ISLAND OF ARRAN FISHING DIRECTORY

Write for information to:
Arran Angling Club,
A J Andrews, Park House, Corriecravie,
Arran
For Permission

Call at the Tourist Office in Brodick and at
the Post Office at Sliddery

FISHING DIRECTORY FOR CLONSAY

For all fishing contact:
The Isle of Colonsay Hotel,
Colonsay, Argyll, Colonsay
(09512) 316

FISHING DIRECTORY FOR TIREE AND COLL

For information contact:
The Factor,
Argyll Estate Office, Heylipol, Scarimsa,
Isle of Tiree
(08792) 516

THE SMALL ISLES FISHING DIRECTORY

RHUM
EIGG
MUCK
Nature Conservancy Council,
Fraser Darling House, 9 Culduthel Road,
Inverness
(0463) 239431

GIGHA
Gigha Hotel,
Gigha, Argyll
(05835) 254

FISHING DIRECTORY FOR LEWIS AND HARRIS

Areas 20–68

Trout fishing in the vast majority of Lewis and Harris Lochs is free of charge. The exceptions are: the private fishings on the estate rivers and lochs mentioned in the text. For permission to fish these waters contact the estates direct:

Stornoway Trust,
Estate Office, Stornoway,

Garynahine Estate,
Estate Off, Isle of Lewis, Hebrides

Uig Lodge,
c/o Renton Finlayson, Estate Off, Bonar Bridge, Sutherland

Soval Estate,
Balallan, Isle of Lewis

Grimerta Estate,
Grimerta Lodge, Callanish, Isle of Lewis

Borve Lodge Estate,
Borve, Harris

The Horsacliet Estate,
Per: Neil MacDonald, 7 Diraclett, Harris

Other information on game fishing in Lewis and Harris may be obtained from
The Sports Shop,
6 North Beach Street, Stornoway, Isle of Lewis
(0851) 5464

FISHING DIRECTORY FOR NORTH UIST, BENBECULA, SOUTH UIST AND ISLANDS

North Uist – Areas 11–19
Benbecula, South Uist and Islands Sections
1–10

NORTH UIST Areas 11–19
Permission for fishing on North Uist may
be obtained from:
**Department of Agriculture and
Fisheries**
Area Office, Balavanich, Benbecula
(0870) 2346
The Lochmaddy Hotel,
Lochmaddy, North Uist
(08963) 331

Sections 1–19
Permission to fish Benbecula, South Uist
and other Islands may be obtained from:
The Secretary,
The South Uist Angling Club, Balavanich,
Benbecula
The Lochboisdale,
Lochboisdale, South Uist
(08784) 332

GAME FISHING IN THE OUTER HEBRIDES

Area 1 SANDRA
Loch na Culice

Area 2 BARRA
Loch Obe
Lochan nam Fadileann
Lochan na Cartach
Loch an Duin
Loch na Doirlinn
Loch Tangusoalg

Area 3 ERISKY
Loch Douvat
Loch Crakvaig

Area 4 SOUTH UIST
Grogarry Loch
Loch Stilligarry
Loch an Eilean
Loch Roag
Loch Altabrug
Loch Dobhrain
West Loch Ollay
Loch a'Chlachain
Mid Loch Ollay
East Loch Ollay
Loch na Duchasaich
Loch an Lusgair
Loch an Turic
Loch Tornish

Upper Loch Bornish
Loch Bornish
Loch Kildonan
Loch Aird an Sgairbh
Loch Baimaleg
Loch Eilean an Staoir
Loch nan Uan
Loch na Uina Moire
Loch na Eilean
Loch na Cuithe Moire
Loch na Tanga
Loch Hallan
Loch nam Faoileann
Loch Trosaridh
Loch Dun na Cille
Loc na Eilgan
Loch na Cafull
Loch na Bagh
Loch Aisavat
Loch a'Choire

Area 5 SOUTH UIST
Loch Moreef
Loch Marulaig
Loch Kearnsinish

Area 6 SOUTH UIST
Loch Eynort
Loch an Mth-Ruaidh
Loch Cnoca Buidhe

Mill Loch
Loch nan Caorach
Loch Snigisclett
Loch Shuravat
Loch Fada
Loch Crogavat
Loch Stulaval
Loch Coragrimsaig
Loch an Clacha-Mora
Loch na Lice
Loch Beouin Mhoir
Loch Beinne an-Oitir
Lochan Goblach
Loch a'Barph
Loch nan Smalag

Area 7 SOUTH UIST
Loch Druidibeg
Loch Teanga
Loch Bein
Loch an Eilein
Loch Spotal
Loch Fada
Loch a'Chnoic Bhuidhe
Loch nam Breac Ruaoh
Loch Arigh Amhlaibh
Loch a'Cheann-Dubhain
Loch Corodale
Loch Hellisdale
Loch Ceann a'Bhaigh
Loch a' Chlachain

Area 8 SOUTH UIST
Loch an Ose
Loch nam Breac Mora
Loch Bee
Loch Shnathaid
Loch Sheilavaig
Loch nam Balgan
Loch Rueval
Loch Clach an Duilisg
Loch an Uisge-Ghil
Loch nan Bgeirgag
Loch Arigh Ard
Loch Cille Bhamotin
Loch an Dun Mhoir
Loch na Lice Baine
Lochh Naid
Loch Druim an Lasgair
Loch Dubh an Loinaire

Area 9 BENBECULA
Loch Langavat
Loch an Fhgidh
Loch na Beiste
Loch Meaneruagh
Loch Ba Alasdair
Loch Uacrach nan Caorach
Loch Olavat
Loch na Faoilinn
Loch Heouravay
Loch Hermidale
Loch a'Bhursta
Loch Ba Una
Loch Dubh Haka
Loch na Deighe Thuath
Loch na Beire
Loch Olavat

Area 10 BENBECULA
Loch Olavat
Loch Fada
Loch Mor
Loch na Uana Moire
Loch Borosdale
Loch a'Mhuilinn
Loch nan Clach Corr
Loch Eilean Iain
Loch nam Faoileann
Loch Dun Mhurchaidh
Loch Smalaig

Area 11 BENBECULA
Loch an Fhaing
Loch Nighe
Loch Mornary
Loch na Faoileag

Area 12 NORTH UIST
Loch Ghoill
Loch a'Chladaich
Loch Crogavat
Loch a'Ghlinne-Dorcha
Loch an Droma
Loch an Laegaich
Loch na Coinnich
Loch a'Chnoic Mhoir
Loch na Buaile Duibhe
Loch na Lairg Baine
Loch Dubh Cnoc Na File
Loch Obisary
Loch an Tomain
Loch Colla

Loch Gheamis
Loch nan Gealag
Loch Fada
Loch nan Garbh Chlachan
Loch an t-Sgasgain
Loch Cravat
Loch nan Clach
Loch an Fhaing Bhuidhe
Loch nan Struban
Loch na ba Ceire
Loch na h-Loaire
Loch Toim
Loch Faoa
Loch na Buail Lochdraich
Loch a'Ghaill
Loch a'Chladdaich
Loch a'Phobuill

Area 13 NORTH UIST
Loch nam Smalag
Loch Tormasad Beag
Loch Langass
Loch Tarruinn ān Eithir
Loch Hunder
Loch Deorauat
Loch Scadavay
Loch nan Ceithir Eilean

Area 14 NORTH UIST
Loch na Moracha
Loch a' Bharpa
Loch Tormasad
Loch na Ba Ceire
Loch nan Strùban
Loch na Bà Ceire
Loch na h-lolaire
Loch an Toim
Loch na Buail' lochdraich
Loch Fada
Loch nan Athan
Loch Dusary
Loch Huna
Loch nan Eun
Loch Hinda
Loch Scadavay
Loch na Garbh-abhainn Ard
Loch na Maighdein
Loch Skealtar
Loch an Strumore
Loch Ousary
Loch nan Athan

Area 15 NORTH UIST
Loch à Bhurd
Loch a' Chonnachair
Loch ha Hostrach
Loch Nighe
Loch Gheornish
Loch an Daimh
Loch Hingauat
Loch Fada
Loch nan Geadh
Loch Lalaidh
Loch Galtarsay
Loch an t-Searraich
Loch Mousgrip
Loch nan Geireann
Loch nan Gobhar
Loch Aonghais
Locha Dubh
Loch Eashader
Loch Uisdein
Loch a Chapull
Loch Sandary
Loch Veirgauat
Loch Dubh
Loch Feirma

Loch Mhic Gille-bhride
Loch Mhic à roin
Loch a Charra
Loch Horisary
Loch Bruist
Loch Trosavat
Loch Ullaveg
Loch Vausary
Loch Steaphain
Loch na Beiste (i)
Loch nan Clachan
Loch Eik
Loch Fada na Gearrachun
Loch Hosta
Loch na Beiste (ii)
Loch Eaval
Loch Grunavat
Loch nan Magarlan
Loch Bhiorain
Loch na Gearrachun

Area 17 NORTH UIST
Loch Beag nan lan
Loch nan Garnach
Loch Olavat

Loch an Eilean
Loch Scolpaig
Loch Skilivat
Loch Grogary
Loch Scarie
Loch nam Feithean
Loch na Cille
Loch Runavat
Loch Sandary
Loch Paible

Area 18 NORTH UIST
Loch an Sticir
Loch Camas-duibhe
Loch losal an Dùin
Loch Aird an Duin
Loch na Carnaich
Loch Dub'h na Moine
Loch Steinavat
Loch na h-Airde Mòire
Loch an Armuinn
Loch an Oiin
Loch Bru
Loch na Buaile
Loch na Creige
Loch na Morgha
Loch Nighe

Area 19 BERNERAY
Loch Bhruist
Little Loch Borve

Area 20 HARRIS
Loch Steisevat
Loch na Cartach
Loch na Moracha
Loch Langavat
Loch Thorsagaeàrraidh
Loch Vallarip
Loch na Craidhach
Loch an Duin
Loch Cistavat
Loch Borve
Loch Sgeireagan Mòr
Loch a' Mhorghain
Loch na Ciste
Loch an Ruisg

Area 21 HARRIS
Loch Alatair
Loch na h-Uidhe
Loch Aoghnais Mhic Fhionnlaidh

Loch a' Gheoidh
Loch Meurach
Loch Dubha
Loch Holmasaig
Loch Huamavat
Loch Dubh Sletteval
Loch Dubh Mas Holasmul
Loch na Mòine
Loch Gleannma Moine
Loch Heileasbhal
Loch Carran
Loch nam Breac
Loch na Callich

Area 22 HARRIS
Loch a' Bhealaich
Loch Mhànais
Loch na Creige Briste
Loch Tarbert
Loch nan Caor
Loch Beacravik
Loch Stochinish

Area 23 HARRIS
Loch Laxidale
Loch Bealach Stocklett
Loch na h-Aibhne Gairbhe
Loch Bearasta Mor
Loch Glumra Beg
Loch Glumra More
Loch Creavat
Loch Geimisgarave
Loch Udromul
Loch a' Gharaidh
Loch a Chlachain
Loch Cartach
Loch Nighe
Loch Sáile

Area 24 HARRIS
Loch Grosebay
Loch Strath Steachran
Loch na Craoibhe
Loch Chollaim
Loch a' Mhuilt Duibh
Loch Mhic Neacail
Loch an Rothaid
Loch Mula
Loch Chluar

Area 25 HARRIS
Loch Grosebay
Loch nan Craobhag
Loch na h-Iolaire
Loch na Larach Léithe
Loch a Mhonaidh
Loch Drinishader
Loch Cul na Bennie
Loch Cnoc na Silgean
Loch Harmasaig
Loch nan Uidhean
Loch na Cro
Loch Plocrapool
Loch Scadaby
Loch na h-Uamha
Loch Grannda
Loch Diraclett

Area 26 HARRIS
Loch nan Learg
Loch nan Uidhean
Lochanan Móra
Loch Uamadale
Loch nan Caor
Loch an Tairbh Duinn
Loch Stioclett

Area 27 HARRIS
Loch nan Eang
Loch Maaruig
Loch an Ruisg
Loch na Ciste
Loch a Mhorghain
Loch Sgeireagan Mor
Loch Torasclett
Laxadale Lochs
Loch na Cartach
Loch an Reithe
Loch Braigh na h-Imirch
Loch Beag
Loch Mor
Lochan an Fheoir

Area 28 HARRIS
Loch Brunaval
Loch a Sgàil
Loch nan Eang
Loch Vistem
Loch Stuladale
Loch an Teine
Loch Ruairidh
Loch nan Learg

Loch Chleistir
Loch an Truim
Loch nam Vidhean
Loch a'Cheiula
Loch Ulladale
Loch Ashavat
Loch Scourst
Loch an Fheoir
Loch Voshimid

Area 30 HARRIS
Loch Maolaig
Loch nan Gille
Loch Uiseader
Loch Bràigh Bheagarais
Loch na Sgàil
Loch à Ghlinne
Loch Cleavag
Loch Cravadale

Loch Bun Abhainn-Eadar
Loch Meavaig
Loch nan Caor
Loch Leosavay
Loch Linnarich
Loch Halladale
Loch nan Sligean
Loch Langavat
Loch Geodha Beag
Loch a Ghoirtein
Loch na Beiste

Area 31 LEWIS
Loch a Mhuin
Loch an Eich
Loch Druim nan Caorach
Loch Druim nan Goban Rainich
Lochan Chipeagi Bheag
Locha Chipeagi Mhor

Area 32 LEWIS
Loch Oil
Loch a' Gharaidh
Loch Cleit an Aiseig
Loch a' Bhaird
Loch na Creig na Ruaidhe

Area 33 LEWIS
Loch nan Eilean
Loch a' Bhroduinn
Lochan Sgeireach
Loch na Sroine

Loch Aigheroil
Loch Bhrollum

Area 34 LEWIS
Loch nan Rin
Loch Allt nan Bearnach
Loch Braigh nan Ron
Loch an Eilein Bhig
Loch na Bà Rhuaidhe
Loch Doimhne
Loch Linngrabhaidh
Loch Ucsabhat
Loch nan Faoileag
Loch Ruadh
Loch Chumraborgh
Loch Cleit à Ghuib Choille
Loch Chlachan Dearga
Loch a' Bheannan Mhòir
Loch Lacasdail
Loch nan Uidhean

Area 35 LEWIS
Loch Fhoirabhal Bheag
Loch nam Breac
Loch Raòinabhat
Loch na Beirighe
Loch Fath
Clar Loch
Loch Airigh Thormaid
Loch Shròmois
Loch a' Ghiuthais
Loch an Eilean
Loch Eishken
Lochan nan Uidhean Beaga
Loch Mór Stiomrabhaigh
Loch Shaghachain
Lodan Stionrabhaigh
Loch Bhreacaich
Loch Mór na Muilne
Loch Gaineamhaich
Loch an Eilean Duibh
Loch à Choin Bhàir
Loch nan Lub
Loch Shandabhat
Loch Caol
Loch Sealag (Loch Shell)

Area 36 LEWIS
Loch na h-Ola
Loch a' Mhadie
Loch an Lar
Loch na Muilne

Loch Oyavat
Loch Dubh
Loch na Craolbe
Loch Mòr an Iaruin
Loch Clach na h-Iolaire
Loch Sgibacleit
Loch Ciste
Loch na Cartach
Loch Chragol
Loch an Fheoir
Loch Dubh
Loch Ealaidh
Loch na h-Inghinn
Loch Airigh Fhearchair
Loch Leathain
Loch Errisort
Loch an Tairbeirt
Loch Totaichean Aulaidh
Loch nan Iolairean
Lochan Tana
Loch nan Eilean
Loch a Ghobhainn
Loch nan Caor

Area 37 LEWIS
Loch an Tairbh
Loch Craidha
Loch nan Stearnag
Loch an Uisge Mhaith Mor
Loch Kinneastal
Loch Tota Ruairdh Dhuibh
Loch Lochain
Loch a Chrochaire
Loch Cartach
Loch nan Eilean
Loch nan Cnamh
Loch Caol
Loch Beinne Buidhe
Loch Dubh

Area 38 LEWIS
Loch Mòr an Tanga
Loch na Muilne
Loch na Beiste
Loch Cromore
Loch Mharabhig
Loch Thorasdaidh
Loch Loch Uaille Mhor
Loch Caol Eishat
Loch Sgorr Ni Dhonnachaidh
Loch Crois Ailein
Loch nam Faoileag

Loch Mòr Dintaka
Loch Feoir
Loch Lite Sithinn
Loch na h-Airigh
Loch na Craoibhe
Loch Mirkavat
Loch Beag Catisval
Loch a Ghruagaich
Loch na Buaile Duibhe
Lochan Saeireach
Loch Druim nam Bideannon
Loch Catisval
Loch Daimh
Loch na Ba Riabhaich

Area 39 LEWIS
Lochana Cràgach
Loch Choilleigar
Loch na Faing
Loch Cheann Chuisil
Loch na Craobhaig
Loch Cro' Criosdaig
Loch Cleit Duastal
Loch a' Gharaidh
Loch nan Ramh
Loch Grunavat
Loch Benisval
Loch Bodavat
Loch na Caillich
Loch nan Geodhannan
Loch an A th Ruaidh
Loch à Fhraoich
Lochan Cleit on Eoin
Loch Snehaval
Loch Creagach
Loch Snehaval Baeg
Loch Lamadale
Loch na h-Airigh

Area 40 LEWIS
Dubh Loch
Loch Braighe Griomaval
Loch nan Ramh

Area 41 LEWIS
Loch na Muilne
Loch Tana
Lochan Lundule
Loch Dibadale
Loch nan Allt Ruadh

Area 42 LEWIS
Loch Longavat
Loch Lomhain
Loch Cràgach
Loch Dubh
Loch a Tuath
Loch a' Bhoineid
Loch Tiorsdam
Loch Tana
Loch Rathaid
Loch Beag Sheilabrie
Loch nan Creaganan Gròid
Lochan a' Chleite Tuath
Loch Letha
Loch na h-Aibhne Ruaidhe
Loch nan Faoileag
Loch Cleit na Struire

Area 43 LEWIS
Loch Scaslavat
Loch a' Gheòidh
Loch Ribavat
Loch Camasord
Loch Rangavat
Loch Sandavat
Loch na Cloich Airde
Loch a' Bheannain
Loch Melavat
Loch Brinnaval
Loch Faoirbh
Loch Mòr na Clibhe
Loch Sandavat
Loch Raonasgail
Loch Mor Bràigh an Tarain
Loch Clibh Cravacal
Loch na Clibhe
Loch Uladale
Loch a' Chama
Loch Greivat

Area 44 LEWIS
Loch à Bheanmich
Loch Nasavig
Loch Mheacleit
Loch Deireadh Bànaig
Loch Mor
Loch a' Gheoidh
Loch Sgailler
Loch Baravat
Loch Buaile nan Caorach
Loch Camasord
Loch Steishal

Loch Trialavat
Loch Linish
Loch a' Choin
Loch nan Eilean

Area 45 LEWIS
Loch à Pheaulir Mor
Lochan Sgeireach
Dubh Lochan
Loch Stacsavat
Loch Suainaval
Loch Granavat
Loch na Ciste
Loch Coirgavat
Loch Airigh an Uisge
Loch an Eilein Choinnich
Loch Sanclavat
Little Loch Roag
Loch na Craobhaige Móire
Loch Ruadh
Loch Dubh
Loch Geshader
Loch nan Uidhean
Loch Chadtartan
Loch Uamasbroc
Loch Scanadale
Loch Beag Ruadh
Loch Fuaroil
Loch na Muilne

Area 46 LEWIS
Caol Loch
Loch an Fhorsa
Lochan Traighidh
Loch Gainmhich
Loch Ruairidh
Loch Morsgail
Lochan Dubh
Loch Ru na Deas
Lochan nan Learga
Loch Airigh à Ghille Ruaidhe
Loch Strandavat
Loch Ruadh Meadhonach
Loch a' Sguair
Loch Coirigerod
Loch Cul Laimhe Bige
Loch Brùiche Breivat
Loch Moglavat
Loch Hestaval

Area 47 LEWIS
Loch Ceann Hulavig

Loch na Muilne
Loch Colloval
Loch Roag
Loch Smuaisaval
Loch Speireag
Loch Sgàire
Loch Beag na Beiste
Loch na Beiste
Loch Tingavat
Loch Suirstavat
Loch Ruadh
Loch na Ciste
Loch Uamsbroc
Loch na Sròine Moire
Loch na Craobhaig
Loch Allagro
Loch Ochàn
Loch Crocach
Loch Ahaltair
Loch Tana
Loch a' Mhairt
Loch Fhreunadail
Loch a' Bhraghad
Caol Loch
Loch Hamasord
Loch na Fang
Loch Aird
Loch Chaphail

Area 48 LEWIS
Loch an Eilein
Loch Ruadh
Loch Mohal Beag
Loch an Fhir Mhaoil
Loch Airigh a Bhealaich
Loch na Ciste
Loch Esa Ghil
Loch Faoghail an Tuim
Loch Ruadh Gheure Dubh Mor
Loch nan Eilean
Loch Mòr Airigh nan Linntean
Loch Beag Airigh nan Linntean
Loch Faoghail Charrason
Loch na Plaide
Loch Fuoghail Kirraval
Loch Fuoghail nan Caorach
Loch Airigh na h-Airde
Loch nan Fiasgan
Loch an ois Crhuirm
Loch an Earbull
Loch nan Eilean
Loch a Choir

Loch Cleit Steirmeis
Loch Tana na Gile Ruaidhe
Loch an Taobh Sear
Loch Roineval
Loch Cleit
Loch Cleit Eirmis
Loch Fadagoa

Area 49 LEWIS
Loch Cul a Cheit
Loch Crogach
Loch an Sgath
Loch na Ciste
Loch an Tairbeart
Loch an Tuim Aird
Loch an Fhada Bhig
Loch à Bhroma
Loch Gobhlaich
Loch an Drunga
Loch Skapraid
Loch Ibheir
Loch Tomain
Loch Culaidhean
Loch Tana
Loch Sgriachach
Lochovat
Loch Tana
Loch Trealand
Loch Cuil Airigh à Flod
Loch an Daimh
Loch a h-Iolare
Loch Cuthaig
Loch Aingh na Ceardaich
Loch nan Faoileag
Loch na Croibhe

Area 50 LEWIS
Loch na Creige Guinme
Loch Iosal a' Bhruic
Loch nan Tri Tom
Loch Geal
Loch à Gheoidh
Loch Dhomhnuill Bhig
Loch Ahmore
Loch nan h-Airigh Uisge
Loch Foid
Loch Fada
Loch na Cairteach
Loch Keadrashal
Loch nan Deaspoirt
Loch Ulapoll
Loch Tràighte

Loch nan Falcag
Loch na Craoibhe
Loch Tom nan Aigheap
Loch na Gainmhich
Loch na Speireig
Loch nam Fiasgan
Loch nam Breac
Loch an Eilean Liath
Loch Eastaper
Dubh Loch Subhal
Loch na h-Airigh Uir
Loch Cnoc na h-Iolaire

Area 51 LEWIS
Loch a Leadharain
Loch Cocn à Choilich
Loch Beag Cnoc Choilich
Loch a Chalachain
Loch Speireag
Loch Uisg an t-Soluis
Loch Briodag
Loch Airigh Riabhach
Loch nan Ramh
Loch Breugach
Loch Faoileag
Loch Leiniscal
Loch a' Chnoic Duibhe
Loch a' Bhuna
Loch Tana
Loch na Linn

Area 52 LEWIS
Loch Cnoc Iain Duibh
Loch nan Muilne
Loch nan Ritheanan
Loch nam Breuc
Loch Holavat
Loch nan h-Inghinn
Loch Keose
Loch Cnoc Berul
Loch Collie Shuardail
Loch Leurbost
Loch Lighigeag
Loch Sgeireach
Loch Grimshader
Loch Harmarshader
Loch Soval
Loch Valtos

Area 53 LEWIS
Loch Mor a' Ghrianain
Loch Airigh an Sgairbh

Loch Mor a' Chrotaich
Loch nan Cnàmh
Loch an Fheoil
Loch Beinn Bhieac
Loch Lobhair
Loch Innseag
Loch Tom an Fheidh
Loch na h-Earaig
Loch Cnoc lain Duibh
Loch Mòr Soval
Loch nan Eilean
Loch nan Starr
Loch nan Deareag
Loch Buaile Bhig
Loch a' Bhlair Bhuidhe
Loch Airigh nan Gleann
Loch Lathamul
Loch nan Capull
Loch na Cois
Loch Beag
Loch Orassy
Loch Beag na Craoibhe
Loch nan Laogh
Loch Airigh on t-Sagairt
Loch Beinn na Gainmheich
Loch Ard Airghigh a' Ghille Ruaidh
Loch Sandavat
Loch Oichean
Loch Crogavat
Loch Skavat
Loch na Buaile Gharbha
Loch Grunavat
Loch An Duna
Loch a Bhlàr Bhuidhe
Loch nan Cnámh (ii)

Area 54 LEWIS
Loch an Tiumpan
Loch an Duin
Loch an t Sidhein
Loch an Duin (ii)
Loch Cuilc
Loch Swordale

Area 55 LEWIS
Loch na Muilne
Loch Sgail
Loch Geal
Loch Tana
Loch a Chnuic
Loch Ruig Sandavat
Tob Valasay

Loch Buàile Miravat
Loch Breaclete
Loch nan Geardraisean
Loch Risay
Loch Gobhlach
Loch na Craobhaig
Loch Mharooil
Loch Nishavat
Loch Baravat
Loch Sgeireach
Loch Ionail
Loch na Ceannamhoir
Loch Barraglom

Area 56 LEWIS
Loch na Miulne
Loch a' Bhaik
Loch Chulain
Loch an Dùnain
Loch Honagro
Loch an Duin
Loch Carloway

Area 57 LEWIS
Loch Mhurchaidh
Loch an Laoigh
Loch Bhravat
Loch Amhastar
Loch an Fhraoich
Loch Beinn nar Sgalag (i)
Loch Laxavat Lorach
Loch Druim à Ghrianain
Loch Tom Liaurat
Loch Fusgro
Loch Borasdale
Loch Cliasan Creag
Loch Erraid
Loch Almaistean
Loch Fionnadeit
Loch na Muilne
Loch Eilaster
Loch Amar Sine
Loch Beinn nan Sgalag (ii)
Loch Dubh

Area 58 LEWIS
Loch Toma Dubh
Loch na Leamhain
Loch Airigh Brocaig
Loch Cleadaich
Loch Sgeireach
Loch Mhurchaidh

Loch an Tairbeart
Loch an Laoigh
Loch an Tuim
Loch na Ba Riabhaich
Loch Gainmheach Eitseal Bheag
Loch an Tairbeart nan Cleitchean
Loch Mhich Léoid
Loch Beag
Loch Rahacleit
Loch Dubh Vishal
Feath Loch Gleaharan
Loch Sandavat
Loch Mór Connaidh
Loch Ceann Allavat
Loch Airigh Seibh
Loch Laxavat Ard
Loch nan Caorach
Loch Mór a' Ghrianain
Loch na Béiste
Loch nan Cleitichean
Loch na Braiste
Loch Sandavat
Loch Clacharan
Loch a'Ghularr

Area 59 LEWIS
Loch nan Càoran
Loch Gil Speireig Mhór
Loch nan Eilean
Loch Beag Thoma Dhuibhe
Loch an Ois
Loch Vatandip
Loch Uravel
Loch nan Cnàmh
Loch Rhuadh Eitseal Bheag
Loch Airigh nan Sloc
Loch na Mòine
Loch Tana
Loch an Tobair
Loch nan Uidhean
Loch Mòr a' Chòcair
Loch Beag a' Chcair
Loch na Cairteach
Loch na Caorann
Loch na Beiste Mòire
Loch Garvaig
Loch nan Geadh
Loch nam Breac
Loch Airigh Mhic Fhionnlaidh Dhuibh
Loch na Moineach
Loch Gainmheach nam Faoileag
Loch na Gainmhich

Loch nan Steall
Loch Dubh nan Stearnag

Area 60 LEWIS
Loch Grinnavat
Loch Sgeireach
Loch Mur an Stàirr
Loch Roisnavat
Loch Beag an Stàirr
Loch nan Clach
Loch na Brathan Mòr
Loch na Scaravat
Loch Dubh an Duine
Loch nan Caorann
Loch Leitir
Loch an Fhraocit
Loch nan Leac
Loch Galavat
Loch Tulagaval
Loch Suiainagadail
Loch Sgaravat Beag
Loch na Brathan Mòr

Area 61 LEWIS
Loch Eagasgro
Loch Bacavat
Loch Aoraidh
Loch Muavat
Loch Breivat
Loch Spealtravat
Loch Bhruthadail
Loch Spealtravat Mòr
Loch Casgro
Da Loch an Fhéidh
Loch Urrahag
Loch an Dùna
Loch Grinavat
Loch Vanalair
Loch Nighean Shomhairle
Loch Ahavat Beag
Loch Ahavat Mor
Loch an Sgeireich Mhòir
Loch Eidhbhart
Loch Dubh Gormilevat
Loch Kearstavat

Area 62 LEWIS
Loch Risord
Loch Neadavat
Loch Carn nan-Eilidean
Loch Grinnavat
Loch Tuamister

Area 63 LEWIS
Loch na Muilne
Loch a' Bhaile
Loch Shader
Loch Chulain
Loch an Dunain
Loch Chulain
Loch Honagro
Loch an Dùin
Loch na h-Airde
Loch Runageo
Loch Breivat
Loch Skorashal
Loch Longavat
Loch Dubh à Chleite
Loch Dalbeg
Loch Raoinavat
Loch na Muilne (i)
Loch a' Bhaile
Loch na Muilne (ii)
Loch Ordais
Loch Arnol
Loch na Muilne (iii)
Loch Sgeireach
Loch Mor Barvas
Loch Sminig
Loch Dubh na h-Airde
Loch Baravat
Loch Drollavat
Loch Dibadale
Loch Scriachavat
Loch Stiapavat

Area 64 LEWIS
Loch Milleho
Loch Tom an Rishal
Loch Gunna
Loch nam Breac
Loch an Fheoir Mhoir
Loch an Fheoir Bheag
Loch a' Ghainmhich
Loch an Tuim
Lochan a' Sgeil
Loch Fada Caol
Loch an Tobair
Loch na Fola
Loch Mòr Sandavat
Loch nan Stearnag
Loch an Umhlaich
Lochan an Fhleasgaich
Loch nan Leac
Loch Stearnag

Loch na Faing
Loch Allavat
Loch Sléitir
Loch na Craoibhe
Loch Dubh Thorraidh
Lochan Dubh
L Niosavat
Upper Loch Hatravat
Lower Loch Hatravat
Loch Foisnavat
Loch Gress

Area 65 LEWIS
Loch Tanavat
Loch Grosavat
Loch nan Geadh
Loch Dubh Skiasgro
Loch an Eilein
Loch Ullavat a' Clith
Loch Ullaval a' Deas
Loch Chulapuill
Loch Beinn Lobheir
Loch Bacavat
Loch Corrasavat
Loch Langavat
Loch Tarstavat
Loch Sandavat
Loch Airigh Choinnich
Loch nan Geadh
Loch Dubh Skiasgro
Loch a' Chitear
Loch Ionadagro
Loch Scarrasdale
Loch Fad Oram
Loch Nic Dhomhnuil
Loch na Cloich
Loch Diridean
Loch Vatacolla
Loch Lingavat Mòr
Loch Lingavat Beg
Loch Mòr Sgeireach
Loch Mor a' Ghoba
Loch Beag Gainemhaich
Loch Gainemhaich
Loch Beag Sgeireach
Loch na Miulne
Loch Garmag Mòr

Area 66 LEWIS
Loch Ben Tearbert

239

Area 67 LEWIS

Loch Fada nam Faoileag
Loch Tana nan Leac
Loch Sgeireach a
Ghlinn Mhóir
Loch Chearasaidh
Loch Leisavat
Loch Rumsagro
Loch Striamavat
Loch Ruiglavat
Loch Kearsavat
Loch Leisavat
Loch Eileavat
Loch Glinnavat
Loch Maravat
Loch an Duin
Loch an Lobain
Loch a'Chlachain
Loch an Fheòir
Loch Eileatier
Loch Dubh Thurtail
Loch Beag Sandavat
Loch a'Ghille Ruaidh
Loch nan Cabrann
Loch Mor Sandavat
Loch Mòr Léig Tàdh
Loch Beag Léig Tàdh

Area 68 LEWIS

Loch na Muilne
Loch Dubh
Loch Leinavat
Loch Shiavat
Loch nan Claban
Loch Sgeireach na Creige Brist
Da Loch Fuimavat
Loch nan Luig
Loch Mór
Loch Néill Bhàin
Loch Bacavat Lorach
Loch nan Learga
Loch Bacavat Ard
Loch nan Learga
Loch Tana
Loch Grassavat
Loch Ruisavat
Loch Bacavat Cross
Loch Longavat
Loch Hatravat
Loch Caol Duin Othail
Loch Eillagual
Loch Mor Eileavat
Loch Beag Eileavat
Lochan Vataleois
Lochan Meadhonach
Loch Dubh a'Ghobha

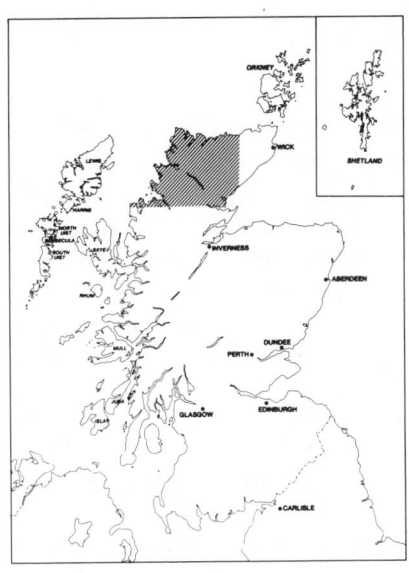

THE GREAT
ESCAPE

Sutherland moors and mountains

When anglers shuffle off this mortal coil and present themselves, wadered and rod-poised ready before the Pearly Gates, the lucky ones will be invited in to spend eternity fishing; and, in my opinion, the paradise St Peter has prepared for them will look a lot like Sutherland.

The South Land of the Vikings has thousands of lochs and lochans, full of hard-fighting wild brown trout, scattered amidst some of the world's most dramatic scenery: desolate moorlands; the sudden shock of Suilven and Inverpolly peaks; glorious Assynt and mighty Ben More, the highest mountain in Sutherland; the gentle shoulder of Canisp, towering over Cama, the crooked loch; and long, wind-swept Veyatie.

Salmon and sea-trout crowd rivers and estuaries. Tumbling Highland streams, rushing from remote moors, through deep pools and silent glades, heather-edged and rowan-graced. Delightful spate streams such as Naver, Borgie, Dionard, Inver and Kincraig. The lovely rivers of the Kyle of Sutherland; Carron, Shin, Oykle and Cassley. Flowing from Sutherland heartlands to mingle at Bonar Bridge with the waters of the Moray Firth.

Wild lands: Cape Wrath and the Parph Peninsula, the norse name for 'turning point'. In 1263 King Haakon of Norway led his great fleet along Sutherland's north coast, determined, once and for all, to establish his right to the Lordship of the Hebrides. They stopped to provision in Loch Erribol, but not for long. The party sent ashore were attacked by Clan MacKay and sent scurrying, bleeding, shipwards. Several vessels were wrecked, rounding the Parph, and the few who managed to reach the foot of hundred-feet-high cliffs, scrambled upwards to safety. Some say marks of their axes can still be seen on the rocks, as they struggled up. What became of these survivors is not known; but, if I'm any judge, it is unlikely that the Mackays would have rolled out a red carpet for their unexpected

241

guests. Generally, it was heads that did the rolling.

The fleet sailed south, past glorious Sandwood Bay, and rested in tide-marked Loch Inchard, near the present-day village of Kinlochbervie, glowered over by the long, grey ridge of Foinaven and conical Arkle. Juniper, scrub oak, alder, willow and birch scattered moors and valleys; growing strongly in warm corners, awaiting the later depredations of sheep and man which stripped the countryside bare. Relics of these ancient forests can still be seen throughout Sutherland, on isolated islands, loch-sprinkled throughout the north: Assynt, Caladail, Cama, Fionn, Seilge, Meadie and many others, safe from the attentions of flourishing farming. The countryside changed over the centuries, cattle giving way to sheep, moorlands reclaimed for growing oats and potatoes. Only the Flow Country, where the eastern boundary of Sutherland mingles with its neighbour Caithness, remains unchanged.

I first discovered Sutherland more than 30 years ago when we had a family holiday in Strathnaver. The lady of the house, a devout member of the Free Church of Scotland frowned mightily upon any Sunday jollity; but at one minute past midnight she was perfectly happy to take a net down to the River Naver to fill her larder.

We fished a number of the surrounding hill lochs for brown trout and tried our luck with salmon on the estuary beat of the river. Caught no salmon, and lost my first fishing hat, whipped from my head in a huge gale. The locals referred to the wind as a 'good drying breeze'. That night, on radio, the BBC weather man called it a force eight storm.

Long, fertile Sutherland straths finger northwards to Pentland Firth and North Sea and each cradles a stream, some of which have runs of sea-trout, all of which play host to Atlantic salmon, fresh from ice-cold Greenland feeding grounds. Fish run the rivers from March onwards and most of these streams used to have the reputation of giving good spring sport. Now the best catches are taken during autumn months with August and September being most productive.

Strath Halladale, the most easterly of the North Sutherland glens, has had a chequered history and from the early years of the 19th century until the present day, absentee landlords and commercial business interests have used Strath Halladale for private pleasure and profit. Most of the Strath was cleared by the Sutherland family to make way for sheep and, more recently, a Lowland company, Basil Baird & Sons, bought the Forsinard Estate to turn peat moorlands into grass-growing fields. Their efforts, after costing the tax-payer upwards of £500,000, were soon abandoned; as was the litter attendant upon their enterprise and the derelict peat-fuelled drying plant at Forsinain remains as yet another memorial to man's insensitivity to his environment.

However, the next owners made more far-reaching changes to the hills and moorlands. Fountain Forestry Limited, a private tree-farming company, bought the two principal Strath Halladale estates in the early 1980s, Forsinard and Bighouse, and they now control most of the game fishing, both in the glen and in the surrounding hills. A massive programme of ploughing, drainage and tree-planting has devastated once open moorlands. Hundreds of miles of seven-feet-high deer fences surround many of the lochs and lochans. New roads scar the hills and access is restricted—by permit only—via locked forestry gates.

The Halladale River runs through the Strath and can give good sport, depending upon water levels. It has always been prone to drying up and, at times, almost disappears in mid-summer; but when conditions are right then good numbers of fish may be taken.

On the credit side, Fountain Forestry has stopped all netting at the mouth of the river and has done some work repairing dams and weirs. They also propose to try and re-establish a system of flow compensation by using water from the hill lochs to maintain a better level in the river. This, in my view, will soon be essential as the flash-flooding effect forestry ploughing has will badly damage traditional rates of flow from the moors.

The Lower Halladale produces most fish, from Trantlemore down to Melvich. There are a number of good holding pools and although the river is mostly slow-moving, it fishes well to the fly, particularly in a strong north or south wind. The Upper River is in the hands of Forsinard Hotel, also owned by Fountain Forestry Limited, and has a limited number of small pools and runs but in good water levels, excellent sport may be had, mostly in the high-sided, gorge-like section of the stream.

Halladale produces about 150 salmon each year and there is also a run of sea-trout. They are best caught in the tidal water, below the new bridge that carries the Thurso/Bettyhill road across the river. Salmon average about 8 lb in weight; sea-trout, 1 lb 8 oz. Larger salmon are taken most seasons, with fish of up to 15 lb and the heaviest Halladale fish on record weighed 30 lb 8 oz. Best flies to use to tempt them to their doom are Willie Gunn, Munro Killer, Shrimp Fly and Stoats Tail. For sea-trout, standard pattern Scottish flies work well. Pack a few Black Pennel, Grouse and Claret, Peter Ross, Teal Blue and Silver, Alexandria and Butchers. That should do the trick.

Strath Halladale has a number of top-quality trout lochs, many now sadly surrounded by tree-farming operations. It is hard to say yet what the long-term effects of this afforestation will be but there is ample evidence from other areas, further south, to allow cause for great concern. Over a period of 11 years, 1971–1982, in Wales, three lakes surrounded by conifers became almost fishless. The same could happen at Forsinard. Tragically, by the time 'time tells', the damage will have been done.

Of equal importance, in my opinion, is the aesthetic effect these new, foreign conifers have on the pleasure of fishing the Forsinard lochs. I suppose, if you are of an insensitive turn of mind, or have not seen the

Loch Stack from Ben Stack, Sutherland

Flow Country in pre-tree farming days, then you may not mind your fishing hemmed in by closely packed Christmas trees.

Sletill, the best of the Forsinard waters, used to involve an hour's walk over the moorland to reach; but the way over the moors was a continual delight. Banks of yellow flag, tormentil, orchids and heather. Grey wagtails in the streams, golden plover and curlew on the hill. Almost certainly we would fish in company with a black-throated diver; often we saw an otter. Part of St Peter's paradise. Now a new road passing through several gates leads almost to the shore of the loch.

This also applies to the other lochs on the Forsinard estate: Leir, Talaheel, Lochan Ealach Mor and Loch na Cloiche; and, to the west, Loch Croach, the Cross Lochs and Breac. Visit them if you wish. There are still good fish to be caught. Perhaps if you do, you will begin to appreciate the utter devastation that mass tree-farming has caused to these once magnificent moorlands.

There are a few excellent lochs at the north of Strath Halladale which have, as yet, been unaffected by tree-farming.

This series of trout lochs offers first-class sport amidst superb surroundings. You will have to work legs and lungs a bit in order to reach them, but the rewards at the end of the hike are well worth the effort involved. My favourites are Eaglaise Mor and Eaglaise Beag, two delightful waters, about 40 minutes' walk south from Melvich. Beag is full of trout which average 10 oz whilst nearby Beag has much larger fish. I have taken trout of over 2 lb here and have happy memories of even larger fish splashing fiercely at my flies.

On the east side of Strath Halladale, lie three further good trout lochs. Akran is the ideal place to introduce a newcomer to the gentle art. Large baskets of bright little trout, three to the pound. Close to Akran are Lochs Caorach and na Seilge, great waters with good numbers of fish which average 10 oz and often surprise you with much larger trout. A short walk to heaven.

West from Strath Halladale is Strathy. A small, spate river which holds few salmon but does have some decent pools. The mouth of the river is often blocked by sand and this restricts both access of fresh fish and the exit of smolts from the system. But in the headwaters of the river there are some good trout lochs, the best of which is Loch Meala.

The fish are of a very high quality and average 12 oz. My best day on Meala produced a lovely basket of trout: six fish weighing 9 lb. Happy memories of wonderful days, sadly now gone forever.

The Naver is one of Scotland's finest salmon streams; and also one of the saddest. At daybreak, on a cold April morning in 1819, Mr Patrick Sellar 'accompanied by the fiscal, a strong body of constables, sheriff officers and others' arrived at the small village of Grumore on the north shore of Loch Naver. The inhabitants of the 16 dwellings were ordered to remove themselves and their belongings from their homes and half an hour later the cottages were set on fire and destroyed. Thus began the infamous Strathnaver Clearances when 2,000 men, women and children were made homeless and their ruined cottages still scar the Strath to this day. But it was not the first time that Clan MacKay had been asked to 'move along'. King Malcolm IV had them evicted from their original homes in Morayshire nearly 700 years earlier due to their lawless behaviour.

Close by the ruined village of Grumore stands evidence of much earlier times, the Grumore Broch, a magnificent Pictish fort on the shores of Loch Naver; with walls estimated to have been 10 feet thick and 40 feet high. A safe, almost impregnable fortress. Romans also knew the wild people of Strathnaver and, ironically, called them the Cereni—'sheep people'. Over the centuries this proud, independent highland race squabbled and fought amongst themselves, their neighbours, Sinclairs, Gunns and Keiths, Lowland Scots, English, Dutch, Spanish, Russian, Americans, French,

Germans; anyone and everyone foolish enough to incur their wrath.

Today, fierce battles still rage amongst the crags and corries of Ben Klibreck, Ben Loyal and the Choire Forest. But now the adversary is stag, grouse, salmon, sea-trout and brown trout and the centre of all this activity is the Altnaharra Hotel which lies at the west end of Loch Naver, 21 miles north of Lairg, where the A836 and B873/Bettyhill road meet. There has been a coaching inn at Altnaharra as far back as 1815 and it has evolved into a comfortable modern hotel; game fishing records covering the past 100 years may be seen at the hotel and are carefully preserved by the proprietor, Paul Panchaud.

Anglers fishing the River Naver often stay at Altnaharra and the river is divided into six beats, fished in rotation by fly only. Obtaining fishing on the Naver is a lot easier than describing it. The cost puts it outwith most anglers and even if one did have the money, then it is still very much a matter of waiting to fill dead men's fishing boots. However, it is sometimes possible to obtain a day on the estuary beat and, if you wish to try your luck, ask the Fishery Manager for permission to do so; and keep an eye open for my fishing hat. It's got to be kicking about somewhere.

Altnaharra Hotel offers good fishing to its guests on both river and loch. Salmon fishing is sometimes available on the River Mallart, a tumbling tributary of the famous Naver; and although the Mallart is a spate river, many fine fish are taken each season. The start of the Mallart fishing is a short walk from the B873 at the north end of Loch Naver and the best pools are Falls Pool and the Washing Pool.

At the other end of Loch Naver, the slow-flowing River Mudale meanders its way between the heights of Sorn an Turic and Cnoc an t-Sabbhail, entering the loch in a wide, shallow, sand and silt-filled bay. This little river can also produce good salmon fishing in the right conditions and is well worth a 'whack'.

The principal water at Altnaharra is Loch Naver itself; six miles long by half a mile wide, easily accessible, with excellent fishing and readily available to visiting anglers. Spring produces the best results and salmon of more than 16 lb are caught. The most notable basket taken from the loch in recent years fell to the rod of Mr Gilbert Sorrin: nine salmon weighing close on 80 lb. The gillie with Mr Sorrin on that memorable day was the late Willie Ross, one of the best known and most respected of all the Altnaharra gillies.

Loch Naver also has a very good sea-trout run, starting from about the middle of June with the best sport being had in August; depending upon weather conditions and all the other excuses we anglers make for our lack of skill. Brown trout also abound in the loch and their average weight is in the order of three to the pound; but watch out for larger specimens since fish of over six pounds have been taken.

When salmon and sea-trout in Naver and Mallart are dour and unresponsive, head north from Altnaharra along the A836 road towards

Tongue. There are dozens of good trout lochs along the way, all waiting for your carefully presented fly. Some, like Craggie and Loyal, are wild and wind-swept; others, such as Meadie, Staink and Plantation Loch can be sheltered and calm, even in stormy weather. All have one thing in common: good stocks of hard-fighting wild brown trout.

Loch Eileanach is a lovely water, 25 minutes walk from the road, to the east of Staink. Eileanach is shaped like a hurrying heather moth and the north section has a scattering of five small islands. Arrange your drift in order to give the shallows round these islands a good thrashing. In the southern section, fish down the west shore towards the outlet burn. This area can produce good results. Further west lie a delightful series of small lochs, 35 minutes' tramp from the road, between the shores of Loch Loyal and the crags of Cnoc Bad na Gallaig. The smallest water, Loch nam Breac Buidhe, contains the largest trout. There is a boat on Breac Buidhe but the other lochs are easily fished from the bank.

The best of the Altnaharra trout waters is Plantation Loch, near Cnoc a'Mhoid. The loch is evenly shallow, about 4–5 ft deep and fish average 1 lb. The best taken recently weighed 3 lb and this loch offers really first-class sport in most conditions. Meadie is a long straggle of water running from the little road that winds from Altnaharra north-east to Ben Hope. Full of little trout where large baskets are the rule, rather than the exception. But, for me, the most lovely of the trout lochs in the area is Tarbhaidh, nestling in a little upland valley south of Loch Naver, between Beadaig and Klibreck. The walk out takes about an hour, but the fish are splendid. Even the smaller ones fight like trout three times their weight and on a good day fish of over 1 lb will bend the strongest rod.

Tongue, on the north coast of Sutherland consists of a small collection of houses on the east shore of a wide, shallow, sandy inlet. There are two hotels, a post office, shop, church and that's about it. But if you've not visited this part of Scotland then you are in for a very pleasant surprise, because Tongue and the surrounding area has something for every member of your 'tribe'. The perfect place for a perfect family holiday.

There are superb beaches at Coldbackie, Melness and Torrisdale; magnificent scenery with hill walking and climbing on Ben Loyal, Ben Hope and Ben Klibreck; a wealth of interesting sites for botanist, archaeologist and ornithologist; or just simply taking it easy amongst friendly, welcoming people.

All this and, for us anglers, much, much more. Sea-trout may be caught in the Kyle of Tongue and there are a dozen fine trout lochs in the immediate vicinity. Fishing is in the hands of the Tongue and District Angling Association and their principal water is Loch Loyal. Loyal is a deep loch, dropping to more than 200 ft at the north end and bank fishing can be very productive. However, best results come from boat fishing and it is the best way to explore the eastern shore; otherwise, it's a long, hard hike round the loch. My favourite fishing area on Loyal is at the south end. Here the loch is shallow and you should mount your assault from where the water begins to deepen, about a couple of hundred yards from the mouth of the inlet burn from Loch Coulside. This area is also good for bank fishing and wading is relatively safe. There are big fish, waiting to be tempted among the weedy shallows.

To the north of Loyal, separated from it by a narrow bar, lies Loch Craggie. When the wind rages down Loyal, retreat to Craggie where there is often shelter. Trout in both lochs are average Highland fish, weighing about 8oz; but pay attention, because there are very much larger trout and fish of up to 7 lb have been taken.

If you like your fishing more remote and less public, then tackle some of the Angling Club's hill lochs; Loch a'Bhualaidh, on the west side of the Kyle; or a quick scramble up the hill to Loch h-Airigh Bige. Then there are also a number of good lochs contained within the road which leaves the A836 at Borgie and passes northwards through Skerry and Modsarie before rejoining the main road before Loch Buidhe.

East from Tongue, the little River Borgie runs into the sea at Torrisdale Bay. The Borgie is one of the most productive spate salmon rivers in the north and is born amongst the hills and moorlands south from Ben Loyal. The river begins life as a modest burn, Allt Dionach-caraid, flowing through Loch Coulside, under the A836 Altnaharra/Tongue road, into dark Loch Loyal, the largest of the three waters draining through Craggie and Sliam; from whence Borgie blossoms, a bright shining stream, dashing northwards to the Pentland Firth. There are 50 named pools and fishing stances on the river, many of them constructed during the early years of the century, and in 1960 a dam was built across Loch Sliam to control water flow. This helps to keep the water in the river at a respectable level during peak fishing months: spring-time May and June and heathered August and September.

The ten-year average catch for the system is in the order of 140 salmon, although in good years upwards of 500 fish have been caught and 1987 produced 221 salmon. A big plus point on the Borgie is the fact that there is no netting at the mouth and returning salmon have freedom of access to their spawning grounds at all times. Gillies are not provided but the water bailiff is on hand to show fishing tenants the water and generally point them in the right direction. Most of the pools and lies are obvious, but in high water fish can be caught almost anywhere in the river. Inch up; stalk the fish; keep back from the bank; crouch; present your fly delicately. I often sing to them. It all helps. At least, I think so.

The river is divided into four, two rod beats and autumn fishing is usually well booked in advance. However, there are cancellations and spring and early summer fishing is often available. June 1987 produced 40 fish. The most important thing to remember is that the Borgie is a spate

All in a day's work. David Aird with Plantation Loch trout

stream. You pay your money and take your chance. No water, no fish. Nevertheless, fish or not, Falls Pool on Borgie is one of the most lovely places to fish in the north.

Just as lovely is nearby Loch Hope, one of the best sea-trout fisheries in Europe. A short stream, just over a mile in length, joins Hope to Loch Eriboll and although fishing on the river is preserved, boats are available at both north and south ends of the loch. South End fishing has traditionally produced best results but in recent years, with more anglers fishing North End, returns are more evenly balanced. Loch Hope is six miles long by three-quarters of a mile wide across Middle Bay. The loch has an average depth of 60 ft and the deepest part is 187 ft, between Creagan na Speireig and Meall Bad a'Mhuidhe, half way down the loch. Strathmore River, very much a spate salmon stream and largely private, feeds Hope, down the strath.

Close to the shores of the river stand the ruins of gaunt Dun Dornaigil Broch, a well-preserved Pictish fort. The broch was between 50–60 ft high, with 15-ft-thick walls encircling a roofless, inner court. Here, in green Strath More, the Dicaledonae, the northern Picts, cultivated their crops, hunted red deer and no doubt netted the stream in a wilderness land unpenetrated even by the might of Rome.

One of Scotland's most famous Gaelic poets, Robb Donn, 'the bard of Sutherland' was born near Dun Dornaigil; in that time after the 1745 Rebellion when Gaelic poetry flourished in the aftermath of Culloden. Alexander MacDonald, John MacCodrum, Dugald Buchanan, Duncan Ban MacIntyre and Willie Ross. They created a great lyrical history of immense beauty, as alive today as when it was first written, more than 200 years ago.

Fishing on Loch Hope is divided into five beats: North End, Middle Bay, Beats 1, 2 and 3. The main runs of sea-trout arrive mid-June with best fishing being from August until September and each season sees 400–500 fish caught. Salmon are also taken, although they must always be considered a bonus, and dapping is a favoured fishing method. The classic technique is for the gillie to operate the dapping rod from the middle of the boat whilst bow and stern rods fish traditional wet fly patterns. When the gillie spots a fish at the dap, he removes the fly and the sea-trout turns either right or left to grab the wet flies—or should. In my case, it's like a post office counter queue. No matter which end of the boat I'm stationed, the fish always seems to go the other way. It is also very important to offer the gillie a dram, before setting out. Otherwise, his memory might fail him at the crucial moment and he may, accidentally, hook the fish himself. Got to be careful, sea-trout fishing.

Loch Hope can be very windy and on some of the beats, to avoid upsetting ultra-shy sea-trout, outboard motors are not allowed. Therefore, when fishing Hope you must have a reasonable amount of experience in small boat handling. And wear a floatation jacket. Better still, ask for the services of a gillie. Not only will his strong arms be a comfort on the oars, but he will also take you quickly to the best lies. Money well spent and, in my experience, the Hope/Altnaharra gillies are expert at their job and really know their waters well.

Driving west from Hope, around the shore-line of narrow sea-Loch Eriboll, you might be forgiven for failing to notice the little River Polla. This tiny spate river from time to time produces large surprises. For instance, a couple of years back, a magnificent salmon of 17 lb. Fishing is worth while after heavy spate and because of high falls, only the lower half of the stream produces results. A question of being in the right place at the right time. Difficult if you happen to live south.

Nevertheless, if you are in the area and water levels are right, ask Jack Watson at the Cape Wrath Hotel to try and arrange a few hours' fishing for you. It may be worth while and you never know your luck. Certainly, the Polla is a lovely place to be; surrounded by fine mountains, running down from Creag Staonsaid and Meall Tarsuinn. Better, though more modest sport, may be had amongst the trout lochs that scatter the high tops: Loch Bealach na Sgeulachd, na Creige Duibhe and Croach. You will need proper permission before fishing, and proper stamina to get there. But it is worth every step of the way.

Far better sport with salmon and sea-trout is just round the corner, at the Kyle of Durness, in Dionard, Grudie, Diall and Loch Dionard; and the fishing is readily available to guests staying at the Cape Wrath Hotel. The hotel is perfectly situated standing amid green fields, looking southwards down Strath Dionard, a splendid Highland panorama of sunlight and sparkling waters. The horizon is lined with the wild peaks of Cranstackie and the massive bulk of Foinaven. Over the shining sands of the Kyle lie the beautiful hills of the Parph Peninsula; crags of Beinn an Amair, Fashven, Beinn Dearg and Creag Ribbach, and the narrow road leading out to remote Cape Wrath lighthouse.

The River Dionard rises deep in the hills flowing through Loch Dionard, cradled between Conamheall east and Foinaven west. A desolate, superb land of wildcat, eagle and red deer. In days past, reaching this magnificent loch involved a long, hard, damp tramp up the strath from Gualin; or a pony-trekked hike from Gobernuisgach Lodge to the south.

Anglers stayed overnight in a comfortable bothy, to make the journey worth while and spent their time fishing for salmon and sea-trout, accompanied by the magical piping of greenshank and curlew. Now an argo-cat track is being built into the wilderness to ease the weary feet of wealthy fishers not inclined to work for their pleasure.

A number of proprietors own the Dionard fishings and upwards of 100 salmon are taken most years. Sea-trout also run the river to the loch and many visit Durness more for sea-trout fishing than for salmon. Two other streams enter the Kyle on the west side: Grudie and Diall. The hotel has rights on both of these waters and, given decent flows, good sport may be had.

The Grudie has a reputation of producing large salmon, fish of up to 17 lb, whilst best fishing on the Diall is to be found in Loch Bad an Fheur-loch, a steep climb up from the ford at Achiemore; occasionally, salmon ascend further to the source of the river, Loch Airigh na Beinne. Salmon and sea-trout enter the system from June onwards and the best fishing is probably during the months of July and August. All depends upon water levels.

Apart from the high quality of salmon and sea-trout fishing, Durness offers what is, in my view, some of the finest and most challenging wild brown trout fishing in Britain. The four limestone lochs of Keodale are crystal clear and will test your skill, knowledge and patience to their uttermost; but rewards can be dramatic. Trout of over 3 lb are common-place and on the smallest water, Loch Lanlish, fish of more than 8 lb are still caught. Loch Borralie is the largest and is a short walk over the fields behind the hotel. Fish average 1 lb 8 oz and sample baskets over recent years read like an angler's dream: two fish at 8 lb 8 oz; four fish at 12 lb; one fish at 5 lb.

The next largest loch is Caladail, easily accessible from the main road and containing trout which are particularly lovely; golden in colour, beautifully marked, with bright pink flesh. Dry fly does well on Caladail and a sample of what you may expect is a perfect basket of six fish at 14 lb, taken in 1983.

The fourth Keodale water, Croispol, lies to the west of the village of Balnakeil and offers its own, unique type of challenge. The fish are smaller, relatively speaking, but they fight with great dash and spirit and in 1981 Norman Simonds landed a beauty weighing 4 lb 8 oz, from the edge of the very deep hole half-way down the east bank.

If the strain of trying to outwit salmon and sea-trout in Dionard and limestone loch trout proves too much, then journey over the Kyle of the Parph. There are more than a dozen lochs here and all contain good stocks of fish, some of which will not have seen an artificial fly for years. The most delightful aspect of fishing here, however, is the complete remoteness of the setting; and providing that you are well shod, you may walk safely all day, fishing and exploring.

The most productive of the Parph waters is Loch Keisgaig, which also involves the longest walk but contains some excellent trout of up to 2 lb in weight. If it is a fine day, walk on and visit that most remote and lovely of all Scottish beaches at Bay of Keisgaig. The hill lochs of the Parph Peninsula are a complete contrast to the well-ordered luxuriant and accessible limestone waters; but they are some of the most fascinating lochs to fish in the north. Take a compass and map, let people know where you are going and have a good day out in the hills; or two or three.

South now, over the watershed at Meal na Moine, down to Rhiconich. Most of the fishing here is let by the Oldshoremore Estate, Scourie Hotel, Scourie and District Angling Club and Reay Forest Estate. Oldshoremore has a number of good trout lochs and sea-trout fishing on Lochs Garbert Mor and Garbert Beag, which can also hold large numbers of salmon, given good water levels in the Inchard River. Fishing on the lochs is by rotation on the basis that at least one of the sea-trout lochs will be available to guests at Oldshoremore Lodge each day of the week, with Garbert Beag being available on a minimum of two days each week.

The estate has also introduced fishing on Loch Sandwood which can produce salmon and sea-trout when water levels are right. Sandwood is probably the loveliest fishing location in Scotland. The loch lies at the end of a four-mile track and is close to the sea by the wide, golden sweep

The Sutherland Flow country

253

of Sandwood Bay. The River Shinary runs through the loch and in spate conditions good sport may be had. If you require your fishing remote and beautiful, then Sandwood is the place to go. Even without the added attraction of fishing, Sandwood is one of the special places on planet Earth and a day there is an all-enduring, pleasurable memory.

As is fishing round Scourie. Indeed, if you fished a different water every day, every week between April and September for several years, you still wouldn't do justice to all the fishing available, and if you spent the rest of your life wandering and fishing amongst these hills and mountains you would never tire of their ever-changing beauty and majesty.

The village of Scourie lies in the A894, 44 miles north-west of Lairg and 40 miles north from Ullapool. There are a few scattered houses, a petrol-filling station, shop and hotel and I knew of few other areas in Scotland which offers such a wide variety of excellent game fishing amid such spectacular scenery.

High above the valley of the Laxford River, magnificent peaks crowd the horizon; Arkle (757 m), Foinaven (867 m), Creagen Meall Horn (729 m) and Ben Stack (721 m) towering over gentle Loch Stack. The western vista from the hills is one of moorlands and crags, silver-specked with lochs and lochans, sweeping towards the Atlantic. The hills are alive with the sound of greenshank, curlew and larks; ravens haunt the high corries and golden eagles wheel and turn in ever watchful readiness for glimpse of prey. A sudden, tiny lochan will hold a pair of red-throated divers and signs of deer, wildcat and otter mark your way. For angler and naturalist alike, this corner of north-west Sutherland is a wonderland of interest and delight.

The Laxford River is strictly private and mere mortals may only dreep over Laxford Bridge, drooling. However, fishing is available in the fine lochs at the head of the river, Stack and More and both these waters produce good numbers of sea-trout and salmon each season.

Stack is undoubtedly one of Scotland's premier sea-trout fisheries, whilst More is better known for salmon. Both offer excellent sport and bookings can be made either through the Reay Estate Office at Achfary or at Scourie Hotel. About 100 salmon and 500 sea-trout are taken each year and dapping is a favourite method of catching them. Be warned, however, both waters can be very wild, and outboard engines are not allowed. Be prepared for some hard work on the oars or ask for a gillie. The estate does not provide gillies but Ian May at the Scourie Hotel can often arrange one. Local knowledge on Stack is important and you should seek advice from the estate before setting out. There are a number of good lies, particularly in the vicinity of underwater shallows and these should be noted before launching your assault.

Scourie Hotel offers good salmon fishing on the Duart System, south from the village towards Kylestrome; and also on a number of other waters including Clashfern, Badnabay and nan Ramh. In recent years the hotel has established a grilse fishery at Cardhu Loch and this has proved to be very popular with visitors. For me, however, the best of the Scourie fishing is to be found out in the hills amidst the hundreds of trout lochs, where fish to suit all tastes may be caught; frying-pan sized, brightly marked tiddlers up to huge fish of 6lb or more. One of the great joys of Scourie fishing is the element of uncertainty. Another one to put back, or one for the glass case?

It would be a long task to detail all the Scourie waters. Most of the best involve a hard walk and you must be ready for up to seven miles hiking a day to get them. One afternoon, watched over by Arkle, I climbed steeply to reach a tiny loch, un-named on the map. The moment my flies landed on the surface, two, 12oz trout grabbed, simultaneously. As long as I cast, so the fish rose and I kept three of the best to take back to show the rest of our party, fishing 500 ft lower. That day ended with a basket of 11 trout weighing 9lb, wet feet, tired legs and wind-burnt faces. Evening sunlight shadowed grey mountains and golden plover called plaintively as we made our way homewards. The path wandered through the hills, past mirror-calm lochs, stippled with rising trout. A black-throated diver swept by, neck outstretched, calling hauntingly. It was one of those paths where your only desire was that it should go on forever. There are many like that by Foinaven, Arkle and Stack, in the far north-west.

A new bridge has been constructed over the narrows at Kylesku, but the old ferry has not been abandoned and works on, in Caithness, as a private vessel, transporting sheep to and from the uninhabited island of Stroma, off the coast from John o' Groats. The journey south is quicker, but I miss the magic of the little boat; chugging over Loch Glencoul and Glendhu to Assynt, under the dreadful tower of Quinag.

Turn right off the bridge and follow the little road out towards Drumbeg, the coast road to Lochinver. A complete adventure in itself. Seaton Gordon, in his marvellous book, *Highways and Byways in the West Highlands*, first published in 1935, described his journey over the tortuous track: 'At first the road was very narrow, but the gradients were not alarming. Then we descended what appeared to be a sheer precipice, crossed a narrow bridge, and found barring our way a great hill which must have been at least one in three. At the first attempt the ancient Wolsley faltered at the steepest corner. A cautious descent in reverse was made to the foot of the hill, and a second gallant effort met—but only just—with the success if deserved.'

Not much has changed thereabouts and this road can still draw a scream from nervous passengers. But, at the end, sanity returns as you pass through the village of Nedd and reach Drumbeg. There is a comfortable small hotel, a lot of midges, and some excellent trout fishing on about 16 lochs. Some, like Loch Drumbeg, are easily accessible; others make you

Falls Pool on the River Borgie

pant a bit, like Gorm Loch Mor and Gorm Loch Beag. But they offer splendid fishing in splendid isolation; and a perfect base for exploring this least visited part of Sutherland.

If you drive due south from the new Kylesku Bridge, the road climbs also, but not so steeply, between Quiang and Glas Bheinn and at the summit there is a wonderful view of Assynt and Inchnadamph; fore-grounded by the blue loch, back-dropped by Canisp and Suilven. A warm welcome to one of my most-loved areas of Sutherland.

Inchnadamph is surrounded by eleven miles of continuous mountains none of which drop below 600 m. Ben More Assynt (1,000 m), Sutherland's highest peak, towers over the grey ruins of Ardvreck Castle by the shores of the loch. Ardvreck was the home of the MacLeods of Assynt, who betrayed the Marquess of Montrose for the sum of £20,000 and a few sacks of meal. Montrose was tied to the back of a pony, where his head was removed and taken to Edinburgh. Happily, there is no record of Macleod ever having received his reward for such an un-Christian, un-Highland, un-charitable act.

Inchnadamph is famous for its limestone caves, dug out over the years by the busy Trailgall Burn, and they have produced a wealth of prehistoric remains. Pot-holes, cave and underground passages extend to over 460 m. Above them alpine flowers grow in profusion: hawkweed, purple saxifrage, mountain saxifrage, sedges and rare grasses. 'Trailgall' is derived from the Norse, meaning Troll's Gill or Giant's Ravine and the caves were believed to have been inhabited by man more than 6,000 years ago.

Inhabiting the depths of Loch Assynt are a multitude of small brown trout and a few very large ferox. Over recent years a number have been caught, mostly by anglers spinning for salmon and most of these fish weigh around the 8–9 lb mark; but there are probably bigger ones lurking in the cold waters of the loch.

Salmon reach Assynt by way of the River Inver, and some 40–50 fish are taken each season, mostly from the Inchnadamph Hotel boats. Fish even run the Loanan Burn and reach Loch Awe where they sometimes are caught in an unguarded moment by trout fishers; thus providing a red-letter day and the danger of a heart attack to the unsuspecting angler. Doesn't do the fish much good either.

Main runs of Inver salmon don't start until June and from then on until the end of the season fish enter the river constantly. However, they are not caught constantly although upwards of 250 fish are taken most seasons. A dam across Loch Assynt at the west end helps to maintain reasonable water levels in the river and much improvement work has been carried out over the years to pools and lies, the best of which are probably Loch an Iasgaich, where the river widens below Little Assynt and Deer, Star and Ladder, further downstream.

There are more than 60 trout lochs in the vicinity of Lochinver and

Assynt which are available to visiting anglers. Many are managed by the Assynt Angling Club and they range from roadside waters, such as Loch a'Choin and an Arbhiar, the 'cat and dog' lochs, to more remote waters such as an Tuirc and scattered Beannach.

The Assynt Estate offers even more, between the heights of Suilven and Canisp; the long fingers of Fada and Gainimh, the little pools of Choire Dhuibh and na Barrack below Caisteal Liath, Suilven's summit, 'the grey castle'; Leothaid and Loch Gorm, to the north of the track that leads eastwards from Glencanisp Lodge. Packed with bright, small trout, offering splendid sport.

Fishing is also readily available to anglers visiting Elphin, near Leadmore Junction. There are a series of four splendid trout waters: Borralan, Urigill, Cama and Veyatie, each offering good sport in marvellous surroundings. They all have thousands of traditional Highland wild brown trout averaging three to the pound, and a few monsters, rarely seen and even more rarely caught. Veyatie produced one a couple of years back and it weighed 9 lb.

Take care fishing these waters, particularly Cama and Veyatie. The water is very deep and close to the shore, and wading can be dangerous. Even getting out of the boat at the wrong end could spell disaster. The bow might be safely aground. However, the stern could be floating over 20 feet of water. Be warned. My favourite Lochinver loch lies at the head of the Kirkaig River, Fionn—'the white loch'. Fionn is a long, straggling water, a myriad of bays and corners, collecting together waters from thousands of acres; Loch Borralan, by the site of the ill-fated Altnacealgach, burnt down a few years ago; Loch Urgill on the northern slopes of the Cromalt Hills; Cama, 'the crooked loch'; windswept Veyatie, lurking below Cul Mor. All meet and mingle in Fionn before plunging seawards down the river.

Fionn has something for everyone. Bright, well-marked wild brown trout averaging 8–12 oz; fine fish of over 3 lb; and in the depths, ferox, caught by the old Scottish fishing method, trolling. Some good baskets are taken and in 1985 one lucky angler returned from Fionn with 19 splendid fish weighing 16 lb.

The walk out to Fionn follows the north bank of the Kirkaig River, a lovely Highland spate stream; past deep, silent pools, where salmon lie. They enter Kirkaig from March onwards with main runs coming in July. Fishing on the river is divided into three beats, from the estuary to Kirkaig Falls, a dramatic, 60-ft torrent barring any further upstream progress for returning salmon. Fishing the Upper Beat requires strength, skill and a head for heights. Instructions for landing salmon from Kirkaig Falls Pool are: 'To gaff a fish one slides down to the right of the fishing stance, and on to a ledge. There is a rope attached to the rock as a hand-hold. When

Three men and a dog—boat work at Durness, Sutherland

gaffed, the gaff and the fish are handed up to the angler who must take care not to let the fish off the gaff and drop on the head of his gillie!'

The lower river is less hazardous to fish and there are many fine pools and runs. Kirkaig produces about 150 salmon each season and fishing is available through the Culag Hotel in Lochinver. Book well in advance. Say the appropriate prayers for rain.

As you travel eastwards from Ledmore, down Strath Oykel, the range and quality of trout fishing diminishes. This is more than compensated for by the quality of sport with salmon and sea-trout because the rivers of East Sutherland provide some of the best game fishing in Scotland. The Oykel rises in Loch Ailsh, tucked under the southern shoulder of Ben

259

More, surrounded by the wonderful stalking country of Benmore Forest. Ailsh used to give excellent sport, particularly with sea-trout, but is now, sadly, but a poor shadow of its former self.

The Oykel produces up to 1,000 salmon most seasons and fishing is well booked in advance. Nevertheless, you should inquire at the Oykel Bridge Hotel for a rod and early-season fishing is sometimes available. The setting is perfect and the river meanders quietly through the Strath, collecting in the waters of numerous hill lochs on its way, draining steep hillsides, hurrying the stream to the Kyle of Sutherland and its meeting with the waters of Shin and Carron.

There are upwards of 70 named pools and the Oykel is the boundary between Ross-shire and Sutherland. Between Caplich Wood and Cnoc a'Bhith, the river charges through a spectacular gorge before gathering in Einig and Mulzie, both of which can produce good salmon fishing, given the right water conditions; flowing down from the wilderness of Freevater Forest and corries of Seana Bhraigh and Meall nam Bradhan in Ross-shire.

Another famous salmon stream, the Carron, starts life on the southern slopes of Seana Bhraigh and sweeps eastwards through Gleann Mor, Glencalvie and Amat to reach the sea in the Kyle of Sutherland, upstream from Bonar Bridge. The Carron also has its contributory streams: Alladale, Water of Glencalvie and Black Water, all of which can fish well after heavy rain.

For me, the most attractive of Kyle rivers is the Cassley; a true 'Highland River', dashing down the glen from a group of the most remote lochs in the north: na Sroine Luime, Fionn Loch Beag, Gorm Loch and Loch Bealach a' Mhadaidh, near to one of Scotland's highest waterfalls, Eas a' Choal Aluinn, 'the maiden's tresses' cascading in a gigantic leap from the heights of Glas Bheinn. Some years ago, whilst staying at Duchally, I walked this way, out to Carn nan Conbhairean, a tiny, dark, deep loch nestling below the massive south-east face of Ben More, cupped in a corrie formed by Meall an Aonaich and Carn nan Conbhairean. Didn't catch anything, but the memory of that remote, magnificent corrie will stay with me forever.

Cassley fishing is shared by Glenrossal and Rosehall. Glenrossal have the upper Cassley, Rosehall from the estate boundary at Glenrossal Kennels. There are a number of waterfalls on the river; at Glenmuick, where Amhain Gleann na Muic enters, and below Glencassley Castle. Fly only, some really super pools and an annual catch in the region of 500 salmon.

The last of the rivers entering the Kyle is Shin; a short, narrow river which has been much altered in character due to the damming of Loch Shin in 1959 by the Hydroelectric Board. The river has its true source in the hills above Loch Merkland, 20 miles further west along the road to Scourie and is also fed by Loch Fiag and Loch Chorm-choire, on the east slopes of Ben Hee.

260

Fishing the river can be a bit of a stumble at times, particularly below Achany Lodge where the stream is forced through a narrow gorge and the famous Falls of Shin, a favourite salmon-spotting site for visitors. For those wishing to have a closer look at salmon, inquire at the Sutherland Arms Hotel in Lairg which can often offer rods. The river can produce over 500 fish in a good year. There is bound to be one for you.

There are a number of trout lochs near Lairg, not least of which is vast Loch Shin itself, 17 miles long, often wild and windy. Trout in Shin are small but each season produces a few surprises with fish of 5 lb and heavier taken. It is best to seek advice before setting out and the Lairg Angling Club will be happy to oblige as well as provide sound boats and outboard motors for hire.

But for a really special day out, visit Loch Craggie, one of the best trout lochs in the area and a short drive from town. Craggie covers an area of 170 acres, is easily accessible and delightfully remote. As you leave Lairg heading northwards to Loch Shin, turn right on the road signposted to Saval. A mile or so up the hill, through a locked gate, a track on the right leads out to Savalbeg Farm. The road passes the farm and you eventually arrive at Loch Dola, a shallow, rocky water, with two small islands in the south bay. Dola is full of splendid trout averaging 8–12 oz and when I last fished it I had more than a dozen fish within the hour. The track goes on, further into the hills, to yet another loch which will send you home with breakfast, Tigh na Creige.

Magnificent Craggie is to the east of Dola, over the crest of a small hill, about 15 minutes' walk from the car. A good boat is moored by a bad boathouse at the west end of the loch and trout in Craggie average 1 lb in weight. Much heavier fish are taken, all over the loch.

The Saval Estate was sold recently to Fountain Forestry Limited and several thousand acres are being planted with the usual rows of lodge pole pine and Sitka spruce. So far, the fishing has maintained its high quality, and I can unhesitatingly recommend Craggie to you as a rewarding and lovely place to fish. There is always a catch, however, and in this case it is the price: £28 per day for a boat with two rods. Nevertheless, in my opinion, it is good value for money.

North from Bonar Bridge, the A9 leads on to greater fishing things, Brora and Helmsdale. On the way, there are a number of good trout waters, the best of which are the Glas Lochs, available through the Sutherland Estate Office in Golspie. A hard walk/climb to reach but worth the effort involved. Also, available from the Dornoch Angling Club, is fishing on Lochs Buidhe, Laoigh, Lannasidh, Lagain, Laro and Cracail Mor, with sea-trout fishing in the Firth at Littleferry. But the real prize here, is Loch Brora and its attendant river; and the best place to start fishing them is in the middle of the village, at Rob Wilson's tackle shop. Colin Taylor is the new owner of this famous north-of-Scotland anglers'

261

Lazy days on Loch Corispol, Durness

Mecca and he will give visiting anglers all the help and advice they need to mount their attack.

Occasional rods on the Lower River are difficult to obtain and the Upper Brora is almost a closed shop, the fishing being let with Estate Lodges. Still worth inquiring, nevertheless, and Colin will keep you right. The Lower Brora has 26 named pools and fishing is organised so that tenants start at opposite ends each day, changing sides at the midway point. Sounds a bit like a rugby match, but this makes sure that no two anglers fish the same pool from opposite banks.

The largest salmon taken from the Brora was a fish of 45 lb caught in the Bengie Pool before the last war; but Rob Wilson's brother, John, landed a huge salmon of 40 lb in 1958. A remarkable fish. Even more remarkable is the fact that John Wilson landed the monster on a new two-and-three-quarter-ounce rod that Rob had just built.

Fishing on Loch Brora is more readily available to visiting anglers, although even here it is better to make sure by booking in advance. The loch is more than three and a half miles long and naturally divides into three sections: Bottom Loch, Middle Loch and Top Loch. Finding your way around and, more important, where the fish are, requires considerable knowledge.

If time is limited, ask Colin Taylor to try and arrange for you to share a boat with a local angler. This could make the difference between a red-letter day and an empty basket. Fishing is from boats only and anglers have the chance of sport with salmon, sea-trout and brown trout. Salmon fishing is best from April until mid-June and then from August until the end of the season in October.

Whilst most salmon are caught in Top Loch, sea-trout are more difficult to find and anglers will have to use all their skill, and oar and arm power to spot them. Generally speaking, they lie in the shallows, fairly close to the bank and in the vicinity of where the three lochs are linked together. Flies that do the damage include Mallard and Claret, Butchers and Black Pennel. Colin Taylor always has a good supply of these and other 'flies of the moment'.

North from Brora is the Helmsdale River, one of the most productive of all Scottish salmon streams. However, like the Naver and Laxford, it is almost impossible for 'normal' anglers to obtain fishing on the famous stream. Rods are sometimes available to the public on the lower, estuary beat and although fish tend to run quickly upstream, this part of the river can fish very well indeed and most seasons it produces upwards of 200 salmon. However, the remainder of the Helmsdale is a closed book and although it is tempting to list its delights, I see little point in doing so if it is not available to visiting game fishermen.

Water flow in Helmsdale is controlled and the source of this munificence is a series of lochs to the west of Kinbrace, in the area known as Badanloch. Here, the visiting angler will be made welcome, particularly at mainland Scotland's most remote hotel, the Garvault, noted in the *Guinness Book of Records* as such. The hotel lies close to the twisting road from Kinbrace into Strathnaver, on the slopes of Ben Griam Mor. Southwards the mountains of the Ben Armine forest and crags of Coire na Saidhe Duibhe crowd the horizon. Eastwards lie the gentle hills of Borrobal and Caithness, Morven and the Scarabens.

The Garvault Hotel offers fishing in its own right and by arrangement with neighbouring estates, to suit all states of physical fitness and ability. The principal waters, Badanloch, Nan Clar and Rimsdale are easily accessible. Out in the hills are a number of other waters which contain trout which vary in size from 8 oz up to 3 lb: Druim a'Chliabhain, Coire

Loch Cama, The Crooked Loch, Assynt

nam Mang, Fhearna, Palm Loch, Rosail, Gaineimh, Coal-loch Beag and Coal-loch Mor, Sgeireach and Rhifail.

The Achentoul Estate has more, all waiting for your best efforts: Ruathair, Arichlinie, Lucy and Culaidh. But if you really want to restore your fishing self-confidence, or introduce a novice to fly fishing, head for Loch Ascaig, south from Kinbrace. Here, even the greatest duffers in the world, people like me, should catch fish; amidst the glorious peace and solitude of wonderful Sutherland.

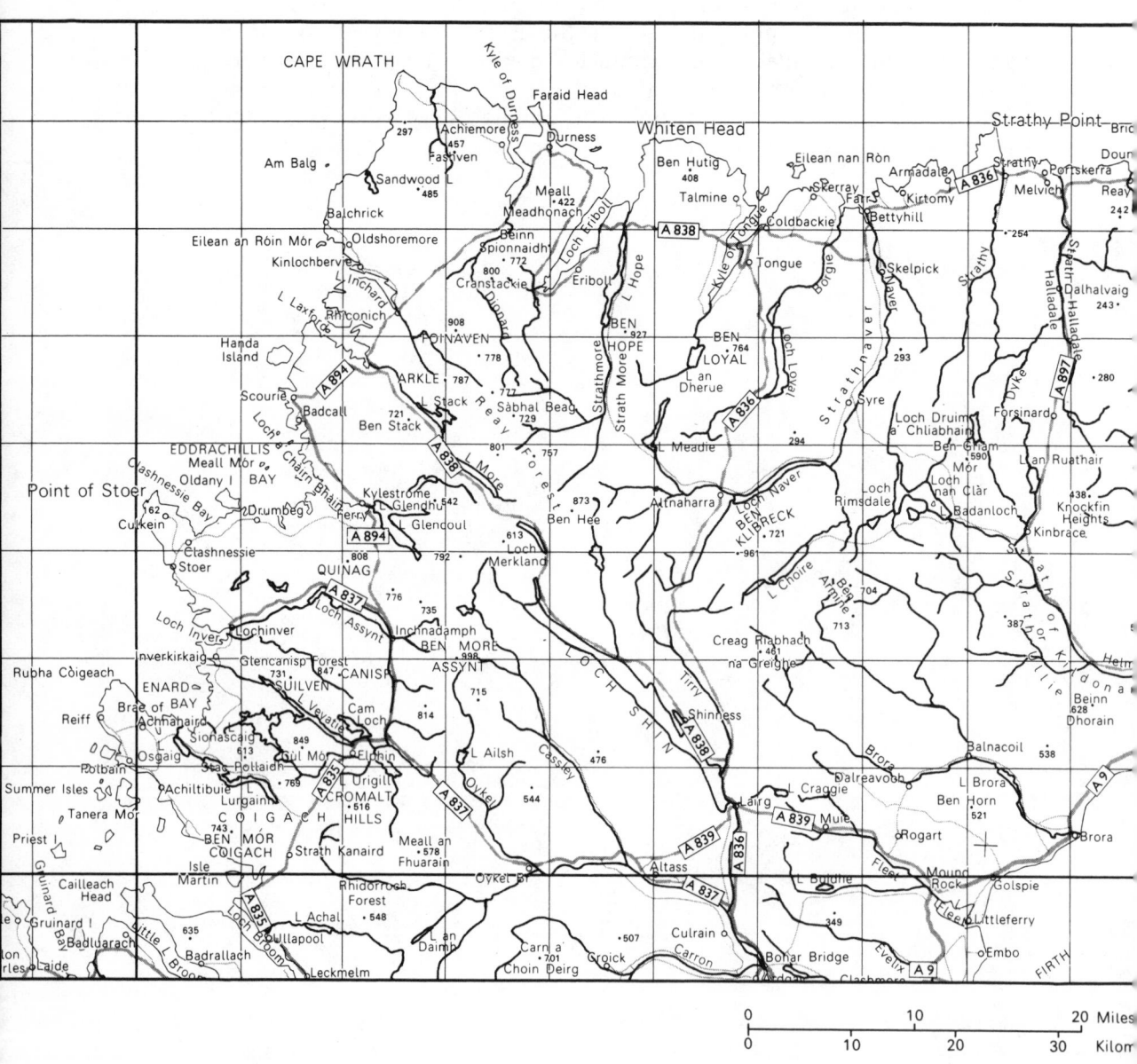

THE GREAT ESCAPE

FISHING DIRECTORY

RIVER HALLADALE
(Lower River)
Mrs Atkinson,
c/o Bradford & Bingley Building Society,
Sinclair Street, Thurso, Caithness
(0847) 63291

RIVER HALLADALE
(Upper River)
Forsinard Hotel,
Forsinard, Strath Halladale, Sutherland
(06417) 221

STRATHY RIVER
CAOL LOCH
LOCH AKRAN
LOCH NA CAORACH
LOCH NA SEILGE
LOCH ACHRIDIGILL
LOCH NA h-EAGLAISE MOR
LOCH NA h-EAGAISE BEAG
Mrs Atkinson,
c/o Bradford & Bingley Building Society,
Sinclair Street, Thurso, Caithness
(0847) 63291

LOCH CROCACH
THE CROSS LOCHS
LOCH TALAHEEL
LOCH LEIR
LOCH SLETILL
LOCHAN EALACH MOR
LOCH NA CLOICHE
Forsinard Hotel,
Forsinard, Strath Halladale, Sutherland
(06417) 221

RIVER NAVER
Naver & District Fishery Board,
Fishery Office, Dalvina Strathnaver,
Kinbrace, Sutherland
(06416) 200

RIVER BORGIE
LOCH SLIAM
Jamie & Partners,
Rectory Place, Loughborough, Leics
(0509) 233433

LOCH NAVER
RIVER MALLART
RIVER MUDALE
LOCH HOPE (South End)
LOCH LOYAL
LOCH CRAGGIE
LOCH STAING
LOCH MEADIE
PLANTATION LOCH
LOCH NAM BREAC BUIDHE
LOCH AN ACHAIDH MHOR
LOCH BAN NA GALLAIG
LOCH EILEANACH
LOCH TARBHAIDH
Altnaharra Hotel,
Altnaharra, by Lairg, Sutherland
(054981) 222

LOCH HOPE (North End)
Osberton Grange Farms Limited,
Scofton Village, West Relford, Workshop,
Notts
(0909) 485621

LOCH LOYAL
LOCH CRAGGIE
LOCH HAKEL
LOCH BUIDGE BORGIE
LOCH CHAORUINN
LOCHAN TIGH-CHOMILD
LOCH NA ARIGH BUIE
LOCH a'MHUILINN
LILY LOCH
LOCH DUBH BEUL na FAIRE
LOCH SKERRAY
LOCH MODSAIRE
LOCH a BHUOLAIDH
Tongue & District Angling Club,
c/o Ben Loyal Hotel, Tongue, Sutherland
(084755) 216

LOCH MEADIE
LOCH MOR
LOCH DUINTE
KIRKTOMY LOCH
CAOL LOCH
LOCH NAN LOAGH
LOCHAN KIRIDH CREAGAIN
LOCH CREITE MEADIE
Bettyhill Fishings,
c/o Bettyhill Hotel, Bettyhill, Sutherland
(06412) 202

KYLE OF DURNESS
RIVER GRUDIE
RIVER DIALL
RIVER DIONARD
RIVER POLLA
LOCH CALADAIL
LOCH LANLISH
LOCH CROISPOL
LOCH BORRALIE
LOCH INSHORE
LOCH BAD AN FHEUR-LOCH
LOCH AIRIGH NA BEINNE
LOCH NA GLAC GAINMHICH
LOCH NA GLAC TARSUINN
LOCH NA GLAMHAICHD
LOCH KESGAIG
Cape Wrath Hotel,
Keodale, Durness, by Lairg, Sutherland
(097181) 274

SANDWOOD LOCH
GARBERT BEAG
GARBERT MOR
OLDSHOREMORE HILL LOCHS
Oldershoremore Estate,
Bury Farm, Hertingfordbury, Hertford,
Hertfordshire
(0992) 582829

CARDHU LOCH
LOWER DUART
UPPER DUART
CLASHFERN
BADNABAY
NAN RAMH
LOCH NA THULL
LOCH AN TIGH SHELG
LOCH NA TUADH
LOCH AN EASAIN UAINE
LOCH NA CLAISE FEARNA

GORM LOCH
LOCH NA SELIGE
LOCH EILEANACH
LOCH NAN UIDH
LOCHAIN DOIMHAIN
LOCH NA h-AIRIGH SLEIBHE
LOCH CROCACH
Scourie Hotel,
Scourie, by Lairg, Sutherland
(0971) 2396

LOCH NAM BRAC
LOCH GOBHLOCH
LOCH DUBH
LOCH a'PHREASAIN
LOCH LAICHEARD
LOCH BEALACH AN EILEIN
LOCH DRUIM NA COILLE
Scourie & District Angling Club,
c/o A Thompson, 2 Handa Terrace,
Scourie, by Lairg, Sutherland
(0971) 2420

LOCH DRUMBEG
LOCH RUIGHEN AN AITINN
LOCH BHRAIGHE
GORM LOCH MOR
GORM LOCH BEAG
LOCH NA LOINNE
LOCH TORR NA L'EIGIN
LOCH SKERRACH
LOCH FEARNA
LOCH BAD AN OG
LOCH DARRAICH
LOCH AN FADA
LOCH TOLLA BHAID
LOCH ODHAR
LOCH NAM BREAC
SHOE LOCH
The Drumbeg Hotel,
Assynt, Sutherland
(05713) 236

LOCH STACK
LOCH MOR
The Factor,
Reay Forest Estate, Achfary, Lochmore, by
Lairg, Sutherland
(097184) 221

RIVER INVER
RIVER KIRKAIG
LOCH FADA
LOCH GAINIMH
LOCH CHOIRE DUBH
LOCH NA BARRACK
LOCH LEOTHAID
LOCH GORM
FIONN LOCH
LOCH CULAG
LOCH CROCACH
LOCH DRUIM SUARDALAIN
LOCH SUILEAG
LOCH ASSYNT (West end)
Assynt Estate,
Estate Office, Lochinver, Sutherland
(05712) 203

LOCH ASSYNT (East end)
LOCH AWE
LOCH BEALACH CORNAIDH
THE a'CHOIRE LOCHS
LOCH MOAL a'CHOIRE
CAM LOCH
LOCH VEYATIE
Inchnadamph Hotel,
Inchnadamph, Assynt, Sutherland
(05712) 202

LOCH BORRALAN
Bruce Ward,
Altnacealgach, by Lairg, Sutherland
(085486) 220

LOCH URIGILL
Tom Strang,
Birchbank Activity Holiday Lodge,
Knockan, Elphin, by Lairg, Sutherland
(085486) 215

LOCH CUL FRAOICH
MANSE LOCH
LOCH SGEIREACH
LOCH NA CREIGE LEITHE
LOCH POLL AN TOBAIR
LOCH ROIB
LOCH a'PHOLLAIN
LOCH SGEIREACH
LOCH THORMIAD
LOCH a'CHOIN
LOCH AN ARBHAIR
LOCH DUBH

LOCH AN TURIC
LOCH BEANNACH
The Tourist Office,
Lochinver, by Lairg, Sutherland
(05714) 330

LOCH AILSH
UPPER RIVER OYKLE
Oykle Bridge Hotel,
Rosehall, by Lairg, Sutherland
(059984) 218

LOWER RIVER OYKLE
Finlayson & Hughes,
Estate Office, Bonar Bridge, Sutherland
(08632) 553

RIVER CASSLEY
N W Graesser,
Rosehall, by Lairg, Sutherland
(054984) 202

RIVER CARRON
Cornhill & Braelangwell
Finlayson & Hughes,
Estate Office, Bonar Bridge, Sutherland
(08632) 553

RIVER CARRON
Gledfield
R MacLeod & Son,
14 Lamington Street, Tain, Ross-shire
(0549) 2171

RIVER SHIN
LOCH SHIN
LOCH NA FUARALACHD
LOCH BHEAG NA FUARALACHD
LOCH BEANNACH
LOCH TIGH NA CREIGE
LOCH CRAGGIE
Sutherland Arms Hotel,
Lairg, Sutherland
(0549) 2291

LOCH SHIN
LOCH a'GHRIAMA
LOCH MERKLAND
MERKLAND HILL LOCHS
Overskaig Hotel,
by Lairg, Sutherland
(054983) 210

GLAS LOCHS
LOCH NAM BREAC BEAGA
Sutherland Estates Office,
Golspie, Sutherland
(04083) 3265

LOCH BUDHIE
LOCH LAOIGH
LOCH LANNASIDH
LOCH AN LAGAIN
LOCH CRACAILMOR
LOCH LARO
Dornoch Angling Association,
c/o Wm A MacDonald, Ironmonger, Castle
Street, Dornoch, Sutherland
(0862) 810301

LOCH FARLARY
LOCH LUNNDAIDH
LOCH HORN
Lindsay & Co,
Main Street, Golspie, Sutherland
(04083) 3212

RIVER BORORA
LOCH BRORA
Colin Taylor,
Rob Wilson Guns & Tackle, Fountain
Square, Brora, Sutherland
(04082) 21373

LOCH BADANLOCH
LOCH NAN CLAR
LOCH RIMSDALE
LOCH DRUIM a'CHLIBHAIN
LOCH COIRE NAM MANG
LOCH AN FHEARNA
PALM LOCH
LOCH ROSAIL
LOCH GAINEIMH
CAOL LOCH BEAG
CAOL LOCH MOR
LOCH SGEIREACH
LOCH RHIFAIL
Garvault Hotel,
Kinbrace, Sutherland
(04313) 224

LOCH AN RUTHAIR
LOCH ARICHLINIE
LOCH CULIADH
LOCH LUCY
The Factor,
Langwell Estate, Berriedale, Caithness
(05935) 237

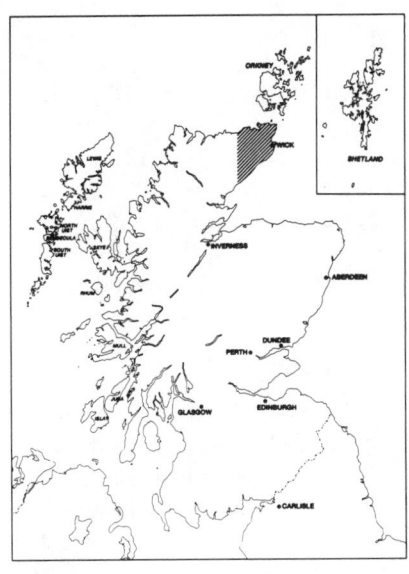

THE LAND OF CAT

Lochs and rivers of Caithness

A great skua winged darkly across the loch, pirating shores in search of prey. Rising trout stippled a mirror-calm surface. our boat drifted silently past Yarrows Broch, a Neolithic burial chamber, guarded by carolling curlew. Mingled amongst grassy mounds and lichen-covered stones lay outlines of a Pictish village, busy with farmer-fishermen 2,500 years before our coming.

A golden finger of sunlight sparkled warmly through gathering clouds, sending myriad colours, reds and blues, shimmering over smooth waters, highlighting the old ruins. June in Caithness. The northern simmer-dim. Almost midnight and still time for a few more casts. Caithness is like that. Always time for a few more casts.

It may be a long way north to the land of John o' Groats, but every mile is a mile nearer to some of the finest game fishing in Scotland. Sea-liced salmon, fresh from ice-cold Greenland seas; sparkling sea-trout and a vast abundance of pink-fleshed, hard-fighting wild brown trout, all waiting to grab your well-presented fly.

With the exception of Loch Calder, game fishing in Caithness, river or loch, is by fly only. Most fishing is readily available to visiting anglers and the charges (1988) vary from £1 for bank fishing on a hill loch, to up to £35 per day for salmon fishing during prime months. A boat on the main trout lochs, with two rods fishing, costs about £10. Nothing to break the bank and real value-for-money sport.

The county has a wide range of accommodation to suit all tastes and pockets. There are comfortable self-catering cottages, guest houses, bed and breakfast establishments and hotels. They have one thing in common: visitors will be greeted with friendly Caithness courtesy and every effort will be made to make your visit to the county as enjoyable as possible.

271

And if your are saddled with a non-fishing family, then fear not, Caithness has plenty to offer them whilst you get on with man's proper function in life, the removal of fish from their natural habitat. The county has a vast array of fascinating archaeological sites, brochs, standing stones and burial chambers to visit. There are dramatic cliff-top castles, such as Sinclair and Girnigoe, near Wick; cresting a narrow promontory, thrusting aggressively in the North Sea, complete with dark, murder-reeking dungeons. Wonderful, empty, long sandy beaches, where you may wander by the shore, often accompanied by a curious seal, watching your progress from the surf.

The county is deservedly famous for its variety of bird life. Golden eagle, hen harrier, peregrine, black and red-throated diver, great northern diver. Firework-beaked puffin stare moodily from burrows above the waves amidst the multitude of other sea birds that scream and fight for nesting space on jagged spring cliffs.

During winter months Caithness is an ornithological 'crew station', the first landfall for Arctic migrants. Huge flocks of grey-lag geese arrive in October, along with Icelandic whooper swans. They scrounge and squabble a living from stubble fields by day and night's frost-fingered darkness is filled with a magical symphony of their haunting, mystical, Nordic music.

Wick is the county town and administrative centre of Caithness, a town steeped in the traditions of the days of the great herring fishings of the 19th century, when upwards of 1,200 small boats crowded harbour piers. Thousands of Highlanders flocked to the town, women and girls to work as herring gutters and packers, men to crew tiny sailing boats.

The industry was so well organised that herring caught off Wick in July were on the menu in Belgrade by September, a distance of 1,500 miles further south. A Heritage Centre displays evidence of this proud history and it is one of the finest of its kind in the north. Priceless photographs from the famous Johnson Collection; furnished interiors of fishermen's homes; complete boats in mock harbour, fully rigged and crewed. There is also a full-scale model of a herring curing house; costumes, documents and personal belongings including the sad little school bag of a child who died, the books of his brief life spilling from the open flap. Just the place for a rainy day.

Caithness Glass Works, at Harrowhill, welcomes visitors and has a breathtaking range of beautiful glassware, often at startlingly inexpensive prices. There are riding schools, three golf courses, a swimming pool in Thurso, tennis courts and more than enough to keep every member of the family happily occupied.

The principal salmon river in Caithness is the Thurso, one of the north's best salmon streams with a ten-year average catch of 868 salmon. The Thurso is born amidst the hills and moorlands of the Flow Country, a wild, desolate scattering of lochs and lochans, alive with the sound of greenshank, golden plover, and dunlin. Peopled by otter, wild cat and deer. The infant Thurso River tumbles from Knockfin Heights over the Flow Country, on its 40-mile-long journey to the broken waters of the Pentland Firth; passing through Loch More, dammed in 1907 to provide a reservoir of water for the river in times of drought, full of brightly marked little wild brown trout.

The top section of the river, below Loch More, gives wonderful sport during early months of the season. The pool below the bridge has produced magnificent, silver spring fish for many a first-time angler; and in Loch Beag, an extension of the stream, I have watched, spellbound, as dozens of autumn salmon battled their way to up-river redds.

One of the most scenically attractive beats is Beat 8, by the bridge at Westerdale. Busy water, churning under the arch, boiling round vast, sandstone boulders, past the old mill wheel, on through fertile fields to the village of Halkirk and ancient Braal Castle. Braal was the home of the Earls of Caithness during the 14th century and in 1395 King Robert II gave the castle to his son, David, when he created him Earl. The old castle passed into the hands of Sir George Crichton, Lord High Admiral of Scotland, a notorious scoundrel who devoted most of his life to unprincipled barbarity: 'As destitute of faith, mercy and conscience as of fear and of folly.'

The Thurso is a well-behaved river, divided into 14 beats, each fishing two rods. Beat 1 is reserved for the use of the Thurso Angling Association and Beat 14, above Loch More, is let separately in conjunction with some delightful self-catering cottages. The river is fished on a rotation system, allowing anglers to fish most of the water, depending upon the length of their stay.

In the past the Thurso was regarded as one of Scotland's classic spring salmon rivers but in recent years, like everywhere else, autumn months now produce best results. However, given the choice, I would prefer to catch one April salmon rather than ten, September-red fish. The power of spring salmon is almost frightening and a 15 minute tussle with an angry 8-lb spring salmon leaves both arms and nerves tingling.

The Ulbster Arms Hotel in Halkirk has been looking after anglers for nearly a hundred years and still does so today with style, old-world courtesy and charm; and, when salmon are dour, with even greater commiseration. The hotel is well furnished, comfortable, and cooking is of a good standard. The river is carefully managed and easily accessible, offering excellent sport. The heaviest fish caught in recent years weighed a massive 47 lb and most seasons produce salmon of over 20 lb. Go thou and do likewise. Seek a booking well in advance of your planned visit and arrive, fingers crossed, rod poised, the light of battle shining in your eye.

A few miles west of Thurso is Forss River, a delightful little spate stream. Under the watchful eye of the historic mill, salmon leap the torrent of Forss Falls; magnificent bars of silver, fighting urgently onwards to breeding grounds in remote moorland streams. The Forss runs north from the flat lands beyond Dorrery Hill, for a distance of approximately 20 miles, winding across the marshlands of Broubster to the sea at Crosskirk Bay. Above the bay, where Forss and the grey Atlantic mingle, stand the ruins of one of Scotland's earliest places of worship, the 12th-century chapel of St Mary's.

Cormorant and seal dive into the bay amongst returning salmon. In spring and summer the cliffs blossom with wild flowers; rare *Primula Scotica*, the Scottish primrose, thrift, scabious and bugle, warmed by welcome northern sun. Otters ply the river bank and a pair of buzzards lord the little woodlands on the east bank of the lower river, floating silently over the quiet valley in endless search for prey.

The Upper River is preserved, but rods are sometimes available to visiting anglers on the Lower River. This is managed by Salar Properties who have time-shared their three-mile stretch; but often, owners do not wish to fish and their rods are then let on a first come, first served basis.

Lower Forss is divided into two beats: above the falls to the bridge over the river in Lythmore Strath, and from Falls Pool at Bridge of Forss to the sea. Four rods fish each beat, changing over after lunch. The upper beat is my favourite, a narrow, everchanging stream, wandering through the valley, where every corner and pot can hold fish. After the turmoil of Forss Falls, the river slows to walking pace as it reaches the sea. The technique of backing up can be used effectively here, particularly when there is a strong north or south wind to disguise your murderous intent.

Some huge fish have been caught in this little river and a cast of the largest is on display in Forss House Hotel, which overlooks the river: 45 lb 8 oz, taken in tiny Corner Pool in 1956. Forss salmon are of more modest size today but most seasons see fish of over 15 lb landed. Success on the Forss is very much a question of being in the right place at the right time, when there are good water levels. You pay your money and take your chance. But when conditions are right, then sport can be fast, furious and spectacular.

On the east side of the county, Wick River can also produce great sport, given decent water levels, and most years see upwards of 200 fish landed with the best fishing coming towards the end of the season in October and early November. The total length of the system is approximately 25 miles, including the Camster Burn; and the dominant flora of the upper river above the village of Watten are rushes, mosses, wet-land grasses, shrub willow, whin, gorse and creeping thistle.

Sadly, now, much of the headwater areas of the river has been afforested and the stream is ever more prone to dry up after flash-flooding. In days past, the peatlands slowly metered out available rain into the feeder burns.

Bruce Sandison on a Caithness hill loch

Now the level of the river falls very quickly after heavy rain.

Close to the moorland road that winds up from Watten, past Strath, by Camster Burn, lie some of the most dramatic Neolithic burial chambers in Europe: the Grey Cairns of Camster. There are two cairns, both remarkably intact and wonderfully preserved. Open, if you dare, the black-painted iron gate into the round cairn and crawl on hands and knees to the inner chamber. Although a rooflight has been fitted, you would be dull of soul indeed not to sense the ghosts of Iron Age men, lingering in the twilight. Recently, the all-pervading march of forestry has surrounded the old cairns, despoiling a view that has lain unchanged for almost 5,000 years.

Fishing on Wick River is controlled and managed by the Wick Angling Association and permission to fish is readily available to visitors. Because of the slow-flowing nature of the stream, bait fishing is probably the most productive method of tempting salmon to their doom; but there is also some delightful fly water.

There are more than 20 well-defined pools from Watten to the estuary: Bulls Hole, Durrans, Otter Island, Dyke End, Willie's Pool, The Wellies, Jasper's Pool, Hughie's Pool, Bridge Pool, McPhails, Willow Pool, Sand End Hole, Ingimister, Sheperds Pool, Windmill, Wash Pool, Quarry Hole, Tarrool, Kate Gows, Borgie and The Pot. The largest fish ever caught in the Wick was a magnificent salmon of 39 lb 8 oz; more recently, Watten angler Willie More caught a fish of 22 lb 2 oz in 1979. The average weight of salmon is in the region of 9 lb although most seasons produce fish of double figures.

Wick River also provides good sport with brown trout and some excellent fish are taken each year. In 1988, a local youngster took a lovely trout of 4 lb 8 oz in the tidal reaches of the river, between the two bridges that cross the stream in the town itself; and I have known of good-sized flounders being caught six miles upstream from the harbour mouth. So treat each rise with great caution; you never know what might be heading your way!

North from Wick, towards John o' Groats, the road passes through the village of Keiss; a neat cluster of houses, hugging the end of the long sand-sweep of Sinclair Bay. Keiss was the birthplace of one of Caithness's most famous sons, James Bremner, ship builder, designer, inventor and thoroughly respected member of the community. Bremner built many of the harbours along the Moray Firth and also advised Isambard Kingdom Brunel during the construction of the Blackwall Tunnel, the first tunnel ever driven under the River Thames. But James's greatest moment came when he and his son visited Ireland, to refloat the SS *Britain*, which had run aground on the rocks.

The best engineering brains in the world had failed to refloat the huge vessel. The Bremners did so, and sailed the ship back to Liverpool, inventing a massive-capacity pump to pump out water flooding in through jagged scars in the hull. As a child, James Bremner used to play in home-made boats in Sinclair Bay and no doubt he caught his fair share of the sea-trout that nose round the coast, heading for Wester River. The Wester is a classic sea-trout system and the only substantial sea-trout river in Caithness. It is a short river, leading to a gravel loch with easy access for returning fish, provided that the sand bar on Keiss beach is kept cleared. Winter storms and high tides sometimes block the river mouth and it takes a day with a digger to get the water flowing again.

This is a late river and runs of fish don't really start until September. Then the system fishes superbly, right through until the end of October.

Some local anglers fish in the sea, at the river mouth, and take good numbers of fish at the right time of the tide, using traditional Scottish patterns of wet flies: Black Pennel, Invicta, Zulus and Butchers. The lower river is very slow-moving and anglers must approach the pools with caution. An ill-considered movement or cast frightens ultra-shy sea-trout, sending them scurrying for safety, trailing mighty wakes through the weeds.

High dunes protect Keiss Golf Course, one of the oldest links courses in Scotland which borders the south bank of the river, and they host a wide range of beautifully wild flowers, such as grass of parnasus, sea-holly, thrift and scabious. Purple and spotted orchid abound the winter and summer, visiting and resident birds crowd the margins of river and bay.

Also crowding the margins, are the ghastly buildings associated with Kestrel Marine Limited, a company engaged in the fabrication of under-sea pipes. They have constructed a long miniature railway, from shore to loch, where they build their pipes preparatory to towing them out to sea. Whilst this industrial activity has reduced the beauty of the river, the high quality of sport goes a long way in compensation. Good boats on the loch are readily available to visiting anglers, and fishing from a boat on the loch probably produces best results.

The area in the vicinity of the outlet burn is a happy place to launch your assault; catch them as they arrive. On the north shore there is a headland where a small feeder stream enters and this is a noted salmon lie. Loch Wester also holds salmon and they sometimes may be found off the mouth of the burn. Brown trout in Wester tend to be small and white-fleshed and not much sport. Save your energies for their larger cousins and book a boat well in advance for autumn fishing. Given the right conditions, you could have a day to remember.

South from Wick, down the road that winds over the magnificent Caithness cliffs, lies the small village of Dunbeath, birth-place of one of Scotland's most famous and enigmatic authors, Neil Gunn. His book *The Silver Darlings* is a fine record of the 19th-century herring fishing, when every cove and inlet held its complement of fishing boats braving sudden summer storms to reap the silver harvest of the seas. But for me his most dramatic story is *Highland River* centred on Dunbeath Water, a lovely spate salmon stream that, given good water levels, can produce marvellous sport. The first chapter of *Highland River* describes the hero, a young boy, finding and killing a huge salmon in one of the upstream pools, dashing into the river and wrestling the fish ashore with his bare hands.

Dunbeath Water rises below the twin hills of Beinn Glas-choire and Ben Alisky, in the heart of Caithness, flowing through dark Loch Dubh, mingling the waters of Allt a Bhuic and Raffin Burns at Achnaclyth, hurrying them down the strath to the cold waters of the North Sea. Fishing is sometimes available to visiting anglers and you should inquire at the Portland Arms Hotel in Lybster for permission. However, wait for rain first or you will have a wasted journey.

Further south lies one of the most scenically attractive Caithness salmon streams, Berriedale Water; another little spate river that offers excellent sport in high-water conditions. There are three beats covering almost 12 miles of water, including over 40 pools and lies. Some heavy salmon have been landed with fish of over 20 lb taken; and, an added bonus, Berriedale Water also holds some super brown trout. A trout of 6 lb 8 oz was landed recently in the pool above the falls on the lower river. Fishing is often available, either on a daily or weekly basis and your best opportunity is to seek spring or early summer fishing when more rods are available. Check the weather forecast first and then speed down the A9, rod at the ready. There are few more delightful salmon streams in the north and a day on Berriedale Water is a day to remember, fish or not.

Fine though Caithness salmon fishing may be, for me, the finest game fishing Caithness has to offer is for wild brown trout. The county has an amazing array of top-quality fishing, on magnificent waters such as Watten and delightful, moorland-girt hill lochs like Ruard where you may fish all day without seeing another soul.

As I write, I look out from my work-room window over Loch Watten, three miles long by up to half a mile wide, full of hard-fighting, sea-trout-silver fish. Pink fleshed, perfectly shaped and averaging 12 oz, they fight with great dash and spirit. Many years ago the loch was stocked with Loch Leven trout and these fish have thrived mightily in the lime-rich, shallow waters.

The loch has an average depth of 8 ft and fish rise and may be caught all over, from the shallows to the deep. Many anglers swear that the best drift is right down the middle. Others extol the virtues of the 'Golden Triangle' at the north end: an imaginary line from Sandy Point on the north shore, over to John Steven's boathouse, south, and then back across the loch towards Shearer's Pool. But no matter where you fish, cast with confidence; trout are there, waiting to grab.

My favourite drift is along the Whin Bank, on the north shore near the little island. Then off the fence that runs into the loch at the east end in the first large bay, known as Factor's Bay. At the start of the season, in late May, at about 9.30 p.m., I catch my first Watten fish of the year, just off this point, generally on a Ke-He, rowing slowly past the fence about 50 yards from the shore.

There are some large trout in Watten and in 1985 a fine fish of 4 lb 8 oz was caught from one of the West Watten boats. In 1986 I was fortunate enough to hook a lovely fish of just over 3 lb, when I wasn't looking, and the memory of that beautiful trout will stay with me to the day I depart for the 'great trout loch in the sky'. So be alert, and concentrate all the time. That's the way to catch fish.

There are about 30 boats on the loch and visiting anglers should have little trouble in booking a day. An outboard motor is essential because Watten can be a windy, dangerous place. Also, take along that best of boat fisher's friends, a drogue; to slow the drift and keep the boat properly set, sideways on the wind.

Watten is jointed to Wick River by a short outlet stream and in high-water conditions, particularly during early and late months, it is possible for salmon to enter the loch. A local angler, Sandy Mieklejohn, proved the point a few years ago by taking a fresh 7-lb fish on a Black Pennel and I'm sure that substantial numbers of salmon reach Watten. There are endless stories of anglers being broken on huge fish and I suspect that these have been angry salmon, escapees from Wick River.

North of Watten, is little Loch Scarmclate, known locally as Stemster; a nursery for Loch Watten and joined to it by a narrow stream. Scarmclate has the same high-quality trout as its 'big brother' Watten, and this is the ideal loch to introduce a newcomer to the gentle art of fly fishing. Best to launch your attack during the early months of the season because, as autumn approaches, Scarmclate becomes heavily weeded. The loch is very shallow and, in days gone by, farmers used to extract marl to use as fertiliser. Therefore, bank fishing is not advisable since there are sudden, unexpected holes.

Scarmclate is an important resting and breeding place for wildfowl and often, in winter, the loch is covered with the graceful images of Icelandic whooper swans. During summer months, Scandinavian fieldfare, redwing and buntings flit and feed in the well-cultivated fields that surround Scarmclate and a pair of binoculars are almost as important as a fishing rod, when afloat. Fish average about 8 oz although there are larger trout. Catch them anywhere on the loch; but the best area is to the east end. Inch down the shore and into the bay where the burn tumbles out to Watten. Water is deeper here and I have taken fish of over 1 lb on small, size 16, flies.

South from Watten village is another beginner's paradise, Loch Toftingall. Sadly, this moorland loch has been affected by forestry and in some places the trees are planted very close to inlet streams and the shore. Thus, silt from forestry ploughing has been washed into the loch causing massive discoloration. Nevertheless, there is still a good stock of excellent brown trout although at times it is like fishing in a bowl of Brown Windsor soup, rather than in a Highland loch. A road leads down to a parking place and boathouse and the loch covers an area of 145 acres, shallow in depth and much given to weed as the season advances. I have always had best results bank fishing and, before afforestation, it was possible, with care, to wade from one side to the other, because you could see every stone on the bottom. Not so today, but wading is safe so, if it is windy, splash in and get at them. Trout average about 10 oz and there is a bag limit of 10 fish per rod.

Toftingall used to be an ornithologist's delight and I have had the great

Jo and Bill Kirk with a fine basket of Loch St John's wild brown trout

pleasure of watching osprey fishing there; black throated divers used to swoop down and spend an hour or so watching your efforts. Hen harriers quartered the moorlands. Greenshank piped from grassy tussocks.

Loch St John's, near Dunnet Head, is the most northerly trout loch on mainland Britain, in a dramatic setting, 150 acres in extent and full of fine fish. The waters of the loch are reputed to have curative powers and in days gone by invalids were carried to the loch to drink the waters. St John's is also supposed to be able to cure the depressed or sad in spirit. Walk once round the loch and then leave, without looking back; all cares instantly vanish.

However, there is nothing depressing about the quality of fishing, particularly during late June and early July when there are large hatches of mayfly; trout rise hungrily, filling the air with the sound of their feelings. And anglers' shouts fill the air with the sound of their excitement as baskets are filled and landing nets work overtime.

During recent years, Loch St John's has been under the management of an improvement association and great work has been done restoring the loch to its former glory. Some complain that the average weight of fish has gone down, but that is to be expected, due to the stocking policy. However, in a few years' time these fish will have grown and provide some of the finest quality wild brown trout fishing in the north. And there are still some of the St John's monsters, renowned of old, with most seasons producing fish of over 3 lb.

Facilities for anglers are good and the association has built a road down to the loch, a parking area and first-class harbour; it is possible to step straight from the car, almost into the boat. Even better, and most unusual for a Highland loch, it is possible to get afloat without bursting a blood vessel heaving the boat over rocky shallows.

Loch St John's has an average of about 5 ft in depth, and like most of our Caithness waters, fish are caught all over the loch. If there is one drift better than others, then it is from the mooring bay, north to Kili Cairn on the north shore. Easy to find: as you row out of the harbour, the bow of the boat is pointing straight down the drift. Turn sideways on and get into action. A few miles south from St John's, lies the dourest loch in Caithness, Heilen, where it is possible to fish for days without ever seeing a fish; where many a heart and line has been broken by the sudden tug of an unexpected monster, grabbing furiously as you doze and dream fishless hours away. But Heilen fish are superb and in May of 1988 a trout of 8 lb 8 oz was landed by a Halkirk angler fishing from the bank. That same week saw fish of 5 lb 4 oz and 4 lb 8 oz taken and throughout the season Heilen consistently produces the heaviest trout in Caithness. It is just catching them that is the problem. Expert's water.

The loch is shallow, averaging 4 ft in depth and covers an area of about 170 acres. Weed growth is prolific and one has to find the gaps, where a fly may be properly fished. The effort involved can be well worth the trouble and my best ever wild brown trout came from Heilen, a fine specimen of 4 lb 8 oz. Each year, the size of the fish grows as I relate the tale of its catching to anyone daft or unsuspecting enough to listen.

There are two good fishing areas on the loch, comparatively weed-free and they are easy to find. From the boat mooring bay on the west shore, angle quarter right across the loch. Where an old fence runs down into the water, there are some deep holes where good fish lurk. Drift down this far bank, towards the middle of the loch. The other area is down the west bank, in the area of the old army building/boathouse.

Best results on Heilen, lies catching a single fish, come during the early months of the season and generally, late at night, from 9 p.m. onwards. This tends to be cold hard work in May, but remember to take along the glass case. This might just be the place where you finally fill it.

The deepest loch in the county is Calder, to the west of Halkirk; a vast, deep, peaty expanse which supplies the town of Thurso with water. The depth at the north end is over 120 ft and Calder has the reputation of holding large ferox. Few people fish for them properly and it would be interesting to see exactly what is down there. If you wish to do so, fish in the old Scottish way, 'trolling'. Use a sinking line, a herring-sized lure (or indeed herring) on a large hook, and motor slowly up the loch fishing the bait at a depth of about 20 ft. Largest trout caught to-date on Calder weighed over 7 lb but I am convinced that there are much larger fish, lurking in the depths.

Arctic char live in Calder and the average size of brown trout is in the order of 8 oz and they are often white-fleshed although there are pink-fleshed fish as well, depending upon the area you fish. They rise well and large baskets are frequently taken. Therefore, Calder is another good starting place for newcomers to fishing. They are almost certain to catch fish.

I would not recommend bank fishing, due to the fact that fluctuations in water levels leave much of the bank soft and spongy. Also, the loch shelves steeply and an ill-considered step too far could land you in 10 ft of water with little chance of getting back safely to terra firma. Best to fish Calder from a boat and best place to concentrate your efforts is in the finger-like bay running off the west shore. In high-water levels, this can give superb sport. Fish this bay, then drift down the west bank, paying particular attention to the little headlands and weed banks.

South from Calder is another dour Caithness water, Loch Olginey, stocked in days past by that great Caithness fisherman, the late Dan Murray. Olginey can be a nightmare and one will often swear that it is entirely fishless. Until it produces a trout of over 5 lb, then all is forgiven. Olginey is easy of access and best fished from the bank. The loch is full of huge underwater boulders, ready to catch the boat fisher unawares and it is just as easy to spend a day catching nothing from the bank as it is from a boat; and a lot safer.

To the south of Wick lie a series of exciting lochs, on the Hempriggs Estate, which offer something for everyone, beginner and expert alike. The largest water is wind-swept Hempriggs, full of small, accommodating trout and a few much larger fish. Hempriggs is most often fished from the bank and is easily accessible from the A9. Wading down the east bank can be a bit of a stumble, the bottom is uneven and rocky. The south shore is mainly peat hag and water deeper. Try both.

Turning right after the village of Thrumster eventually brings you to possibly the easiest of the Caithness lochs, Yarrows, the main water supply for Wick. Large baskets of brightly marked trout are the rule rather than the exception on Yarrows, and the setting is lovely. Best results come from boat fishing and bank fishing is uncomfortable and downright dangerous due to the depth of water close to the shore. My favourite area is at the south end, enfolded by the slopes of Battle Moss and Yarrows Hill. In the immediate vicinity there are more than 40 sites of archaeological interest: cairns, forts, brochs and standing stones. Obviously, our ancestors knew a good source of fish when they saw it and arranged their dwellings accordingly.

Close to Yarrows, and formed by blocking the main inlet burn, is the Marl Loch, also known as Brickigoe. This was re-established a few years ago and stocked with trout from Yarrows. The feeding is much better in Marl and consequently, the fish are of a much better quality, both in size and eating. The only problem is tempting them to take the fly. Marl is shallow, weedy and difficult to fish. No boat, all from the bank. Still worth the effort, and you may well be rewarded with a basket of six fish weighing over 6 lb for your trouble. Hurry along.

A rutted track leads past Marl Loch, following the west shore of Yarrows, ending at South Yarrows farm. Park here and climb into the hills. Just before the top of Yarrows Hill is one of my favourite Caithness waters, tiny Loch of Warehouses. Favourite, not because it contains vast numbers of trout, indeed, there are very few, but because it is such a beautiful, peaceful place to fish. The view from the Warehouse Hill is wonderful. On a clear day, over the spires and chimneys of Wick, beyond the wide, golden sweep of Sinclair Bay, lie the Orkney Islands, dominated by the red-scarred hills of Hoy. White-fingered, Pentland Skerries Lighthouse, deserted Stroma, near John o' Groats; one of the most dramatic views in Caithness. To be treasured. Some good fish in the loch too.

The hardest Hempriggs water is Sarclet, six miles south from Wick, left in the village of Thrumster. This small loch lies high above the waves on Sarclet Head, and all day long you are lulled by the deep sound of the sea, stroking mighty cliffs. The loch has some of the finest quality brown trout in Caithness and they average 12 oz in weight. Not so easy to catch (where are fish easy to catch?) and weed is a problem as the season advances. Also, in the early months, model yachts can be a problem because Sarclet is the home of the local club and great battles are regularly fought amidst the calm waters of the loch, mini-Americas Cups and myriad Blue Ribands. But do pay Sarclet your respects. The largest fish taken recently weighed over 6 lb and where there is one there is bound to be at least another. Has it your name, neatly inscribed along the lateral line?

The A895 is a long, straight road running from Latheron in the south to Georgemas and Thurso in the north. It is known locally as the Causiemire, 'the way across the mire'. Before the road was built horse passage over the moor could be dangerous and difficult and beasts were laden with brush wood to pile into the wettest bogs to effect safe passage.

A few miles up the new road are two delightful little lochs, easy to fish and offering great sport to visiting anglers. The first, Rangag, to the left of the road, is packed with little fish where even the greatest duffers in the world, people like me, will be assured of catching fish.

A rocky promontory on the east shore is the site of a Pictish Broch and reputed home of a Caithness robber baron of the Middle Ages, Grey Steel. His stock-in-trade was to greet visitors to Caithness on the high cliffs of the Ord. You either paid up or had a one-way passage to your Maker over the cliff-top. He eventually met his own Maker, headless, when a bank of outraged Watten men raided the castle late at night and put an end to Grey Steel's merry pranks.

Right from Rangag, hidden from the road, is Loch Stemster, the perfect place for fishing on a windy day or for a family picnic. The loch is circular, surrounded by hills and no matter from which direction the wind howls, there is always a fishable bank. There is a boat as well, but I rarely use it, finding that bank fishing produces better results.

To the south of the loch is a dramatic ring of standing stones and an ancient burial chamber and a track leads round the lochside, out into the moorlands. You fish whilst the rest of the tribe explore. Trout in Stemster average about 10 oz although there are larger fish. My son Charles had one of just under 2 lb a few years back and I obtained eternal glory once by landing two fish of over 1 lb each, on the same cast.

A number of rocky points poke out into the loch from the south shore and these can produce excellent results. The first extends some way out and, with care, you can wade out a considerable distance covering a lot of water as you do so. The trick is not to stray too far left or right. Bad, wet news if you do.

Travelling north from Rangag and Stemster, past the farm at Achavanich, there are two ruined cottages on your right. Directly opposite, a track leads down the hill to the foot of the wide valley. This is the way out to one of the best Caithness trout lochs, Ruard; just over the first line of hills and an easy 40-minute walk. Make for the green, cultivated patch in the distance and follow the Land-Rover track that criss-crosses the Loop-Burn. At the old steading, follow the little stream up the valley, keeping to the right-hand bank. The other side is very hard walking and should be avoided at all costs. This is a delightful valley, with the stream burbling crystal clear through trout-darting pools, fringed with yellow flag, bordered with purple-bright orchids. At the loch, turn left and follow the shore round to the boathouse.

Ruard is one of those extra-special places; remote, beautiful, surrounded

Two before breakfast for Edinburgh angler Mike Shepley

by empty, heather-clad moorlands and full of hard-fighting wild brown trout. They are not large but you should manage to catch breakfast and, more often that not, also catch a glimpse of an otter or red-throated diver. If I was asked to choose but one Caithness loch to fish, then it would probably be Ruard and I have no hesitation in recommending it to you.

In 1975, the choice would have been less easy. Then the moorlands at Altnabreac, in the heart of the Flow Country, were our playground; lochs such as Skyline, Garbh, Caol and Caise our delight. Now the whole area has been afforested and as years advance the magnificent views of the Caithness mountains, Morven and the Scarabens will be obscured. A new forestry road crosses the hill and access is easy. The trout are still there and you may wish to fish them. I can tell you that they have some superb fish. Skyline, where the average weight is 2 lb and where my wife Ann and I have seen the whole surface of the loch alive with cruising, feeding trout. Little Caise, now edged by the road, with hundreds of eager, small trout.

Dark Garbh, one of our best-loved lochs, where we once foundered in a leaky punt; lazed warm summer days away, buzzed by heather bees and dusky moths. I once hooked an enormous trout which almost pulled me into the loch. Where a basket of a dozen, nice fish was always assured, almost regardless of the weather.

The majority of the Flow Country lochs are now in the ownership of tree-farmers; Fountain Forestry Limited who claim to own some 43 Caithness and East Sutherland waters. However, there are still a few which have not been affected by forestry, or are only marginally affected. Loch Glutt is one, at the end of the long track out from Loch More past Dalnaha and Dalnawillan.

Glutt is a small loch, crystal clear, spring-fed, deep and difficult to fish but there are large fish there, of over 3 lb and you may still experience the magic of the hills and the wonderful peace of the Caithness moorlands. Similarly, Thulachan and Sand, close neighbours, at the end of of a track south from Loch More. I have seen whooper swans, whiling away summer months on Sand, and the fish are sparkling and free rising. Follow the track west from Altnabreac Station, to Loch Eun, Rumsdale and a'Mhadaidh. Dozens of little fish in the latter two, fish of 1 lb and more in Eun. But all set amidst some of God's most magical scenery. Happy memories of long, wonderful days in the hills.

Closer to Westerdale, but edged by the forest, are Loch Meadie and the 'dusky loch' a'Cherigal. Meadie will always produce sport, from either boat or bank; whilst a'Cherigal is a fickle lady, one moment gracious with beautiful 1-lb trout, the next moment as dour as death. Gaineimh and Eileanach, divided by the new forest road that leaves Loch More by the Sleach Water is full of traditional Highland brown trout, averaging three to the pound; with the occasional monster. Eddie MacArthy had a superb fish from Gaineimh in 1987, a trout of 3 lb 8 oz. So be prepared and consider every rise carefully.

Game fishing in Caithness is outstanding; both from the point of view of quality of fish and scenic beauty. It would take a lifetime to do it proper justice. So if you haven't fished there yet, it's about time you got started. Not a moment to lose.

THE LAND OF CAT

FISHING DIRECTORY

THURSO RIVER
LOCH EUN
LOCH RUMSDALE
LOCH a'MHADAIDH
LOCH MEADIE
LOCH a'CHERIGAL
LOCH GAINEIMH
LOCH EILEANACH
LOCH THULACAN
LOCH SAND
LOCH GLUTT
Ulbster Arms Hotel,
Halkirk, Caithness
(084783) 206

FORSS RIVER
Salar Management Services Limited,
Lochloy House, Lochloy, Nairn
(0667) 55355

WICK RIVER
The Sports Shop,
High Street, Wick
Hugo Ross,
Fishing Tackle Dealer, Breadalbane
Terrace, Wick.

RIVER WESTER
LOCH WESTER
A Dunnet,
Auckhorn Farm, Keiss, by Wick, Caithness
(095583) 208

DUNBEATH WATER
Portland Arms Hotel,
Lybster, Caithness
(05932) 208

BERRIEDALE WATER
The Factor,
Estate Office, Berriedale, Caithness
(05935) 237

LOCH WATTEN
Loch Watten Hotel,
Watten, by Wick, Caithness
(095582) 237
D Gunn,
Watten Lodge, Watten, by Wick, Caithness
(095582) 217
J A Barnetson,
Lynegar Farm, Watten, Caithness
(095582) 205

J Swanson,
Banks Lodge, Watten, by Wick, Caithness
(095582) 326

LOCH SCARMCLATE
LOCH CALDER
Harper's Fly Fishing Services,
The Drill Hall, Sinclair Street, Thurso,
Caithness
(0847) 63179

LOCH OLGINEY
D G Mackay,
Achaguie, Scotscalder, by Halkirk
(084783) 650

LOCH ST JOHN'S
Northern Sands Hotel,
Dunnet, Caithness
(084785) 270

LOCH HEILEN
Hamish Pottinger,
Greenland Mains Farm, Castletown,
Caithness
(084782) 210

LOCH TOFTINGAL
LOCH RANGAG
LOCH STEMSTER
LOCH SKYLINE
LOCH GARBH
LOCH CAISE
LOCH CAOL
LOCH THORMAID
LOCH SORACH
Mrs Atkinson,
c/o Bradford & Bingley Building Society,
Sinclair Street, Thurso, Caithness
(0847) 63291

LOCH OF YARROWS
MARL LOCH
LOCH SARCLATE
LOCH OF WAREHOUSES
LOCH HEMPRIGGS
Thrumster Garage,
Thrumster, by Wick, Caithness
(095585) 252

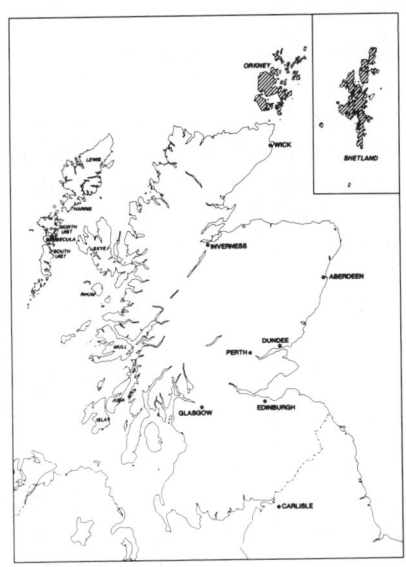

BEYOND THE PENTLAND FIRTH

Orkney and Shetland Isles

Over the sea to Orkney; and I hope that you are a good sailor because the vagaries of the Pentland Firth test the strongest sea-legs. I remember, with fond horror, a passage in 1967. Our car was lifted onboard by sling and dumped, none too ceremoniously, in the hold; but that was as nothing compared to the dumping we received when the boat left the comparative calm of Scrabster Harbour in Caithness.

House-high waves, mad walls of tormented, flying spray roared in from all quarters as the vessel cork-screwed and bobbed crazily northwards. My five-year-old son Blair and I wedged together top-side, trying to pretend it was really all good fun; meanwhile, wife Ann and three-year-old daughter Lewis-Ann weathered it out below, reading, as though a force eight gale was an every-day occurrence. Strong stuff, females.

Eventually, the boat pitched drunkenly into the lee of Hoy, and, slowly, calmer waters settled pounding hearts. We were not, as I had previously expected, every minute, doomed to a watery grave. Ashore, surrounded by the solid stones and cobbles of the old grey town of Stromness, I felt like Mr Fletcher Christian waving farewell to Captain Bligh and his Bounty. Then, from a great height, they dropped the car on the pier: a final gesture of disgust from proper seamen to fair-weather sailors and landlubbers like me.

In spite of that violent introduction to the Orcades, this magic land has held us enthralled ever since and the journey from mainland Scotland is not always so stormy. We have sailed, mill-pond calm amidst myriad sea birds, chased and chivvied by porpoise and gannets, lazing sun-burnt past sentinel stacks, barely aware of time passing. What finer way to go fishing; and few islands offer such a warm welcome to anglers.

Most people think of the Orkney Islands in terms of the mainland view from Caithness; across the firth to the russet-red crags of Santoo Head, Sneuk Head and Robie Geo on the island of Hoy. But beyond the hills of Hoy lies a vista of gentle fields and soft moorlands; of farmlands, filled with safely grazing sheep, handsome cattle and fine crops. This is the scene that unfolds as you drive north from Stromness. At the crest of Cairston Hill, before you glints Loch of Stenness, incredibly blue, with Loch Harray beyond, stretching into hazy distance; and between these two waters, the ancient Stenness standing stones, forming a 100-ft circle at the centre of which is a stone square where cremated bones have been found; and nearby Ring of Brodgar, built before the time of the great Pyramids of Egypt.

There are more than a thousand known sites of prehistoric man scattered throughout the islands. Recently, farmer and antiquarian Ronnie Simison from South Ronaldsay, discovered a 5,000-year-old burial chamber, now known as 'The Tomb of the Eagles' because it contained the talons of sea eagles. It also contained the remains of 340 people; and in 1986 a Bronze Age house was discovered on the Island of Sanday.

Further afield lies Maeshowe, described as the most magnificent chambered tomb in Europe, and on the island of Rousay, Midhowe, the 'Great Ship of Death', a 100-ft-long stalled burial cairn, divided by stone slabs into 12 sections, perfectly preserved.

But the Stone Age village of Skara Brae in Sandwick is perhaps one of Orkney's most dramatic monuments. A huge storm uncovered the remains of ten houses, buried under the sand dunes for almost 5,000 years. They have been carefully excavated and nestle on a bluff overlooking the Bay of Skaill, half a mile of golden sand washed by green Atlantic waves. Visit Skara Brae on a mid-summer evening, amidst the cry of seagull and twittering late larks. Then, it is as though a small, axe-carrying, sheepskin-clad man will come to greet you, prehistoric dogs yapping around calloused, sandalled feet.

Orkney is an ornithologist's delight. I remember, as a small boy in 1949, lying on the cliffs east of Birsay, watching fulmers sweeping along the cliffs. Had my first glimpse of a hen harrier, floating ghost-like over the moors. There are many rare species to be seen, including great northern diver, red-throated diver, purple sandpiper, golden plover, great skua, Arctic terns and puffin.

A super way to see puffins is to book a seat with Puffin Watch. This is a guided trail-walk of one and a half miles with spectacular views of Hoy and the northern coastline of Scotland. It includes transport, use of bird-hides and binoculars and takes about three hours. Ask at the tourist office for details. The wildflowers are just as inviting; that Scottish jewel, *Primula Scotica*, grass of parnassus, Scottish lovage, Alpine bearberry, mountain everlasting, spring squill, oysterplant and bog pimpernel. Everywhere you turn on these lovely islands, some new pleasure greets you and Orkney is a holiday venue for all seasons.

For anglers, much more; for Orkney boasts some of the most exciting wild brown trout fishing in Britain and also offers excellent sport with sea-trout among the bays and seaweed-fringed shores round the islands. There are five principal trout lochs, Harray, Stenness, Swannay, Boarhouse and Hundland; and many other smaller waters, both on Mainland and outer islands.

However, before setting out to explore these waters, I must issue a warning: fishing in Orkney can severely affect your mind. A few years ago, after a visit with Roy Eaton, then editor of the magazine *Trout and Salmon*, I was standing on the upper deck of the *St Ola*, watching the bustle of imminent departure. As mooring ropes were unloosed, I saw, to my horror, Roy scuttling townwards, apparently unaware of the distinct possibility of missing the boat. 'Roy!' I shouted, 'where on earth are you going? Get back here now or you will miss the boat.'

Later, over warm, sweet tea, I asked him what he had been playing at. 'Bruce,' he replied through choked breath, 'when I thought of these last few days, of fishing and the people, and the mountain of work waiting for me in the office, something just sort of snapped. And if you hadn't shouted I would have been half way to Swannay by now. Next time, do me a favour. Mind your own business and let me go.'

Of all Orkney lochs, Swannay is my favourite. Not only because of the quality of fish but also because of the serenity of the surroundings. My wife and I know Swannay in its every mood: from mill-pond calm to raging turmoil; and yet, even in the worst of weather, Swannay has never sent us home supperless.

One wild April morning we arrived at the shores of the loch in the middle of a snow storm and sat dejectedly in the car, muttering crossly about the impossibility of fishing. Ann ended the family rebellion that was about to explode by leaping from the car and, rod clutched firmly, head bent against the gale, staggering off into the blizzard like some latter-day piscatorial Titus Oates. Within 20 paces she was lost from view. 'Now look what you have done,' I scolded the tribe. 'If you never see your mother again, you have only yourselves to blame.'

Half an hour later, blue-nosed but triumphant, Ann returned, with three lovely fish, each weighing about 1 lb, all in perfect condition and taken on a Black Pennel. We almost got stuck in a snowdrift at Setter on the way back to our cottage, but dinner that night was wonderful. The next day, warmed by thin Easter sunlight, I fished from the bank near Dale and was rewarded with two of the most beautiful trout I have ever seen, each weighing just under 2 lb. Given my angling ability, my success was probably due more to luck than any skill on my part; at least that's what the rest of them said and being outnumbered six to one, including Ann's Yorkshire terrier Heathcliff, I was in no position to argue.

But Swannay, like most lochs, can be fickle and there are times, when conditions seem perfect, that you would swear that there wasn't a fish in the place. Nothing could be further from the truth and boat fishing brings the best results. I discovered this fact many years ago, fishing from the shore at the north end. The bottom is uneven and rocks slippy. Good place for a ducking. Best fishing areas are at the south end. The bay where burn of Etheriegeo enters is the place to start. Fish from the burn-mouth westwards and then tackle the drifts between the island of Muckle Holm and Loudenhill Farm. The east shore should be given careful attention, from the association site down past Southend and Dale.

Swannay trout do not give themselves up easily and you will probably count your catch on the fingers of one hand, rather than two. However, they make a meal fit for a king and one of the best baskets in recent years contained 42 fish weighing 69 lb 10 oz. Our last visit ended more modestly, with four fish in the boat. But I shall remember that day for many years to come due to the astonishing weather. One moment we were bathed in brilliant sunlight, the next shivering, hunched in torrential rain. At times the sun was so hot that perspiration flowed down our faces; the next minute, ice-cold rain was dripping from jackets and sleeves whilst distant thunder rattled and rumbled.

At the end of the day we retired, stunned but happy, marvelling at the perversity of nature and the perfidy of trout. Nevertheless, a local angler, fishing throughout the same conditions had a lovely basket of 12 fish, the heaviest being a beauty of 2 lb 8 oz. I had been watching him during the afternoon; he told me that he had taken most of his fish on a small Blue Zulu fished very rapidly across the surface, hardly allowing the flies to settle before beginning to retrieve. I made rapid mental notes for my next visit. The most productive flies on the loch are: Black Pennel, Black and Blue Zulu, Ke-He, Loch Ordie and Butchers.

Wherever you fish on Swannay, travel slowly and cautiously. Swannay is shallow and full of underwater skerries and because the water tends to be peaty, they are difficult to detect. So hasten slowly and take along a bag-full of spare sheer-pins for the outboard motor. Boat and outboard hire may be found at Dale on the west shore. Could be confusing, because there are two Dales, the other one being on the east shore. The boats are sound and there is a good jetty; and in decent water levels it is even possible to enjoy the luxury of motoring away from the harbour, rather than the usual grunting, heaving and pushing required to get boats afloat on most Scottish lochs.

As always, be selective about the fish you keep. Swannay can produce fish of up to 6 lb and most seasons fish of 3 lb are caught. Be generous. Return the smaller ones to fight another day, and encourage your companions to do likewise. When you finally arrive at that Great Trout Loch in the sky, St Peter will bless you mightily and perhaps direct you immediately to a celestial 'one for the glass case' for your mortal consideration.

During our first visit to Orkney, we hired a caravan on the shores of Loch Boardhouse; near the Viking island of Birsay and Earl's Palace, home of the 16th-century rulers of Orkney. We had asked to be sited as near to the shores of the loch as possible and could not have wished for a better position; we were almost able to cover rising fish from the living-room. Boardhouse is two miles long, lying north-west/south-east, divided by narrows. The south bay is three-quarters of a mile wide, between Nicol Point and Midhouse, whilst the north bay is just under half a mile across from the standing stone at Stanger, north-east to Newhouse.

Unlike other Orkney waters, Boardhouse is almost entirely free of skerries, underwater outcrops of jagged rock and the loch has an average depth of 8–12 ft. The bottom is soft and an ideal habitat for insect life. Consequently, trout thrive mightily and, frequently, so do anglers. Fish average 12 oz although each season much larger specimens are landed and trout of 4 lb are by no means uncommon.

One evening, fishing with my young son, things were very dour and we were considering giving in and returning to the caravan when I noticed a particularly inviting looking daddy-long-legs, struggling on the waves. A few moments manoeuvring with the oars and I had the delicate insect in my hands. I carefully tied it to a bare hook and prepared to cast. The daddy-long-legs came adrift on the back-cast and landed on the surface; whereupon one of the largest trout I have ever seen, swirled up and gulped it down. 'Not really fly fishing, though Dad, is it?' questioned the rising young Walton from the bow. There is no justice in fishing, I thought.

In days past, sea-trout and the occasional salmon found their way into Boardhouse but since the loch was used as a water supply, few migratory fish enter. There is a fish pass but sea-trout seem reluctant to use it. However, the quality and strength of brown trout more than compensate for lack of their larger cousins and they fight hard and long before coming to the net.

One of the principal pleasures of fishing Boardhouse is the sure and certain knowledge that trout may be caught throughout the whole loch, from margins to middle. Some areas are perhaps better than others; for example, during August, when weed grows strongly in the middle of the south bay, good baskets may be taken by carefully inching round their edges. There is also considerable weed growth in the north bay during the back end, and good sport may be had there as well.

Bank fishing on Boardhouse is bad news and uncomfortable, due to the depth of water close to the shore and the muddy nature of the bottom. Nevertheless, I remember catching fish near the stone surround by the waterworks—in a howling gale—so, if all else fails, go thou and do likewise. When trout are in the mood, sport is fast and furious so it is important to be selective about which fish you keep.

East of Boardhouse, and joined to it by a little stream, is Loch of Hundland;

a small, skerried water and, towards the end of the season, given to high weed growth. When we visited in 1967 the loch had all but disappeared, due to a long, dry spell. Things have much improved since then and Hundland is noted for the size and quality of its fish; heavier than Boardhouse trout with occasional monsters sometimes caught unawares in the weeds.

Because the loch is shallow, fish rise and may be caught all over, from middle to margins. So cast with confidence, everywhere. The bottom is soft and this promotes prolific hatches of flies. Another plus-point with Hundland is that it produces good results in bright conditions, when other Orkney waters tend to be dour.

The Loch of Harray is Orkney's largest and most popular freshwater loch and each season it produces upwards of 25,000 trout. These fish are of a very high quality, silver and pink fleshed, marvellous to catch and to eat. Their average weight is in the order of 10–12 oz but some huge fish have been taken over the years: in 1964 a magnificent trout of 17 lb 8 oz was landed and fish of over 5 lb are caught most seasons.

Harray is six miles long by up to one and a half miles wide encompassing an area of 2,500 acres. The loch is shallow and consequently warms up quickly and spring fishing can be spectacular. All depends upon the weather. Fish may be caught throughout the whole system and most anglers launch their attack from boats.

However, bank fishing can be just as productive and, in high winds, one of the most delightful aspects of fishing Harray is that it is always possible to find a sheltered corner from which to cast. One of the most popular bank fishing areas is at the south end of the loch, close to the Standing Stones and Maeshowe. Fish round to the mouth of the burn that feeds Harray from the moors of Nisthouse and Heddle. Good fish are waiting.

In a strong west wind, make for Mill of Rango, close to the A967 and fish down past Whilliastane to Pontooth on Ness of Tenston. When the storm howls in from the east, head for Bigging and ply the shoreline southwards past Nistaben to Ballarat House. There are endless numbers of points, headlands and fishy corners, where trout lie, all waiting for your well-presented fly. You do not need to cast far to be amongst them, so wade sparingly.

Afloat is a different matter. The loch is full of skerries and round them is where most fish are caught, just as the water begins to deepen. Finding these feeding areas is not easy and my best advice is to seek local knowledge. The way to do this is to join the Orkney Trout Fishing Association. The high quality of Orkney sport is maintained and supported by the association, a group of unpaid, keen local anglers who expend much time, energy and effort in looking after the island's fisheries. Membership of the association allows visitors access to all the association sites on all the major lochs and fellow members are always willing to guide the newcomer to the most productive drifts. Merkister Bay, at the north-east end of the loch is a popular fishing area; very shallow and downright dangerous in low water conditions. Buoys mark the safe channel out from the jetty. Stick to it.

Halfway down the loch, between Ballarat House on the east shore and Ness of Tenston on the west shore can be a highly productive drift; as are the skerried bays of Ling Holms west and Long Holm by Grimeston on the east. As a general rule, when fishing Harray, if you can't see the bottom you are probably fishing too far out; keep to the margins and shallows.

1983 International Fly Fishing Competition, Loch Harray, Orkney Islands

In recent years, more and more sea-trout are being caught in Harray and they enter from Loch of Stenness, where the B9055 ribbons between the two waters at the south end. Kirk Bay is one of the best places to search for them, as they congregate at the mouth of Tormiston Burn, waiting to dash upstream past Masehowe to spawn.

When Loch of Harray is good, it is very, very good and you could happily spend all your time on Orkney fishing this perfect water and never become bored or dejected. Harray must rate as one of the top ten Scottish trout waters and a Mecca for any angler venturing north of Mr Hadrian's Wall in search of sport. If Loch of Harray is a lady, then her near neighbour, loch of Stenness can be an infuriating, maddening, perverse child. It probably has the finest quality trout of all Orkney waters but they are also the most difficult to catch. Blank days, even for local anglers, are frequent. But when Stenness decides to behave, then rewards can be outstanding. It is all a matter of being in the right place at the right time. Fishing.

The famous standing stones at the south end of the loch dominate the view; and when we visited Orkney in 1967, the centre-piece of the circle was two upright slabs, topped by a flat stone. The flat stone was placed recently by a local historian, in the mistaken belief that a similar stone had been removed from the site centuries previously. Not so. There never was such a 'table' and the offending slab has since been taken down.

North of the Standing Stones is the majestic Ring of Brogar, a collection of more than 30 upright stones laid out in a perfect mathematical circle; and on a small promontory, jutting out into the loch near Bridge of Waith are the remains of a Chambered Cairn. Round the margins of Stenness, other relics of times past crowd the shoreline, burnt mounds, tumili and cairns. Positive proof that prehistoric man was well established on these green and fertile lands more than 6,000 years ago.

Orcadians still greet visitors today with wonderful warmth and kindness; soft, musical voices soothing strained city nerves. Arrange your holiday in June and hear a hundred glorious voices resounding through the red stones of St Magnus Cathedral in Kirkwall. The annual Festival of Music, guided by composer Peter Maxwell-Davies, is now an established part of the Scottish cultural scene; as is the Drama Festival, supported by that most marvellous of Scottish writers, George Mackay Brown.

Other musical sounds, dearer to the hearts of anglers, may be heard on Loch of Stenness; the wild scream of singing reels as superb sea-trout, bars of silver, charge off into the depths. For Stenness is joined to the Atlantic by the Bush, a short stream connecting the loch to the Bay of Ireland and Scapa Flow.

Loch of Stenness water is brackish, providing an excellent environment for the production of food beloved by fish, including shrimp, midges, snails, sea-weed fly and daddy-long-legs; even eels and shore crabs. The largest trout ever caught on Orkney came from Stenness and was reputed to have weighed 29 lb. Fish of up to 7 lb are still taken and most seasons produce trout weighing 4 lb or more.

The bad news is that they are very hard to catch. With such an abundance of natural food available, under the noses, your artifical flies, no matter how lightly danced overhead, are often studiously ignored; and I have had more despairing, blank days on Stenness than on almost any other loch in Scotland. However, to help you on your way, I suggest that you concentrate your murderous efforts round the margins. Fish lie in very shallow water, so whether fishing from bank or boat, stay close the shore and pay attention. Stenness fish tend to follow the fly, waiting until the last moment before grabbing greedily—or not as is more often the case. So remember to pause before casting again. Otherwise, you might spend the whole day pulling the fly from the fish's mouth. Annoying for expectant trout but infuriating for expectant anglers.

Sea-trout are most prolific during autumn months and tend to gather in the area of the outlet burn, the south-east bay, close to the Standing Stones Hotel, where Stenness is linked to Loch of Harray, and round the Ness, a peninsula near Voy in the north end of the loch.

Wading is uncomfortable, particularly at the south end where seaweed makes one stumble about a bit—much to the amusement of the mute swans which invariably grace the loch. But persevere, creep up on them, because bank fishing here often produces better results than fishing from a boat.

Don't expect large baskets of fish, although, like everywhere else, on its day, Stenness can produce great results. Do expect trout of matchless quality, finely marked and fighting fit. If the fates are unkind, take comfort in the knowledge that perhaps even the early inhabitants of Orkney experienced similar problems in removing fish from Stenness. In fact, I have this theory that the Standing Stones and Ring of Brogar have nothing whatsoever to do with ancient rites or mathematical calculations. They are really a memorial to demented Neolithic anglers—driven daft after returning fishless from Stenness. Prove me wrong if you can!

When things get tough on Stenness, take comfort in the fact that little Loch of Kirbister will welcome you and restore your angling self-confidence. This delightful water lies to the south of Stenness close to the A964 road midway between Stromness and Kirkwall. Kirbister is the ideal place to take newcomers to the gentle art and the fish, though not large, give a good account of themselves. There is even the odd chance of a sea-trout, but they seem loath to use the fish ladder from Waulkmill Bay and few are taken. The loch is, however, a very pleasant place to spend a few hours and, most days, breakfast will be assured.

Mainland Orkney has a series of other small waters, all of which have their own particular attractions. Clumly, north of Stromness has a reputation of holding some excellent trout; Loch of Tankerness, east of

Kirkwall, Peerie Water and Loch of Wasdale. But the best of the smaller waters is undoubtedly Skaill, six miles north of Stromness and this water has some good fish; seek permission well in advance from Skaill House and look out for action.

If you like your trout fishing more remote, then the outlying islands of Orkney offer some fine sport. The Island of Rousay has three good lochs, all containing stocks of wild brown trout. The largest is Muckle Water, close to its little brother, Peerie Water, and they are approached by a track that leaves the island's circular road at Westness a few miles west of the ferry landing stage. Trouble is, the bus goes anti-clockwise round the island, so you will have to be patient. Or stop off at Loch of Wasbister, in the north and have a few casts there on the way round.

For me, the most dramatic of the outlying lochs are those on the island of Hoy, south from Stromness, across the Bring Deeps, past the little island of Graemsay. There are three trout lochs here and they all involve a good hike to reach. The most accessible is Sandy Loch, to the south of the track out to Rackwick. Deep, dark and dour, but some with some large fish.

In the south of Hoy are Heldale Water and Hoglinns Water, on the cliffs above Sweinn Geo and Little Rack Wick. A good track invites you out onto the hill from Heldale, following the Burn of Heldale westwards up Cairn Hill, and both waters can be easily fished during the course of one day. The only problem will be leaving. The setting is magnificent and it is unlikely that you will meet another soul. Meeting the fish will also be a problem for they are few and far between. However, if you should be fortunate enough to tempt one, it will be well worth catching and I unhesitatingly recommend these lovely waters to you as a perfect place to fish.

Shetland has some of the best game fishing to be found in Scotland. Ask a Shetland angler how often he changes his flies during the course of a day's fishing and he is most likely to reply 'Oh, no, we don't bother changing our flies up here. If the fish aren't rising we just change the loch.' That is easy to do when there are more than 300 lochs to choose from and they all contain excellent quality, hard-fighting wild brown trout which vary in size from bright half-pounders right up to monsters of more than 10 lb.

Sea-trout are present throughout the year and in autumn the voes and burns can be full of fish returning to spawn. Although they are not often caught, salmon also run the larger burns to the lochs and the variety of fishing in Shetland is unsurpassed throughout Britain, offering the best value-for-money sport in the land.

Most people have only a vague idea of where Shetland really is —apart, that is, from being in the little box at the top right of maps of UK. The islands lie on the same latitude as Bergen in Norway and the southern tip of Greenland, 200 miles north of Aberdeen and some 230 miles west of Bergen.

Nevertheless, due to the warming influence of the Gulf Stream, extremes of temperature are unusual; it is never too hot, or too cold. Rather less can be said for local temperature variations; Shetland weather is as fickle and devious as midgeing trout, with bright sun one minute and pouring rain the next. But there is one constant factor—the ever-present wind; and what the Shetlander refers to as a gentle breeze, BBC weathermen in London report as a force-eight gale.

The Shetland Islands have provided home and haven for the world's travellers for more than 4,000 years. At Jarlshof, near to Sumburgh Airport, lie the impressive ruins of Bronze Age dwellings, intermingled with the remains of successive settlements, right down to Viking times. The sequence of occupation begins with houses of the Skara Brae type, on Orkney, built nearly 4,000 years ago, used well into the late Bronze Age; Iron Age dwellings came next, followed by the enigmatic builders of the Brochs and a round house and wheel house. Indeed, Shetland belonged to Norway from AD 875 until 1468. Then, the islands were ceded to Scotland as part of the dowry when James III married Margaret, daughter of King Christian I. In ancient times writers referred to Shetland as Ultima Thule and in 400 BC, Pytheas of Marseilles, astronomer and geographer, sailed 'six days from north Britain' to reach them.

These remote northern lands are a wild scattering of more than 100 islands far out into the vastness of the Atlantic Ocean, spread over an area of 550 square miles. The largest island is Mainland and the other principal islands are Yell, Unst, Fetlar, Bressay and Whalsey. They are an endless delight of sunlight, sea and serenity, guarded by sea-bird-clad crags. There are deserted, shining white, sandy beaches; moorlands abound with golden plover, Artic Skua and red-throated divers; springtime is a riot of wild flowers; and during summer months, beneath the magnificent silence of the 'simmer dim' it never really becomes dark.

The old capital of Shetland was Scalloway, on the west coast, but this distinction now belongs to Lerwick in the east. Lerwick is a busy, bustling town and its harbour plays host to most of Europe's fishing fleets. Boats from Russia, Poland, Denmark, Norway, Germany and France ride at anchor of Commercial Street and a dozen different dialects may be heard in shop and bar.

Visitors admire and buy the famous handmade knitware which uses the natural colours of the hardy island sheep. Shetland sheep are not shorn, in the traditional fashion. The wool is gently teased from the animal by hand. There is delicately spun lace from the island of Unst, so fine that a square can be easily passed through a wedding ring. Soft sheepskin rugs and coats and a wide range of traditionally designed silverware.

The islands provide a wealth of interest for archaeologist, ornithologist, botanist, geologist, historian or just plain escapists like me; and there is more than enough to keep every member of the family fully occupied.

The only danger lies in succumbing to the temptation to stay forever, because Shetland casts a mystical spell that is hard to resist.

As a visiting angler your first and most important call should be made to the Shetland Anglers Association. With so many fishing possibilities available it is essential to seek advice on the best place to start. Otherwise, precious days could be lost, thrashing away fruitlessly on one water, whilst the fish are rising on another, but a step over the hill.

The Shetland Anglers Association was formed in 1920 and it now has over 500 members, including 30 ladies and 50 juniors. The association has a comfortable clubhouse and owns fishing rights on some of the best Mainland lochs, with permission to fish on most others. The members do a vast amount of work, managing and maintaining their fishing and are usually in the midst of some ambitious new scheme for improving the quality of island sport.

But, above all, the members are a most friendly and welcoming group, always ready to tell you which flies to use, which fingers to cross and how to get to the lochs that are producing best results at that time. Membership of the association costs under £10 per season and if that is not value-for-money fishing, then I don't know what is. Join the association for the duration of your visit and you will find it money well spent.

But, whatever you do, don't forget your kabes and humlibands. No, they are not strange patterns of Shetland flies and you neither eat them nor wear them. You row with them. A kabe is a wedge of hardwood which acts as a rowlock; the humliband is a looped thong which passes through the centre of the kabe. The oar is slipped between and away you go; well, away you go after a little practice.

The Shetlanders are enormously proud of their boats and they maintain them meticulously. The are also very lovely to look at—boats, that is, although to be sure Shetland has more than its fair share of pretty girls. But the boats are marvellous; sleek, narrow-bowed, finely crafted works of art, owing as much to Viking traditions as to the skill of modern-day boat builders. On the islands, it is said that you may do as you please with another man's wife, but you must never lay a finger on another man's boat.

One of the most popular Shetland waters is Loch of Tingwall, within easy reach of Lerwick and ideal for a few hours' evening fishing. There is a good mooring bay, fishing hut and jetty and access is easy. Tingwall is over one mile long by some 200 yards wide and, south of the boathouse, divides into two sections. The association stocks the loch and the average weight of trout is in the order of 12 oz. Fish are of excellent quality, rise to the fly like rockets and fight very hard indeed.

The north end of the loch is shallow and the water becomes cloudy and coloured, particularly in high winds. Whilst fish may be caught all over this north section, a favoured drift is from the north-east corner, down the shore for some 300 yards to an old dyke. Another good drift here is from the starting point, over towards the boathouse.

The southern part of Tingwall is much deeper and the water is very clear. Drift down either shore, fairly close in, and look out for action. Boat fishing brings best results although bank fishing can be good as well. Take care wading, however, since there are one or two deep holes close to the bank on the east shore.

At the north end of the loch is the site of an ancient Viking court, Law Ting Holm. Summary justice was administered here. Convicted felons had their heads crushed on a convenient stone. So be very careful not to miss any rising fish—never can tell who might be watching, waiting to pounce on miscreant anglers.

South from Tingwall, and joined to it by a little feeder stream is Loch of Asta, sheltered by the Hill of Steinswall. This water also offers good sport and is easily accessible from the B9074. However, the best bank fishing on Asta is down the east shoreline. Cross the feeder burn and stumble around. Both Ringwall and Asta are limestone lochs, with a high pH and excellent feeding.

Further west from Tingwall, beyond Gallow Hill, are a series of delightful waters where you may wander undisturbed all day, apart from the splash of rising fish. Park the car at the north of Tingwall and follow the track out to Griesta; then on to Broo Loch, south to Ustaness, Jamie Cheyne's, Maggie Black's and Garth. A splendid way to spend the day.

Perhaps the best Shetland water is Loch of Benston, complete with scenic island, surrounded by well-cultivated fields, dressed with fishy corners, points and skerries, full of superb trout which average 1 lb and some fish over 3 lb. The last time I fished Benston, within minutes of starting, I had a lovely fish. Then, for no apparent reason, the loch went dead. Nothing daunted, my companion decided that it was time to change lochs. The boat was hauled ashore, loaded on to its trailer, and off we went, down the road to another great Shetland water, Loch of Girlsta. Girlsta is named after a Norwegian princess, drowned on the loch whilst trying to escape to her lover. In Viking times, it must have been very bad news, being a Norwegian princess and in love; for there are many other lochs throughout Scotland, where a similar story is told.

Girlsta is a mile long by about 300 yards wide, narrow, deep and windy. It deepens very quickly from the margins to more than 70 ft, consequently, the best fishing areas are at the shallow north and south ends, or close to the shore down either side. When fishing from a boat, you really must have someone on the oars all the time, to keep the boat in the best fishing position and on this exposed water an outboard motor is essential.

Wading is dangerous. Halfway down the west shoreline is a small cairn which marks the spot where an incautious angler lost his life in the mid-1920s. Searchers found the fisherman's dog, guarding his basket and tackle. The unfortunate angler was never seen again. Stay on terra firma if you bank fish and leave the wading to locals who know their way around.

On its day, Girlsta can produce spectacular sport. We had a long drift down the east shore and were rewarded with two fish, each weighing 1 lb 8 oz. The trout were in perfect condition, fought like demons and were virtually unseen until brought to the net. Well, really, to be truthful, my fishing partner got the reward. I remained fishless. By the following morning the weight of these fish had miraculously risen to 'just under 2 lb' and a month later I distinctly heard him refer to them as 'well over 2 lb'.

My introduction to Girlsta trout came during out lunch break. As we sat by the short, a fish rose a couple of yards from the bank. Over the years, I have noticed that they wait until you have taken a large bite from a soggy tomato sandwich, whilst balancing a cup of scalding coffee on one knee and a large dram on the other. Then they rise. Abandoning the coffee and dram, spluttering sandwich-muffled curses, I grabbed the nearest rod and sprinted, well, lumbered loch-side. One cast, out over the still-widening rings, and my Black Pennel was grabbed with the utmost fury and the rod almost wrenched from my hand. A huge trout set off for the depths, sending the reel screaming in protest.

As always happens in these circumstances, the fly came free and I staggered back, fishless and fuming. My companions, more experienced in these matters, due to their great age and vast knowledge—and the fact that I had got to the rod first—never missed a munch. 'More coffee, Bruce?' was the only comment as I sat sobbing by the shore.

But Girlsta has a reputation for heavy fish. The largest trout ever caught on Shetland came from Girlsta and weighed 12 lb 8 oz. A 6 lb 6 oz fish was landed in 1981 and in 1984 one sad angler lost a trout at the net, estimated to be in the order of 10 lb. I like to think that there was the mark of a small Black Pennel on its lower jaw.

The day after my adventure with the Girlsta monster, Bobby Tulloch of the Shetland Anglers Aassociation accompanied me to a group of small lochs near Black Ward whilst my companion, Roy Eaton, now editor of the magazine *Salmon, Trout and Sea-trout*, went off to do battle with the trout on Loch Grunnavoe and Burga Water. Bobby and I fished the Sma Lochs, a short walk over the moor and in spite of a howling gale we had good sport. We had several good fish from the middle of the chain of three lochs, the heaviest of which weighed 1 lb 8 oz.

In the afternoon, Bobby and I changed lochs and set off to walk round Sulma Water to fish the lochs on the red crags of Smith's Hamar. The scenery here is magnificent and, climbing up the hill, we surprised a pair of red-throated divers on a small lochan. The local name for these birds is 'rain geese', and tradition has it that when they head seawards in large numbers it is a sure sign of an approaching storm.

That afternoon the sun was shining brightly and, heavily clad in fishing gear, I found the going tough. Bobby breasted the ridge ahead of me and stood, arms outstreched, saying 'My, what a fine cooling breeze!' When I caught up with him several minutes later, I was hit by what can only be described as a minor hurricane, never mind a 'fine cooling breeze'. Still, I suppose one gets used to it and I cooled down mighty quick.

To visit Shetland and not fish some of the outer islands would be a serious misdemeanour, but due to the limited amount of time we had we could only manage one day away from Mainland. This we spent in the company of David Pottinger, another expert Shetland angler and we sailed across Bura Voe on the MV *Hendra* to the lovely island of Whalsey; to be greeted on arrival by the island's best known angler, George Irvine; a man who, rumour has it, gets up at midnight, if he is going fishing the next day. Seems to work, for George caught a superb trout of 9 lb 8 oz from Loch of Huxter a few years back.

Our assault on Huxter didn't produce such spectacular results but we were pleased enough with the fish we caught; and in the afternoon we fished another grand Whalsey water, Loch of Isbister—to no avail. But it was a perfect day and the kindness and courtesy of our hosts, David Pottinger, George Irvine, Brian Polson and Bob Irvine made it a day to remember.

In days gone by, Shetland was most famous for the quality and quantity of its sea-trout fishing and for decades a small army of devotees made an annual pilgrimage to fish for these most sporting of all game fish. Moray MacLaren, one of Scotland's most noted angling authors, thrilled me when I was a child with his description of Shetland sea-trout. Sadly, the glory days seem to have gone and sea-trout fishing in Shetland is but a poor shadow of its former self.

Nevertheless, good sport can still be found, if you are in the right place at the right time. Trouble is that the best locations are jealously guarded secrets so it is difficult for the visitor to find decent sport. Shetland Angling Association have attempted to redress matters by publishing a list of the most productive sea-trout venues and most of them are easily accessible and, particularly during the autumn months, well worth visiting.

Twenty-six locations are listed and they cover Mainland and the islands. But the list is by no means exhaustive as sea-trout can be found in most of the voes, inlets and burn mouths throughout Shetland. The best advice I can give is to seek the help of association members. Join the association and ask. Shetland anglers are always ready to help.

However, to start you off in your sea-trout search I suggest that you consider an outing to Loch of Spiggie at the southern end of Mainland. There are two beaches to the north of the loch, approached via the little road that winds past the hotel and Souther House, and as the road turns south you will see the first beach on your right. The bay is enclosed by Cloki Stack and Northern Stack, with the little island of Colsay protecting the entrance. The second location is north from Northern Ness round the

Bay of Scousburgh to Ness of Renwick. Sea-trout may be caught here throughout the season; and if they prove to be dour, then drive over to Spiggie to restore your self-confidence amongst the fine trout on this perfect Shetland loch.

Of all the wonderful fishing Shetland has to offer, for me none is finer than the series of lochs lying at the north of Mainland in the vicinity of Ronas Hill (450 m), the highest point on the isles. It is the end of the road as far as the A970 is concerned. Park your car near Skelberry at grid reference 363864. There is a gate to your left, go through it, walk down the grass field, over the fence, then follow the burn, up the valley in front of you. When you arrive at the top and climb onto the moor, a wonderful vista opens; a scattering of granite boulders, glistening in sunlight; golden plovers flit over rough peat hags; Scootie Allan, the Arctic skua, watches haughtily from tussocks; the song of the wind, tugging persistently at your clothes, urging you on.

Ahead lie more than 30 lochs and lochans, varying in size from the ragged straggle of Many Crooks to half-mile-long, windswept Roer Water. All have good stocks of hard-fighting trout which average 8 oz; some have superb fish of 3 lb and more. Finding out which contain which is half the pleasure of fishing on Ronas Hill.

When I last made the trek out, Bobby Tulloch was my guide and one of the lochs we fished, Birka Water, is a classic Scottish trout loch. The sudden shock of its sheer beauty is almost impossible to describe: 700 yards long by 300 yards wide; crystal clear water; sandy beach at the north end; but the most dramatic aspect of Birka is the magnificent waterfall that drops from high crags along the south shore.

I saw the falls after heavy rain, on a warm, sunny afternoon; full, silver, thunderous, it tumbled into the loch sending urgent wavelets rippling over the calm surface. We climbed up the side of the falls to the upper loch; there, at eye level, a few yards in front of us, unaware of our secret passage, swam a proud pair of red-throated divers. They soared skywards as we breasted the crest of the falls and swung away over the moors calling hauntingly.

Birka Water collects together all the waters from the lochs on the north slopes of Ronas Hill: Many Crooks, Loch of Hadd, Swabbie Water and Sandy Water. They outlet from Birka down a boulder-strewn, narrow defile to Ian Clodie Water, far below; then leap over red-jagged cliffs into the Atlantic.

After a wonderful day we walked slowly homewards, stopping once or twice to cast into small lochans along the way, talking of Shetland past and present and of the marvellous wonder of the moors. Before descending to the road I stopped and looked back, trying to fix the scene firmly in my mind. Of all the places I have wandered, throughout Scotland, few have made such a deep and lasting impression on me than the wide sweep of blue, loch-specked moorlands on Ronas Hill.

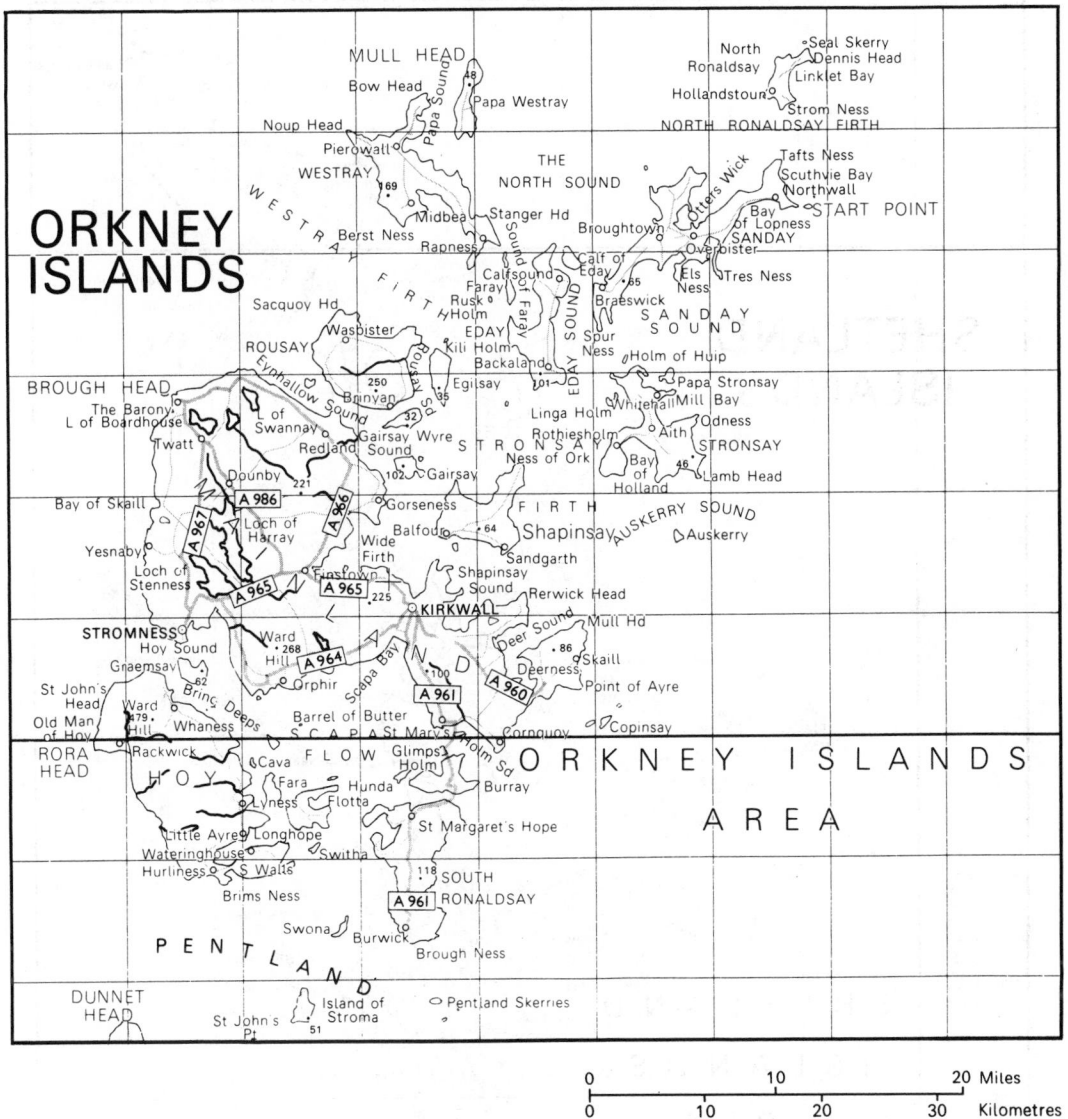

FISHING DIRECTORY

For details of game fishing in Orkney, and membership of the Orkney Trout Fishing Association, write to:

The Secretary,
Orkney Trout Fishing Association, c/o W S Sinclair, 27 John Street, Stromness.

For details of game fishing in Shetland, and membership of the Shetland Anglers' Association, write to:

The Secretary,
Shetland Anglers' Association, c/o Shetland Tourist Board, Lerwick, Shetland.

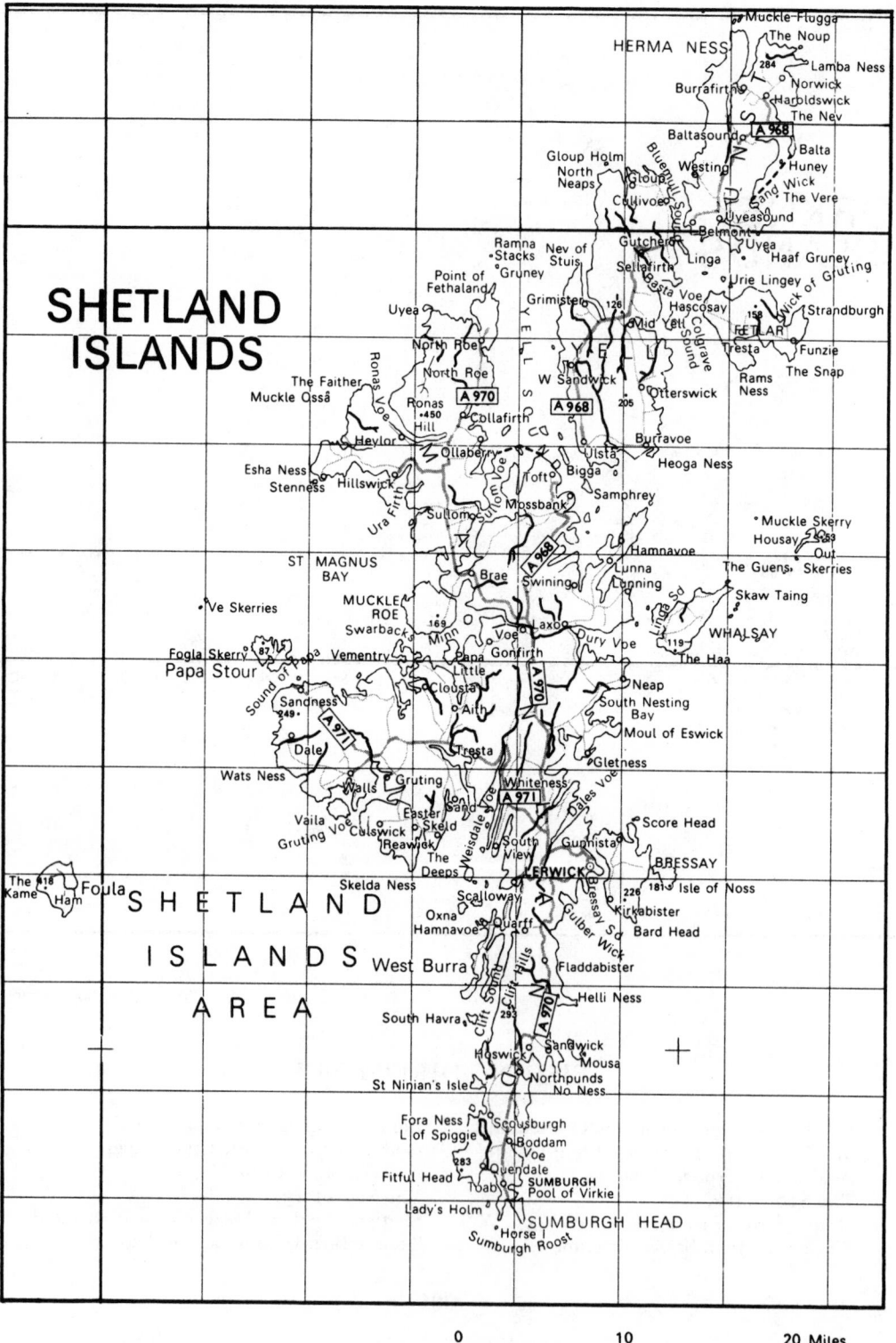

SHETLAND
ISLANDS

HERMA NESS

Muckle Flugga
The Noup
284
Lamba Ness
Burrafirth
Norwick
Harbldswick
The Nev

Baltasound
A 968
Balta
Gloup Holm
North
Neaps
Westing
Huney
Sand
Wick
The Vere
Gloup
Uyeasound

Collivoe
Uyeasound
Belmont
Gutcher
Uyea
Haaf Gruney

Ramna
Stacks
Nev of
Stuis
Sellafirth
Linga
Urie Lingey
Nick of Gruting

Point of
Fethaland
Gruney
Grimister
126
FETLAR
158
Strandburgh

Uyea
Mid Yell
Hascosay
Tresta
Funzie

North Roe
W Sandwick
Rams
Ness
The Snap

The Faither
Muckle Ossa
North Roe
A 970
A 968
205
Otterswick

Ronas
450
Hill
Collafirth
Ulsta
Burravoe

Heylor
Ollaberry
Toft
Bigga
Heoga Ness

Esha Ness
Stenness
Hillswick
Sullom
Mossbank
Samphrey

Muckle Skerry
Housay
Out
Skerries

ST MAGNUS
BAY
Brae
Swining
Hamnavoe
The Guens

Ve Skerries
MUCKLE
ROE
169
Lunna
Lunning
Skaw Taing
WHALSAY

Swarback
Voe
Laxo
Dury Voe
119

Fogla Skerry
87
Vementry
Papa
Gonfirth
The Haa

Papa Stour
Clousta
Aith
Little
Neap
South Nesting
Bay
Moul of Eswick

Sandness
249
Tresta
Gletness

Dale
A 971
Score Head

Wats Ness
Walls
Gruting
Whiteness
A 971
BRESSAY

Vaila
Gruting Voe
Easter
Skeld
Sand
South
View
Gunnista
226
181
Isle of Noss

Calswick
Reawick
The
Deeps
LERWICK
Kirkabister
Bard Head

Skelda Ness
Scalloway
293
Helli Ness
Gulber Wick

The
Kame
118
Foula
Ham
S H E T L A N D
Oxna
Hamnavoe
Quarff
Fladdabister

I S L A N D S
West Burra
Sandwick
Mousa

A R E A
South Havra
Kroswick
Northpunds
No Ness

St Ninian's Isle
Fora Ness
Scousburgh

L of Spiggie
283
Boddam
Voe

Fitful Head
Quendale
SUMBURGH
Pool of Virkie

Lady's Holm
Horse I
SUMBURGH HEAD
Sumburgh Roost

| 0 | | 10 | | 20 | Miles |
| 0 | 10 | 20 | 30 | | Kilometres |

FISHING IN SCOTLAND

District Boards and Close Season for Salmon and Trout

Fishing in Scotland is under the general jurisdiction of the Dept of Agriculture and Fisheries for Scotland, Chesser House, Gorgie Road, Edinburgh EH11 3AW.

The annual close season for **trout** in Scotland extends from October 7 to March 14, both days included. Trout may not be sold between the end of August and the beginning of April, nor at any time if the fish is less than 8 in long.

Visiting anglers are reminded that on Scottish rivers and lochs the owner of the fishing is the riparian proprietor, whose permission to fish should be obtained. The only public right of fishing for brown trout is in those portions of the rivers which are both tidal and navigable, but the right must not be exercised as to interfere with salmon or sea-trout fishing and can be exercised only where there is a right of access to the water from a boat or from the banks.

Salmon. Provision is made in the Salmon Act, 1986, for the formation and amalgamation of District Boards, composed of representatives of proprietors of salmon fisheries in each district. These boards are responsible for the administration and protection of the salmon fisheries in their districts, and boards have been formed for practically all the important salmon rivers. In districts in which boards have not been formed, the salmon fisheries, of which sea-trout fisheries are legally part, are under the direct control of the proprietors.

In the following list, the days fixing the start and finish of the annual close time for net fishing and for rod fishing respectively are in all cases inclusive. The first pair of dates are the limits of the net season and the second pair apply to rod fishing.

Add. Annual close time for net-fishing: From Sept 1 to Feb 15, both dates inclusive. Annual close time for rod-fishing: From Nov 1 to Feb 15, both days inclusive.

Ailort. Aug 27 to Feb 10; Nov 1 to Feb 10.

Aline. Aug 27 to Feb 10; Nov 1 to Feb 10.

Alness. Aug 27 to Feb 10; Nov 1 to Feb 10.

Annan. Sept 10 to Feb 24; Nov 16 to Feb 24.

Applecross. Aug 27 to Feb 10; Nov 1 to Feb 10.

Arnisdale (Loch Hourn). Aug 27 to Feb 10; Nov 1 to Feb 10.

Awe. Aug 27 to Feb 10; Oct 16 to Feb 10.

Ayr. Aug 27 to Feb 10; Nov 1 to Feb 10.

Baa and Goladoir. Aug 27 to Feb 10; Nov 1 to Feb 10.

Badachro and Kerry (Gairloch). Aug 27 to Feb 10; Nov 1 to Feb 10.

Balgay and Shieldaig. Aug 27 to Feb 10; Nov 1 to Feb 10.

Beauly. Aug 27 to Feb 10; Oct 16 to Feb 10.

Berriedale. Aug 27 to Feb 10; Nov 1 to Feb 10.

Bervie. Sept 10 to Feb 24; Nov 1 to Feb 24.

Bladnoch. Aug 27 to Feb 10; Nov 1 to Feb 10.

Broom. Aug 27 to Feb 10; Nov 1 to Feb 10.

Brora. Aug 27 to Feb 10; Oct 16 to Jan 31.

Carradale (in Kintyre). Sept 10 to Feb 24; Nov 1 to Feb 24.

Carron (W Ross). Aug 27 to Feb 10; Nov 1 to Feb 10.

Clayburn Finnisbay, Avennangeren, Strathgravat, North Lacastile, Scalladale and Mawrig (East Harris). Sept 10 to Feb 24; Nov 1 to Feb 24.

Clyde and Leven. Aug 27 to Feb 10; Nov 1 to Feb 10.

Conon. Aug 27 to Feb 10; Oct 1 to Jan 25.

Cree. Sept 14 to last day of Feb; Oct 15 to last day of Feb.

Creed or Stornoway, and Laxay (Island of Lewis). Aug 27 to Feb 10; Oct 17 to Feb 10.

Creran (Loch Creran). Aug 27 to Feb 10; Nov 1 to Feb 10.

Croe and Shiel (Loch Duich). Aug 27 to Feb 10; Nov 1 to Feb 10.

Dee (Aberdeenshire). Aug 27 to Feb 10; Oct 1 to Jan 31.

Dee (Kirkcudbrightshire). Aug 27 to Feb 10; Nov 1 to Feb 10.

Deveron. Aug 27 to Feb 10; Nov 1 to Feb 10.

Don. Aug 27 to Feb 10; Nov 1 to Feb 10.

Doon. Aug 27 to Feb 10; Nov 1 to Feb 10.

Drummachloy or Glenmore (Isle of Bute). Sept 1 to Feb 15; Oct 16 to Feb 15.

Dunbeath. Aug 27 to Feb 10; Oct 16 to Feb 10.

Earn. Aug 21 to Feb 4; Nov 1 to Jan 31.

Echaig. Sept 1 to Feb 15; Nov 1 to Feb 15.

Esk, North. Sept 1 to Feb 15; Nov 1 to Feb 15.

Esk, South. Sept 1 to Feb 15; Nov 1 to Feb 15.

Ewe. Aug 27 to Feb 10; Nov 1 to Feb 10.

Fincastle, Meaveg, Ballanchist, South Lacastile, Borve and Obb (West Harris). Sept 10 to Feb 24; Nov 1 to Feb 24.

Findhorn. Aug 27 to Feb 10; Oct 7 to Feb 10.

Fleet (Kirkcudbrightshire). Sept 10 to Feb 24; Nov 1 to Feb 24.

Fleet (Sutherlandshire). Sept 10 to Feb 24; Nov 1 to Feb 24.

Forss. Aug 27 to Feb 10; Nov 1 to Feb 10.

Forth. Aug 27 to Feb 10; Nov 1 to Jan 31.

Fyne, Shira and Array (Loch Fyne) to Feb 15; Nov 1 to Feb 15.

Girvan. Sept 10 to Feb 24; Nov 1 to Feb 24.

Glenelg. Aug 27 to Feb 10; Nov 1 to Feb 10.

Gour. Aug 27 to Feb 10; Nov 1 to Feb 10.

Greiss, Laxdale or Thunga. Aug 27 to Feb 10; Nov 1 to Feb 10.

Grudie or Dionard. Aug 27 to Feb 10; Nov 1 to Feb 10.

Gruinard and Little Gruinard. Aug 27 to Feb 10; Nov 1 to Feb 10.

Halladale, Strathy, Naver and Borgie. Aug 27 to Feb 10; Oct 1 to Jan 11.

Helmsdale. Aug 27 to Feb 10; Oct 1 to Jan 10.

Hope and Polla or Strathbeg. Aug 27 to Feb 10; Oct 1 to Jan 11.

Howmore. Sept 10 to Feb 24; Nov 1 to Feb 24.

Inchard. Aug 27 to Feb 10; Nov 1 to Feb 10.

Inner (in Jura). Sept 10 to Feb 24; Nov 1 to Feb 24.

Inver. Aug 27 to Feb 10; Nov 1 to Feb 10.

Iorsa (in Arran). Sept 10 to Feb 24; Nov 1 to Feb 24.

Irvine and Garnock. Sept 10 to Feb 24; Nov 1 to Feb 24.

Kanaird. Aug 27 to Feb 10; Nov 1 to Feb 10.

Kilchoan or Inverie (Loch Nevis). Aug 27 to Feb 10; Nov 1 to Feb 10.

Kinloch (Kyle of Tongue). Aug 27 to Feb 10; Nov 1 to Feb 10.

Kirkaig. Aug 27 to Feb 10; Nov 1 to Feb 10.

Kishorn. Aug 27 to Feb 10; Nov 1 to Feb 10.

Kyle of Sutherland. Aug 27 to Feb 10; Oct 1 to Jan 10.

Laggan and Sorn (Island of Islay). Sept 10 to Feb 24; Nov 1 to Feb 24.

Laxford. Aug 27 to Feb 10; Nov 1 to Feb 10.

Leven. Aug 27 to Feb 10; Nov 1 to Feb 10.

Little Loch Broom. Aug 27 to Feb 10; Nov 1 to Feb 10.

Loch Duich. Aug 27 to Feb 10; Nov 1 to Feb 10.

Loch Luing. Aug 27 to Feb 10; Nov 1 to Feb 10.

Loch Roag. Aug 27 to Feb 10; Oct 17 to Feb 10.

Loch Sunart. Aug 27 to Feb 10; Nov 1 to Feb 10.

Lochy. Aug 27 to Feb 10; Nov 1 to Feb 10.

Lossie. Aug 27 to Feb 10; Oct 16 to Feb 10.

Luce. Sept 10 to Feb 24; Nov 1 to Feb 24.

Lussa (Island of Mull). Aug 27 to Feb 10; Nov 1 to Feb 10.

Moidart. Aug 27 to Feb 10; Nov 1 to Feb 10.

Morar. Aug 27 to Feb 10; Nov 1 to Feb 10.

Mullanageren, Horasary and Lochnaciste (North Uist). Sept 10 to Feb 24; Nov 1 to Feb 24.

Nairn. Aug 27 to Feb 10; Oct 1 to Feb 10.

Naver and Borgie (see Halladale).

Nell, Feochan and Euchar. Aug 27 to Feb 10; Nov 1 to Feb 10.

Ness. Aug 27 to Feb 10; Oct 16 to Jan 14.

Nith. Sept 10 to Feb 24; Dec 1 to Feb 24.

Orkney Islands (river from Loch to Stenness etc). Sept 10 to Feb 24; Nov 1 to Feb 24.

Ormsary (Loch Killisport), **Loch Head, and Stornaway** (Mull of Kintyre). Aug 27 to Feb 10; Nov 1 to Feb 10.

Pennygowan or Glentorsa and Aros. Aug 27 to Feb 10; Nov 1 to Feb 10.

Resort. Aug 27 to Feb 10; Nov 1 to Feb 10.

Ruel. Sept 1 to Feb 15; Nov 1 to Feb 15.

Sanda. Aug 27 to Feb 10; Nov 1 to Feb 10.

Scaddle. Aug 27 to Feb 10; Nov 1 to Feb 10.

SALMON FISHERIES

1. *Annual Close Times Applicable to the Salmon Rivers in Scotland*

N.B. In the following List the days fixed for the commencement and termination of the Annual Close Time for Net-fishing and for Rod-fishing respectively, are in all cases inclusive.

	Annual Close Time for Net-fishing	Annual Close Time for Rod-fishing
Add	Sept. 1 to Feb. 15	Nov. 1 to Feb. 15
Ailort (Kinloch)	Aug. 27 to Feb. 10	Nov. 1 to Feb. 10
Aline	Aug. 27 to Feb. 10	Nov. 1 to Feb. 10
Alness	Aug. 27 to Feb. 10	Nov. 1 to Feb. 10
Annan	Sept. 10 to Feb. 24	Nov. 16 to Feb. 24

Applecross	Aug. 27 to Feb. 10	Nov. 1 to Feb. 10
Arnisdale (Loch Hourn)	Aug. 27 to Feb. 10	Nov. 1 to Feb. 10
Awe	Aug. 27 to Feb. 10	Oct. 16 to Feb. 10
Ayr	Aug. 27 to Feb. 10	Nov. 1 to Feb. 10
Baa and Goladoir	Aug. 27 to Feb. 10	Nov. 1 to Feb. 10
Badachro and Kerry (Gairloch)	Aug. 27 to Feb. 10	Nov. 1 to Feb. 10
Balgay and Shieldaig	Aug. 27 to Feb. 10	Nov. 1 to Feb. 10
Beauly	Aug. 27 to Feb. 10	Oct. 16 to Feb. 10
Berriedale	Aug. 27 to Feb. 10	Nov. 1 to Feb. 10
Bervie	Sept. 10 to Feb. 24	Nov. 1 to Feb. 24
Bladenoch	Aug. 27 to Feb. 10	Nov. 1 to Feb. 10
Broom	Aug. 27 to Feb. 10	Nov. 1 to Feb. 10
Brora	Aug. 27 to Feb. 10	Oct. 16 to Jan. 31
Carradale (in Cantyre)	Sept. 10 to Feb. 24	Nov. 1 to Feb. 24
Carron (W. Ross)	Aug. 27 to Feb. 10	Nov. 1 to Feb. 10
Clayburn, Finnisbay,	Sept. 10 to Feb. 24	Nov. 1 to Feb. 24
Avennangeren, Strathgravat, North Lacastile, Scalladale and Mawrig (East Harris)		
Clyde and Leven	Aug. 27 to Feb. 10	Nov. 1 to Feb. 10
Conon	Aug. 27 to Feb. 10	Oct. 1 to Jan. 25
Cree	Sept. 14 to Feb. 28	Oct. 15 to Feb. 28
Creed or Stornoway and Laxay (Island of Lewis)	Aug. 27 to Feb. 10	Oct. 17 to Feb. 10
Creran (Loch Creran)	Aug. 27 to Feb. 10	Nov. 1 to Feb. 10
Croe and Shiel (Loch Duich)	Aug. 27 to Feb. 10	Nov. 1 to Feb. 10
Dee (Aberdeenshire)	Aug. 27 to Feb. 10	Oct. 1 to Jan. 31
Dee ((Kirkcudbrightshire)	Aug. 27 to Feb. 10	Nov. 1 to Feb. 10
Deveron	Aug. 27 to Feb. 10	Nov. 1 to Feb. 10
Don	Aug. 27 to Feb. 10	Nov. 1 to Feb. 10
Doon	Aug. 27 to Feb. 10	Nov. 1 to Feb. 10
Drummachloy or Glenmore (Isle of Bute)	Sept. 1 to Feb. 15	Oct. 16 to Feb. 15
Dunbeath	Aug. 27 to Feb. 10	Oct. 16 to Feb. 10
Earn	Aug. 21 to Feb. 4	Nov. 1 to Jan. 31
Echaig	Sept. 1 to Feb. 15	Nov. 1 to Feb. 15
Esk, North	Sept. 1 to Feb. 15	Nov. 1 to Feb. 15
Esk, South	Sept. 1 to Feb. 15	Nov. 1 to Feb. 15
Ewe	Aug. 27 to Feb. 10	Nov. 1 to Feb. 10
Fincastle, Meaveg, South Lacastile, Borve and Obb (West Harris)	Sept. 10 to Feb. 24	Nov. 1 to Feb. 24
Findhorn	Aug. 27 to Feb. 10	Oct. 7 to Feb. 10
Fleet (Sutherlandshire)	Sept. 10 to Feb. 24	Nov. 1 to Feb. 24
Fleet (Kirkcudbrightshire)	Sept. 10 to Feb. 24	Nov. 1 to Feb. 24
Forss	Aug. 27 to Feb. 10	Nov. 1 to Feb. 10
Forth	Aug. 27 to Feb. 10	Nov. 1 to Jan. 31
Fyne, Shira and Aray (Loch Fyne)	Nov. 1 to Feb. 15	
Girvan	Sept. 10 to Feb. 24	Nov. 1 to Feb. 24
Glenelg	Aug. 27 to Feb. 10	Nov. 1 to Feb. 10
Gour	Aug. 27 to Feb. 10	Nov. 1 to Feb. 10
Greiss, Laxdale or Thunga	Aug. 27 to Feb. 10	Nov. 1 to Feb. 10
Grudie or Dionard	Aug. 27 to Feb. 10	Nov. 1 to Feb. 10

Gruinard and Little Gruinard	Aug. 27 to Feb. 10	Nov. 1 to Feb. 10
Halladale, Strathy, Naver and Borgie	Aug. 27 to Feb. 10	
Helmsdale	Aug. 27 to Feb. 10	Oct. 1 to Jan. 10
Hope and Polla or Strathbeg	Aug. 27 to Feb. 10	Oct. 1 to Jan. 11
Howmore	Sept. 10 to Feb. 24	Nov. 1 to Feb. 24
Inchard	Aug. 27 to Feb. 10	Nov. 1 to Feb. 10
Inner (in Jura)	Sept. 10 to Feb. 24	Nov. 1 to Feb. 24
Inver	Aug. 27 to Feb. 10	Nov. 1 to Feb. 10
Iorsa (in Arran)	Sept. 10 to Feb. 24	Nov. 1 to Feb. 24
Irvine and Garnock	Sept. 10 to Feb. 24	Nov. 1 to Feb. 24
Kannaird	Aug. 27 to Feb. 10	Nov. 1 to Feb. 10
Kilchoan or Inverie (Loch Nevis)	Aug. 27 to Feb. 10	Nov. 1 to Feb. 10
Kinloch (Kyle of Tongue)	Aug. 27 to Feb. 10	Nov. 1 to Feb. 10
Kirkaig	Aug. 27 to Feb. 10	Nov. 1 to Feb. 10
Kishorn	Aug. 27 to Feb. 10	Nov. 1 to Feb. 10
Kyle of Sutherland	Aug. 27 to Feb. 10	Oct. 1 to Jan. 10
Laggan and Sorn (Island of Islay)	Sept. 10 to Feb. 24	Nov. 1 to Feb. 10
Laxford	Aug. 27 to Feb. 10	Nov. 1 to Feb. 10
Leven	Aug. 27 to Feb. 10	Nov. 1 to Feb. 10
Little Loch Broom	Aug. 27 to Feb. 10	Nov. 1 to Feb. 10
Loch Duich	Aug. 27 to Feb. 10	Nov. 1 to Feb. 10
Loch Luing	Aug. 27 to Feb. 10	Nov. 1 to Feb. 10
Loch Roag	Aug. 27 to Feb. 10	Oct. 17 to Feb. 10
Lochdunart	Aug. 27 to Feb. 10	Nov. 1 to Feb. 10
Lochy	Aug. 27 to Feb. 10	Nov. 1 to Feb. 10
Lossie	Aug. 27 to Feb. 10	Oct. 16 to Feb. 10
Luce	Sept. 10 to Feb. 24	Nov. 1 to Feb. 10
Lussa (Island of Mull)	Aug. 27 to Feb. 10	Nov. 1 to Feb. 10
Moidart	Aug. 27 to Feb. 10	Nov. 1 to Feb. 10
Morar	Aug. 27 to Feb. 10	Nov. 1 to Feb. 10
Mullanageren, Horasary and Lochnaciste (North Uist)	Sept. 10 to Feb. 24	Nov. 1 to Feb. 24
Nairn	Aug. 27 to Feb. 10	Oct. 1 to Feb. 10
Naver and Borgie see Halladale		
Nell, Feochan and Euchar	Aug. 27 to Feb. 10	Nov. 1 to Feb. 10
Ness	Aug. 27 to Feb. 10	Oct. 16 to Jan. 14
Nith	Sept. 10 to Feb. 24	Dec. 1 to Feb. 24
Orkney Islands (River from Loch of Stenness, etc)	Sept. 10 to Feb. 24	Nov. 1 to Feb. 10
Ormsary (Loch Killisport) Loch Head and Stornoway (Mull of Kintyre)	Aug. 27 to Feb. 10	Nov. 1 to Feb. 10
Pennygowan or Glenforsa and Aros	Aug. 27 to Feb. 10	Nov. 1 to Feb. 10
Resort	Aug. 27 to Feb. 10	Nov. 1 to Feb. 10
Ruel	Sept. 1 to Feb. 15	Nov. 1 to Feb. 15
Sanda	Aug. 27 to Feb. 10	Nov. 1 to Feb. 10
Scaddle	Aug. 27 to Feb. 10	Nov. 1 to Feb. 10
Shetland Islands (River of Sandwater, etc)	Sept. 10 to Feb. 24	Nov. 1 to Feb. 24
Shiel (Loch Shiel)	Aug. 27 to Feb. 10	Nov. 1 to Feb. 10

✓ Sligachan, Broadford and Portree (Isle of Skye)	Aug. 27 to Feb. 10	Nov. 1 to Feb. 10
✓ Snizort, Orley, Oze and Drynoch (Isle of Skye)	Aug. 27 to Feb. 10	Nov. 1 to Feb. 10
Spey	Aug. 27 to Feb. 10	Oct. 1 to Feb. 10
Stinchar	Sept. 10 to Feb. 24	Nov. 1 to Feb. 24
Tay (except Earn)	Aug. 21 to Feb. 4	Oct. 16 to Jan. 14
Thurso	Aug. 27 to Feb. 10	Oct. 6 to Jan. 10
Torridon, Balgay and Shieldaig	Aug. 27 to Feb. 10	Nov. 1 to Feb. 10
Tweed	Sept. 15 to Feb. 14	Dec. 1 to Jan. 31
Ugie	Sept. 10 to Feb. 24	Nov. 1 to Feb. 9
Ullapool (Loch Broom)	Aug. 27 to Feb. 10	Nov. 1 to Feb. 10
Urr	Sept. 10 to Feb. 24	Nov. 30 to Feb. 24
Wick	Aug. 27 to Feb. 10	Nov. 1 to Feb. 10
Ythan	Sept. 10 to Feb. 24	Nov. 1 to Feb. 10

SELECT BIBLIOGRAPHY

Northern Scotland and the Islands, Francis Thompson, Michael Joseph, London

The Great Salmon Rivers of Scotland, John Ashley Cooper, Victor Gollancz, London

Culloden, John Prebble, Secker & Warburg, London

The Steel Bonnets, George MacDonald Fraser, Barrie & Jenkins, London

History of the Highland Clearances, Alexander MacKenzie, A & W MacKenzie, Inverness

Trout Lochs of Scotland, Bruce Sandison, Allen & Unwin, London

The Sporting Gentleman's Gentleman, Bruce Sandison, Allen & Unwin, London

The Salmon Rivers of Scotland, Mills & Grasser, Cassel Limited, London

Guide to Prehistoric Scotland, Richard Feachem, B T Batsford, London

The Caithness Book, Donald Omand, Highland Printers, Inverness

The Southern Uplands, Andrew & Thrippleton, Scottish Mountaineering Trust, Edinburgh

Chambers Biographical Dictionary, ed. Thorne & Collocott, Wm Chambers, Edinburgh

Wild Sports & Natural History of the Highlands, Charles St John, The Mercat Press, Edinburgh

Angler's Companion to Forth Country, Crammond, Edinburgh

Where to Fish in Caithness, Duncan Speirs, Thurso

Fishing in Perthshire, Perthshire Tourist Board, Perth

Angling in the Lothians, Graham Priestly, Balerno, Midlothian

Angling in the Scottish Borders, Borders Regional Council, Newton St Boswells

A Trout Fishing Guide to Orkney, Stan Headley, Eccles, Inverness

Game Fishing in Sutherland, Bruce Sandison, Sutherland Tourist Board, Dornoch

Game Fishing in Ross-shire, Bruce Sandison, Ross-shire Tourist Board, Dingwall

Pattie's Guide to Fishing in South West Scotland, Pattie's of Dumfries, Dumfries

Highways and Byways in the West Highlands, Seaton Gordon, MacMillan, London

The Companion Guide to the West Highlands of Scotland, W H Murray, Collins, London

Fort William Fishing Guide, Rod & Gun Shop, Fort William

A Guide to Trout Fishing in South Uist, John Kennedy

Portrait of Spey, Francis Thompson, Robert Hale, London

Portrait of the Lothians, Nigel Tranter, Robert Hale, London

Scotland for Fishing, Pastime Publications, Edinburgh

Where to Fish, D. A. Orton, Harmsworth Publishing, London